Language Origins

Studies in the Evolution of Language

General Editors
James R. Hurford, *University of Edinburgh*
Frederick J. Newmeyer, *University of Washington*

Published

The Origins of Vowel Systems
Bart de Boer

The Transition to Language
Edited by Alison Wray

Language Evolution
Edited by Morten H. Christiansen and Simon Kirby

Language Origins
Perspectives on Evolution
Edited by Maggie Tallerman

The Discovery of Language
Robbins Burling

In Preparation

The Origins of Language
Jean-Louis Dessalles
translated by James Grieve

Published in Association with the Series

Language Diversity
Daniel Nettle

Function, Selection, and Innateness
The Emergence of Language Universals
Simon Kirby

The Origins of Complex Language
An Inquiry into the Evolutionary Beginnings of Sentences, Syllables, and Truth
Andrew Carstairs McCarthy

Language Origins

Perspectives on evolution

Edited by
Maggie Tallerman

OXFORD
UNIVERSITY PRESS

OXFORD

UNIVERSITY PRESS

Great Clarendon Street, Oxford OX2 6DP

Oxford University Press is a department of the University of Oxford.
It furthers the University's objective of excellence in research, scholarship,
and education by publishing worldwide in

Oxford New York

Auckland Cape Town Dar es Salaam Hong Kong Karachi Kuala Lumpur
Madrid Melbourne Mexico City Nairobi New Delhi Shanghai Taipei Toronto

With offices in

Argentina Austria Brazil Chile Czech Republic France Greece
Guatemala Hungary Italy Japan Poland Portugal Singapore
South Korea Switzerland Thailand Turkey Ukraine Vietnam

Oxford is a registered trade mark of Oxford University Press
in the UK and in certain other countries

Published in the United States
by Oxford University Press Inc., New York

British Library Cataloguing in Publication Data

Data available

Library of Congress Cataloging in Publication Data

Data available

Typeset by SPI Publisher Services, Pondicherry, India
Printed in Great Britain on acid-free paper by Biddles Ltd., King's Lynn, Norfolk

ISBN 0-19-927903-9   978-0-19-927903-6
ISBN 0-19-927904-7 (Pbk.)   978-0-19-927904-3 (Pbk.)

1   3   5   7   9   10   8   6   4   2

Contents

Part IV
Learnability and diversity:
How did languages emerge and diverge?

Preface and acknowledgements

This volume represents a cross-section of current work in the field of language evolution, written from the differing perspectives of cognitive scientists in a number of academic disciplines. All of the chapters started life as papers presented at the Fourth International Conference on the Evolution of Language, held in March 2002 at Harvard University in Cambridge, Massachusetts; thanks are due to the local organizer Tecumseh Fitch, and to Michael Studdert-Kennedy for his invaluable support. A total of thirty-five papers (around a third of the number presented at the conference) were submitted for consideration in the current volume, and following two rounds of independent anonymous review, these were whittled down to the sixteen chapters (plus editor's introduction) that appear here. All have been considerably revised and updated to take into account developments in the most recent literature.

I would like to take this opportunity to thank the several dozen individuals who participated in the review process, and whose perceptive and stimulating comments enabled the authors to revise their chapters to a very high standard. All the chapters were rewritten following the first round of reports, and all were subsequently revised in light of the final reports received from OUP's two anonymous reviewers. Thanks to each of the authors for their patience and willingness to rewrite their chapters in order to comply with the exacting demands of both the reviewers and the editor!

I owe a particular debt of thanks to Michael Studdert-Kennedy, who has been fantastically kind and supportive over the past two years, reading and providing extensive editorial assistance on papers written by non-native speakers, commenting on drafts of mine and other people's, advising and encouraging me, and always being polite, erudite, and cheerfully optimistic. Michael, you are a scholar and a gentleman.

Many thanks to the series editors, Jim Hurford and Fritz Newmeyer; Jim's help and practical support in particular was invaluable, and if anyone would like to obtain the unpublished version of our joint fruit salad project, please contact me (but you'll need the strawberries from Jim's garden). Thanks also to Alison Wray for her advice and for sharing the relevant details of her own edited volume in this series, and to John Davey at Oxford University Press for his patient support.

A further big thanks goes to Michael Studdert-Kennedy, Alison Wray, and Jim Hurford for agreeing to write (at quite short notice) the tremendously helpful Introductions to Parts I, III, and IV.

On a personal note, this volume was constructed during some of the hardest months of my life, when totally unexpectedly in June 2003, the University of Durham announced its inexplicable decision to close the highly successful Linguistics Department where I had worked for twenty years, and to get rid of the personnel. I would like to thank the many people in the linguistics community who wrote letters, emailed the administration, and offered their support and encouragement to me and my colleagues during this miserable time. All came to nought, and an excellent department was closed down, despite international pressure to save it. But we felt the full force of the friendship and appreciation shown by the community, and for that, I will always be grateful.

Finally, I extend my heartfelt gratitude to my husband, S. J. Hannahs, whose love, support, interest in the intricacies of language evolution, and generosity with his time have enabled me to cope in the darkest of hours.

Maggie Tallerman

Durham,
September 2004

List of Figures

List of Tables

List of Abbreviations

3MS	third-person masculine singular
3rd	third person
ABS	absolutive
ACC	accusative
A.DCL	affirmative declarative
ANAPH	anaphoric
AT	agent topic
C2	Nominal Class 2
C5	Nominal Class 5
COP	copula
COMP	complementizer
DET	determiner
DEF	definite
HAB	habitual
F	feminine
FUT	future
HAB	habitual
IMP	imperfective
INF	infinitive
LAD	language acquisition device
M	masculine
NEG	negative
NOM	nominative
NONFIN	non-finite
NP	Noun Phrase
PASS	passive
PAST/PST	past
PF	perfective
PL	plural
POSTREL	post-relative

PREP	preposition
PRES	present
PROG	progressive
PRT	particle
REL	relative
RELPRON	relative pronoun
SG	singular
SUB	subordinator
SUBJ	subject
TNS	tense
TT	theme topic
UG	universal grammar
V/N	Verb/Noun
VP	Verb Phrase

Notes on the contributors

MICHAEL ARBIB was born in England, grew up in Australia and lives in the USA. He has worked in the theory of computation, vision and motor control, schema theory, and neuroinformatics. He is currently at work on the book *Beyond the mirror: biology and culture in the evolution of brain and language.*

BART DE BOER defended his PhD on self-organization in vowel systems at the AI-lab of the Vrije Universiteit Brussel in 1999. He then worked as a postdoctoral research fellow at the Center for Mind, Brain and Learning at the University of Washington in Seattle. He is now working as an assistant professor at the Artificial Intelligence Department of the Rijksuniversiteit Groningen in the Netherlands.

HENRY BRIGHTON is interested in machine learning and the foundations of cognitive science. He gained his PhD from the University of Edinburgh. Currently, he is a postdoctoral research fellow within the Center for Adaptive Behavior and Cognition at the Max Planck Institute for Human Development, Berlin. He is also author of *Introducing artificial intelligence,* published by Icon Books, Cambridge.

TED BRISCOE is Reader in Computational Linguistics in the Computer Laboratory, University of Cambridge. His research interests also include natural language processing and information extraction. He is joint editor of *Computer Speech and Language* and book review editor for *Natural Language Engineering.* He has published nine papers on evolutionary linguistics and recently edited *Linguistic evolution through language acquisition: formal and computational models* (CUP, 2002; see <http://www.cl.cam.ac.uk/users/ejb>.

ANDREW CARSTAIRS-MCCARTHY is Professor of Linguistics at the University of Canterbury, in Christchurch, New Zealand. His main research interests are in inflectional morphology, and he is the author of *Allomorphy in inflexion* (1987). The brain's surprising facility in coping with the idiosyncrasies of morphology led him in the 1990s to wonder about how they, and language in general, might have evolved.

NICK CHATER is Professor of Psychology and Director of the Institute for Applied Cognitive Science at the University of Warwick. His research focuses on computational and mathematical models of cognitive processes, including language processing, reasoning, and perception. He was an undergraduate at Cambridge and has a PhD in Cognitive Science from the University of Edinburgh. He has held lecturing appointments at University College London, the University of Edinburgh, and Oxford University.

BERNARD COMRIE is Director of the Department of Linguistics, Max Planck Institute for Evolutionary Anthropology, Leipzig, and Distinguished Professor of Linguistics at the University of California Santa Barbara. His main interests are language universals and typology, historical linguistics, linguistic fieldwork, and languages of the Caucasus. Publications include *Aspect* (CUP, 1976), *Language universals and linguistic typology* (Blackwell/University of Chicago Press, 1981, 1989), *The languages of the Soviet Union* (CUP, 1981), *Tense* (CUP, 1985), *The Russian language in the twentieth century* (with Gerald Stone and Maria Polinsky, OUP, 1996). He is also editor of *The world's major languages* (Croom Helm/OUP, 1987).

SHIMON EDELMAN is Professor of Psychology at Cornell University, where he is also active in the Cognitive Studies and Information Science programs. He works on developing computational understanding of cognition, in particular vision (including object and scene recognition and perceptual learning) and language (including acquisition and processing).

BRADLEY FRANKS is a senior lecturer in the Department of Social Psychology at the London School of Economics. His background is in cognitive science and social psychology. He has published widely in cognitive science, cognition and culture, evolutionary psychology, and philosophical psychology.

DAVID HORN has been Professor of Physics at Tel Aviv University since 1971, where he has also served as Dean of Exact Sciences and as Director of the Brain Studies Center. His current research interests include analysis of spatiotemporal patterns, clustering techniques, and motif and syntax extraction from texts and biological sequences.

JAMES R. HURFORD is Professor of General Linguistics at the University of Edinburgh, and was the founder of the Language Evolution and Computation Research Unit there. He has a broad interest in reconciling various traditions in linguistics which have tended to conflict. In particular, he has worked on articulating a framework in which formal representation of grammars in individual minds interacts with statistical properties of language as used in communities. The framework emphasizes the interaction of evolution, learning, and communication. He is perhaps best known for his computer simulations of various aspects of the evolution of language, and was also the co-editor of two general collections of papers on language evolution, Hurford et. al (1998) and Knight et al. (2000).

SIMON KIRBY is a Reader in the Language Evolution and Computation Research Unit, University of Edinburgh. In addition to his numerous shorter articles on linguistic evolution, he is author of *Function, selection, and innateness* (OUP, 1999) and co-editor (with Morten Christiansen) of *Language evolution* (OUP, 2003).

TANIA KUTEVA was born in Bulgaria, and studied English and Russian philology, typology, cognitive linguistics, and Slavistics in Bulgaria and at Heidelberg, Germany. She completed her PhD in 1996. She has been an assistant professor of English at Sofia, Bulgaria; research assistant at the Institute for African Studies, University of Cologne, Germany; visiting professor of English at the University of Texas at San Antonio, USA; and since 2000 has held the post of Professor of English Linguistics at the Institute for English and American Studies, University of Düsseldorf, Germany.

DANA McDANIEL is Professor of Linguistics at the University of Southern Maine, where she has been teaching since 1990. Her primary research interest is children's acquisition of syntax. Her recent work focuses on the developing production system, as well as on children's grammatical knowledge.

Luca Onnis is a Postdoctoral Research Associate in the Department of Psychology, Cornell University. He has a degree from the University of Bologna and a PhD in Psychology from the University of Warwick. He studies statistical language learning incorporating computer simulations, neural networks, corpus analyses, brain imaging, and behavioural data.

Pierre-Yves Oudeyer studied theoretical computer science at Ecole Normale Supérieure de Lyon, then obtained his PhD in artificial intelligence at University Paris VI; this presented a computational theory of the origins of speech sounds. He studies the role of self-organization as crucial support for natural selection in the origins of language. He is also engaged in research in developmental robotics, where he is investigating how a robot can autonomously set up its own tasks, so that the complexity of its behaviour increases in an open-ended manner.

Irene Pepperberg received her SB from MIT, her MA and PhD from Harvard University, and is currently a Research Associate Professor at Brandeis University. She has won NSF, Whitehall, Selby, Radcliffe, John Simon Guggenheim, and Harry Frank Guggenheim Fellowships, is a Fellow of six societies, is on the editorial board of four journals, and has over 100 publications.

Kate Rigby completed her PhD in the Department of Social Psychology at the London School of Economics in 2002. She is currently a postdoctoral research fellow in the School of Psychology and Human Development at the Institute of Education, University of London.

Matthew Roberts is a PhD candidate at the University of Warwick. His research on computational models of language acquisition focuses on the ubiquitous 'u-shaped' pattern of overgeneralization and recovery as it is applied to grammar acquisition. After obtaining a first degree in Psychology and Education from Warwick, he completed a postgraduate teaching certificate and subsequently a masters degree in cognitive science from Birmingham University.

Eytan Ruppin is a Professor in the School of Computer Science and School of Medicine, Tel Aviv University, Israel. His research encompasses computational studies of brain and cognitive disorders, evolutionary models of neural processing in embodied agents, and the analysis of genetic and metabolic networks.

ANDREW SMITH is a postdoctoral research fellow at the Language Evolution and Computational Research Unit, University of Edinburgh. His research uses computational simulations to explore the acquisition and emergence of language-like communication systems, and how the inference of meaning drives semantic and linguistic variation and change.

KENNY SMITH is a research fellow in the Language Evolution and Computation Research Unit, University of Edinburgh, where he obtained his PhD. His research concerns the impact of learner biases on the structure of language, possible evolutionary explanations for these biases, and the influence of population dynamics on linguistic evolution.

ZACH SOLAN is a PhD student in the School of Physics and Astronomy at Tel Aviv University, Israel. His research focuses on developing an unsupervised method for the acquisition and representation of syntactic knowledge, and on models of language evolution.

MICHAEL STUDDERT-KENNEDY received his BA in Classics, at Cambridge University (1951), and his PhD in experimental psychology from Columbia University (1961). He was a Research Associate (1961-1986) and President (1986-1992) of Haskins Laboratories, New Haven, and has taught at Barnard College, the City University of New York, University of Connecticut, and Yale University. His research interests include speech perception, the early development of speech perception and production, and the evolution of language. He has published numerous articles and has been editor or co-editor of six books.

MAGGIE TALLERMAN taught for twenty years at the University of Durham, and is currently a Reader in Linguistics at the University of Newcastle upon Tyne. She has worked extensively on the syntax and morphosyntax of Welsh, which was the subject of her 1987 PhD thesis (University of Hull). She is also the author of *Understanding syntax* (Hodder/OUP, 1998/ 2005). Her interests in language evolution centre on the evolution of syntax, and stem from a view that linguists have a duty to inform—and be informed by—work in this burgeoning field.

ALISON WRAY's main area of research is theoretical psycholinguistics, particularly the modelling of units of language processing. Her recent publications, including *Formulaic language and the lexicon* (CUP, 2002), focus on wordstrings that seem to be processed holistically. In relation to language evolution, she has extended this theme into the human proto-language period, proposing that humans expressed semantically complex messages before they had grammar or individual words. She is a Reader at Cardiff University.

KLAUS ZUBERBÜHLER received his undergraduate degree in Zoology from the University of Zurich in 1993. He obtained a doctorate in Psychology from the University of Pennsylvania in 1998. He then worked at the Max Planck Institute for Evolutionary Anthropology in Leipzig. Since 2001, he has been a lecturer in Psychology at the University of St Andrews, Scotland.

1 Introduction: Language origins and evolutionary processes

MAGGIE TALLERMAN

In this volume, researchers from a wide variety of academic backgrounds investigate the origins and evolution of complex language in *Homo sapiens*. The chapters that follow are written by linguists, speech scientists, neuroscientists, psychologists, biologists, cognitive scientists, and computer scientists. The volume is divided into four parts, with themes as follows:

- Part I: Evolution of speech and speech sounds
- Part II: Evolution of grammar (syntax and morphology)
- Part III: Analogous and homologous traits in other species
- Part IV: Learnability and diversity

The volume reflects a broad sweep of the research being undertaken across all the academic disciplines listed above. Moreover, it shows how researchers are taking serious note of work in fields other than their own, narrowly defined one: when a linguist takes on board the theories of evolutionary biology, or a neuroscientist understands the principles of generative grammar, then we know that we are truly beginning to attempt cross-disciplinary work.

What is perhaps most noticeable is the growing maturity of this rapidly developing field. It is no longer good enough to present (even a plausible) just-so story for one's own favourite piece of the evolutionary puzzle: instead, researchers in the field of evolutionary linguistics are looking for real evidence. But what counts as evidence in a branch of knowledge where the relevant details lie deep in prehistory, and cannot fossilize? For linguists working on language evolution, evidence is language structure as we know it: we have a special duty to ensure that hypotheses are consistent with the observed properties of fully evolved languages, and with what we know of their acquisition by infants. This means that universal features should be taken into account (see for instance Chapters 4 and 5, on the properties of vowel systems); that theorists should work at a level of abstraction which is sufficient to account for the diversity of linguistic properties, but also that they take into account the remarkable homogeneity of linguistic structure. Around a third of the chapters in this volume (particularly in Part IV) look to computer modelling to underpin their hypotheses; although not all readers will be familiar with the technicalities of simulation studies, all the chapters have a discussion which summarizes the findings in plain terms. Of course, any model is only as sound as its initial assumptions, which obviously affect the way the simulation turns out. No doubt some of these assumptions will be challenged by other researchers; yet the field is a young one, and its terms of reference are still under construction. Researchers in language evolution also need to ensure that their theories are compatible with the tenets of evolutionary biology: despite being a unique system, language is nonetheless a biological system. Individual languages, of course, exhibit the additional property of being culturally transmitted: the tensions between our genetic linguistic inheritance, the cultural transmission of language, and the timescale on which individual languages undergo change are explored in a number of the chapters that follow.

Although in general the authors in this volume are not in any doubt that language did evolve—in other words, that it is not a phenomenon which somehow stands completely outside the normal Darwinian mechanisms through which complex systems come into being—they are also aware that diverse forces are at work. If there is any consensus at all in the most recent work on language origins, it is surely that a variety of factors which *do* have parallels elsewhere in the natural world are responsible for the emergence of this biologically unique phenomenon.

The field of scientific investigation into language origins has been developing steadily since the last decades of the twentieth century. Without doubt, a major impetus for the renewed interest in the field has been the realization that language is *not* merely a 'communication system' which can be likened to the vocalizations of non-human primates, or the intricate system of 'dancing' used by honeybees to communicate information about sources of nectar. For this realization, we are particularly indebted to the work of the linguist Noam Chomsky (for instance, Chomsky 1965, 1986, 1995), who has done more than anyone to foster a research programme which sets out just how complex in 'design' the human language faculty really is. From the Chomskyan revolution it has become clear exactly how much we have to account for, particularly in the realm of syntax: no serious account of language evolution can say 'and then syntax (or phonology or morphology) just happened'. For instance, the following remarks by the psychologist Robin Dunbar and the phonetician Philip Lieberman, playing down the complexity, the relevance, and the uniqueness of linguistic structure, would seem naive to most linguists:

[W]e can already see many hallmarks of human speech in the Old World monkeys. In the vervet's calls we have an archetypal protolanguage. [...] It seems but a small step from here to formalizing sound patterns so that they can carry more information. And from there to producing language is but another small step (Dunbar 1996: 141).

[N]othing that linguists study is relevant to any of the questions [concerning the evolution and function of language].... [T]he grammatical structures of languages [...] are not, in themselves, relevant to questions about the functions of language or its evolution (Dunbar 1998: 107).

[T]he ability to comprehend simple aspects of syntax can be observed in living apes [...]. Ape–human lexical and syntactic abilities differ, but are quantitative. [...] Syntax is not the touchstone of human language (Lieberman 2000: 130, 156).

The chapters in this volume do not regard the development of speech sounds and speech, or of syntax and morphology, as 'small steps', and nor do they underestimate the intricate blend of factors leading to full language in our species. For the most part, issues of how observed properties of language arose are regarded by the authors as directly relevant: we want to understand what language is, and account for how it got to be that way. So for instance, when Studdert-Kennedy looks at the articulatory origins of discrete consonants and vowels, using the particulate principle (Chapter 3), when Oudeyer (Chapter 4) and de Boer (Chapter 5) examine the evolution of vowel systems, when McDaniel suggests an account of the development of syntactic movement which stresses the role of production (Chapter 7), when Carstairs-McCarthy asks why languages have morphology (Chapter 8), or when Roberts et al. (Chapter 15) examine the development and retention of linguistic idiosyncrasies and quasi-productivity, all are stressing that the structure of language is *directly* relevant to questions about its evolution. Yet this does not prevent the authors from examining the societal context in which language evolves and is acquired, and considering the relevance of extra-linguistic properties in shaping its attributes.

Paradoxically, though the Chomskyan revolution in linguistics seems to have led to renewed interest in the origins of language, in many cases this interest was a reaction against the views expressed by Chomsky himself. In his earlier work, small comments made here and there (e.g. Chomsky 1975: 59; 1982: 18–23; 1988) indicate Chomsky's apparent disbelief in the idea that language evolved via natural selection. For instance:

Evolutionary theory is informative about many things, but it has little to say [...] about questions of this nature [i.e. language evolution]. The answers may well lie not so much in the theory of natural selection as in molecular biology, in the study of what kinds of physical systems can develop under the conditions of life on earth and why, ultimately because of physical principles. It surely cannot be assumed that every trait is specifically selected (Chomsky 1988: 167).

Human language has the unusual, possibly unique, property of discrete infinity [...]. It may be that at some remote period a mutation took place that gave rise to the property of discrete infinity, perhaps for reasons that have to do with the biology of cells, to be explained in terms of properties of physical mechanisms, now unknown. [...] Quite possibly other aspects of [the] evolutionary development [of language] again reflect the operation of physical laws applying to a brain of a certain degree of complexity (Chomsky 1988: 169–70).

For many, the idea that language cannot be explained by Darwinian mechanisms is an anathema. One of the most significant milestones in the recent canon of work in language evolution, Pinker and Bloom (1990), came about expressly as a counter-argument to the non-selectionist views of language emergence put forward by Chomsky and also by the palaeo-biologist Stephen Jay Gould (e.g. Gould 1979, 1993). Pinker and Bloom's sketch of an adaptationist account of language emergence, and the hugely diverse peer commentaries that follow their article, triggered a resurgence in the field of language evolution (though their actual argumentation has recently been criticized extensively by Botha 2002). Amongst the latest literature, another paper that has excited a great deal of debate is Hauser, Chomsky, and Fitch (2002), which is discussed by a number of the authors in this volume (although it appeared after the original submission of papers for review). Hauser et al. make the astonishing claim that the 'faculty of language in the narrow sense' consists solely of recursion, a *exaptation*

view which is criticized at several points in this volume; see in particular Arbib (Chapter 2) and Studdert-Kennedy (Chapter 3).

Although Pinker and Bloom (1990) aim to present an account of language evolution which is fully consistent with a Darwinian theory of natural selection, there are, as they acknowledge, other evolutionary forces. One of these, akin to Darwin's own notion of 'preadaptation', is *exaptation* (e.g. Gould and Vrba 1982); this is the process whereby an organism adopts some feature to serve a function which the feature did not originally fulfil, but for which its form makes it particularly useful. Classic examples are the evolution of wings in insects and the evolution of feathers (and thus wings) in birds. Both of these were features that did not evolve to serve the function of flight: insect wings were solar heat exchange panels, as Pinker and Bloom discuss, and bird feathers evolved for insulation. Both features are exapted, over time, for flight, but of course this process is both gradual and also subject to natural selection, so consistently Darwinian in that sense: 'An exaptation [...] comes about by means of natural selection, has a primary utility when it arises, but is recruited for a secondary function' (Wilkins and Dumford 1990: 763).

Processes of exaptation are explicitly discussed or implicitly assumed in a number of chapters in this volume. Opening Part I, Arbib's Chapter 2 outlines his proposal for the *mirror system hypothesis*: 'an account of the evolution of the brain mechanisms that gave humans a language-ready brain'. This hypothesis claims that an ancient primate neural mechanism which handled manual gesture in our prehominid ancestors was ultimately adapted to serve a quite different function in (proto)humans—language. A brain area known as F5 in non-human primates is known to regulate the manual grasping of objects, and this area is known to be *homologous* (i.e. it has the same evolutionary origin) as part of the human Broca's area: thus, neural structures with one function may have been exapted for (aspects of) language. Arbib details the hypothetical stages in the *Homo* line which could have led to the system of vocalization under volitional control that is characteristic of language (but not of primate vocalization). Various other examples of exaptation are discussed in Part II. Tallerman (Chapter 6) argues against an earlier proposal by Andrew Carstairs-McCarthy which claims that the structure of the syllable was exapted for the structure of the clause. McDaniel (Chapter 7) suggests that syntactic movement arose from a kind of protolanguage in which copies of words occurred frequently in each utterance: essentially, movement for discourse purposes (e.g. focalizing or topicalizing a constituent) is an exaptation of an earlier method of production which allowed copies/traces of items. Carstairs-McCarthy (Chapter 8) proposes that 'morphophono-logical' alternations arose simply because adjacent items in an utterance affected each other's pronunciation, even before morphology existed: morphology then exploits this by assigning *meaning* to the variations in phonetic form, and so is an exaptation because it assigns a new function to these natural variations in form. And Franks and Rigby (Chapter 10) suggest that creativity in problem solving is surely subject to natural selection, but might subsequently have been exapted by sexual selection, in the form of a display of a cognitive trait, the creative use of language.

Another neo-Darwinian force is *genetic assimilation*, or the Baldwin effect (e.g. Waddington 1942, 1975). This is a mechanism whereby plas-ticity (the ability to adapt to changes in the environment) during the lifetime of an individual can speed up evolution: when the learned behav-iour is advantageous, natural selection will ensure that individuals who are genetically predisposed towards this type of learning are more likely to reproduce successfully. In subsequent generations, the acquired ability can become genetically determined (see the comments of Oudeyer in Chapter 4 regarding honeybees and honeycomb formation). Note that it is not the learned behaviour itself that is passed on genetically—such 'Lamarckian inheritance' of acquired characteristics is not a plausible evolutionary route—but rather, the tendency to adapt and learn. Thus, the idea of genetic assimilation is again entirely compatible with a selectionist ac-count of evolution. Briscoe's Chapter 14 (Part IV) is the only chapter in this volume to consider this particular evolutionary force in detail, in an investigation into the relationship between the evolving language faculty and genetic change in individuals.

'Ordinary' natural selection unsurprisingly also plays a role in this volume, and the majority of authors certainly assume that it was a (if not necessarily the) driving force in the emergence of language. For example, in Part IV both Chaper 14 (Briscoe) and Chapter 16 (Solan et al.) assume that communicative success leads to reproductive success. A similar assumption is explored in an interesting set of experiments discussed by Franks and Rigby in Chapter 10, only in the context of sexual selection. The authors suggest that the creative use of language could be an indication of genetic fitness (for instance, showing intelligence and an adeptness at problem solving), and would thus be attractive to a potential mate. Moreover, linguistic 'displays' meet with the requirements of the *handicap principle* (e.g. Zahavi 1975) in that they are not readily faked, and so they are reliable as signals of genetic fitness. Franks and Rigby therefore suggest that sexual selection affected cognitive evolution, including aspects of language. On the other hand, Comrie and Kuteva in Chapter 9 argue against the simplistic extension of adaptive Darwinian explanations to account for the ways in which individual grammatical categories (such as tenses) or grammatical constructions (such as the relative clause) have developed. Their cogent argument is that individual aspects of grammar do not evolve to fulfil any functional need or 'gap' in the grammatical structure of a language; instead, they emerge for historical (not biological) reasons, and particular constructions are often just the result of historical accident.

All the chapters in Part IV also examine a variety of external factors (other than an evolving language being adaptive for its speakers), as Jim Hurford outlines in his introduction to that section. These authors address such issues as the property of stable irregularity in language (Roberts et al., Chapter 15); the property of language diversity (why so many languages have emerged: Solan et al., Chapter 16); and the issue of how children can learn the meanings of words, even though meanings are not explicitly transferred from one individual to another (Smith, Chapter 17). The chapters by Roberts et al. and Solan et al., as well as Briscoe's Chapter 14, are all broadly concerned with issues of the cultural transmission of language. And Smith argues that children operate a *mutual exclusivity bias*, which essentially means that a new label (word) is associated with an unfamiliar object, rather than a familiar object for which they already know the label. Thus, a general learning bias is again seen to aid the evolution of language.

In Chapter 13 in Part IV, Brighton et al. discuss the basis for a relatively recent (and intriguing) insight which has emerged from evolutionary linguistics: the idea that languages themselves adapt to be learnable (which they term *linguistic evolution*); see, for instance, Kirby (1999) and much subsequent work. To be sure, the role of biological mechanisms in language evolution is important, but these should not be assumed to be the *only* mechanisms in operation: since languages are culturally (and not biologically) transmitted from generation to generation, there have to be effects which stem from this mode of transmission. Arbib (Chapter 2) likewise suggests that 'language has evolved to match basic language structures to the learning capabilities of the infant human brain'. De Boer's Chapter 5 in Part I is also relevant here: the finding is that infant-directed speech (which has special properties) appears to facilitate learning, and thus is likely to be an evolutionary adaptation in the transmission of languages across generations.

The two papers that form Part III look for relevant evidence outside the evolutionary line leading to modern *Homo sapiens*: these are studies in comparative biology. In Chapter 11, Pepperberg indicates that if we look only at the primate lineage, 'we may miss insights into the evolutionary pressures exerted in the development of complex cognitive and communicative processes'. The behaviour of an avian species is clearly not directly relevant to the evolution of language. But the fact that certain behaviours which are highly developed in language (word + word vocal combinations) also appear (in a simpler form) in an unrelated species does tell us something about language evolution. For instance, it should tell us not to assume that developments and evolutionary pressures which occurred *solely* in the primate line (specifically, in the hominid line) are responsible for observed properties of language; it should make us alert to evolutionary pressures that we might be missing if we concentrate solely on primate abilities. Note also that Pepperberg argues on the basis of her work with Grey parrots that the 'necessary neural substrates for behavioural precursors to language can evolve in any reasonably complex vertebrate brain, given the right socio-ecological selection pressures'. In fact this comment echoes a number of remarks of Chomsky's, for instance that

The elementary materials that enter into thought may very well be primitive and available for other animals. That is, it is perfectly possible for example that perceptual categorisation or object identification is similar among a lot of organisms. They have all more or less the same perceptual world and they have the same problems to deal with (Chomsky 1982: 19).

An interesting perspective on this is offered by Zuberbühler, in Chapter 12. Looking at the way in which (in his interpretation) certain monkey alarm calls can be semantically modified, he suggests that actually, 'many of the cognitive capacities that are prerequisite for language are phylogenetically much older, and evolved in the primate lineage long before the advent of modern humans'; note that the last common ancestor between humans and Old World monkeys is dated to at least twenty-five million years ago, whilst chimpanzees and humans diverged around six million years ago. It may be that a close examination of natural (rather than laboratory) behaviour in non-human primates can point us in the direction of some previously unsuspected precursors to linguistic abilities. Relevant discussion on the capabilities of non-human primates can also found in Chapter 2 (Arbib) and Chapter 3 (Studdert-Kennedy). Arbib investigates which features are shared with other primates, and which are uniquely human, while Studdert-Kennedy considers how the movements of the primate oral tract could have given rise to movements which are used in speech.

Some of the ideas about non-adaptationist evolutionary pressures in language development which were put forward as conjecture by Chomsky (as in the earlier quotations) emerge forcefully in this volume, supported by experimental evidence. For instance, the idea that linguistic systems are subject to *self-organization*, or to other 'laws of form', appears at several points. The most advanced expression of this comes in Part I, in Oudeyer's Chapter 4. Oudeyer studies (via computer modelling) the evolution of vowel systems, assuming only the development of a modern vocal tract: no tendency to imitate or even communicate with other individuals is built into this scenario, yet the results are robust, and vowel systems which have the properties observed in human systems (such as discreteness and universal tendencies) reliably emerge. Oudeyer explicitly likens this approach to studies of other, 'natural', self-organizing systems, such as the formation of snowflakes or the structure of honeycomb—systems which are not guided by natural selection, but are entirely due to physical properties of the world. He terms this the 'blind snowflake-maker approach'. What is interesting is that observed properties of human language can emerge with no functional pressures at all, at least in this one sphere of the sound system: in Oudeyer's model, the agents do not play language games, and they have no inbuilt social skills—they simply vocalize.

Studdert-Kennedy (Chapter 3) examines a different (but germane) physical principle, the *particulate principle*, and shows how the linguistic property of discrete infinity (or duality of patterning) is derived from this. All natural systems that 'make infinite use of finite means' exploit the particulate principle, using small discrete units that are combined into larger units, which are then recombined to form hierarchies (such as syllable, word, phrase, clause, in the case of language). So duality of patterning, which language exploits so successfully, is not a biologically isolated feature after all, and thus instantiates one more way in which aspects of language can be seen as natural phenomena with parallels (though not exact counterparts) elsewhere in the biological and physical world.

Not every single recent trend or line of interest will occur in any one volume. The chapters here reflect some of the main preoccupations of scholars interested in language evolution; other current topics include recent genetic findings (e.g. Enard et al. 2002, noted by Zuberbühler, Chapter 12), and the idea of manual gestural origins for language (Arbib, Chapter 2; the notion is also strongly supported by Pepperberg, Chapter 11).

In summary, this volume on language origins is subtitled *perspectives on evolution* for a clear reason: it does not purport to give the answers to how, or why, or when language evolved, but it does aim to shed light from a variety of different academic perspectives on all of these questions. Hopefully, the work presented here will suggest fruitful avenues for future research in an exciting—and rapidly maturing—field.

FURTHER READING

For an overview of recent work in the field of language origins, the chapters in Christiansen and Kirby (2003) provide the most up-to-date survey of the field.

PART I

Evolution of speech and speech sounds:
How did spoken language emerge?

Introduction to Part I: How did links between perception and production emerge for spoken language?

MICHAEL STUDDERT-KENNEDY

We study evolution to understand the present as much as the past, about which we shall be forever uncertain. Each of the following four chapters indeed bears, in one way or another, on a central puzzle of modern speech research: the link between perception and production implicit in the capacity to replicate the behaviour of a model. I say *replicate* to avoid the connotation of intention in *imitate*. The ten-month-old infant whose babble drifts towards the sound pattern of the ambient language (Jusczyk 1997: 177–8) is replicating (as I shall use the word) rather than imitating the sounds it hears. We should also distinguish between replication of function and replication of form. Among primates, replication of function, as in the famous potato-washing of certain Japanese macaques or the nut-cracking of certain chimpanzees, may not be uncommon. But untutored replication of form in facial, vocal, and manual mimicry is confined to humans.

A neurophysiological requirement for replication of form would seem to be a direct link, unmediated by function, between input and output. Yet the dimensions of perception and action, of listening and speaking, seem incommensurable. How might the necessary links have evolved for spoken language?

The broadest and most ambitious answer comes from Arbib's heuristic framework for the evolution of language, grounded in 'brain mechanisms for action and perception that we share with other primates'. The chapter is an exemplary exercise in comparative biology, unusual in studies of language evolution because relevant homologies across primates are rare. Two facts inspired Arbib's endeavour. First was the discovery in area F5 of the macaque's brain of so-called 'mirror neurons', which fire not only when a monkey grasps or manipulates an object, but also when it sees another monkey, or a human, do the same. Second, area F5 in monkey brain is arguably the homologue of Broca's area in human brain. Broca's area is, of course, well known to be involved in control of articulatory movements in speech and of manual movements both generally and in sign languages. Recently, the area has also been found, in brain-imaging studies, to be the site of a mirror system for grasping. These facts invite at least two observations. First, mirror neurons seem to provide neurophysiological evidence of 'parity' between actions of perceiving self and perceived other, a natural ground for the evolution of imitation. Second, the facts are compatible with the familiar, if contested, hypothesis that language first evolved as a system of manual signs, and this in turn may explain why language, as we now know it, is both spoken and signed.

Accordingly, Arbib proposes an evolutionary account, encompassing both observations, of what he terms 'language readiness... those properties of the brain that provide the capacity to acquire and use language'. He excludes from biological purview many properties of language, such as words, compositionality, syntax, that have rendered its Darwinian evolution problematic among some linguists, and assigns their emergence to culture and history. He proposes a path from a mirror system for manual grasping (shared by the common ancestor of human and monkey) through simple manual imitation (shared by the common ancestor of human and chimpanzee) to complex manual imitation, then to protosign, including pantomime, and protospeech (all peculiar to hominins, including early *Homo sapiens*).

Protosigns in Arbib's account have no syntax: they are unitary structures that convey meaning directly. Initially no more than single iconic gestures, later combined into longer pantomimic displays, protosigns gradually came to be amplified by conventional non-iconic gestures, constituting a first move toward linguistic abstraction. Protosign thus provided the 'scaffolding' on which protospeech (often holophrastic) and, eventually, language built. 'True language' began in diverse cultures with the fractionation of holophrastic utterances into words. As words fractionated from longer strings of gestures, protosyntax coevolved to combine them.

Arbib's 'Mirror System Hypothesis', then, is a biological, neurolinguistic hypothesis concerning how evolution carried primates to the brink of phonology and syntax. For Arbib, the rest is history. We should note that several steps in his proposed sequence, though logically plausible, as yet lack the necessary bridging evidence. These include steps: (1) from a mirror system for action recognition to a mirror system for imitation; (2) from imitation to pantomime (Arbib remarks 'the transition to pantomime does seem to involve a genuine neurological change'); (3) from iconic gestures and pantomime to conventional, non-iconic gestures, analogous to the arbitrary sounds of speech; (4) from manual and facial gestures to vocalization, engaging what became Broca's area with the vocal apparatus. Each of these steps may eventually be more firmly grounded in neuropsychological and neurophysiological data, but remains at present speculative.

Studdert-Kennedy takes up where Arbib leaves off, with the fractionation of holistic utterances into their components. He develops an action-oriented evolutionary hypothesis similar to that of Arbib, but quite without the detailed neurophysiological modelling and argument. Studdert-Kennedy's purpose, moreover, is different. His aim is to understand the nature and origin of the meaningless discrete phonetic categories on which all spoken language is based. Consonants and vowels are valid units of function, as the alphabet attests, but, as usually conceived, they are static, cognitive entities, purely linguistic and therefore precisely what an evolutionary account must explain. Adopting the theory of articulatory phonology, Studdert-Kennedy proposes the gesture as the dynamic unit of action from which consonants and vowels are formed. He draws on child speech errors among other facts as evidence, arguing that gestures emerged through differentiation of holistic utterances, precipitated by and in step with the evolution of imitation, perhaps much as we observe them develop in the child today. Imitation of holistic utterances entails discovery that different target utterances can be parsed into different combinations of the same set of gestural components; this leads to behavioural and neuroanatomical differentiation of the organs (lips, tongue tip/body/root, velum, larynx) by which gestures are executed. The physical, precognitive, prelinguistic evolutionary basis for discrete phonetic categories in every spoken language then is the particulate neuroanatomy and neurophysiology of the vocal apparatus, ultimately affording universal gestural categories of voicing, nasality, lip action, and place of articulation.

Both Arbib and Studdert-Kennedy draw on morphological, physiological and behavioural properties of living primates to infer a possible course of evolution. The next two chapters have quite different goals and methods: they use computer simulation to explore questions that we cannot otherwise realistically address. Oudeyer asks how certain key phonetic properties might emerge 'from scratch' among creatures that can vocalize and hear, but have no communicative capacity at all; de Boer asks how vowel systems, once evolved, remain stable in the face of the rapid, reduced speech of everyday life.

Central for Oudeyer is a question briefly touched on towards the end of Studdert-Kennedy's chapter: How might an articulatory–acoustic continuum, executed by a single organ (as in a vowel height series, for example) come to be divided into discrete phonetic categories? Earlier papers by Lindblom (1986; Liljencrants and Lindblom 1972) showed that the distribution of discrete vowels in continuous auditory–phonetic space can be predicted with impressive accuracy for systems of up to nine vowels by maximizing contrastive dispersion across the space. De Boer (2001a) extended Lindblom's seminal work through computer simulation of a process by which vowels self-organize within a population of 'agents' who 'imitate' each other's randomly emitted vowels. Thus de Boer demonstrated that imitation, shaped by selective reinforcement, might serve as the discriminative mechanism driving vowel dispersion in the Lindblom model.

Both Lindblom and de Boer assumed the prior existence of discrete phonetic units; de Boer further assumed a capacity for vocal imitation supported by a perceptuomotor link specific to speech. Oudeyer, by contrast, assumes neither. His goal is to explore, through computer simulation, the self-organizing properties of a generic (i.e. not specific to speech) coupling between perception and production, with no pressure to discriminate, to imitate, or even to communicate with others. His account of the architecture and function of his artificial system will call for careful reading by those unfamiliar with the language of dynamical systems theory (for which see Kauffman 1995, for example), but, very roughly, here is how it goes.

Oudeyer assumes a world of artificial 'agents'. Each agent is endowed with a working model of the vocal tract and of the cochlea (a mechanism for acoustic wave analysis), connected to a 'brain'. The brain consists of two sets of interconnected neurons: a perceptual 'map' to accept input from the cochlea and a motor, or articulatory, 'map' to send 'commands' to the vocal tract. Every neuron in each map is connected to every other neuron in each map. Connections differ only in their 'weight', or strength, that is, the degree to which the activities of connected neurons are correlated. Initially, weights are random throughout, so that the system is in equilibrium. But the balance is unstable, susceptible to upset by the biasing effects of producing and perceiving vocalizations.

The agents are set in a world where they wander freely, randomly emitting random vocalizations. Each agent hears itself and its neighbours. Initially, a vocalization is a continuous, unsegmented trajectory through articulatory–acoustic space, but the dynamics of the set-up are such that three types of change gradually occur in the neural maps, and so in the form of vocalizations. First, perceptual neurons become increasingly sensitive to vocalizations they have already heard and less sensitive to those they have not. Second, all changes in the perceptual map propagate to the motor map, so that the more often an agent hears a sound, the more often it produces that sound. Third, perception of a self-produced vocalization (or 'babbling') increases the weight of connections between the perceptual neurons activated by that vocalization and the motor neurons that produced it; in other words, the agent learns the mapping from perception to motor commands by 'babbling'.

Oudeyer reports the results of two types of simulation, each engaging twenty agents in some 2000 interactions. In the first, relations between the perceptual map and the motor map are random and 'linear'. Under these conditions, vocalizations produced and perceived gradually converge and stabilize in all agents on the same few discrete, articulatory–acoustic clusters, or categories; the number and placement of categories vary randomly from one simulation to another. Several aspects here deserve emphasis. First, discrete phonetic categories self-organize in a space that lacks the natural discontinuities of the vocal apparatus. Second, and especially important, categories self-organize in a single agent, even if it has never heard another agent, so that the individual, not the community, is the locus of discrete phonetic capacity, as well as a possible source of language diversity—a striking analogy with Chomsky's (1986) view of language form as devoid of function and a property of the individual (I-language). Third, since in any given simulation all agents converge on the same categories, sounds evidently radiate through a population not by mutual imitation, but by perceptuomotor coupling between individuals, such that speakers simply replicate what they hear. Finally, because categories are few, longer vocalizations now demand category reuse, that is, combinatoriality, a critical property of natural phonologies.

In the second type of simulation, relations between articulation and acoustics modelled those of the human vocal tract, and so were non-linear. Oudeyer here used the standard articulatory phonetic dimensions of tongue height, tongue front–back position, and rounding to synthesize vocalizations. Each vocalization was thus an articulatorily 'possible vowel' (Lindblom 1986: 17) within the space defined by these dimensions. Notice, however, that not every possible vowel was an actual vowel in human languages. The task of Oudeyer's agents therefore was to discover the 'correct' vowels, as it were, by the same process of random vocalization and random interaction as in the previous simulation. Remarkably, under these conditions the categories that emerged in 500 simulation runs predicted with fair accuracy the relative frequencies and qualities of vowels in standard descriptions of human languages. Thus, Oudeyer demonstrated that neither maximized dispersion nor mutual imitation is necessary to yield the balanced system of vowel contrasts found in every language. Given an evolved vocal tract, perceptuomotor coupling within and between agents may alone suffice.

Before we consider Oudeyer's view of the possible origins of perceptuomotor coupling within a speaker, we turn to de Boer who is concerned with the role of such coupling both within and between speakers in maintaining the stability of vowel systems across generations. De Boer asks how children learn the prototypic vowels of their language in spite of ubiquitous vowel reduction in the speech of adults. Why don't vowel systems collapse toward the centre of the vowel space over time? At least two answers seem plausible. First, children may learn their vowels from the careful unreduced speech often directed toward infants, in which vowels are louder, longer, higher in pitch, and less variable in formant structure than in adult-directed speech. Second, children may automatically compensate for vowel reduction, correcting for dynamic undershoot by perceptual overshoot.

De Boer's first question was whether the vowels of infant-directed speech are easier to learn than those of adult-directed speech. He used a standard statistical machine-learning algorithm to compare natural vowels, /i, a, u/, excerpted from adult-directed speech of ten mothers, with the same vowels excerpted from infant-directed speech of the same ten mothers. For every mother and every vowel infant-directed speech was more readily learned than adult-directed speech.

In a second, rather more complicated experiment, de Boer studied the stability of the five-vowel system most frequently occurring in the world's languages, and of three types of frequently occurring seven-vowel systems. He used a population of twenty 'adult agents' and twenty 'infant agents'. Each adult has a set of five or seven synthetic vowels at the start of a run and each infant has none. Adults randomly produce vowels specified by appropriate settings of the standard articulatory parameters (tongue height, tongue front–back position, lip rounding); infants extract and store formant values of the vowels they hear. After roughly 500 pairwise interactions per agent between randomly chosen speaking adults and listening infants, the adults are removed. Each infant's stored acoustic exemplars are then categorized by a statistical learning mechanism and converted into settings of the articulatory parameters it will use as a new adult. A new set of infants is added and the next generation begins.

De Boer compared three conditions: infant-directed speech; adult-directed, reduced speech with some automatic compensation for reduction; slightly reduced infant-directed speech with slight automatic compensation. The five-vowel system remained stable over 100 generations under all conditions. With either infant-directed or compensated adult-directed speech alone, the seven-vowel systems tended to collapse quite rapidly into six-vowel systems over the first fifty generations; but with speech both infant-directed and compensated, seven-vowel systems remained fairly stable over 250 generations. Evidently, then, infant-directed speech may facilitate phonetic learning and, aided by some degree of compensation, may contribute to the long-term stability of larger vowel systems.

Notice that each of de Boer's 'infants' comes equipped, like a real infant, to transform a formant pattern into a pattern of articulation. But where did this capacity of infants come from? How were the first perceptuomotor links established in evolution? One possibility, as we have seen, is that the links evolved from lower primate mirror neurons under pressure for imitation (whether for language or not). Presumably, this would be the answer of Arbib and Studdert-Kennedy. An alternative (although perhaps not ultimately incompatible) answer comes from Oudeyer: the links are a side-effect of general architectural properties of the brain. On this view, all neurons in all modalities are connected as the brain develops; structure emerges through stimulation and through pruning by cell death, that is, through activity-dependent neural epigenesis (Changeux 1985). This, of course, is precisely the process modelled by Oudeyer's simulations. Such a model finesses the central problem of vocal imitation, the mechanism of the transform from acoustic signal to articulation, by building the transform into the neural structure. Perception and production are never separate, never incommensurable: input pervades and shapes output.

How this model will play out neurophysiologically remains to be seen, but, generalized across both consonants and vowels, its implications for the origins of phonological structure are profound. Discrete phonetic elements, their combinatoriality, their universality, and perhaps even their diversity across languages would seem to be implicit in formal correspondences between the neural substrates of speaking and hearing. Balanced systems of phonological contrast would then be purely formal in origin, whatever their present function. That speakers within a community, despite their natural diversity, converge on the same limited set of contrasts follows from their compulsion, evident already in infants, to replicate what they hear.

2 The Mirror System Hypothesis: how did protolanguage evolve?

MICHAEL ARBIB

2.1 Action-oriented neurolinguistics in context

We ask: how much of language rests on brain mechanisms that evolved specifically to serve language, and how much rests on human 'inventions' that exploited brain mechanisms that evolved for other purposes? For example, reading is the fruit of historical developments of the last few thousand years and must thus exploit brain mechanisms extant in early *Homo sapiens* which had evolved for other purposes. The present chapter offers an evolutionary framework for language which relates it to the brain mechanisms for action and perception that we share with other primates.

Let us define a protolanguage as a system of utterances used by a particular hominid species (possibly including *Homo sapiens*) which we may recognize as a precursor to human language, but which is not itself a human language in the modern sense. The approach offered here extends the Mirror System Hypothesis of Rizzolatti and Arbib (1998), to be explained below, and provides a neurological basis for the claim (e.g. Hewes 1973; Stokoe 2001) that hominids had a (proto)language based primarily on manual gestures before they had a (proto)language based primarily on vocal gestures. However, this claim remains controversial and one may contrast two extreme views on the matter:

(i) Language evolved directly as speech (MacNeilage 1998).
(ii) Language evolved first as signed language (i.e. as a full language, not protolanguage) and then speech emerged from this basis in manual communication (Stokoe 2001).

My approach is closer to (ii) than to (i). I shall argue that our distant ancestors (for example, *Homo habilis* through to early *Homo sapiens*) had a protolanguage based extensively on manual gestures ('protosign') which—contra (i)—provided essential scaffolding for the emergence of a protolanguage based primarily on vocal gestures ('protospeech'), but that the hominid line saw advances in both protosign and protospeech feeding off each other in an expanding spiral so that—contra (ii)—proto-sign did not attain the status of a full language prior to the emergence of early forms of protospeech. (For more on this issue, see Arbib 2004; Fogassi and Ferrari 2005; MacNeilage and Davis 2004.)

I will use the term *language readiness* for those properties of the brain that provide the capacity to acquire and use language. Then the hypothesis offered here is that the 'language-ready brain' of the first *Homo sapiens* supported basic forms of gestural and vocal communication (protosign and protospeech) but not the rich syntax and compositional semantics and accompanying conceptual structures that underlie modern human languages.

Some authors use the term Universal Grammar as a synonym for the ability to acquire language whether or not this rests on innate syntactic mechanisms, but I think we should reserve 'grammar' for a mental representation that underlies our ability to combine words to convey or understand meaning, or the systematic description of the commonal-ities of individual grammars of the members of a community. Some use the term Universal Grammar in the sense of a syntactic framework rich enough to describe (most of) the variations seen in all the recorded history of human languages. Yet others go further, and claim that universal grammar is a biological property of humans fixed in the ancestral genome of *Homo sapiens*. The most interesting formulation (though I believe it is wrong) of this claim for an innate universal grammar is the principles and parameters hypothesis, namely that the human genome encodes a grammar, the universal grammar, that will yield at least the core syntax of any specific language as soon as certain parameters are set. A further claim here is that these parameters are set so easily on the basis of the child's early experience of language that the poverty of the stimulus problem is solved. I espouse an alternative view of what the genome encodes.

Chomsky's Minimalism (Chomsky 1993a, 1995), the latest in his series of theories of 'competence', characterizes what strings of lexical items are 'grammatically correct' as follows (Figure 2.1(a)): a set of lexical items is

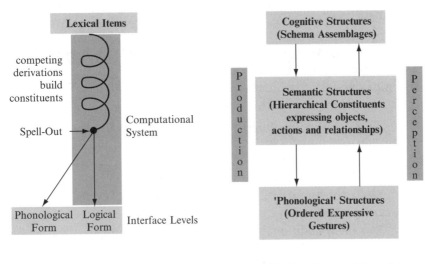

(a) Chomsky's Minimalism   (b) A Performance Viewpoint

FIG. 2.1 Contrasting (a) Chomsky's Minimalism which provides a 'competence characterization' of the phonological and logical forms of well-formed sentences, and (b) a performance viewpoint which relates the phonological and semantic forms of an utterance to cognitive form through production and perception.

taken at random, the computational system then sees whether legal derivations can be built, each of which combines all and only these elements.

Spell-Out occurs when one of the legal derivations, if any, is chosen on the basis of some optimality criteria. The computational system then transforms the result into two different forms, the phonological form, the actual sequence of sounds that constitutes the utterance, and the logical form, which provides an abstract semantics of the sentence in some quasi-logical notation. There is no attempt here to model actual sentence production—the process starts with words chosen at random and only at the end do we see whether or not they can be arranged in some way that yields a semantic structure. The aim here is to provide a framework in which one can characterize all and only those strings of symbols which constitute the well-formed (i.e. grammatical) sentences of a given language, irrespective of how such sentences are produced or understood.

Chomsky's definition of grammar has changed radically over the years, and so it would seem that whatever was done to argue that an earlier version of universal grammar was genetically encoded actually militates against the claim that a Minimalist-style universal grammar would be genetically encoded. But might it be countered that the trend of work on universal grammar has been such as to make the demands on genetic encoding and the complexity of learning a specific language less demanding with each innovation? To the contrary, Webelhuth (1995: 83–5) shows that functional head theory (a key feature of the Minimalist program) buys increased explanatory adequacy at the price of requiring many additional decisions to be made by language learners— the parameters that distinguish one grammar from another when these grammars are defined by the Minimalist program are much further from overt language than for the early grammars of Chomsky (1965), thus making it less plausible that an innate universal grammar solves the poverty of the stimulus problem. The counter claim here (shared by Deacon 1997) is that language has evolved to match basic language structures to the learning capabilities of the infant human brain, and that for such a learning system there is indeed a richness of the stimulus rather than a poverty of the stimulus. But what is that richness? Hauser, Chomsky, and Fitch (2002: 1577) assert that

No known 'general learning mechanism' can acquire a natural language solely on the basis of positive or negative evidence [they cite Gold (1967) and Nowak and colleagues (e.g. Nowak et al. 2001) in support of this claim] and the prospects for finding any such domain-independent device seem rather dim. The difficulty of this problem leads to the hypothesis that whatever system is responsible must be biased or constrained in certain ways. Such constraints have historically been termed 'innate dispositions', with those underlying language referred to as 'universal grammar'.

What is not made explicit here is that both Gold and Nowak consider very unnatural learning problems, such as 'Given strings w_1, w_2, ..., w_n, ... of some formal language, process these strings and stop at some stage having inferred a grammar G that generates the language $L(G) = \{w_1, w_2, ..., w_n, ...\}$'. However, the child does not learn a language by seeking to parse meaningless strings. Instead, it starts by building up the capacity to understand and use very simple utterances, one then two words long. These initially refer to specific wants and needs, actions and objects that it is learning about in its world. In general, it makes sense of the sentences by mapping them onto its cognitive understanding. At first, then, *milk* may really stand for *want milk* or *drink milk* rather than the liquid itself. As the child progresses to *want red box*, *red box* is at first a single 'word' and only later is the child's colour understanding ready to support that *red box* combines *red* and *box*. In short, the child does not seek to learn to parse arbitrary un-annotated strings, but rather to make sense of strings by pairing some of the words it hears with possible 'cognitive forms' to provide an implicit 'bracketing' for parts of the string. More generally, I think it reasonable to argue that as the child learns a language, it knows what words 'go together'. Given this, it is important to balance the results of Gold and Nowak with the result of Levy and Joshi (1979) showing that, given a bound *n* on the number of non-terminals, if one had the constituent structure for all strings of depth at most *n* (i.e. parse trees with no labels on the non-terminal nodes), rather than just the strings themselves, then the grammatical categories and the rules that link them can indeed be inferred. Thus, while I agree that constraints on human learning mechanisms are needed, I argue that it is a mistake to expect the constraints to operate purely within the domain of autonomous syntax. Instead, I see language as grounded in the need to 'translate' cognitions into words, thus providing the child with cues even richer than those operative in Levy and Joshi's result.

In any case, a neurolinguistic approach should provide a performance approach which explicitly analyses both perception and production (Figure 2.1(b)). Production starts with a cognitive form which includes much that we want to talk about; from this is extracted a semantic form which structures the objects, actions, and relationships to be expressed in the next utterance, and this provides the basis for creating the phonological form, the ordered series of expressive gestures (spoken, signed, oro-facial or some combination thereof) which constitutes the overt utterance.[1] Conversely, perception will seek to interpret the phonological form as a semantic form

---

[1] Note the formulation 'cognitive form which includes...'. In most linguistic models of production, it is assumed that a semantic structure is given in some 'internal code' and that this must be translated into well-formed sentences. However, in an ongoing conversation, our current mental state and our view of the mental state of our listeners create a richness which our next sentence can only sample, and the generation of that sentence may

which can then be used to update the perceiver's cognitive form. For example, perception of a visual scene may reveal 'Who is doing what and to whom/which' as part of a non-linguistic action–object frame in cognitive form. By contrast, the verb-argument structure is an overt linguistic representation in semantic form—in modern human languages, generally the action is named by a verb and the objects are named by nouns (or noun phrases). A production grammar for a language is then a specific mechanism (whether explicit or implicit) for converting verb-argument structures into strings of words (and hierarchical compounds of verb-argument structures into complex sentences) and vice versa for perception.

In the brain there may be no single grammar serving both production and perception, but rather a 'direct grammar' for production and an 'inverse grammar' for perception. Thus the value of a single competence grammar as a reference point for the analysis of perception and production remains debatable. Jackendoff (2002) offers a competence theory with a much closer connection with theories of processing than has been common in generative linguistics and suggests (his section 9.3) strategies for a two-way dialogue between competence and performance theories. Jackendoff's approach to competence appears to be promising in this regard precisely because it abandons 'syntactocentrism', and instead gives attention to the interaction of, for instance, phonological, syntactic, and semantic representations.

2.2 Language, protolanguage, and language readiness

2.2.1 *Views of protolanguage*

Earlier, I defined a protolanguage as the system of utterances used by a hominid species (including *Homo sapiens*) which (could we only observe them!) we could recognize as a precursor to human language in the modern sense. Bickerton (1995) has a different definition—for him, a protolanguage is a communication system made up of utterances comprising a few words in the current sense placed in a sequence without

---

reflect many factors which change our thoughts even as we express them in attempting to reach some communicative goal. To borrow the terminology of motor control, a sentence is not so much a preplanned trajectory as a more or less clumsy attempt to hit a moving and ill-identified target.

syntactic structure. Moreover, he asserts that infant language, pidgins, and the 'language' taught to apes are all protolanguages in this sense; compare McDaniel, Chapter 7, on the notion of protolanguage. Bickerton hypothesizes that the protolanguage of *Homo erectus* was also a protolanguage in his sense and that language just 'added syntax' through the evolution of Universal Grammar. My counter-proposal is that the 'language readiness' possessed by the first *Homo sapiens* did include the ability to communicate both manually and vocally—I use the terms *protosign* and *protolanguage* for the manual and spoken forms of protolanguage, with the prefix 'proto' here having no Bickertonian implication—but I propose that such protolanguages were composed mainly of 'unitary utterances' (a view shared, for example, by Wray 2000, who relates these to formulaic utterances in modern human languages), and I further propose that words co-evolved culturally with syntax through fractionation. The following, very hypothetical, example may clarify what I have in mind (similar examples with much more argumentation are provided by Wray 2000). Imagine that a tribe has two unitary utterances concerning fire which, by chance, contain similar substrings which become regularized so that for the first time there is a sign for 'fire'. Now the two original utterances are modified by replacing the similar substrings by the new regularized substring. Eventually, some tribe members regularize the complementary gestures in the first string to get a sign for 'burns'; later, others regularize the complementary gestures in the second string to get a sign for 'cooks meat'. However, because of the arbitrary origin of the sign for 'fire', the placement of the gestures that have come to denote 'burns' relative to 'fire' differs greatly from those for 'cooks meat'. It thus requires a further invention to regularize the placement of the gestures in both utterances—and thus as words fractionate from longer strings of gestures, at the same time the protosyntax emerges which combines them.

2.2.2 *Criteria for language readiness*

I next offer characterizations of (a) language readiness (in this section: properties LR1 to LR6), and (b), full Language (section 2.2.3: properties LA1 to LA4). Of course, both characterizations are preliminary. What is important here is the underlying distinction between the capabilities which the brain has developed as a result of natural, biological selection to support protolanguage, and the capabilities it manifests not because of genetic changes but rather because of historical accumulation (as is the case for computer programming and space flight). I do not prove that LR1-LR6 and LA1-LA4 are on opposite sides of the divide, but my hope is to encourage scholars to recognize that there is a divide and debate where it lies.

First, the properties I hypothesize as supporting protolanguage:

LR1:   Symbolization: The ability to associate an arbitrary symbol with a class of episodes, objects or actions. (At first, these symbols may not have been words in the modern sense, may have been very few in number, and may have been based on manual and facial gestures rather than being vocalized.)

LR2:   Intentionality: Communication intended by the utterer to have a particular effect on the recipient.

LR3:   Parity (Mirror Property): What counts for the speaker/signer must count (approximately) for the listener/viewer.

The remainder are more general properties, delimiting cognitive capabilities that underlie a number of the ideas which eventually find their expression in language:

LR4:   From hierarchical structuring to temporal ordering: perceiving that objects and actions have subparts; finding the appropriate timing of actions to achieve goals in relation to those hierarchically structured objects.

My point here is that a basic property of language—translating a hierarchical conceptual structure into a temporally ordered structure of words or articulatory gestures (whether signed or vocalized)—is in fact not unique to language but is apparent whenever an animal takes in the nature of a visual scene and produces appropriate behaviour.

LR5:   Beyond the here-and-now 1: the ability to recall past events or imagine future ones.

LR6:   Paedomorphy and sociality: paedomorphy is the prolonged period of infant dependency which is especially pronounced in humans; this combines with social structures for caregiving to provide the conditions for complex social learning.

Where Deacon (1997) makes symbolization central to his account of the co-evolution of language and the human brain, the present account will stress LR3: Parity, since it underlies the sharing of the meaning. As in this chapter, Deacon stresses the componential homology which allows us to learn from relations between the brains of monkeys and humans.

2.2.3 *Criteria for Language*

I then suggest that 'true language' involves the following further properties:

LA1:   **Symbolization and compositionality**: the symbols become words in the modern sense, interchangeable and composable in the expression of meaning.

LA2:   **Syntax, semantics, and recursion**: the matching of syntactic to semantic structures co-evolves with the fractionation of utterances, with the nesting of substructures making some form of recursion inevitable.

Where Hauser, Chomsky, and Fitch (2002) assert that recursion is the one uniquely human component of the faculty of language in the narrow sense (FLN), I stress that recursion is not restricted to language. Consider the task of chipping one stone with another. The instructions might amount to something like:

1. Pick a stone to be flaked and a stone to flake it with (the 'tool').
2. Chip awhile.
3. Is the flake finished? If so stop.
4. Is the tool still OK? If so, return to [2]. If not, find a better tool, then return to [2].

More generally, actions of a given type may call on other actions of the same type to be repeated until some criterion of success is attained, thus opening the way to recursion. In a similar way, once one comes to perceive actions or objects at increasing levels of detail, recursion follows (recall LR4: From hierarchical structuring to temporal ordering). The key transition, on this view, is the compositionality that allows cognitive structure to be reflected in symbolic structure (the transition from LR1: Symbolization to LA1: Symbolization and compositionality), as when perception (not uniquely human) grounds linguistic description (uniquely human) so that, for example, the NP [noun phrase] describing a part of an object may optionally form part of the NP describing the overall object. From this point of view, recursion in language is a corollary of the essentially recursive nature of action and perception, once symbolization becomes compositional.

LA3:   **Beyond the here-and-now 2**: Verb tenses or other circumlocutions express the ability to recall past events or imagine future ones.

LA4:   **Learnability**: to qualify as a human language, much of the syntax and semantics of a human language must be learnable by most human children.

I shall return to these criteria in the concluding Discussion.

2.3 The Mirror System Hypothesis

The brains and bodies of humans, chimps and monkeys differ, and so do their behaviours. They share general physical form and a degree of manual dexterity, but humans have abilities for bipedal locomotion and learnable, flexible vocalization that are not shared by other primates. Moreover, humans can and normally do acquire language, and monkeys and chimps do not—though chimps and bonobos can be trained to acquire a protolanguage (in Bickerton's sense) that approximates to the complexity of the protolanguage of a two-year-old human infant. A crucial aspect of human biological evolution has been the emergence of a vocal apparatus and control system that can support speech. But did these mechanisms arise directly from primate vocalizations? The hypothesis presented here is that the route was instead indirect, proceeding via a form of protosign. (I will have nothing to say about the biological evolution of the vocal apparatus.)

Since humans can learn language and monkeys and chimps cannot, we seek brain regions that are homologous (i.e. for which there is evidence for a shared ancestry) so that we may learn from analysis of both their similarities and differences. The starting point for the Mirror System Hypothesis is that the system of the monkey brain for visuomotor control of hand movements for grasping has its premotor outpost in an area called F5 (see Figure 2.2 left) which contains a set of neurons, called *mirror neurons*, such that each mirror neuron is active not only when the monkey executes a specific grasp but also when the monkey observes a human or other monkey execute a more-or-less similar grasp (Rizzolatti et al. 1996).

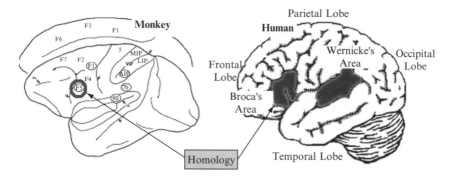

FIG. 2.2 A comparative side view of the monkey brain (left) and human brain (right), not to scale. The view of the monkey brain emphasizes area F5 of the frontal lobe of the monkey; the view of the human brain emphasizes two of the regions of cerebral cortex, Broca's area and Wernicke's area, considered crucial for language processing. F5 is considered homologous to Broca's area.

Thus F5 in the monkey brain contains a mirror system for grasping which employs a common neural code for executed and observed manual actions.

The classic papers on the mirror system for grasping in the monkey focus on a repertoire of grasps—such as the precision pinch and power grasp—which seem so basic that it is tempting to think of them as prewired. However, observation of human infants shows that little more than the sketchiest coordination of reaching with the location of a visual target plus the palmar grasp reflex is present in the early months of life, and that many months pass before the child has in its motor repertoire the basic grasps (such as the precision pinch) for which mirror neurons have been observed in the monkey. Oztop, Bradley, and Arbib (2004) thus argue that, in monkey as well as human, the basic repertoire of grasps is attained through sensorimotor feedback. They provide the *infant learning to grasp model* (ILGM) which explains this process of grasp acquisition. Future modelling will address the issue of how the infant may eventually learn through observation, with mirror neurons and grasping circuitry developing in a synergistic manner (see Arbib, Oztop, and Zukow-Goldring 2004 for a study of infant skill acquisition and further discussion).

The next few paragraphs are designed to show that the functionality of mirror neurons rests on the embedding of F5 in a much larger neural system, and include a brief outline of the Mirror Neuron System (MNS) model (Oztop and Arbib 2002) which demonstrates how neural plasticity can yield mirror neuron functionality through correlated experience rather than through 'pre-wiring'. Readers who wish to omit this part of the argument may go directly to the paragraph starting 'Oztop and Arbib (2002) provide...'.

To introduce the MNS model, it is first useful to distinguish the *mirror neurons* in area F5 of monkey premotor cortex—active both when the monkey executes a specific grasp and when it observes another executing a more-or-less similar grasp—from *canonical neurons* in F5, which are active when the monkey itself is doing the grasping in response to sight of an object but *not* when the monkey sees someone else do the grasping. More subtly, canonical neurons fire when they are presented with a graspable object, irrespective of whether the monkey performs the grasp or not—but clearly this must depend on the extra condition that the monkey not only sees the object but is 'aware', in some sense, that it is possible to grasp it. Were it not for this caveat, canonical neurons would also fire when the monkey observed the object being grasped by another.

Taira et al. (1990) established that AIP (Figure 2.2 left; called AIP because it is in the anterior part of the intraparietal sulcus of monkey parietal cortex[2]) extracts neural codes for 'affordances' for grasping from the visual stream and sends these on to area F5. *Affordances* (Gibson 1979) are features of the object relevant to action, in this case to grasping, rather than aspects of identifying the object's identity. For example, a screwdriver may be grasped by the handle or by the shaft, but one does not have to recognize that it is a screwdriver to recognize its different affordances. These affordances provide the input to the canonical neurons of F5:

(1) AIP $\rightarrow$ F5$_{canonical}$

The FARS model (Fagg and Arbib 1998) provides a computational account of the neural mechanisms, including those in (1), for going from the shape of part of an object to the grasping of that part of the object. By contrast, the task for the mirror system is to determine whether the shape

---

[2] The reader unfamiliar with the neuroanatomy of the monkey brain need not worry about the details of cerebral localization or the anatomical labels in Figures 2.2 and 2.3. The only point important here is that parietal cortex (the 'top right' part of both monkey and human cerebral cortex in Figure 2.2) can be subdivided into many regions and that different parietal regions provide the input to the canonical and mirror neurons, one (AIP) concerned with the affordances of objects and the other (PF) concerned with relations between an object and the hand that is about to grasp it.

of a hand and its trajectory are 'on track' to grasp an observed affordance of an object, and so we have to find other regions of the brain that provide appropriate visual input. One relevant brain region in the parietal cortex is PF, which contains neurons responding to the sight of goal-directed hand/arm actions (Fogassi et al. 1998). MNS (Figure 2.3) is organized around the idea that (1) is complemented by (2):

(2) PF → F5$_{mirror}$

The MNS model (Figure 2.3) shows how the interaction of various brain regions provides mechanisms to evaluate the key criteria for activating a mirror neuron:

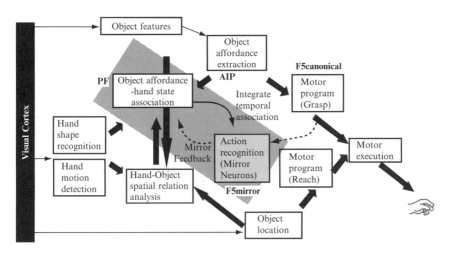

FIG. 2.3 A schematic view of the Mirror Neuron System (MNS) model (Oztop and Arbib 2002), which focuses on the circuitry highlighted by the grey diagonal rectangle. (i) Top diagonal: object features are processed by AIP to extract grasp affordances, these are sent on to the canonical neurons of F5 that choose a particular grasp. (ii) Bottom right. Recognizing the location of the object provides parameters to program arm movements during the reach. Motor cortex can then control the hand and the arm. (iii) Essential elements for the mirror system: bottom left are two schemas, one to recognize the shape of the hand of the actor being observed by the monkey whose brain we are interested in, and the other to recognize how that hand is moving. The schema for hand–object spatial relation analysis takes information about object features, the motion of the hand and the location of the object to infer the relation between hand and object. Together with F5 canonical neurons, the schema for associating object affordances and hand state (posited to be in PF) provides the input to the F5 mirror neurons.

- The preshape that the monkey is seeing corresponds to the grasp that the mirror neuron encodes.
- The preshape that the observed hand is executing is indeed appropriate to an affordance of the object that the monkey can see (or remember).
- The hand must be moving on a trajectory that will indeed bring it to grasp the part of the object that provides that affordance.

Oztop and Arbib (2002) provide an explicit computational model of how the mirror system may learn to recognize the hand–object relations associated with grasps already in its repertoire. The details are irrelevant here. What is relevant is that such learning models, and the data they address, make it clear that mirror neurons are not restricted to recognition of an innate set of actions but can be recruited to recognize and encode an expanding repertoire of novel actions.

With this background on the monkey, I now turn to the question 'Is there a mirror system for grasping in the human brain?' Brain imaging cannot answer the question of whether the human brain contains neurons each matched to specific grasps, but it can seek brain regions that are more active both for grasping an object and for observation of grasping an object when compared to simple observation of an object. Dramatically, the prefrontal area with this 'mirror property' in humans is Broca's area (see Figure 2.2 right), the frontal area most strongly implicated in the production of language. Moreover, there is evidence that part of Broca's area is homologous to monkey F5 (Rizzolatti and Arbib 1998, to which the reader is referred for references to the primary data). This led Rizzolatti and Arbib to formulate the Mirror System Hypothesis thus:

The Mirror System Hypothesis: The parity requirement for language in humans—that what counts for the speaker must (approximately) count for the hearer—is met because brain mechanisms supporting language evolved from the mirror system for grasping in the common ancestor of monkey and human, with its capacity to generate and recognize a set of manual actions.

As such, the Mirror System Hypothesis provides a neural 'missing link' to those (Stokoe 2001, for a recent example) who, struck by the ability of deaf children to acquire sign language as readily as normal children acquire speech, have argued not only that language must be considered as multimodal—with manual gesture on a par with speech—but also that some form of signing could have provided the scaffolding for the evolution of speech. They stress that pantomime can convey a wide range of meanings without recourse to the arbitrary associations that underlie the sound–meaning pairings of most words of a spoken language.[3]

The Mirror System Hypothesis is a neurolinguistic hypothesis—it is an account of the evolution of the brain mechanisms that gave humans a language-ready brain. It claims that a specific mirror system—the primate mirror system for grasping—evolved into a key component of the mechanisms that render the human brain language-ready (but see Fogassi and Ferrari 2005 for the possible role of oro-facial mirror neurons). Note that the hypothesis does not say that having a mirror system is equivalent to having language—monkeys have mirror systems but do not have language. Arbib (2004) explains why it is unlikely that species-specific vocalizations of monkeys, such as the snake and leopard calls of vervet monkeys, provided the basis for the evolution of human speech. To achieve the full implications of the hypothesis, we must go beyond the core data on the mirror system to stress that manipulation inherently involves hierarchical motor structures which are unavailable for the closed call system of primates. The mastery of hierarchical motor structures is not the property of F5 alone but involves its integration within a network of distributed cortical and subcortical structures. To understand this point, we recall Lashley's (1951) critique of behaviourist psychology: if we tried to learn a sequence like $A \rightarrow B \rightarrow A \rightarrow C$ by reflex chaining, what is to stop A triggering B every time, to yield the performance $A \rightarrow B \rightarrow A \rightarrow B \rightarrow A \rightarrow \dots$? A solution is to store the 'action codes' (motor schemas) A, B, C, … in one part of the brain and have another area hold 'abstract sequences' and learn to pair the right action with each element, as in Figure 2.4.[4]

---

[3] However, it is important to stress that the symbols of sign language are no more pantomimes than the characters of Chinese are drawings of objects. In each case, the explicit iconicity of the symbol (to the extent that it exists) is part of its history but is not appealed to in its use within a modern language.

[4] For those readers conversant with neurophysiology, I add that in my group's modelling of visuomotor control of grasping (Fagg and Arbib 1998) we posit that the action codes are in F5, the sequence information is in the region of the supplementary motor area called SMA-proper, and that the management of these sequences involves essential activity of the basal ganglia to manage priming and inhibition. The important point for all readers is that no single brain region holds the 'magic key' for perception and action, let alone language. Both F5 in monkey and Broca's area in human are embedded in much larger neural systems. Indeed, Lieberman (2000) downplays the role of Broca's area in language

Fɪɢ. 2.4 A solution to the problem of serial order in behaviour. Store the 'action codes' A, B, C, … in one part of the brain and have another area hold 'abstract sequences' and learn to pair the right action with each element.

2.4 From grasp to Language: seven hypothesized stages of evolution

How, then, do we get from the brain of our common ancestor with monkeys via the brain of our common ancestor with chimpanzees to the language-ready brain of the first *Homo sapiens*? Arbib (2002) extends the Mirror System Hypothesis to present seven stages of this evolution (S1-S7), with imitation grounding two of the stages. The first three stages are prehominid:

S1: **Grasping**

S2: **A mirror system for grasping shared with the common ancestor of human and monkey**

S3: **A simple imitation system for grasping shared with the common ancestor of human and chimpanzee**

The next three stages then distinguish the hominid line from that of the great apes:

S4: **A complex imitation system for grasping**

S5: **Protosign:** a manual-based communication system, breaking through the fixed repertoire of primate vocalizations to yield an open repertoire

S6: **Protospeech:** resulting from control mechanisms first evolved for protosign coming to control the vocal apparatus with increasing flexibility.

The final stage:

and emphasizes the role of the basal ganglia (the brain region from which different defects may yield Parkinson's disease and Huntington's disease).

S7: **Language**: the change from action–object frames to verb-argument structures to syntax and semantics; the co-evolution of cognitive and linguistic complexity.

S7 is claimed to involve little if any biological evolution, but instead to result from cultural evolution (historical change) in *Homo sapiens*.

Arbib (2002) discusses the distinction between 'simple' and 'complex' imitation—with chimpanzees being capable of the former but not the latter. Rather than rehearse these details here, it is important to distinguish two roles for imitation in the transition from complex imitation to proto-sign (S4 to S5).

Rizzolatti and Arbib (1998) stress the transition from praxic action directed towards a goal object to pantomime in which similar actions are produced away from the goal object. But communication is about far more than grasping! To pantomime the flight of a bird you must use movements of the hand (and arm and body) to imitate movement other than hand movements. You can also pantomime an object using movements which suggest tracing out the characteristic shape of the object. Imitation is the generic attempt to reproduce movements performed by another, whether to master a skill or simply as part of a social interaction. By contrast, pantomime is performed with the intention of getting the observer to think of a specific action or event. It is essentially communicative in its nature. The imitator observes; the pantomimic intends to be observed. This is where the intentionality (LR2) of language readiness comes in.

The transition to pantomime does seem to involve a genuine neurological change. Mirror neurons for grasping in the monkey will fire only if the monkey sees both the hand movement and the object to which it is directed (Umilta et al. 2001). A grasping movement that is not made in the presence of a suitable object, or is not directed toward that object, will not elicit mirror neuron firing. By contrast, in pantomime, the observer infers the goal or object of the action from observation of the movement in isolation.

A further critical (but perhaps non-biological) change en route to language emerges from the fact that in pantomime, it might be hard to distinguish a movement signifying 'bird' from one meaning 'flying'. This would favour the invention of abstract gestures available as elements for the formation of compounds which can be paired with meanings in more or less arbitrary fashion. This requires extending the mirror system to attend to a whole new class of hand movements, those with conventional meanings agreed upon by the protosign community to reduce ambiguity and extend semantic range. (As ahistorical support for this, note that Supalla and Newport (1978) observe that AIRPLANE is signed in American Sign Language with tiny repeated movements of a specific handshape, while FLY is signed by moving the same handshape along an extended trajectory.)[5] The notion, then, is that the manual domain supports the expression of meaning by sequences and interweavings of gestures, with a progression from pantomime to increasingly conventionalized gesture in order to speed and extend the range of communication within a community.

I would then argue that Stage 5 (protosign) provides the scaffolding for Stage 6 (protospeech). Some mirror neurons in the monkey are responsive to auditory input and there are oro-facial neurons in F5 that control movements that could well affect sounds emitted by the monkey (see Arbib 2004; Fogassi and Ferrari 2005, for references and further details). The speculation here is that the evolution of a system for voluntary control of intentional communication based on F5/Broca's area could then lay the basis for the evolution of creatures with more and more prominent connections from F5/Broca's area to the vocal apparatus. This in turn could provide conditions that lead to a period of co-evolution of the vocal apparatus and the neural circuitry to control it. Corballis (2002) offers cogent reasons for the selective advantage of incorporating vocalization into an originally hand-based communicative repertoire and I will not attempt to summarize them here.

Following Hurford (2004), we recall the Saussurean distinction between the sign and the signified, and the linkage between them (Figure 2.5).

For the top row of Figure 2.5, consider how the Mirror System Hypothesis supports the transition from a mirror system for grasping in F5 in the common ancestor of monkey and human to a mirror system for words (in the sense of composites of articulatory gestures) in Broca's area in humans:

- Mirror system for grasping and manual praxic actions
- Mirror system for pantomime of grasping and manual praxic actions
- Mirror system for pantomime of actions outside the pantomimic's own behavioural repertoire
- Mirror system for conventional gestures used to ritualize, disambiguate or replace pantomime

[5] I say 'ahistorical' because such signs are part of a modern human language rather than holdovers from protosign. Nonetheless, they exemplify the mixture of iconicity and convention that, I claim, distinguishes protosign from pantomime.

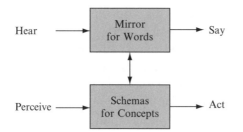

Fɪɢ. 2.5 The Saussurean sign linking word and meaning (adapted from Hurford 2004).

- Mirror system for all manual (and related facial) communicative gestures
- Mirror system for all vocal (and related manual and facial) communicative gestures

Hurford (2004) argues that there is a mirror system for concepts like grasp, run, walk etc., which links the perception and action related to each concept. Extending this, I argue that the bottom row of Figure 2.5 takes us into territory on which the Mirror System Hypothesis has remained silent. First, the Mirror System Hypothesis is agnostic as to whether there are mirror systems for actions other than those bulleted above and, if so, where these might be located in the human brain. Moreover, I do not believe that there is a mirror system for all concepts. Consider that recognizing an object (an apple, say) may be linked to many different courses of action (to place the apple in one's shopping basket; to place the apple in the bowl at home; to peel the apple; to eat the apple; to discard a rotten apple, etc.). Thus there cannot be a mirror system encompassing all concepts. Instead, I visualize the brain as encoding a varied network of perceptual and motor schemas (Arbib 1981, 2003). Only rarely (as in the case of certain basic actions like grasping and walking) will the perceptual and motor schemas be integrated into a 'mirror schema'. In general, a word may be linked to many schemas, with varying context-dependent activation strengths. On this view, a 'concept' corresponds not to one word but rather to a graded set of activations of the schema network.

A major goal for our action-oriented neurolinguistics is, then, to understand what additional mechanisms are employed by the human brain in linking cognitive form to semantic form and phonological form, in part by responding to the challenges in extending the model of Figure 2.4. Returning to Figure 2.5, we also need to explain (i) why it is easy for humans to build a 'mirror system' for 'words', and (ii) how this mirror system can be linked to the perceptual and motor schemas for concepts. In each case, I suggest that this is not a general property spread across the human brain, but instead involves different patterns of plasticity linked to specific brain mechanisms which evolved along the hominid line.

With this, I complete my presentation of the six stages of evolution of the language-ready brain. The details of the passage from protolanguage to language, the posited post-biological stage S7 (Language), are beyond the scope of this article. A preliminary account of the possible transitions from action–object frame to verb-argument structure to syntax and semantics is given in Arbib (2005).

2.5 Discussion

To conclude, we revisit the ten properties, LR1-LR6 and LA1-LA4, hypothesized to support protolanguage and 'true language' and try to reconcile them with the seven stages, S1-S7, of the extended Mirror

TABLE 2.1 *A comparative view of the posited properties of protolanguage and language (left column) and the seven stages of the extended Mirror System Hypothesis (right column).*

LR4: From hierarchical structuring to temporal ordering	S1: Grasping S2: Mirror for grasping
	S3: Simple imitation S4: Complex imitation
LR1: Symbolization LR2: Intentionality LR3: Parity (Mirror property)	S5: Protosign
	S6: Protospeech
LA1: Symbolization and compositionality LA2: Syntax, semantics, and recursion	S7: Language
LR5: Beyond the here-and-now 1 LA3: Beyond the here-and-now 2	
LR6: Paedomorphy and sociability LA4: Learnability	

System Hypothesis. Table 2.1 reorders these elements in a fashion designed to facilitate this comparison. The rows with the right-hand cell filled show the way in which the Mirror System Hypothesis provides an action-oriented framework for the evolution of protolanguage.

2.5.1 *LR4: From hierarchical structuring to temporal ordering → S1: Grasping; S2: Mirror for grasping*

Where Hauser et al. (2002) view recursion as the uniquely human key to the faculty of language, LR4 reminds us that the study of animal behaviour is replete with examples of how an animal can analyse a complex sensory scene and, in relation to its internal state, determine a course of action. When a frog faced with prey and predators and a barrier ends up, say, choosing a path around the barrier to escape the predator (see Cobas and Arbib 1992, for a model) it exemplifies the ability to analyse the spatial relation of objects in planning its action. However, there is little evidence of recursion here—once the frog rounds the barrier, it seems to need to see the prey anew to trigger its prey-catching behaviour. By contrast, the flow diagram given by Byrne (2003) shows that the processing (from getting a nettle plant to putting a folded handful of leaves into the mouth) used by a mountain gorilla when preparing bundles of nettle leaves to eat is clearly recursive. Gorillas (like many other species, and not only mammals) have the working memory to refer their next action not only to sensory data but also to the state of execution of some current plan. Thus when we refer to the monkey's grasping and its ability to recognize similar grasps in others (S1: Grasping and S2: Mirror for grasping) it is a mistake to treat the individual grasps in isolation—the F5 system is part of a larger system that can direct those grasps as part of a larger recursively structured plan. Of course, more needs to be done in understanding the interaction of the diverse neural systems that support grasping and how they each change in the evolution of the language-ready brain.

2.5.2 *S3: Simple imitation; S4: Complex imitation*

The multicausal view of evolution implicit in the above argument is (to simplify) that a change in one part of a complex system (e.g. in working memory) can be exapted to yield improved performance of another system (e.g. planning) in a way which makes a mutation affecting another system (e.g. perception of patterns of social behaviour) beneficial even though it would not have adaptive value had not prior changes (some primary and some secondary) already occurred. Such changes continue in a cascade over tens of millennia. What offers promise of an account in this vein becoming more than a series of just-so stories (which have value in framing our arguments) is the method of comparative biology—we cannot study the brains of our ancestors, but we can compare our brains with those of other species in the search for meaningful homologies (Aboitiz and García 1997; Arbib and Bota 2003) which can anchor and be anchored by the inference of evolutionary relationships. Similarly, we can compare behaviours (see also Pepperberg's Chapter 11 and Zuberbühler's Chapter 12). The fact that monkeys have little or no capacity for imitation, and had their common ancestor with humans some twenty million years ago, while chimpanzees have an ability for 'simple' imitation and had their common ancestor with humans some five million years ago makes it plausible that our evolutionary path took us through the emergence of simple imitation (S3: Simple imitation) before five million years ago, and the emergence of complex imitation (S4: Complex imitation) more recently. The left-hand cell is blank in this row of Table 2.1 because one can certainly entertain many scenarios for why both of these stages would have been adaptive in ways that had no relation to language as such. However, these stages are crucial to the present theory because complex imitation is central to the ability of human infants to acquire language and behaviour in a way that couples these in their increasing mastery of the physical and social world.

2.5.3 *LR1: Symbolization; LR2: Intentionality; LR3: Parity ⇔ S5: Protosign*

The Mirror System Hypothesis as presented above assumes, rather than provides an explanation for, LR2. This is Intentionality, the transition from making praxic movements, for example, those involved in the immediate satisfaction of some appetitive or aversive goal, to those intended by the utterer to have a particular effect on the recipient. As a placeholder, let me note that (as Darwin (1872/1998) observed long ago) the facial expressions of conspecifics provide valuable cues to their likely reaction to certain courses of behaviour (a rich complex summarized as 'emotional state') and that this ability can be observed across a far wider range of mammalian species than just the primates. Moreover, the F5 region contains oro-facial cells as well as manual cells. One might thus posit a progression from (i) control of emotional expression by systems that exclude F5 to the extension of F5's mirror capacity from manual to oro-facial movement and then, via its posited capacity (achieved by stage S3: Simple imitation) for simple imitation, (ii) ability to support the imitation of emotional expressions. This would then provide the ability (iii) to affect the behaviour of others by, for example, appearing angry. This would in turn provide the evolutionary opportunity to (iv) generalize the ability of F5 activity to affect the behaviour of conspecifics from vocal expressions to a general ability to use the imitation of behaviour (as distinct from praxic behaviour alone) as a means to influence others. This in turn makes possible (v) reciprocity by a process of backward chaining, where the influence is not so much on the praxis of the other as on the exchange of information. With this, the transition described by LR2 (intentionality) has been achieved in tandem with the achievement of LR1: Symbolization, the ability to associate an arbitrary symbol with a class of episodes, objects or actions (but without, at this stage, compositionality).

In the present theory, the crucial ingredient in LR1: Symbolization is the extension of imitation from the imitation of hand movements to the ability to in some sense project the degrees of freedom of movements involving other effectors (and even, say, of the passage of the wind through the trees) to create hand movements that could evoke something of the original in the brain of the observer. As my discussion of Hurford (2004) showed, this involves not merely changes internal to the mirror system but its integration with a wide range of brain regions involved in the elaboration and linkage of perceptual and motor schemas. With this, LR3: Parity follows automatically—what counts for the signer must count (approximately) for the observer.

The transition to protosign (S5) may not require further biological changes but does involve the discovery that it is more efficient to use conventionalized gestures for familiar objects, actions, and episodes than to initiate an original pantomime. With time and within a community these gestures would become increasingly stylized and their link to the original pantomime would be lost. But this loss would be balanced by the discovery that when an important distinction cannot be conveniently pantomimed, an arbitrary gesture may be invented to express the distinction. Deixis presumably plays a crucial role here—what cannot be pantomimed may be shown when it is present so that the associated symbol may be of use when it is absent. Protosign, then, emerges as a manual-based communication system rooted originally in pantomime but which is open to the addition of novel communicative gestures as the life of the community comes to define the underlying concepts and makes it important to communicate about them.

2.5.4 *S6: Protospeech*

I have placed S6: Protospeech, the evolution of protospeech, in a separate row of the table from S5: Protosign, the evolution of protosign, to stress that the role of F5 in grounding the evolution of a protolanguage system would work just as well if we and all our ancestors had been deaf. However, primates do have a rich auditory system which contributes to species survival in many ways, of which communication is just one (Ghazanfar 2003). The hypothesis here, then, is not that the protolanguage system had to create the appropriate auditory and vocal-motor system 'from scratch' but rather that it could build upon the existing mechanisms to derive protospeech. My hypothesis is that protosign grounded the crucial innovation of using arbitrary gestures to convey novel meanings, and that this in turn provided the scaffolding for protospeech.

Consistent with my view that true language emerged during the history of *Homo sapiens* and the observation that the vocal apparatus of humans is especially well adapted for speech, I suggest that the interplay between protospeech and protolanguage was an expanding spiral which yielded a brain that was ready for language in the multiple modalities of gesture, vocalization, and facial expression (Arbib 2004).

2.5.5 *LA1: Symbolization and compositionality; LA2: Syntax, semantics and recursion ⇔ S7: Language*

I claim that stage S7: Language, the transition from protolanguage to language, is the culmination of manifold discoveries in the history of mankind, arguing that it required manifold incremental changes to yield the full structure of language: the symbols which were developed so painfully in prehuman societies become words in the modern sense, interchangeable and composable in the expression of meaning (LA1: Symbolization and compositionality). This fractionation of the vocabulary made necessary the development of syntax and semantics to gain the benefits of putting the pieces together in novel combinations without an explosion of ambiguity

(LA2: Syntax, semantics, and recursion). What I stress is that there was no sudden transition from holophrastic utterances to an elaborate system of principles and parameters. Rather, languages emerged through a process of bricolage (tinkering) which yielded many novelties to handle special problems of communication, with a variety of generalizations amplifying the power of groups of inventions by unifying them to provide tools of greatly extended range. Clearly, I have not offered a comprehensive argument for this position here, and plan to develop a fuller argument elsewhere.

2.5.6 *LR5: Beyond the here-and-now 1; LA3: Beyond the here-and-now 2*

LR5 and LA3, the two forms of 'Beyond the here-and-now', together make two points: the first is that language involves many powerful devices that extend the range of communication but that might not be considered as touchstones to the definition of language. Thus, if one took a human language and removed all reference to time, one might still want to call it a language rather than a protolanguage, even though one would agree that it was thereby greatly impoverished. Similarly, the number system of a language can be seen as a useful, but not definitive, 'plug in'. LA3: Beyond the here-and-now 2 nonetheless suggests that the ability to talk about past and future is a central part of human languages as we understand them. Secondly, LR5: Beyond the here-and-now 1 reminds us that these features of language would be meaningless (literally) without the underlying cognitive machinery—in this case the substrate for episodic memory provided by the hippocampus (Burgess, Jeffery, and O'Keefe 1999) and the substrate for planning provided by the frontal cortex (Passingham 1993: chapter 10). Thus the neurolinguist must not only seek to learn from the syntactician how time is expressed in a variety of languages, but also seek to understand how these verbal structures are linked to the cognitive structures which give them meaning and thus, presumably, grounded their evolution—irrespective of what autonomy the syntactic structures may have when severed from the contingencies of communication.

2.5.7 *LR6: Paedomorphy and sociality; LA4: Learnability*

The final row of Table 2.1 again links a biological condition with a 'supplementary' property of human languages. This supplementary property is that languages do not simply exist—they are acquired anew (and, as we saw above, may be slightly modified thereby) in each generation (LA4: Learnability). The biological property is an inherently social one about the nature of the relationship between parent (or other caregiver) and child (LR6: Paedomorphy and sociality); the prolonged period of infant dependency which is especially pronounced in humans has co-evolved with the social structures for caregiving that provide the conditions for the complex social learning that makes possible the richness of human cultures in general and of human languages in particular.

I deny that there is any single 'magic mutation' or change of brain or body structure that created the capacity for language as humans know it today, and the rows in Table 2.1 with the right-hand cell empty indicate some of the further work that must be done. However, the above discussion should make clear that the evolution of the mirror system is one important aspect of brain changes underlying the evolution of language readiness and that the Mirror System Hypothesis does indeed provide an action-oriented framework for the evolution of protolanguage, which should in future serve to anchor new contributions to linguistics through enriched attention to neurolinguistics.

ACKNOWLEDGEMENTS

Preparation of this chapter was made possible in part by a Fellowship from the University of Southern California Center for Interdisciplinary Research. Travel to the Harvard meeting was funded by a grant from VPRO Dutch Television for travel to the Netherlands to tape a programme on mirror neurons. Some of the material presented here was further developed for a pre-conference workshop entitled 'Conversations on language, brain, culture' held in association with ASFLA 2002, Macquarie University, Sydney, Australia, on July 4th, 2002. I want to express my gratitude to the two referees and, especially, to Maggie Tallerman for the probing comments that led me to recast the original draft in a form that greatly clarifies what I am trying to say.

FURTHER READINGS

- Rizzolatti and Arbib (1998) is an early statement of the Mirror System Hypothesis.
- Aboitiz and García (1997) gives an alternative view of the evolution of brain mechanisms supporting human language, with special emphasis on com-

paring the macaque and human brain, and on the importance of specialized working memories.

- Bickerton (1995) gives an account of the best-known view of protolanguage, which the present chapter seeks to oppose.
- Deacon (1997) provides an excellent exposition of the evolution of language and brain, especially strong on presenting the relevant neuroscience in an accessible manner.
- Finally, Arbib (2005) presents an expanded version of many of the arguments of the present chapter, accompanied by critiques of the theory by experts from a wide range of disciplines, and the author's attempt to defend and, where appropriate, update the theory in light of these commentaries.

3   How did language go discrete?

MICHAEL STUDDERT-KENNEDY

'Human language is based on an elementary property that also seems to be biologically isolated: the property of discrete infinity.'

(Chomsky (2000: 3))

3.1 Introduction

'Discrete infinity' refers to the creative property of language by which speakers construct and hearers understand, from a finite set of discrete units, an infinite variety of expressions of thought, imagination, and feeling. This is the property that Chomsky has been endeavouring to describe and explain throughout his career. For Chomsky, the central, 'biologically isolated' property of language and the source of its infinite scope is syntax, the abstract, linguistic, computational system by which discrete, meaningful units (morphemes, words) are combined to form an infinite variety of phrases and sentences. An important mechanism of syntax is recursion, the embedding of a phrase within a phrase that permits, in principle, sentences of infinite length and affords language much of its power to express new thoughts appropriate to new situations. Indeed, in a recent paper, Hauser, Chomsky, and Fitch (2002: 1571) term recursion a 'core property' of language. They defend the hypotheses that (1) 'FLN [the faculty of language in a narrow sense] comprises only the core computational mechanisms of recursion', (2) 'only FLN is uniquely human', and (3) 'most, if not all, of FLB [the faculty of language in a broad sense] is based on mechanisms shared with non-human animals' (2002: 1573).

Hypotheses limiting the 'uniquely human' properties of language to a single syntactic mechanism without regard to phonology or semantics have no empirical basis, however. The hypotheses derive rather from the purely formal 'architecture', the 'syntactocentric' model of language that generative linguistics has assumed, without evidence or argument, since its inception (Jackendoff 2002: 107–11). Hauser et al. (2002: 1570) illustrate the model in their figure 2 with concentric circles: recursion at the centre, surrounded by 'conceptual-intentional', 'sensory-motor', and other 'broad' processes at the periphery. Such a model does not lend itself to evolutionary interpretation because it suggests no path from sensory-motor primitives to elaborated cognitive syntax by which supporting neural structures might have grown and evolved. In fact, the model is simply one of many possible descriptions of language form. Yet what we need, if we are to understand how language became part of the human genetic endowment, is a model of language function. Form follows function, not function form.

The present chapter attempts to contribute to a model of function by starting from the bottom up instead of the top down. The chapter argues that phonology, though it lacks recursion, has its own mode of discrete infinity (cf. Jackendoff 2002: 111–17), no less 'biologically isolated' than that of syntax, namely, its capacity to form an unbounded set of meaningful words by combining a finite set of meaningless discrete phonetic units. Indeed, it is in words rather than in syntax that the child first evinces, by systematic speech errors, a combinatorial capacity for discrete infinity (see section 3.8, below). Moreover, as Bickerton has remarked, 'Syntax could not have come into existence until there was a sizable vocabulary whose units could be combined into complex structures' (1995: 51). And, we may add, a sizable vocabulary, beyond the 30–40 vocal signals typical of modern primates, could not have come into existence until holistic vocalizations had differentiated into categories of discrete phonetic units that could be organized into words (Lindblom 1992, 1998; Studdert-Kennedy 1987; Wray 2000). Thus, discrete phonetic units are, logically and biologically, necessary precursors of syntax and therefore the ground of Chomsky's discrete infinity.

The combination of discrete phonetic units into a functional hierarchy (gestures, segments, syllables) seems, moreover, to be an example of a biologically unique mode of behavioural organization. Several studies, seeking analogues in animal behaviour, have discovered statistically defined, higher-order groupings of elementary behavioural units in, for example, blowfly grooming (Dawkins 1976), mouse grooming (Fentress

1983), chickadee calls (Hailman and Ficken 1987), and gibbon 'song' (Mitani and Marler 1989). But none has found new levels of structure or function in higher-order units analogous to the structure of a syllable or the meaning of a word. Of course, even if chickadee calls, gibbon 'song', or any other animal communication system were indeed analogues of human language, the prospects for further behavioural studies along these lines would still not be good—at least if we assume for animal systems what Chomsky has long (correctly) maintained for language (e.g. 1965: 21) that, in principle, no objective procedures for discovery of linguistic structure beyond a speaker-hearer's intuition are possible.

Not surprisingly, then, 'duality of patterning' (Hockett 1958), the two-tiered hierarchy of phonology and syntax that affords language its infinite expressive scope, is commonly taken to be a 'fundamental universal characteristic' of language (Hurford 2002a: 319). The origin of this 'universal characteristic' is seldom considered, however (although see Carstairs-McCarthy 1999, and also Tallerman, Chapter 6, for a critique). Certainly, Hauser et al. (2002) have nothing to say on the matter. The purpose of what follows is to suggest how this hierarchy might have begun to evolve. My key assumptions are two: (i) The elements of cognitive structure initially arise *in evolution*, directly or indirectly, from sensorimotor experience: brains evolved to perceive the world and to control action; (ii) functional (articulatory and acoustic) properties of speech give rise to phonological form, not vice versa. I will propose that discrete phonetic units evolved in step with vocal imitation, a capacity unique among primates to humans (Hauser 1996), by differentiation of the vocal apparatus into six discrete, independently controlled organs, and that vocal imitation evolved out of the manual and facial imitation characteristic of an earlier hominid mimetic culture (Donald 1991), perhaps supported by systems of mirror neurons such as those recently discovered in macaques (Rizzolatti and Arbib 1998; Arbib, Chapter 2 above).

3.2 The analogy between language and the genetic system

3.2.1 *Meaningless discrete units*

That speech can be broken into strings of phonetic units, consonants, and vowels was, of course, known to ancient Greek and Roman grammarians;

the latter, indeed, gave them their names, *littera vocalis* and *littera con-sonans*, in which letters of the alphabet are explicitly identified with sounds of speech. And, as a matter of fact, until x-rays and magnetic resonance images of speech became available, the transcription of speech by a listener into a string of discrete alphabetic symbols and its recovery by a reader were our only evidence for the standard assumption that we speak by permuting and combining a finite number of discrete elements of sound.

The 'potential infiniteness' of language as 'a system of sound–meaning connections' was recognized, as Hauser et al. (2002: 1571) observe, by Galileo and the seventeenth-century 'philosophical grammarians', among others. Yet, unlike Hauser et al. (2002), these writers saw 'potential infiniteness' as arising, in the first instance, not from the combination of meaningful units or from syntactic recursion (of which they knew noth-ing), but from the combination of meaningless letters of the alphabet or speech sounds to form words. In passages quoted elsewhere by Chomsky (1966: 84), we find Galileo (1632/1953: 119) attributing the vast scope of written language to 'the various collocations of twenty-four little charac-ters upon a paper', and the 'philosophical grammarians' admiring '... cette invention merveilleuse de composer de vingt-cinq ou trente sons cette infinie variété de mots... n'ayant rien de semblable en eux-mêmes à ce qui se passe dans notre esprit...' ['... this marvellous inven-tion of forming an infinite variety of words from twenty-five or thirty sounds that in no way resemble in themselves what goes on in our mind...']. (Arnauld and Lancelot 1660/1997: 23). Here, the authors stress that the basic combinatorial elements they are thinking of are arbitrary and have no intrinsic meaning, a point that Hauser et al. (2002) fail to mention.

Similarly, in the analogy between language and the genetic system with which they open their paper, Hauser et al. (2002: 1569) remark on certain correspondences—hierarchy, generativity, recursion, limitless scope—but ignore the correspondence that makes all the others possible, namely, the intrinsic lack of meaning in both gene and phonetic segment. If meaning, or function, inhered in the elementary units, they could hardly commute across contexts to form larger structures with new meanings or functions. Thus, Jakobson (1970: 438), a linguist, remarked that both 'the genetic code and the verbal system are... based upon the use of discrete compo-nents... devoid of inherent meaning', and Jacob (1977: 188), a biologist writing of language and heredity, stressed that 'for such a system to function implies that the basic units, phonemes or chemical radicals, are by themselves devoid of meaning'. Yet Hauser et al. (2002) propose a model in which the basic mechanism, common to both genetics and language, of combining meaningless units to form a hierarchical structure of meaning (or function) above them, is not even mentioned.

3.2.2 *The particulate principle*

The analogy between language and the genetic system, captured in the now standard textbook metaphor of the 'genetic code' and adopted without question by Hauser et al. (2002: 1569), was a source of puzzlement to Jakobson (1970), one of the first to remark it. He raised the question of 'whether the isomorphism exhibited by these two different codes, genetic and verbal, results from a mere convergence induced by similar needs, or whether, perhaps, the foundations of the overt linguistic patterns superimposed upon molecular communication have been modelled directly on its structural principles' (1970: 440). The answer, convergence of function rather than homology of form, was implicit in Jacob's observation that the principle of a combinatorial hierarchy '. . . appears to operate in nature each time there is a question of generating a large diversity of structures using a restricted number of building blocks' (Jacob 1977: 188). But it was Abler (1989) who spelled out the logic of the answer, and so invited a more illuminating and evolutionarily tractable model of language than the syntactocentrism of Hauser et al. (2002).

Abler (1989) was the first to extend to other domains Fisher's (1930) arguments concerning the discrete combinatorial (as opposed to blending) mechanisms of heredity. He recognized that a combinatorial and hierarchical principle is a mathematically necessary condition of all natural systems that 'make infinite use of finite means', including physics, chemistry, genetics, and language. He dubbed it 'the particulate principle of self-diversifying systems'. Briefly, the principle holds that all such systems necessarily display the following properties: (i) Discrete units drawn from a finite set of primitive units or elements (e.g. atoms, genes, phonetic segments) are repeatedly permuted and combined to yield larger units (e.g. molecules, proteins, syllables/words) above them in a hierarchy of levels of increasing complexity; (ii) at each level of the hierarchy, larger units have structures and functions beyond and more diverse than those of their constituents from below; (iii) units that combine into a larger unit do not disappear or lose their integrity: they can re-emerge or be recovered through mechanisms of physical, chemical, or genetic interaction, or, for language, through the mechanisms of human speech perception and language understanding. (For fuller discussion, see Studdert-Kennedy 1998, 2000.)

For an evolutionary account of language the importance of the particulate principle is twofold. First, it brings language within the natural sciences by generalizing its combinatorial, hierarchical structure across other domains; in other words, *it derives duality of patterning from a broad extra-linguistic physical principle rather than accepting it as a language-specific cognitive axiom.* Second, the principle invites a view of language as a hierarchy of increasing scope, and complexity, evolving by stages from basic symbolic reference, or 'naming' (Terrace 1985, 2005), and a combinatorial phonetics, through the simple word combination of a proto-language (Bickerton 1990), to the elaborate combinatorial phrase structures of recursive syntax (cf. Dessalles 2000: part II; Jackendoff 2002: chapter 8). On such a model, each step in the evolution (or ontogeny) of the 'language organ' sets up the structural conditions for the next step.

3.3 The elements of speech and language

3.3.1 *The linguistic status of consonants, vowels, and features*

Whether we acknowledge the particulate principle, as logic demands, or simply accept the dual pattern as an unexplained, language-specific axiom, as does Hurford (2002a), we cannot avoid the question of what the elements of spoken language actually are. Curiously, a common answer, even among writers concerned with the evolution of language (e.g. Hurford 2002a; Kohler 1998; MacNeilage 1998), is that the basic units are consonants, vowels, and their descriptive features.

The answer is curious for at least three reasons. First, consonants and vowels have no existence outside language: they are purely linguistic entities and therefore precisely what an evolutionary account of phonology must explain. No one undertaking an evolutionary account of syntax takes its major word classes, such as nouns and verbs, for granted. They attempt rather to ground the classes in properties and events of the external world to which early hominids may be presumed to have been sensitive, by invoking such extralinguistic notions as Agent, Patient, Goal (e.g. Bickerton 1990). Similarly, consonants and vowels must have arisen from prelinguistic primate perceptuomotor capacities. How did this come about?

A second reason for rejecting consonants and vowels as basic elements is that they are compound units, analogous to molecules, not atoms. They are commonly said to be bundles or strings of features. But, as the adjectival nomenclature of feature systems reveals (labial, coronal, nasal, etc.), features are descriptive properties, not substantive entities, and necessarily therefore, like the segments they describe, purely linguistic. Features too must derive from prior non-linguistic perceptuomotor capacities.

A third reason for rejecting consonants and vowels is that we have known for over fifty years, since the publication of Joos' *Acoustic phonetics* in 1948, that discrete units corresponding to consonants and vowels are not to be found in the acoustic signal (Liberman, Cooper, Shankweiler, and Studdert-Kennedy 1967). The standard response to this paradox, implicit but not always acknowledged, has been a retreat into cognition. The retreat was sounded by Hockett (1958: 210) in his famous simile likening a string of phonemes passing through the speech apparatus to a row of variously coloured, but unboiled Easter eggs passing through a wringer. On this view, discrete units exist only in the minds of speakers and hearers. Special implementation rules are applied by the speaker and special (or, for some authors, general) perceptual mechanisms are deployed by the listener. But, for an evolutionary account, the retreat into cognition will not do. How, after all, did discrete units get into the mind?

3.3.2 *Insights from reading machines for the blind*

Clues to the true nature of the units of speech came from work on reading machines for the blind, devices designed to transform optic print into an acoustic alphabet—a sort of auditory Braille (Cooper, Gaitenby, and Nye 1984). Despite years of work in several countries, no one succeeded in devising a set of acoustic patterns more efficient than the dots and dashes of Morse code, for which highly skilled professional users may reach reception rates of some 30–40 words/minute, roughly one fifth of a normal English speaking rate and intolerable for extended listening. Why is speech so much more efficient than any artificial acoustic code? In English, we readily produce and comfortably understand 120–180 words/minute or 10–15 phonetic segments/second. (Readers may want to check these numbers by reading a text out loud at a brisk rate for a minute.) If we break the phonetic segments down into discrete movements of lips, tongue, velum, and larynx, we arrive at a rate of some 15–20 movements/second. By way of comparison, a violinist's tremolo may reach 16 Hz and a hummingbird may beat its wings at over 70 Hz. But these are identical repetitive movements of a single organ. Speech, by contrast, engages half a dozen organs (lips, tongue blade/body/root, velum, larynx) in as many different combinations as there are different phonetic segments in the speech stream, all nicely executed within a tolerance of millimetres and milliseconds. In fact, it is precisely the distribution of action over different articulators that makes the high rates of speech possible.

Such rates can be achieved only if separate parts of the articulatory machinery—muscles of the lips, tongue, velum, etc.—can be separately controlled and if a change of state for any one of these entities, together with the current state of others is a change to another phoneme . . . it is this kind of *parallel processing* that makes it possible to get high-speed performance with low-speed machinery (Liberman et al. 1967: 446, italics added).

Here, departing from the purely sequential processing usually assumed for patterns of sound distributed over time, the authors propose both for speech production and, by implication, for speech perception (as many subsequent studies have indeed confirmed) a mode of parallel processing such as enables us to perceive patterns of light distributed over space so rapidly—most notably in reading. The authors see the greater rate of speech compared with arbitrary acoustic alphabets as due to rapid moment-to-moment changes in vocal tract configuration (and so in spectral structure) effected by the orchestrated actions or momentary positions of *all vocal organs simultaneously* (cf. Lindblom 1998: 261). They propose, as a basic phonetic element, a change in position by an articulator, that is, a unit of action. Importantly, unlike the static acoustic alphabets devised for reading machines, the proposed unit is dynamic.

Notice also that, unlike consonants, vowels and features, movements of the vocal apparatus are not intrinsically linguistic. Almost every movement of the articulatory machinery, later refined and adapted to speech, may be found in crude form in primate cries and calls (glottal action, lip protrusion, mandible lowering and raising) or in primate sucking and feeding (smacking the lips, lowering and raising the mandible for chewing; raising, lowering, humping, and retroflexing the tongue to prepare a bolus of food for swallowing, and so on). Thus, many speech gestures are adaptive variants of prior non-speech units of action (cf. MacNeilage 1998).

3.3.3 *The gesture in articulatory phonology*

Once a movement has been selected for linguistic use, it may properly be termed a gesture, that is, a movement made with communicative intent. The word 'gesture' has been widely used informally in the speech literature for many years to refer to articulatory movements. Only recently has the term been given a precise, technical definition and formally adopted by Browman, Goldstein, and their colleagues, as the central concept in the new and still developing theory of articulatory phonology (Browman and Goldstein 1986, 1991, 1992, 1995).

In that theory the gesture serves as a unit of motoric, phonetic, and phonological function. Motorically, a gesture is the act of forming and releasing a constriction of variable location and degree, at some point in the vocal tract, thus effecting a dynamic sequence of vocal tract configurations. (The reason for including both formation and release of a constriction within a single gesture is the fact, established by many perceptual studies, that acoustic information specifying any given gesture is distributed over the spectral structure both before and after the peak or centre of the gesture itself.) Phonetically and phonologically, a gesture achieves some communicative goal, such as lip closure, velum lowering, tongue raising, glottal abduction, and so on. Thus, the gesture is simultaneously a concrete unit of phonetic action and an abstract unit of phonological contrast.

I will not rehearse here arguments and experimental evidence for the gesture, all readily available in the substantial literature on articulatory phonology and in several recent papers (e.g. Browman and Goldstein 2000; Goldstein, Pouplier, Chen, Saltzman, and Byrd, forthcoming; Studdert-Kennedy and Goldstein 2003). I note only the following points that distinguish gestures from the purely linguistic entities of consonants, vowels, and features. First, as a unit of phonetic action the gesture can be directly observed by a variety of techniques, including x-ray, magnetic resonance imaging, and palatography. (In fact, it was by copying the movements of discrete articulators from x-ray microbeam data for use in articulatory synthesis of speech by a vocal tract model that the gesture of articulatory phonology was first described and defined.) Second, because the gesture is not intrinsically linguistic, we can trace a continuous path from infant prelinguistic mouthings and vocalizations through babbling and early speech to the mature phonological system (e.g. Nittrouer 1993; Studdert-Kennedy 2002; Studdert-Kennedy and Goodell 1995). Third, the gesture takes a step toward the desired evolutionary account of the origins of consonants and vowels, and their descriptive features, by viewing them as recurrent, complex, cohesive patterns of gesture and sound. The last point is particularly important because it allows us to see consonants and vowels as dynamic units of phonetic action, spatially and temporally coordinated gestural structures, rather than as static 'beads on a string', as the saying goes.

3.4 Where do gestures come from?

A fair conclusion from the argument up to this point is that the shift from continuously variable primate signalling to particulate human language required an integral anatomical system of discrete, independently movable parts that could be coordinated to effect rapid sequences of expressive global action. The only candidate systems among primates (perhaps, indeed, in the entire animal kingdom) are the hands, the face, and the vocal apparatus. One might readily develop an argument for signing with hands and face similar to what follows for speech with face and vocal apparatus, but I focus on the latter, if only because facial expression and vocalization (together with bodily posture) are the principal means of communication among our closest primate relatives. How then, we must ask, did the human face and vocal apparatus come to be so much more highly differentiated than those of other primates? How did we come to have independent control over the several parts, or organs, of these two systems? And how did we come by the capacity to coordinate the actions of these organs into cohesive facial expressions and vocal tract configurations?

Ultimately, the evolution of such capacities must rest on changes in morphology and neurophysiology. 'The crucial factor, however, in the

acquisition of most evolutionary novelties is a shift in behavior...
[C]hanges in behavior generate new selection forces which modify the
structures involved' (Mayr 1982: 611-12). My hypothesis is that the
'crucial factor' in differentiation of the human face and vocal apparatus
was the evolution of facial and vocal imitation, both behaviours unique
among primates to humans (Hauser 1996). How and when did the
capacity to imitate first arise?

3.5 Mimetic culture

The gap between the collective habits of ape and human social groups is so
wide that we are compelled to posit intervening stages of prelinguistic
hominid social organization. By far the most deeply thought-out account
of such an intervening culture is Donald's (1991) hypothesis of a mimetic
culture in *Homo erectus*, generally believed to have been an immediate
predecessor of *Homo sapiens*. *Homo erectus*, a stable species for more than
a million years, spread out over the entire Eurasian land mass, leaving
evidence of a complex nomadic life well beyond the reach of apes: they
made stone tools, practised butchery, and used fire. What held groups of
these creatures together? How did individuals communicate with one
another? How did they plan group activities? We shall probably never
know the answers to these questions, but here I adopt Donald's (1991)
well reasoned, though necessarily speculative, account of how the capacity
for bodily imitation first arose.

Donald sees the modern human mind as a hybrid of its past embodi-
ments. In the brachiomanual gestures, facial expressions, pantomime and
inarticulate vocalizations to which modern humans readily resort when
deprived of the use of language, Donald sees a powerful and coherent
mode of communication and thought that he terms mimesis. The capacity
for mimesis, Donald proposes, first arose in *Homo erectus*. The mode
requires conscious and intentional control of expressive behaviours, including facial mimicry and inarticulate vocalization, which we still use and
understand in dance, pantomime, and even daily life. We are justified in
regarding mimesis as a possible independent mode of communication
that evolved before language, because it emerges naturally in deaf and
aphasic individuals who cannot speak or use a formal sign language, and

in normal individuals who find themselves among speakers of a language they do not know.

Mimesis is a continuous, analogue, iconic mode of representation, instantaneous in its effect, holistic and idiosyncratic. Language, by contrast, is particulate (or digital), non-iconic, linear and hierarchical, analytic and conventional (grammatical). How did the face and vocal apparatus go from analogue to discrete? How did they differentiate into discrete independently controllable organs? For this we must consider what little we know about the mechanism of imitation.

3.6 How do we imitate?

Imitation is central to human life and culture. Almost everything we do in our daily lives, other people also do. We are creatures of conformity who have learned to live by copying others. Yet we know remarkably little about how we do this. We wave goodbye to a one-year-old infant, in its mother's arms, and we are not surprised when the infant waves back. But how does the child do this? How does it transduce the optic pattern falling on its retinae into the matching pattern of movements in its own hand and arm? How does light get into the muscles?

'I would not be surprised if specific neurons were found that carry out some of the basic tasks of imitation, such as relating observed facial expressions or actions to one's own...' (Blackmore 1999: 80-1). When Blackmore published these words, evidence for such neurons had already been found in the macaque monkey by Rizzolatti and his colleagues at the University of Parma (Rizzolatti, Fadiga, Gallese, and Fogassi 1996).

3.6.1 *Mirror neurons*

Certain neurons in ventral premotor cortex (area F5) of the macaque brain fire not only when the monkey performs an action, but also when it sees another monkey or another creature with similar gross anatomy, a human experimenter, perform the same action (Rizzolatti et al. 1996; Arbib, Chapter 2). The first actions for which these so-called 'mirror neurons' were reported were manual actions, such as grasping, twisting, tearing, or otherwise manipulating pieces of food. Later studies found F5 neurons (i) for both seeing and producing mouth actions, including communicative mouth actions, such as lip protrusion and lip-smacking (Ferrari, Gallese, Rizzolatti, and Fogassi 2003), and (ii) for both hearing and/or seeing and producing sound-making actions, such as ripping paper, dropping a stick, or breaking a peanut (Kohler, Keyser, Umiltá, Fogassi, Gallese, and Rizzolatti 2002).

According to Rizzolatti and Arbib (1998), area F5 is somatotopically organized: its dorsal part contains a representation for hand movements, its ventral part a representation for mouth and larynx movements. The rostral part of the macaque ventral premotor cortex is believed by many to be the homologue of human Broca's area. Importantly, 'in most F5 neurons, the discharge correlates with an action, rather than with the individual movements that form it' (Rizzolatti and Arbib 1998: 18). In other words, F5 is organized not only *somatotopically*, but also by *function* or *action*. Since macaques are not known to imitate the actions they observe, either in the wild or in the laboratory, Rizzolatti and Arbib (1998: 190) postulated 'a fundamental mechanism for action recognition' in these monkeys.

Evidence consistent with both manual and vocal mirror neuron systems in humans comes from transcranial magnetic stimulation (TMS) studies. TMS, focused on specific cortical sites, can either excite or inhibit the neurons that activate specific muscles of which the response can then be measured by changes in electrical potential associated with muscle contractions, that is, by motor-evoked potentials (MEPs). Fadiga and his colleagues have shown that MEPs recorded from hand muscles are significantly increased over the levels induced by TMS alone, if subjects are simultaneously observing, or even simply imagining, movements normally executed by those muscles (Fadiga, Fogassi, Pavesi, and Rizzolatti 1995). Similarly, listening to words or pseudowords (nonsense) containing medial linguapalatal trills (e.g. Italian *birra* (beer) or *berro* (pseudoword)) significantly increases MEPs, recorded from the tongue muscle that effects the linguapalatal constriction, over the baseline TMS level for that muscle, as compared with listening to words containing medial labiodental fricatives (e.g. *baffo* (moustache) or *biffo* (pseudoword)) or with listening to a pair of non-speech tones (Fadiga, Craighero, Buccino, and Rizzolatti 2002). This result is consistent with a system of mirror neurons underlying both our capacity for vocal imitation and, perhaps, a motor mechanism of speech perception (Studdert-Kennedy 2002).

We should, however, strike two notes of caution. First, the putative speech mirror neurons do not explain how the transform from sound to phonetic action is actually effected; for example, we do not know how they solve the puzzle of the so-called 'inverse transform'. The puzzle arises because, although a given vocal tract configuration gives rise to a unique acoustic spectral pattern, the inverse does not hold: a given spectral pattern may arise from two or more different vocal tract configurations. Of course, the ambiguity may be reduced, or even eliminated, under the dynamic constraints of gestures moving from target to target, so that there would then be no puzzle to solve. Nonetheless, in their perceptual function, speech mirror neurons evidently represent the output from a process of acoustic-to-articulatory transformation that we still do not fully understand.

A second note of caution accompanies the inference from mirror neurons to imitation. For, as remarked above, although macaques (the only creatures in which single mirror neurons have so far been directly observed) recognize, they do not imitate the actions that their mirror neurons represent. On the other hand, recognition that a conspecific shares the same motor repertoire as oneself would seem to be a first and necessary step toward imitation (and, incidentally, toward a 'theory of mind'). We may reasonably hypothesize therefore that mimesis evolved in the hominid line by exploiting mirror neuron systems inherited from primate ancestors. Mirror neurons seem indeed to provide precisely the type of intermodal representation that Meltzoff and Moore (1997) posit in their model of human facial imitation.

3.7 From facial to vocal imitation

3.7.1 *Facial imitation in infants*

Infants can imitate manual, facial, and vocal actions. Facial imitation is unique among the three modalities because the child cannot feel the face that it sees and cannot see the face that it feels. Facial imitation is therefore necessarily cross- or intermodal.

Much of what we know about infant facial imitation comes from the sustained research programme of Meltzoff and Moore (1997 and many references therein). Among the characteristics of infant facial imitation, they list the following (1997, table 1): (i) infants imitate a range of specific, isolated, and arbitrary acts, including tongue protrusion, lip protrusion, mouth opening, eye blinking, cheek and brow movements; (ii) infants, presented with a model to imitate, quickly activate the appropriate facial organ (indicating somatotopic representation of facial organs); (iii) infants spontaneously correct their erroneous imitations; (iv) infants imitate absent actions, that is, actions previously, but not currently, observed. These last two characteristics demonstrate that facial imitation is mediated by a representation of the target. We recognize in this list characteristics familiar, *mutatis mutandis*, from infants' early imitations of words.

Indeed, Meltzoff and Moore (1997) propose a model, the active intermodal matching (AIM) model of facial imitation, that can readily be extended to vocal imitation. Their model is particularly appropriate because it deals not with the 'rational imitation' of function described by Gergely, Bekkering, and Kiraly (2002), for example, but with mimicry of arbitrary facial actions similar to the intrinsically meaningless gestures of vocal mimicry and vocal accommodation (Locke, 1993: chapter 4; Vihman 1996: 115-18). Among the concepts central to AIM are *organ identification, body babbling*, and *organ relations*. Organ identification evidently draws on somatotopic representations similar to those by which infants recognize correspondences between their own vocal organs and those of adults. Body babbling, like vocal babbling, is spontaneous activity by which the infant discovers the relations between its movements and the resulting organ configurations. Organ relations (e.g. tongue between lips, tongue protruded beyond lips, eyebrows raised, and so on) are analogous to the vocal tract configurations that the infant learns to recognize in an adult spoken utterance; organ relations are the metric by which infant and adult actions are perceived as commensurate.

3.7.2 *The facial–vocal link*

Given the importance of facial expression in primate communication (Darwin 1872/1998; Hauser 1996: chapters 4 and 7), and the evidence for mirror neurons responding to and producing communicative mouth actions in macaques, we may reasonably suppose that the capacity for facial imitation, postulated by Donald (1991) for the mimetic culture of *Homo erectus*, would have been supported by a system of facial mirror neurons, such as that of the modern macaque.

We also know that changes in position of the lips, jaw and teeth in rhesus monkeys, as in humans, affect the spectral structure of vocalizations (Hauser, Evans, and Marler 1993). Indeed, the close relation between facial expression and the quality of vocalizations was remarked by Darwin (1872/1998: 96). Thus, we may reasonably hypothesize that, as systematic vocal communication was gradually added to the mimetic repertoire in the transition from *Homo erectus* to *Homo sapiens*, the facial mirror neuron system was gradually coopted and extended to the vocal organs. Thus, the capacity for vocal imitation may have evolved out of the capacity for facial imitation, leading crucially to differentiation of the vocal tract. The end result of this process, as we have seen, seems to be a finely differentiated mirror neuron system for speech in *Homo sapiens*.

3.8 Grounding phonetic categories

3.8.1 *The role of imitation in vocal tract differentiation*

Imitation has often been dismissed as a factor in language acquisition because the child learning syntax quite evidently does more than imitate: it extracts and applies rules. Nonetheless, imitation is the key to building a lexicon large enough to trigger the onset of word combination and syntax. Imitation of a spoken word requires implicit parsing of the perceived act into its component gestures and their reassembly in correct spatiotemporal sequence (cf. Byrne 2003). We see this quite clearly in the systematic errors of a child attempting its first words (Studdert-Kennedy 2002; Studdert-Kennedy and Goodell 1995). Typically, the child recognizes which articulatory organs to activate, but fails to execute the correct amplitude or the correct relative phasing of gestures. Consider, for example, a twenty-two-month old girl who says ['weːn'di] for ['rezn̩] (*raisin*). She evidently recognized the organs to be activated (lips, tongue-tip, velum), but she omitted the initial tongue-tip retroflexion, while correctly rounding the lips, to give [w] instead of [r]; she correctly closed the tongue tip against the palate, while lowering the velum correctly, but too early, to yield an anticipatory [n], then raised the velum while holding the tongue-tip closure to give a delayed stop, [d], instead of the required fricative, [z]; finally, she released the tongue tip, but delayed opening the glottis, to give an unwanted final vowel, assimilated to the preceding point of tongue-tip constriction. Such errors indicate that the child has recognized the correspondences between organs of the adult vocal apparatus and its own, but cannot control the amplitude and phasing of its gestures.

In another attempt at [r], word-medial rather than word-initial, the same child offered ['bu'di] for ['bɛrɪ] (*berry*). Here, lip rounding for [r] slides into alignment with tongue raising toward the palate, yielding [u] for [ɛ], and full closure of the tongue tip replaces approximant retroflexion, giving [d] for [r]. Thus, the same combination of gestures for [r] gives rise to different errors in different words. Evidently, the child's target is the word as a whole, and gestures have not yet been fully differentiated from the contexts in which they appear. In due course, repeated use of the same organ in many different contexts leads to independent, context-free control of that organ (Lindblom 1992, 2000). Taking the child's development as an epitome of evolution, we may hypothesize that the six components of the vocal apparatus emerged as independently controlled organs in step with the evolution of vocal imitation. But why was it just these components that emerged?

3.8.2 *Why did the vocal tract differentiate as it did?*

Imitation suggests an account of *how* increasingly fine motor control of already existing primate vocal organs may have evolved, but does not explain *why* the vocal apparatus differentiated into the universal set of six independent organs (lips, tongue tip/body/root, velum, larynx), most or all of which are used in every spoken language. A start has been made toward a perceptuomotor account of vocal tract differentiation by the Distinctive Regions Model (DRM) of speech production (e.g. Carré and Mrayati 1990). The model idealizes the vocal tract as a uniform tube 18 cm long, open at one end, closed at the other. Acoustic theory then defines eight discrete regions of such a tube where deformations, or constrictions, afford greatest acoustic contrast for least articulatory effort. Articulatory effort is minimized by positing that tongue movements are discrete transverse gestures (constrictions), perpendicular to the wall of the vocal-tract, rather than continuous longitudinal movements of the tongue through vocal tract space. Thus, the diphthong [ai], for example, consists of a discrete, narrow constriction by the tongue root or the tongue body in the pharynx, rapidly followed by a discrete narrow constriction of the tongue tip at the front of the palate rather than by a continuous longitudinal movement of the tongue from back to front. Talkers' systematic use of discrete transverse movements of the tongue has been confirmed through analysis of lateral x-rays by Iskarous (forthcoming). The eight distinct regions of the DRM include all discrete places of articulation known to be used in the world's languages, executed by gestures of the lips and the three organs of the tongue.

3.8.3 *The origins of discrete phonetic units*

Evolutionarily, the initial basis for discrete phonetic units, we may now hypothesize, was differentiation of the discrete organs of the vocal tract. *Discrete organs constitute the universal basis of a particulate phonology in every spoken language.* Not only do they afford a biologically unique speed of serial action, but they also offer a range of contrasting phonetic categories, some or all of which are used in every language. These categories include contrasts in voicing, in nasality and in 'place of articulation' executed by different organs (lips, tongue tip/body/root).

Differences among languages have arisen, due to diverse, unknown historical contingencies, partly from different ways of dividing gestural continua into categories, partly from differences in the degree to which languages have elaborated the gestural structure of their segmental phonetic repertoires (Lindblom and Maddieson 1988).

Different gestural continua afford different phonetic possibilities. Some continua give rise to the abrupt acoustic discontinuities postulated by Stevens's (1989) 'quantal theory': for example, differences in degree of gestural constriction give rise to abrupt switches from laminal to turbulent to interrupted airflow in the vowel–fricative–stop sequence of the English word *eased* ([izd]). Other gestural continua give rise to acoustic continua: for example, the tongue-body front–back continuum for vowels, the tongue-tip continuum for alveolopalatal fricatives (/s/-/ʃ/), and the temporal continuum of gestural phasing between different organs in voice onset time (cf. Browman and Goldstein 2000).

Different processes of phonological attunement (or accommodation) among speakers-hearers in different language communities then give rise to different phonological categories along gestural continua, either through mutual vocal mimicry (Browman and Goldstein 2000) or, perhaps, simply through low-level sensory-motor interactions without functional pressures to communicate (Oudeyer, Chapter 4). Importantly, these studies of attunement indicate how discrete categories may develop along gestural continua that are devoid of natural category boundaries. Categories may emerge as automatic self-organizing consequences of random search through phonetic space and of random interactions among speakers-hearers under certain perceptuomotor constraints (cf. de Boer 2001a, Chapter 5 below; Lindblom 1992, 2000).

3.9 Summary and conclusions

What are the elementary combinatorial units at the base of the two-tiered hierarchy of phonology and syntax that affords language its infinite expressive scope? The traditional answer (consonants, vowels, and their descriptive features) will not do, from an evolutionary point of view, because these are purely linguistic (i.e. cognitive) units and therefore part of what an evolutionary account must explain. How did these discrete units get into the mind?

This chapter proposes a dynamic unit of phonetic action, the gesture, as defined in the developing theory of articulatory phonology, and as observed in x-ray or other images of an active speaker's vocal tract. A gesture is the formation and release of a constriction of variable location and degree produced by one of the six organs of the vocal apparatus (lips, tongue tip/body/root, velum, larynx). A key question for an evolutionary account is: how did these organs differentiate as independently controlled components of the vocal apparatus? The chapter proposes that the organs differentiated in step with the evolution of facial and vocal imitation, both behaviours unique among primates to humans.

The capacity for analogue mimicry of facial expressions perhaps first emerged in the hypothesized mimetic culture of *Homo erectus*, with the support of a system of mirror neurons as observed in modern macaque monkeys. Repeated use of the same facial organs (lips, cheeks, eyebrows, etc.) in many different expressive contexts led to their independent control as discrete components of an expression. The close link between facial expression and the quality of simultaneous vocalizations led to the beginnings of vocal mimicry. Eventually, repeated reuse of the same six vocal organs in many different contexts led to their emergence as independent organs, supported by a system of mirror neurons such as seems to underlie the speech of modern humans.

These six discrete organs, composing an integral vocal apparatus, are the universal basis of discrete phonetic actions, and so of discrete units of meaning, in every spoken language. Differences among languages arise through diverse, unknown historical contingencies from different processes of phonological attunement among speakers-hearers in different language communities, and from differences in the complexity with which languages elaborate the gestural structure of their segments.

ACKNOWLEDGEMENTS

I thank Louis Goldstein and Björn Lindblom for inspiration and discussion, René Carré, Marc Hauser, John Locke, Pierre-Yves Oudeyer, Maggie Tallerman, and two anonymous reviewers for valuable comments. Preparation of the chapter was supported in part by Haskins Laboratories.

FURTHER READING

I have assumed that early evolutionary steps into language entailed differentiation of the primate vocal apparatus and its neural support, both central and peripheral; but surprisingly little is known about the comparative peripheral neuroanatomy of the vocal tract. For some first steps, see Ramsay and Demolin (2002), Sanders (2002, 2004), Zur, Mu, and Sanders (2004).

On the possible role of mirror neurons in the evolution of imitation in humans, see Rizzolatti, Craighero, and Fadiga (2002); for their possible role in the evolution of language see several papers in Stamenov and Gallese (2002).

For discussion of gestural coordination and the emergence of segments within the framework of articulatory phonology, see Fowler (1996); also papers by Browman and Goldstein, cited above.

For moves toward a functional rather than purely formal account of the sound patterns of language, including computational modelling of phonological systems and the emergence of phonetic gesture, see Lindblom (1992, 1998, 2000) and references therein; also, de Boer (2001a), Browman and Goldstein (2000), Carré and Mrayati (1990), and Oudeyer (Chapter 4 below).

4 From holistic to discrete speech sounds: the blind snowflake-maker hypothesis

PIERRE-YVES OUDEYER

4.1 The speech code

Sound is a medium used by humans to carry information when they speak to each other. The existence of this kind of medium is a prerequisite for language. It is organized into a code, called speech, which provides a repertoire of forms that is shared in each language community and that allows its users to encode content information. This code is mainly conventional, and thus intuitively requires coordinated interaction and communication to be established. How, then, might a speech code be formed prior to the existence of communication and of language-like interaction patterns?

Moreover, the human speech code is characterized by several properties which we have to explain. Here are some of them:

Property 1: Discreteness and systematic reuse. Speech sounds are phonemically coded as opposed to holistically coded. This implies two aspects: (i) in each language, the continuum of possible sounds is broken into discrete units; (ii) these units are systematically reused to build higher-level structures of sounds, like syllables.

For example, in articulatory phonology (see Studdert-Kennedy and Goldstein 2003; Studdert-Kennedy, Chapter 3), a vocalization is viewed as multiple tracks in which gestures are performed in parallel (the set of tracks is called the gestural score). A gesture is the combination of several articulators (e.g. the jaw, the tongue) operating to execute a constriction somewhere in the mouth. The constriction is defined by the place of obstruction of the air as well as the manner. Given a subset of organs, the space of possible places of constrictions is a continuum (for example, the vowel continua from low to high, executed by the tongue body), though each language uses only a few places to perform gestures. This is what we call discreteness.[1] Furthermore, gestures and their combinations, which may be called 'phonemes', are systematically reused in the gestural scores that specify the syllables of each language. Some researchers call this 'phonemic coding'.

Property 2: Universal tendencies. Reoccurring units of vocalization systems are characterized by universal tendencies. For example, our vocal tract makes it possible to produce hundreds of different vowels. However, each particular vowel system typically uses only three, four, five, or six vowels, and extremely rarely more than twelve (Schwartz et al. 1997a). Moreover, some vowels appear much more often than others. For example, most languages contain the vowels [a], [i] and [u] (87 per cent of languages) while other vowels are very rare, such as [y], [œ] and [ɯ] (5 per cent of languages). Also, there are structural regularities: for example, if a language contains a front unrounded vowel at a certain height, for example the [ɛ] in *bet*, it will also usually contain the back rounded vowel at the same height, which would be the [ɔ] in *hawk* in this case.

Property 3: Sharing. The speakers of a particular language use the same phonemes and they categorize speech sounds in the same manner. However, they do not necessarily pronounce each of them exactly the same way.

Property 4: Diversity. At the same time, each language categorizes speech sounds in its own way, and sometimes does this very differently from other languages. For example, Japanese speakers categorize the <l> of *lead* and the <r> of *read* as identical.

This chapter addresses the question of how a speech code with these properties might have formed from non-speech prior to the ability to have linguistic interactions. The mechanism I present is based on a low-level model of sensory-motor interactions. I show that the integration of certain very simple and non-language-specific neural devices allows a population of agents to build a speech code that has the properties

---

[1] The fact that the audible speech stream is continuous and produced by a mixture of articulatory movements is not incompatible with 'discreteness': 'discreteness' applies to the command level, which specifies articulatory targets in time, which are then sequentially and continuously reached by the articulators under the control of a low-level motor controller.

outlined above. The original aspect is that this presupposes neither a functional pressure for communication, nor the ability to have coordinated social interactions (agents do not play language or imitation games). It relies on the self-organizing properties of a generic coupling between perception and production both within agents and in the interactions between agents.

4.2 Existing approaches

4.2.1 *The reductionist approach*

One approach is 'reductionist': it tries to reduce properties of the speech system to properties of some of its parts. In other words, this approach hopes to find a physiological or neural structure, the characteristics of which are sufficient to deduce the properties of speech.

For example, cognitive innatism (Chomsky and Halle 1968; Pinker and Bloom 1990) defends the idea that the brain features a neural device specific to language (the Language Acquisition Device) which 'knows' at birth the properties of speech sounds. This 'knowledge' is supposed to be pre-programmed in the genome. A limit of this approach is that its defenders have remained rather imprecise on what it means for a brain to know innately the properties of language. In other words, this hypothesis is not naturalized. Also, no precise account of the origins of these innate devices has ever been provided.

Other researchers focus on the vocal tract physics as well as on the cochlea electro-mechanics. For example, they claim that the categories that appear in speech systems reflect the non-linearities of the mapping from motor commands to percepts. Phonemes would correspond to articulatory configurations for which small changes lead to small changes in the produced sound. Stevens (1972) defends this idea. There is no doubt that the morphoperceptual apparatus influences the shape of speech sounds. However, this reductionist approach has straightforward weaknesses. For example, it does not explain the large diversity of speech systems in the world's languages (Maddieson 1984). Also, there are many experiments which show that the zones of non-linearity of perception in some languages are not compatible with those of certain other languages (e.g. Japanese [l] and [r], as noted above).

Another example of this approach is that of Studdert-Kennedy and Goldstein (2003); see also Studdert-Kennedy (Chapter 3) for the origins of discreteness, or 'particulate speech' in his terms. Studdert-Kennedy and Goldstein remark that the vocal apparatus is physiologically composed of discrete independent articulators, such as the jaw, the tongue, the lips, the velum, etc. This implies that there is some discrete reuse in complex utterances due to the independent articulators that move. I completely agree with this remark. However, other aspects of discreteness are not accounted for. Indeed, as Studdert-Kennedy and Goldstein (2003) note, once you have chosen to use a given set of articulators, there remains the problem of how the continuous space of possible constrictions or timings between gestures is discretized. Goldstein (2003) proposes a solution to this question that I will review later in the chapter (since it is not reductionist but is a mixture of self-organization and functionalism).

One has to note that this 'reductionist' approach proposes answers concerning the presence of properties (1) and (2) of the speech code, but addresses neither the diversity of speech sounds nor the fact that they are shared across communities of agents. This approach also does not provide answers to the chicken-and-egg problem of the formation of a code, although this was, of course, not its goal.

4.2.2 *The functionalist approach*

The functionalist approach attempts to explain the properties of speech sounds by relating them to their function. Basically, it answers the 'why' question by saying 'the system has property N because it helps to achieve function F'. It answers the 'how' question by saying 'systems with property N were formed through Darwinian evolution (genetic or cultural) under the pressure to achieve function F'. This approach could also be called 'adaptationist':[2] systems with property N were designed for ('ad') their current utility ('apt'). Note that typically, functionalist explanations take into account constraints due to brain structure, perceptual, and vocal systems.

Typically, in the case of the four properties of speech sounds we are interested in, this function is 'communication'. This means that the sounds

---

[2] I use the term adaptationism in its general form: the adaptation may be achieved through genetic or cultural evolution.

of a speech code should be perceptually distinct enough so that they are not confused and communication can take place. The constraints which are involved typically include a cost of production, which evaluates how much energy is to be spent to produce the sounds. So, under this view, speech sounds are a reservoir of forms which are quasi-optimal in terms of perceptual distinctiveness and economy of energy.

For example, Lindblom (1992) shows that if we search for vowel systems which are a good compromise between perceptual distinctiveness and energy cost of articulation, then we find the most frequent vowel systems in human languages. Lindblom also showed similar results concerning the reuse of units to form syllables.

Operational scenarios describing how Darwinian cultural evolution formed these systems have also been described. For example, de Boer (2001a) builds a computer simulation showing how cultural evolution might have worked, through processes of imitation among agents. In this simulation, the same mechanism explains both the acquisition of vowels and its formation; this mechanism is imitation. As a consequence, he also proposes an answer to the question: 'How are vowel systems acquired by speakers?'.

Note that de Boer's model does not deal with questions concerning discreteness (which is built in) and systematic reuse (indeed, his agents produce only simple static vowel sounds, and systematic reuse is a property of complex dynamic sounds). However, this model is very interesting since it shows a process of formation of a convention, i.e. a vowel system, within a population of agents. This really adds value to the work of Lindblom, for example, since it provides a mechanism for (implicit) optimization which Lindblom merely assumed.

However, the imitation game that agents play is quite complex and requires a lot of assumptions about the capabilities of agents. Each of the agents maintains a repertoire of prototypes, associations between a motor program and its acoustic image. In a round of the game, one agent, called the speaker, chooses an item from its repertoire, and utters it to another agent, called the hearer. Then the hearer searches its repertoire for the closest prototype to the speaker's sound, and produces it (he imitates). Then the speaker categorizes the utterance of the hearer and checks if the closest prototype in its repertoire is the one he used to produce the initial sound. Then he tells the hearer whether it was 'good' or 'bad'. Each item in the repertoires has a score, used to promote items which lead to successful imitations and prune the others. In the case of bad imitations, depending on the scores of the prototype used by the hearer, either this prototype is modified so as to better match the sound of the speaker, or a new prototype is created, as close as possible to the sound of the speaker.

So to perform this kind of imitation game, a lot of computational/cognitive power is needed. First, agents need to be able to play a game, involving successive turn-taking and asymmetric role-changing. Second, they must voluntarily attempt to copy the sound production of others, and evaluate this copy. Finally, when they are speakers, they need to recognize that they are being imitated intentionally, and give feedback/reinforcement to the hearer about the (lack of) success. The hearer must understand the feedback, which says that from the point of view of the other, he did or did not manage to imitate successfully.

The level of complexity needed to form speech-sound systems in this model is characteristic of a society of agents which already possesses some complex ways of interacting socially, including a system of communication (which allows them for example to know who is the speaker and who is the hearer, and which signal means 'good' and which signal means 'bad'). The imitation game is itself a system of conventions (the rules of the game), and agents communicate while playing it. It requires the transfer of information from one agent to another, and so requires that this information be carried by shared 'forms'. So it presupposes that there is already a shared system of forms. The vowel systems that appear do not really appear 'from scratch'. This does not mean that de Boer's model is flawed, but rather that it deals with the subsequent evolution of language (or more precisely, with the evolution of speech sounds) rather than with language origins (in other words it deals with the formation of *languages—les langues* in French—rather than with the formation of *language—le langage*). Indeed, de Boer presents interesting results about sound change, provoked by stochasticity and learning by successive generations of agents. But the model does not address the bootstrapping question: how did the first shared repertoire of forms appear, in a society with no communication and language-like interaction patterns? In particular, the question of why agents imitate each other in the context of de Boer's model (this is programmed in) remains open.

Another model in the same spirit was proposed by Browman and Goldstein (2000) and Goldstein (2003). This model is very interesting since it is one of a small number of studies, alongside the work presented in the present chapter, which tries to approach the question of the origins of the discretization of the continuum of gestures (they call this 'emergence of discrete gestures').[3] It involves a simulation in which two agents could produce two gestures, each parametrized by a constriction parameter taken in a continuous one-dimensional space (this space is typically the space of possible places of constrictions, or the continuous temporal interval between two gestures). Agents interacted following the rules of the 'attunement game'. In one round of the game, both agents produced their two gestures, using for each of them a parameter taken in the continuum with a certain probability. This probability was uniform for both gestures at the beginning of the simulation: this meant that a whole continuum of parameters was used. Next, agents recovered the parameter of the other agent's first gesture, and compared it to the parameter they used themselves. If this matched, then two things occurred: the probability of using this parameter for the first gesture was increased, and the probability of using the same value for the second gesture is decreased. This simulated the idea that agents are attempting to produce both of their gestures differently (so that they are contrasted and can be differentiated), and the idea that they try to produce each gesture in a similar fashion to the corresponding gesture of the other agent (so that a convention is established). At the end of the simulations, agents converged to a state in which they used only one value for each gesture, so the space was discretized, and these pairs of values were the same for the two agents in the same simulation and different in different simulations. Goldstein utilized simulations both using and not using non-linearities of the articulatory to acoustic mapping. Not employing it led to the uniform use of all parameters across all simulations, while employing it led to statistical preference for parameters falling in the stable zones of the mapping.

Like de Boer's simulation, in this model agents have coordinated interactions: they follow the rules of a game. Indeed, they both need to produce their gestures together in one round of the game. Secondly, as in the 'imitation game', a pressure for differentiating sounds is programmed in, as well as a pressure to copy the parameters of the other agent. This means

---

[3] There is also the work of Studdert-Kennedy (Chapter 3), but as explained earlier, this focuses on another kind of discreteness in speech, i.e. that related to the independent and parallel use of different sets of organs to perform gestures.

that it is again presupposed that agents already live in a community in which complex communication exists. However, this was certainly not a concern in that simulation, in the context of research in phonology, whilst the primary concern in the present chapter is the bootstrapping of language. Thus, it remains to be seen how discrete speech, which has been argued to be crucial for the rise of language (Studdert-Kennedy and Goldstein 2003), might have come to exist without presupposing that complex communication had already arisen. More precisely, how might discrete speech appear without a pressure to contrast sounds? This is one of the issues we propose to solve later in the present chapter.

Furthermore, in Goldstein's model, one assumption is that agents directly exchange the targets that they used to produce gestures (there is noise, but they are still given targets). However, human vocalizations are continuous trajectories, first in the acoustic space, and then in the organ relation space. So what a human gets from another's gesture is not the target, but the realization of this target which is a continuous trajectory from the start position to the target. And because targets are sequenced, vocalizations do not stop at targets, but continue their 'road' towards the next target. The task of recovering the targets from the continuous trajectory is very difficult, and has not been solved by human speech engineers. Maybe the human brain is equipped with an innate ability to detect events corresponding to targets in the stream, but this is a strong speculation and so incorporating it in a model is a strong (yet interesting) assumption. In the present chapter, I do not make this assumption: agents will produce complex continuous vocalizations specified by sequences of targets, but initially will be unable to retrieve any kind of 'event' that may help them find out where the targets were. Instead, they use a time resolution filter which ensures that each of the points on the continuous trajectory is considered as a target (while only very few of them actually are targets). This introduces a huge amount of noise (not white noise, but noise with a particular structure). However, I show that our society of agents converges to a state in which agents have broken the continuum of possible targets into a discrete repertoire which is shared by the population. Using the structure of the activation of the neural maps of agents, at the end it is possible to retrieve where the targets were (but this will be a result rather than an assumption).

4.3 The 'blind snowflake-maker' approach

Functionalist models have their strengths and weaknesses, which we are not going to detail in this chapter (for a discussion, see Oudeyer 2003). Instead, I propose another line of research, which I believe is almost unexplored in the field of the origins of language. This is what we might call the blind snowflake-maker approach (by analogy with the 'blind watchmaker' of Dawkins 1986, which illustrates the functionalist approach).

There are, indeed, mechanisms in nature which shape the world, such as that governing the formation of snowflakes, which are quite different from Darwinism (Ball 2001). They are characterized by the property of self-organization, like Darwinism, but do not include any concept of fitness or adaptation. Self-organization is here defined as the following property of a system: the local properties which characterize the system are qualitatively different from the global properties of the system.[4]

The formation of snow crystals is illustrated in Figure 4.1. The local mechanism at play involves the physical and chemical interactions between water molecules. If one looks at these physical and chemical prop-

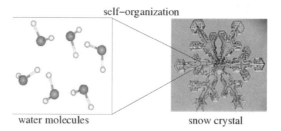

Fig. 4.1 The properties of water molecules and the way they interact are qualitatively different from the symmetrical large-scale structure of snow crystals: this is self-organization.

---

[4] Note that this definition of self-organization is 'non-magical' and differs from a definition stating that this is a property of systems in which the operations of the higher level cannot be accounted for solely by the laws governing the lower-order level, i.e. cannot be predicted from, nor reduced to, its constituents. I do not include any dimension of surprise in the concept of self-organization; when I say that the system described in the chapter self-organizes, this does not mean that its behaviour is surprising or unpredictable from its components, but that its global behaviour has qualitative properties different from the properties of its constituents.

erties, one never finds anything that looks like the structure of snow crystals. However, if one lets these molecules interact at the right temperature and pressure, marvellous symmetrical structures, with a great diversity in exact shapes, form (Kobayashi and Kuroda 1987). This is an example of a mechanism that shows self-organization, and builds very complex shapes which are not adaptive or functional (it would be hard to claim that it helps the water to survive). There is no reason why this kind of 'free' formation of structures would not appear in the biological world too. This idea has been defended by Thompson (1932), Gould and Vrba (1982), and Kauffman (1995).

Thompson (1932) gives the example of the formation of the hexagonal honeycomb of the honeybee. Honeybees build walls of wax made by regular hexagonal cells which tile the whole plane. This is remarkable because (a) there are only three ways to tile the plane with regular shapes (squares, triangles and hexagons), and (b) hexagons are optimal since it takes less material to cover the same area with hexagons than with triangles or squares. There are two possible ways to account for this. First, one might think that honeycomb was designed as an adaptation by the honeybees to minimize their metabolic cost: this is the Darwinist functionalist approach. The honeybees would have tried out many possible shapes until they stumbled on hexagons, which they would have found to be less energy-consuming. This would imply that honeybees would have acquired sophisticated instincts that allow them to build perfect hexagons without compasses and set-squares. This explanation is plausible but elaborate, and requires a time-consuming search in the space of forms by the honeybees.

A second explanation, proposed by Thompson, is much more straightforward for the honeybees. Hexagonal forms are the consequence of purely physical forces: if the wax of the comb is made soft enough by the body heat of the bees, then it is reasonable to think of the compartments as bubbles surrounded by a sluggish fluid. And physics makes the bubbles pack together in just the hexagonal arrangement of the honeycomb, provided that initially the wax cells are roughly circular and roughly of the same size; see Figure 4.2. So it might be that initially, honeybees would just build wax cells which were roughly circular and of roughly the same size, and by heating them they automatically obtained hexagonal cells, owing to the self-organizing properties of the physics of packed cells. Note, this does *not* entail that modern honeybees lack an innate,

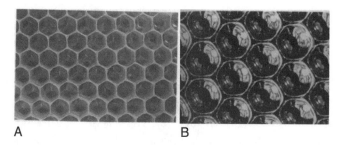

A   B

FIG. 4.2 (a) shows the regular hexagonal tiling of the honeycomb; (b) shows the same pattern taken by a raft of water bubbles.

hard-wired neural structure which allows them to build precisely hexagonal shapes; a proposal for such an innate capacity was suggested by von Frisch (1974). Rather, Thompson's proposal is that long ago in evolutionary history, the honeybees might simply have relied on the self-organization of heated packed wax cells, which would have led them to find the hexagon, but later on in their evolutionary history, they might have incorporated into their genome schemata for building those hexagons directly, in a process similar to the Baldwin effect (Baldwin 1896; see Briscoe, Chapter 14).

The goal of this chapter is to present an approach to the formation of speech codes which is very similar in spirit to the approach taken by D'Arcy Thompson to the formation of honeycomb. We will propose that the formation of sound systems with the properties of discreteness, systematic reuse, universal tendencies, diversity and sharing, may be a result of self-organization occurring in the interactions of modules which were not necessarily selected for communication. The mechanism is not based on manipulation of the genetic material, but results from the interaction of agents and from a number of generic neural and physical modules (which may have a function on their own, not related to speech communication) during the lifetime of agents. Note that the scenario I propose explains how sound systems with the four properties above could have formed before being related to communication, but says nothing about how it could have been recruited later to be used as an information carrier in communication. If we take the example of the origins of bird feathers used by Gould and Vrba (1982), it is like explaining how the feathers came up with the thermoregulation pressure, but not saying how the feathers were recruited to fly.

4.4 The mechanism

The model is a generalization of that of Oudeyer (2001a), which was used to model a particular phenomenon of acoustic illusion, called the perceptual magnet effect. This model was itself a generalization and unification of the earlier models of Damper and Harnad (2000) and Guenther and Gjaja (1996).

It is based on the building of an artificial system, composed of robots/agents endowed with working models of the vocal tract, the cochlea, and some parts of the brain. The complexity and degree of reality of these models can be varied to investigate which aspects of the results are due to which aspects of the model. I stress that while some parts of the model are inspired by knowledge from neuroscience, we are not trying to reproduce faithfully what is in the human brain. Rather, I attempt to build an artificial world in which we can study the phenomenon described at the beginning of the chapter (i.e. the speech code). Because we know exactly what is happening in this artificial world, in particular what the assumptions are, I hope this will enhance our understanding of speech. The model does this by allowing us to give sufficient conditions for the appearance of a speech code, and it can also tell us what is not necessary (e.g. we will show that imitation or feedback are not necessary). Because the mechanisms that formed speech involve the interaction of many components and complex dynamics, artificial systems are a crucial tool for studying them, and it helps to obtain intuitive understanding of them. Our artificial system aims at proving the self-coherence and logical plausibility of the concept of the 'blind snowflake-maker', applied to the origins of discrete speech sounds. For more details on this methodology of the artificial, see Steels (2001) and Oudeyer (2003).

4.4.1 *The architecture of the artificial system*

Here, I summarize the architecture of the system, and in particular the architecture of agents. Technical details can be found in Appendix 4.1 at the end of this chapter. Each agent has one ear which takes measurements of the vocalizations that it perceives, which are then sent to its brain. It also has a vocal tract, the shape of which is controllable and which allows it to produce sounds. The ear and the vocal tract are connected to a brain, which is basically a set of interconnected neurons. There are two sets of neurons. One is called the 'perceptual map', which gets input from the measurements taken by the ear. Then the neurons of the perceptual map send their output to the second set of neurons, the 'motor map' (this could also be called an 'articulatory map'). These motor neurons send signals to a controller which drives the vocal tract. These signals should be viewed as commands specifying articulatory targets to be reached in time. The articulatory targets are typically relations between the organs of the vocal tract (like the distance between the lips or the place of constriction). They correspond to what is called a 'gesture' in the articulatory phonology literature (Browman and Goldstein 2000; Studdert-Kennedy, Chapter 3). Figure 4.3 gives an overview of this architecture. In this chapter, the space of organ relations will be two-dimensional (place and manner of constriction) or three-dimensional (place, manner of articulation, and rounding).

What we here call a neuron is a box which receives several inputs/ measurements, and integrates them to compute its activation, which is propagated through output connections. Typically, the integration is made by first weighting each input measurement (i.e. multiplying the measurement by a weight), then summing these numbers, and applying to

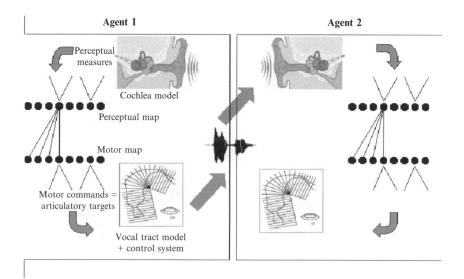

Fig. 4.3 Overview of the architecture of agents in the artificial world.

the sum a function called the 'tuning function'. The tuning function is in this case a Gaussian curve, whose width is a parameter of the simulation. A weight is attached to every connection between neurons. In the model, all weights are initially random.

Also, the neurons in each neural map are all interconnected. This means that they receive inputs from all other neurons in the map. When a stimulus is perceived, this prompts an initial activation of all the neurons in the two maps. Next, the activation of each neuron, after the update of all the weights, is updated according to the new activation of the neurons to which it is connected. This is repeated until the activations stabilize. This is what is called an attractor in dynamical systems language. This attractor, i.e. a set of neuron activations which is stabilized, is the same for a number of different stimuli, called its basin of attraction. This models categorization behaviour. There are as many categories as there are attractors.

The production of a vocalization consists of choosing a set of articulatory targets. To choose these targets, one activates neurons in the motor map of agents sequentially and randomly. This activation is a command which we take as the definition of a gesture in this chapter. A target is specified by the weights of the output connections of the activated motor neurons. Then there is a control system which executes these commands by pulling the organs towards the targets continuously and sequentially.[5] Here, the control system simply amounts to generating a continuous trajectory in the organ relation space which passes through the targets. This is achieved through simple spline interpolation, which is basically a polynomial interpolation. Because initially the weights of the connections

---

[5] It is important to note that this method of producing complex articulation already contains some discreteness. I assume that syllables are specified as a sequence of targets. This is in fact in line with the literature on motor control in mammals (Kandel et al. 2001), which describes it as being organized in two levels: a level of high-level discrete commands (our targets), and a low level which takes care of the execution of these motor commands. So this level of discreteness at the level of commands may not be a feature to be explained in the context of research on the origins of language, since it is already present in the motor-control architecture of mammals. However, I do not assume that initially these targets are organized: the set of commands used to define targets is taken as a continuum of possible commands and there is no re-use of targets from one syllable to another; discreteness and systematic re-use are a result of the simulations. Also, I do not assume that there is discreteness at the perceptual level: agents are not able to detect 'events' in the acoustic stream. (However, at the end they are able to identify the categories of targets which were used to produce the sound.)

are random, agents produce vocalizations with articulatory targets that are spread uniformly across the space of possible targets. This implies that their vocalizations are initially holistic as far as the commands are concerned (the whole continuum of physically possible commands is used). They are not phonemically coded.

Agents produce vocalizations not by a static configuration of the vocal tract, but rather by continuous movement of the vocal tract. This implies that agents receive a continuous trajectory (in the acoustic space) from the vocalizations of other agents. Next I explain how this trajectory is processed, and how it is used to change the weights of the connections between the neurons.

First of all, agents are not able to detect high-level events in the continuous trajectory, which would allow them, for example, to figure out which points were the targets that the other agents used to produce that trajectory. Instead, they segment the trajectory into very small parts, corresponding to the time resolution of perception (this models the time resolution of the cochlea). Then all these small parts are integrated, giving a value in the acoustic space, which is sent to the perceptual neurons. Each perceptual neuron is then activated.

The weights change each time the neurons to which they are connected are activated. The input connections of the perceptual neurons are changed so that the neurons become more sensitive to the stimuli that activated them, and the change is larger for neurons with a high activation than for neurons with a low activation (this is sensitization of neurons). Then the activation of the perceptual neurons is propagated to the motor neurons. Two possibilities ensue: (i) the motor neurons are already activated because the vocalization was produced by the agent itself, and the weights of the connections between the perceptual and the motor neurons are reinforced if they correspond to a link between two neurons whose activation is correlated, and weakened if they correspond to a link between neurons whose activation is not correlated (this is Hebbian learning). This learning rule allows the agent to learn the mapping between percepts and motor commands during babbling. (ii) If the motor neurons were not already activated (the sound comes from the vocalization of another agent), then the weights of the connections between the two maps are not changed, but the weights of the connections between the motor neurons and the control system are changed. The neuron with the highest activation in the neural map is selected, and its output weights, which specify an organ relation, are used as a reference to update the other weights: they are changed so that the organ relation they specify looks a little more like that of the reference neuron, and this change is weighted by the current activation of each motor neuron.

A crucial point is the coupling between the production process and the perception process. Let us term the weights of the input connections of the perceptual neurons the preferred vectors of these neurons. This term comes from the fact that the set of weights of a neuron forms a vector, and the stimulus that has the same values as the weights will activate the neuron maximally. We also call the output weights of the motor neurons their preferred vector. The set-up and the dynamics of the two neural maps ensure that the distribution of preferred vectors in the motor map corresponds to the distribution of preferred vectors in the perceptual map: if one activates all the neurons in the motor map randomly, many times, to produce sounds, this then gives a distribution of sounds that is the same as the one coded by the neurons of the perceptual map. The distribution of the preferred vectors of the neurons in the perceptual map changes when sounds are perceived, which in turn changes the distribution of preferred vectors in the motor map, which then implies that if an agent hears certain sounds more often than others, he will also tend to produce them more often (here, a 'sound' refers to one small subpart of a vocalization, generated by the time-resolution filter described earlier). It is important to see that this process of attunement is not realized through imitation, but is a side effect of an increase in sensitivity of neurons, which is a very generic, local, low-level neural mechanism (Kandel et al. 2001).

Agents are put together in a world in which they will wander randomly. At random times, they produce a vocalization, and agents next to them hear the sound and adapt their neural maps. Each agent also hears its own sounds, using this to learn the mapping from perception to motor commands.

At the start, every agent produces sounds with targets that are randomly spread across the continuum: this means that this continuum is not discretized and there is no systematic reuse of targets. In other words, agents' vocalizations are holistic. I will show that their neural maps self-organize and synchronize so that after a while they produce complex sounds with targets belonging to a small number of well-defined clusters: the continuum is then discretized. Moreover, the number of clusters is small compared to the number of vocalizations they produce during their lifetime, which implies a systematic reuse of targets across vocalizations.

Finally, these clusters are the same for all agents: the code is shared and specific to each agent community, because in each simulation run, the set of clusters that appears is different (so there is diversity).

I use two kinds of model for mapping from motor configurations to sounds and then perception. The first kind is abstract and trivial: this is a random linear mapping from one space to the other. This allows us to see what we can get without any special mapping properties, in particular without non-linearities. In fact, I show that we get quite far without these, obtaining discreteness, systematic reuse, sharing, and diversity. The second kind is a more realistic model of the mapping, using three motor parameters: tongue height, tongue front–back position, and lip rounding. The formants corresponding to any configurations are then calculated using de Boer's (2001a) model, which is based on human data. This model allows us to predict the vowel systems that appear in human languages, thus allowing us to account for some universal tendencies in human vowel systems.

4.4.2 *Non-assumptions*

Agents do not play a language game in the sense used in the literature (Hurford et al. 1998), and in particular do not play the 'imitation game' which is, for example, used in de Boer (2001a). Their interactions are not structured, there are no roles and no coordination. In fact, they have no social skills at all. They do not distinguish between their own vocalizations and those of others. They do not communicate. Here, 'communication' refers to the emission of a signal by an individual with the intention of conveying information which will modify the state of at least one other agent, which does not happen here. Indeed, agents do not even know that there are other agents around them, so it would be difficult to say that they communicate.

4.5 The dynamics

4.5.1 *Using the abstract linear articulatory/perceptual mapping*

This experiment used a population of twenty agents. I describe first what was obtained when agents use the linear articulatory synthesizer. In the simulations, 500 neurons were used per neural map, and $\sigma = 0.05$ (width of their tuning function). The acoustic space and the articulatory space are both two-dimensional, with values in each dimension between zero and one. These two dimensions can be thought of as the place and the manner of articulation.

Initially, just as the preferred vectors of neurons are randomly and uniformly distributed across the space, so the different targets that specify the productions of the agents are also randomly and uniformly distributed. Figure 4.4 shows the preferred vectors of the neurons in the perceptual map of two agents. We see that these cover the whole space uniformly, and are not organized. Figure 4.5 shows the dynamic process of relaxation associated with these neural maps, and due to their recurrent connections. This is a representation of their categorizing behaviour. Each small arrow represents the overall change of activation pattern after one iteration of the relaxation (see the Appendix to this chapter). The beginning of an arrow represents a pattern of activations at time t (generated by presenting a stimulus whose coordinates correspond to the coordinates of this point;

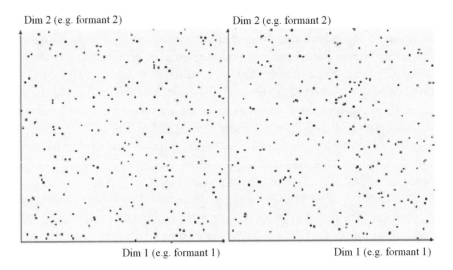

Dim 2 (e.g. formant 2)   Dim 2 (e.g. formant 2)

Dim 1 (e.g. formant 1)   Dim 1 (e.g. formant 1)

FIG. 4.4 Acoustic neural maps in the beginning. As with all other figures, the horizontal axis represents the first formant (F1), and the vertical axis represents the effective second formant (F2'). The unit is the Bark, and they are oriented from low values to high values. (The Bark is the standard unit corresponding to one critical band width of human hearing.)

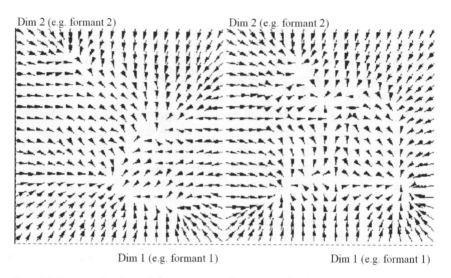

Dim 2 (e.g. formant 2)   Dim 2 (e.g. formant 2)

Dim 1 (e.g. formant 1)   Dim 1 (e.g. formant 1)

FIG. 4.5 Representation of the two agents' attractor fields initially.

this is possible because the population vector is also a decoding scheme which computes the stimulus which activated a neural map). The end of the arrow represents the pattern of activations of the neural map after one iteration of the relaxation. The set of all arrows allows one to visualize several iterations: start somewhere on the figure, and follow the arrows. At some point, for every initial point, you get to a fixed point. This corresponds to one attractor of the network dynamic, and the fixed point to the category of the stimulus that gave rise to the initial activation. The zones defining stimuli that fall into the same category are visible on the figure, and are called basins of attractions. With initial preferred vectors uniformly spread across the space, the number of attractors as well as the boundaries of their basins of attractions are random.

The learning rule of the acoustic map is such that it evolves so as to approximate the distribution of sounds in the environment (though this is not due to imitation). All agents produce initially complex sounds composed of uniformly distributed targets. Hence, this situation is in equilibrium. However, this equilibrium is unstable, and fluctuations ensure that at some point, symmetry breaks: from time to time, some sounds get produced a little more often than others, and these random fluctuations may be amplified through positive feedback loops. This leads to a multi-peaked distribution: agents get into the kind of situation in Figure 4.6 (for

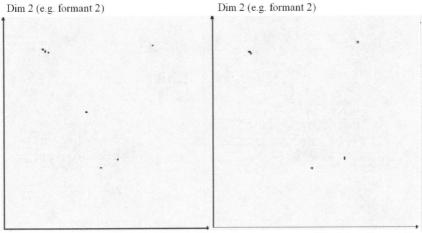

FIG. 4.6 Neural maps after 2000 interactions, corresponding to the initial state of FIG. 4.4. The number of points that one can see is fewer than the number of neurons, since clusters of neurons have the same preferred vectors and this is represented by only one point.

the unbiased case) which corresponds to Figure 4.4 after 2000 interactions in a population of twenty agents. Figure 4.6 shows that the distribution of preferred vectors is no longer uniform but clustered. However, it is not so easy to visualize the clusters with the representation in Figure 4.6, since there are a few neurons which have preferred vectors not belonging to these clusters. They are not statistically significant, but introduce noise into the representation. Furthermore, in the clusters, basically all points have the same value, so that they appear as one point. Figure 4.7 allows us to visualize the clusters better, by showing the attractor landscape that is associated with them. We see that there are now three well-defined attractors or categories, and that these are the same in the two agents represented (they are also the same in the eighteen other agents in the simulation). This means that the targets the agents use now belong to one of several well-defined clusters, and moreover can be classified automatically as such by the relaxation of the network. The continuum of possible targets has been broken; sound production is now discrete. Moreover, the number of clusters that appear is low, which automatically ensures that targets are systematically reused to build the complex sounds that agents

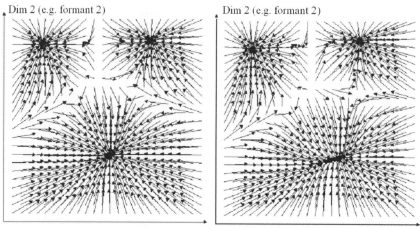

Dim 1 (e.g. formant 1)   Dim 1 (e.g. formant 1)

FIG. 4.7 Representation of the attractor fields of two agents after 2000 inter-actions. The number of attractors is fewer than the number of points in FIG. 4.6. This is because in the previous figures, some points correspond to clusters and others to single points. The broad width of the tuning function ensures that the landscape is smoothed out and individual points which are not too far from clusters do not manage to form their own basin of attraction.

produce. All the agents share the same speech code in any one simulation. However, in each simulation, the exact set of modes at the end is different. The number of modes also varies with exactly the same set of parameters. This is due to the inherent stochasticity of the process. I illustrate this later in the chapter.

It is very important to note that this result of crystallization holds for any number of agents (experimentally), and in particular with only one agent, which adapts to its own vocalizations. This means that interaction with other agents—i.e. the social component—is not necessary for discreteness and systematic reuse to arise. But what is interesting is that when agents do interact, then they crystallize in the same state, with the same categories. To summarize, there are, so far, two results: first, discreteness and systematic reuse arise because of the coupling between perception and production within agents; second, shared systems of phonemic categories arise because of the coupling between perception and production across agents.

We also observe that the attractors that appear are relatively well spread across the space. The prototypes that their centres define are thus perceptually quite distinct. In terms of Lindblom's framework, the energy of these systems is high. However, there was no functional pressure to avoid close prototypes. They are distributed in that way because of the intrinsic dynamics of the recurrent networks and their rather large tuning functions: indeed, if two neuron clusters get too close, then the summation of tuning functions in the iterative process of relaxation smooths their distribution locally and only one attractor appears.

4.5.2 Using the realistic articulatory/acoustic mapping

In the previous subsection, we assumed that the mapping from articulations to perceptions was linear. In other words, constraints from the vocal apparatus due to non-linearities were not taken into account. This is interesting because it shows that no initial asymmetry in the system was necessary to get discreteness (which is very asymmetrical). So there is no need to have sharp natural discontinuities in the mapping from the articulations to the acoustic signals and to the perceptions in order to explain the existence of discreteness in speech sounds (I am not saying that non-linearities of the mapping do not help, just that they are not necessary).

However, this mapping has a particular shape that introduces a bias into the pattern of speech sounds. Indeed, with the human vocal tract, there are articulatory configurations for which a small change effects a small change in the produced sound, but there are also articulatory configurations for which a small change effects a large change in the produced sound. While the neurons in the motor map have initially random preferred vectors with a uniform distribution, this distribution will soon become biased: the consequence of non-linearities will be that the learning rule will have different consequences in different parts of the space. For some stimuli, many motor neurons will have their preferred vectors shifted a lot, and for others, very few neurons will have their preferred vectors shifted. This will very quickly lead to non-uniformities in the distribution of preferred vectors in the motor map, with more neurons in the parts of the space for which small changes result in small differences in the produced sounds, and with fewer neurons in the parts of the space for which small changes result in large differences in the produced sounds. As a consequence, the distribution of the targets that compose vocalizations will be biased, and the learning of the neurons in the perceptual maps will ensure that the distributions of the preferred vectors of these neurons will also be biased.

The articulatory synthesizer used is from de Boer (2001a). This models only the production of vowels. The fact that agents produce only vocalizations composed of vowel sounds does not imply that the model does not hold for consonants. I chose this articulatory synthesizer because it is the only one both fast enough and realistic enough for my computer simulations. The articulatory space (or organ relation space) is three-dimensional here: tongue height (i.e. manner of articulation), tongue front–back position (i.e. place of articulation), and lip rounding. Each set of values of these variables is then transformed into the first four formants, which are the poles of the vocal tract shaped by the position of the articulators. Then the effective second formant is computed, which is a non-linear combination of the second, third, and fourth formants. The first and effective second formants are known to be good models of our perception of vowels (de Boer 2001a). To get an idea of this, Figure 4.8 shows the state of the acoustic neural maps of one agent after a few interactions between the agents (200 interactions). This represents the bias in the distribution of preferred vectors due to the non-linearities.

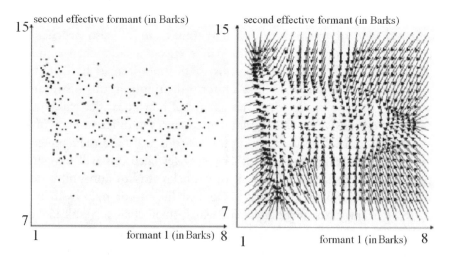

FIG. 4.8 Initial neural map and attractor field of one agent within a population of twenty agents. Here the realistic articulatory synthesizer is used.

A series of 500 simulations was run with the same set of parameters, and each time the number of vowels as well as the structure of the system was checked. Each vowel system was classified according to the relative position of the vowels, as opposed to looking at the precise location of each of them. This is inspired by the work of Crothers (1978) on universals in vowel systems, and is identical to the type of classification in de Boer (2001a). The first result shows that the distribution of vowel inventory sizes is very similar to that of human vowel systems (Ladefoged and Maddieson 1996): Figure 4.10 shows the two distributions (the plain line is the distribution corresponding to the emergent systems of the experiment; the dotted line is the distribution in human languages), and in particular the fact that there is a peak at five vowels, which is remarkable since five is neither the maximum nor the minimum number of vowels found in human languages. The prediction made by the model is even more accurate than that of de Boer (2001a), since his model predicted a peak at four vowels. Then the structure of the emergent vowel systems was compared to the vowel systems in human languages as reported in Schwartz et al. (1997a). More precisely, the distributions of structures in the 500 emergent systems was compared to the distribution of structure in the 451 languages of the UPSID database (Maddieson 1984). The results are shown in Figure 4.11. We see that the predictions are fairly accurate, especially in the prediction of the most frequent system for each size of vowel system (less than eight). Figure 4.9 shows an instance of the most frequent system in both emergent and human vowel systems. In spite of the predictions of one four-vowel system and one five-vowel system which appear frequently (9.1 and 6 per cent of systems) in the simulations and never appear in UPSID languages, these results compare favourably to those obtained by de Boer (2001a). In particular, we obtain all this diversity of systems with the appropriate distributions with the same parameters, whereas de Boer had to modify the level of noise to increase the sizes of vowel systems. However, like de Boer, we are not able to predict systems with many vowels (which are admittedly rare in human languages, but do exist). This is certainly a limitation of our non-functional model. Functional pressure to develop efficient communication systems might be necessary here. In conclusion, one can say that the model supports the idea that the particular phonemes which appear in human languages are under the influence of the articulatory/perceptual mapping, but that their existence, which means the phenomenon of phonemic

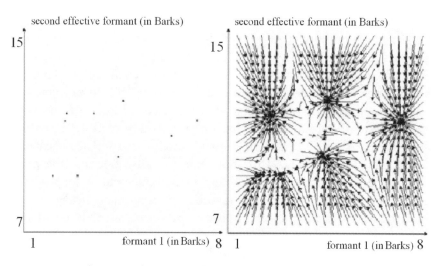

FIG. 4.9 Neural map and attractor field of the agent from FIG. 4.8 after 2000 interactions with the other twenty agents. The corresponding figures for other agents are nearly identical, as in FIG. 4.6 and 4.7. The vowel system produced corresponds to the most frequent five-vowel system in human languages.

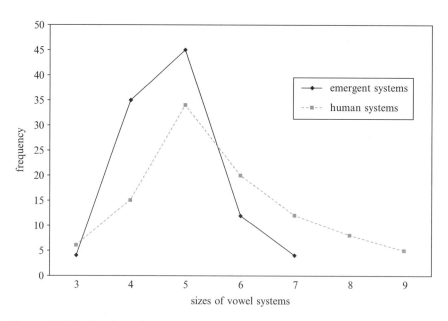

FIG. 4.10 Distribution of vowel inventory sizes in emergent and UPSID human vowel systems.

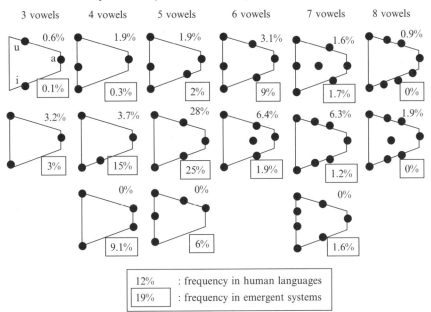

Most frequent vowel systems in human languages and emergent systems

FIG. 4.11 Distribution of vowel inventory structures in emergent and UPSID human vowel systems. This diagram uses the same notations as Schwartz et al. (1997). Note that here, the vertical axis is also F2, but oriented from high values to low values.

coding, is not due to this mapping but to the sensory-motor coupling dynamics.

4.6 Discussion

A crucial assumption of the artificial system presented in this chapter is the fact that there are connections between the motor vocal neural map and the perceptual acoustic map which allow the agents to learn the mapping between the two spaces. How might these connections have appeared?

First, it is possible that they appeared through Darwinian genetic evolution under a pressure for language. But the simplicity and non-specificity of the neural architecture allows other ways of explaining their origins which do not necessitate a pressure for language. These scenarios truly illustrate the 'blind snowflake-maker' approach.

One alternative scenario is that these connections evolved for imitation. Imitation may have appeared for purposes very different from language: for example, it might have evolved to maintain social cohesion. Copying of types of behaviour might have been used to mark friendship, for example, as in some species of birds. Interestingly, this kind of imitation does not require a system of sounds made of discrete units that can be reused to produce infinite combinations. Also, in this kind of imitation, agents do try to copy behaviours or sounds, but do not try to discriminate sounds. This means that there is no pressure to develop a system of sounds that are different from each other and categorized as such. There is no need to have a system of categories as a whole if all that is useful is just evaluating the similarity of the sound you yourself produce to one produced by another individual at a given moment. But discreteness, reuse, and a system of differences and categories are necessary for speech. The artificial system of this chapter shows precisely that with just a simple neural system which may very well have evolved for 'imitation for social cohesion' (it would be difficult to make a simpler system), we obtain freely, through self-organization, a system of sounds that is shared by a population and that is discrete, with systematically reused units and a system of categorization. In other words, we obtain exactly what speech needs without the need for speech.

So, even if the neural devices that are assumed in this chapter evolved for imitation, they produce speech-sound systems without a functional pressure for speech (as used in the context of language). The simulations of de Boer and of Browman and Goldstein do assume this pressure for speech, since their agents do try to produce the sounds of their repertoire differently (and in the case of de Boer, they try to make the repertoire as big as possible). But the agents here do not try to distinguish sounds. The fact that they reach a system of categories that allows them to distinguish sounds is a self-organized result. Furthermore, the notion of repertoire is not pre-programmed, but appears as a result.

A second alternative scenario for the origins of the neural structure which allows the learning of the mapping between sounds and articulatory configurations is possible. The system just needs initially random neurons that are sensitive to sounds, random neurons that are sensitive to motor commands, and random connections between these two sets of neurons.

Then it needs the random connections between these two sets of neurons to adapt by following a very general dynamic: Hebbian learning. Next, activating the motor neurons randomly and uniformly leads to a movement of the vocal tract which produces sounds, which in turn activates the perceptual neurons, and then the connections between the two maps self-organize so that after a while the mapping is effectively learnt. This is what we call babbling.

Crucially, this architecture does not require precise pre-wiring during ontogeny which is pre-programmed by the genes. The neurons in the perceptual map and in the motor map certainly existed well before speech. In fact they have existed since ears and mouths have existed. So the question, of course, is how did they come to be connected? It is quite possible that these connections are a side-effect of general architectural design constraints of the brain; Gould and Vrba (1982) give many examples of other features of the bodies and brains of animals which appeared in a similar manner. Indeed, it is obvious that the connections between certain modalities (for example, vision and the motor control of arms) are necessary and thus existed very early in mammalian evolution. It might very well be that the most efficient strategy to produce these connections is to connect all modalities rather than just to connect particular modalities with other particular modalities. This might be more efficient because it requires fewer specifications for the growth process, and thus might be more robust, and the advantage of this robustness might be superior to the cost of having *a priori* unnecessary connections. In fact, this method of shaping the brain by initial generation of many random neural structures, followed by a pruning phase, is accepted by a large part of the neuroscience community (see Changeux 1983). But then all mammals should have these connections between neurons that perceive sounds and neurons that control the movements of the mouth. So, why are we the only mammal to have such a system of speech sounds? And in particular, why do monkeys or chimps not have speech sounds like ours? It is probable that they do have at birth the connections between the neurons that perceive sounds and those that control the mouth, but that they lose them because the key is somewhere else. The key might lie in *babbling*.

In fact, precisely one of the assumptions that I make (and which monkeys or chimps do not seem to implement) is that the agents activate spontaneously, often, and randomly, the neurons of their motor map. This means that they spontaneously try out many articulatory configurations and repeat these trials. In other words, they practise. Monkeys or chimps do practise certain specific motor activities when they play, but these are very limited and they do not try to practise all the motor activities that their bodies allow, while human children do. For example, once monkeys have thrown a stone towards an objective, they will not try to do it again repeatedly. And it seems that a major evolutionary event which gave rise to primitive humans with increased skills as compared to their ancestors is the ability to practise any new motor activity that they encounter, in particular vocal babbling. Indeed, a general drive to explore all motor activities available to the body may have been very beneficial for the learning of many skills useful for primitive humans, who lived in a dynamic, quickly changing environment (for example, coping with changes in habitat, or living in complex dynamic social structures). This may have pushed them, in particular, to use their vocal apparatus for babbling. And then we come to the beginning of the simulation presented in this chapter, which shows that self-organization takes place and generates 'for free' a system of sounds shared by the agents who live in the same area and which is phonemically coded/discrete. Monkeys or chimps may have the connections, but because they do not practise, the neural structures connecting the two modalities certainly die (through the pruning process of activity-dependent neural epigenesis; Changeux 1983). But humans do practise, which not only allows the neural system to be kept alive, but also allows the generation of a shared speech code.

4.7 Conclusion

This chapter presents a mechanism providing a possible explanation for how a discrete speech code may form in a society of agents which does not already possess the means to communicate and coordinate in a language-like manner. Contrary to other computational models of the origins of language (see Cangelosi and Parisi 2002), the agents do not play language games. They have, in fact, no social skills at all. I believe the mechanism presented may be the kind of mechanism that could solve the language bootstrapping problem. I have shown how one crucial prerequisite, i.e. the existence of an organized medium that can carry information in a conventional code shared by a population, may appear without linguistic features being already there.

Furthermore, this same mechanism allows us to account for properties of the speech code like discreteness, systematic reuse, universal tendencies, sharing, and diversity. I believe that this account is original because (a) only one mechanism is used to account for all these properties and (b) we need neither a pressure for efficient communication nor innate neural devices specific to speech (the same neural devices used in the chapter can be used to learn hand-eye coordination, for example).

Models like that of de Boer (2001a) are to be seen as describing phenomena occurring later in the evolutionary history of language. More precisely, de Boer's model, as well as, for example, that of Oudeyer (2001b) for the formation of syllable systems, deals with the recruitment of speech codes like those that appear in this chapter, and studies how they are further shaped and developed under functional pressure for communication. Indeed, whilst we have shown here that one can go a long way *without* such pressure, some properties of speech can only be accounted for *with* it. An example is the phenomenon of chain shifts, in which the prototypes of sounds of a language are all moved around the space.

However, in de Boer (2001a) and Oudeyer (2001b), the recruitment of the speech code is pre-programmed. How this could have happened in the origins of language is a problem which remains to be solved. A particular instantiation of the problem is: how do agents come to have the idea of using a speech code to name objects? In fact, the problem of the recruitment of features not initially designed for a certain linguistic function is present at all levels of language, ranging from sounds to grammar. The question of how recruitment comes about is a major challenge for research on the origins of language. In this chapter, we have shown one example of recruitment: individual discrete sounds were systematically reused in the building of complex vocalizations, and this was not pre-programmed.

ACKNOWLEDGEMENTS

I would like to thank Michael Studdert-Kennedy for his very helpful comments which helped to improve this chapter greatly. I would also like to thank Luc Steels for supporting the research presented in the chapter.

FURTHER READINGS

For a comprehensive overview of research on the origins of speech sounds, Lindblom (1992), de Boer (2001), and Studdert-Kennedy and Goldstein (2003) are key references.

For the role of self-organization in the origins of patterns in the biological world, and in particular for the relationship between self-organization and neo-Darwinian natural selection, Kauffman (1995) is a good start, presenting the general arguments in an accessible way, and could be followed up by Ball (2001) and Thompson (1932), who present a great many biological examples, with more technical and empirical detail.

Appendix 4.1: Technical Details of the Mechanism

The neurons have a Gaussian tuning function. If we note $tune_{i,t}$ the tuning function of n_i at time t, s one stimulus vector, v_i the preferred vector (the weights) of n_i, then the form of the function is:

$$tune_{i,t}(s) = \frac{1}{\sqrt{2\pi}\sigma} * e^{-\frac{1}{2}v_i * s^2/\sigma^2}$$

The notation $v_1 * v_2$ denotes the scalar product between vector v_1 and vector v_2. The parameter σ determines the width of the Gaussian, and so if it is large the neurons are broadly tuned (a value of 0.05 means that a neuron responds substantially to10 per cent of the input space).

When a neuron in the perceptual map is activated because of an input s, then its preferred vector is changed. The mathematical formula of the new tuning function is:

$$tune_{i,t+1}(s) = \frac{1}{\sqrt{2\pi}\sigma} * e^{v_{i,t+1} * s2/\sigma 2}$$

where s is the input, and $v_{i,t+1}$ the preferred vector of n_i after the processing of s:

$$v_{i,t+1} = v_{i,t} + 0.001 * tune_{i,t}(s) * (s - v_{i,t})$$

Also, when a sound is perceived and through propagation activates the motor neurons, the weights of the output connections of these neurons also change. The preferred vector of the most active neuron is taken as a reference: the other preferred vectors are changed so that they get closer to this preferred vector. The change is made with exactly the same formula as for the neurons in the perceptual map, except that s is the preferred vector of the most active neuron. When an agent hears a vocalization produced by itself, the motor neurons are already activated when the perceived sound activates the neurons in the perceptual map. Then, the weights of the connections between the two neural maps change. A Hebbian learning rule is used. If i is a neuron of the perceptual map connected to a neuron j of the motor neural map, then the weight $w_{i,j}$ changes:

$$\delta w_{i,j} = c_2 * (tune_{i,s_i} - <tune_{i,s_i}>)(tune_{j,\,s_j} - <tune_{j,s_j}>)(\text{correlation rule})$$

where s_i and s_j are the input of neurons i and j, $<tune_{i,s_i}>$ the mean activation of neuron i over a certain time interval, and c_2 a small constant. All neurons between the two maps are connected.

Both the perceptual and the motor neural map are recurrent. Their neurons are also connected to each other. The weights are symmetric. This gives them the status of a dynamical system: they have a Hopfield-like dynamics with point attractors, which are used to model the behaviour of categorization. The weights are supposed to represent the correlation of activity between neurons, and are learnt with the same Hebbian learning rule:

$$\delta w_{i,j} = c_2(tune_{i,s_i} - <tune_{i,s_i}>)(tune_{j,\,s_j} - <tune_{j,s_j}>)(\text{correlation rule})$$

These connections are used to relax each neural map after the activations have been propagated and used to change the weights of these connections. The relaxation is an update of each neuron's activation according to the formula:

$$act(i,\ t+1) = \frac{\sum_j act(j,t) * w_{i,j}}{\sum_i act(i,t)}$$

where $act(i)$ is the activation of neuron i. This is the mechanism of competitive distribution, together with its associated dynamical properties.

To visualize the evolution of the activations of all neurons during relaxation, we use the 'population vector'. The activation of all the neurons in a neural map can be summarized by the 'population vector' (see Georgopoulos et al. 1988): it is the sum of all preferred vectors of the neurons weighted by their activity (normalized as here we are interested in both direction and amplitude of the stimulus vector):

$$pop(v) = \frac{\sum_i act(n_i) * v_i}{\sum_i act(n_i)}$$

The normalizing term is necessary here since we are not only interested in the direction of vectors.

5 Infant-directed speech and evolution of language

BART DE BOER

5.1 Introduction

Language is an extremely complex phenomenon and evolutionary accounts of it are therefore often considered problematic. Previous work by the author has been concerned with finding mechanisms that could suggest a simplification of the way in which language has evolved. One such factor is self-organization in a population, as explored in de Boer (2000, 2001a). However, in this chapter another mechanism is explored, one that is based on bootstrapping. I investigate whether speech might be more learnable if infants are first confronted with an easier-to-learn version, called infant-directed speech. For work on self-organization, readers are referred to Oudeyer's work (Chapter 4) in this volume.

Infant-directed speech is the special way of speaking that is used when caregivers address infants. One can think of several reasons why this should be used, and this chapter investigates one of them: it could be that infant-directed speech facilitates learning and transfer of language across generations.

The learning of unbounded, productive communication systems (such as human language) turns out to be an extremely hard problem. It can be proven mathematically that even relatively simple examples of productive communication systems cannot be learned with complete accuracy. Gold (1967) has shown that this is the case for context-free grammars. Although, of course, the class of context-free languages cannot be equated with human languages, linguists agree that learning human language is at least as hard a problem.

Compounding the problem of learning human language is the fact that most of the linguistic utterances which humans produce consist of rapid,

casual speech in which articulation is reduced and words are concaten-
ated. Also, a lot of language only makes sense if the context is known.
Finally, many words, expressions, and grammatical constructions occur
extremely infrequently. This is known as the poverty of the stimulus (e.g.
Chomsky 1968; but see also Pullum 1996). How children manage to learn
their native language is still very much an open question.

Different theories exist as to how children tackle the task of learning
language. Most of these theories agree that children have a bias towards
learning human languages. Note that the term bias is used here in its
broadest sense. 'Bias' as I use it only means that some things are learned
more easily than others. Within linguistics there is a strong debate about
the form of this learning bias. One extreme position postulates that there
is a very detailed, language-specific bias (e.g. principles and parameters;
for an overview see Baker 2001), while another extreme postulates there is
hardly any bias at all, only that which is caused by general (neural)
learning mechanisms (e.g. Elman et al. 1996). The study of the evolution
of language in turn investigates how these learning biases have evolved.

In order to understand what makes children so good at learning
language, it is necessary to know exactly what input they receive, and
what input they pay most attention to. If input to children is considerably
different from the rapid, casual speech that adults usually hear, children's
learning biases might be quite different from what would otherwise be
expected. In fact, it turns out that infant-directed speech is significantly
different from adult-to-adult speech in a number of respects. The properties that make infant-directed speech special will be treated in more
detail in the next section. A possible explanation for the special characteristics of infant-directed speech is that these make speech easier to learn.
Newport et al. (1977) have argued that infant-directed language (which
they term 'motherese') is not necessarily adapted to be a special 'teaching
language'. They show that only some of its attributes make it easier to
learn. However, they did not look at the acoustic-phonetic and phonological properties of infant-directed language. Here we will focus on its
acoustic-phonetic properties, and try to show objectively whether they
cause infant-directed speech to be easier to learn.

If infant-directed speech is really easier to learn, this has implications
for children's innate biases for learning language. The innate specification
of language can then be less restrictive. Rapid learning could probably be
achieved through a bootstrapping procedure, such that simple construc-

tions are learned first and then used to interpret and learn more complicated constructions. The infant will still need to have a number of learning biases, but these can be simpler. This would have implications for how specializations for language have evolved. However, in our present state of knowledge, we do not know whether infant-directed speech is *really* more learnable than adult-directed speech.

Testing the learnability of infant-directed speech in an experimental setting is problematic. One cannot do an experiment in which one group of infants is deprived of infant-directed speech (but not of ordinary adult-directed speech) while the control group is exposed to both. A different experiment, where one group of infants hears infant-directed speech in a second language, while the other group hears only adult-directed speech in the same second language, is possible. However, it is extremely difficult to ensure that the only differences are due to the difference between the two kinds of speech, and not, for example to the difference in kind of interaction, or to the content of the speech. How, then, is it possible to test differences in learnability? This chapter proposes that it can be tested with a computer model.

Unfortunately, computer models that can learn the semantic or syntactic content of real language are still very much in their infancy (but see e.g. Roy 2000; Steels and Kaplan 2000) so it is not possible to test the difference in learnability for these aspects of language. However, computer models that handle speech sounds are much more advanced. The focus of this chapter is therefore on the learnability of vowel sounds. The work is based on recordings of infant-directed and adult-directed speech that were acquired at the University of Washington in Seattle (Gustafson 1993; Kuhl et al. 1997). The computer model and the data set that were used are discussed in section 5.3.

There is another reason, connected to the learnability issue, why infant-directed speech holds interest for research into the evolution of language. In adult-to-adult speech, articulation tends to be strongly reduced. This is especially noticeable in vowel sounds. If children base the vowel systems that they learn directly on the signals that they perceive most frequently, the vowel system of a language would be reduced in every generation until it collapses. There are two basic ways to counter this: either children could have a mechanism that automatically compensates for the expected reduction of a vowel system, or they could focus on speech registers that are more clearly articulated, for example, infant-directed speech. Again, this is difficult to investigate with real children, but relatively straightforward to do with a computer model. Such a model and some preliminary results are presented in section 5.4.

This chapter is intended for an interdisciplinary audience, but I have found it necessary to include some technical details of the computer simulations used here. Readers who are interested in the main results, and not in the details of the methods used, might wish to skip or only read the first paragraphs of sections 5.3.3 and 5.4.3.

5.2 Infant-directed speech

When talking about infant-directed speech, one must be careful not to confuse it with the meaningless vocalizing towards very young infants that is sometimes referred to as 'baby talk'. This vocalizing is probably meant to draw the infant's attention and to soothe it, but it is unclear whether it plays any role in the acquisition of language. Infant-directed speech, on the other hand, consists of meaningful utterances directed to the infant during, for example, play, explanation, or when the infant needs to be disciplined. Such utterances already occur before the infant can reasonably be supposed to understand what is said.

Infant-directed speech tends to be slower, simpler, more clearly articulated, and has higher and wider intonation contours than adult-directed speech (e.g. Fernald and Kuhl 1987; Fernald et al. 1989). Infants tend to prefer infant-directed speech over adult-directed speech (Fernald 1985; Fernald and Kuhl 1987).

One of the most noticeable differences between adult-directed and infant-directed speech is the intonation. This is immediately obvious, even when one listens to infant-directed speech in a language one doesn't know. The overall pitch of infant-directed utterances is higher, and the pitch range is expanded. Although the extent to which pitch is expanded is culturally determined, expansion itself has been observed in many different languages and cultures, even in languages where pitch can distinguish meaning, i.e. tone languages (Grieser and Kuhl 1988). Infant-directed speech also has a slower tempo than adult-directed speech. In particular, the syllable nuclei are considerably stretched.

The exaggerated intonation and slower tempo make infant-directed speech easier to understand, and probably also to learn. Whereas the higher pitch could be explained as an unconscious attempt by the care-givers to imitate the infant, the other properties of infant-directed speech do serve a useful purpose. Intonation helps the infant to separate sentences, words within sentences, and syllables within words. Slower tempo also makes it easier to divide speech into sentences, words, and syllables. All these are prerequisites for learning speech and language. However, these are not the only useful phonetic and phonological properties of infant-directed speech.

It turns out that in infant-directed speech, the vowels at least are more carefully articulated than those in adult-directed speech. Kuhl et al. (1997) perform experiments in which the speech of mothers talking to other adults was compared with speech of the same mothers talking to their infants. These experiments were undertaken for Russian, English, and Swedish. Acoustic measurements were made of the vowel parts of target words (containing [i], [a] and [u]) in order to estimate the accuracy of articulation. This was done by measuring the area of the triangle in acoustic space that had the three target vowels as its corners. It turned out that, although there was considerable individual variation, articulation was significantly more precise for infant-directed speech than for adult-directed speech. Infant-directed speech therefore contains better information about the exact articulation of vowels.

It is perhaps not surprising that infants prefer to listen to infant-directed speech rather than to adult-directed speech (Fernald 1985; Fernald and Kuhl 1987). This effect is probably amplified when the infant-directed speech is produced during a face-to-face interaction with the infant. Infants pay much more attention to speech in face-to-face interactions than to speech produced around them. During such interactions, caregivers almost invariably modify their speech without necessarily being aware of doing so. The greater attention that infants pay to infant-directed speech, together with its frequent occurrence in face-to-face interactions, probably means that it influences language learning more than would be expected from the relative frequency with which infants hear this type of speech.

All these factors indicate that infant-directed speech facilitates language learning. Further support comes from the fact that special infant-directed speech registers occur almost universally cross-culturally (Ferguson 1964; Fernald et al. 1989; Lieven 1994). There are some reports of cultures in which infants are not addressed directly by adults (e.g. Schieffelin and

Ochs 1983; Schieffelin 1985), although in these cultures older children generally do address infants directly. Such exceptions seem to indicate that infant-directed speech is not indispensable for learning language. However, it appears that special infant-directed speech registers are the norm rather than the exception cross-culturally.

There seem to be important indications that infant-directed speech facilitates learning of language and speech. Infants automatically prefer infant-directed speech and caregivers automatically produce infant-directed speech. The properties of infant-directed speech (tempo, intonation) probably make it easier to detect phrases (see, for example, the papers in Morgan and Demuth 1996: part IV), words (e.g. Morgan and Demuth 1996: part II, III), and syllables. Also, vowels are articulated more carefully. If infant-directed speech really facilitates learning, then it is probably an evolutionary adaptation for transferring language from generation to generation; see also Brighton et al., Chapter 13 in this book. However, testing the learnability of infant-directed speech or the way in which it facilitates the preservation of language across the generations is quite impossible using real human subjects. Therefore these properties are investigated with computer models in this chapter.

5.3 Investigating the learnability of infant-directed speech

The model used for investigating the learnability of infant-directed speech is based on applying a statistical machine-learning method to two data sets. These consist of words taken from adult-directed and infant-directed speech, respectively. This work was first presented in de Boer (2001b) and has been described in more detail in de Boer and Kuhl (2003). Here I will give a brief description of the computational model, the data set, and the results.

5.3.1 *The data set*

The aim of the research was to compare the learnability of infant-directed speech and adult-directed speech. For this, recordings of both types of speech were needed. The recordings used here are the same as those used in Kuhl et al. (1997), first described by Gustafson (1993). They consist of digitized recordings of ten American mothers, talking both to another adult and to their infants. The infants ranged in age from two to five months. The topics of conversation in both cases were everyday objects likely to be familiar to the infants. The words used in the work presented here were *sock*, *sheep*, and *shoe*. These words were selected to have the vowels [a], [i], and [u] occur in roughly similar phonetic contexts. In the adult-to-adult conversation, the experimenter elicited these words, while in the infant-directed session the mothers used toys representing the objects while playing with their infants.

The recordings were made on audio cassettes and digitized at 16 bits resolution and a sampling rate of 16 kHz. After this, the target words were identified and isolated from the recordings. These were then used as input to the signal processing and learning modules of the computer model.

5.3.2 *Signal processing*

Formants are the resonant frequencies of the vocal tract and can be observed as peaks in the frequency spectrum of a speech sound. This is illustrated in Figure 5.1 for the vowel [a].

The resonant frequencies are determined by the sizes and impedances of the different oral cavities formed when the tongue and lips are put in position to articulate. The shape of the vocal tract as it occurs in almost all vowel articulations can be reconstructed from the first three formants, while the first two formants suffice to represent the accuracy of articulation of the vowels [a], [i], and [u]. Hence only the first two formants were used.

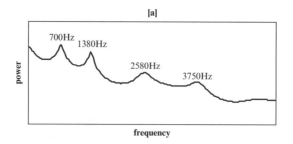

Fig. 5.1 Example of a smoothed spectrum showing formant peaks for the vowel [a] for a male speaker. The power scale is relative and has been omitted. The frequencies of the first four formant peaks are indicated.

The words in the input to the computer model were monosyllabic and had voiceless consonants only. Therefore the target vowels could be identified by the fact that they were voiced. After detecting the voiced part of a word, acoustic properties of the vowel that represent the accuracy of articulation were extracted. The first two formant frequencies (also used by Kuhl et al. 1997) were calculated throughout the length of the voiced part of the words, resulting in hundreds of formant pairs per word. Details of the signal-processing algorithms can be found in de Boer and Kuhl (2003).

The vowels of the target words were of different lengths, the [a] in *sock* being much shorter than the [u] in *shoe*. Also, the number of examples per word differed for each mother and register (see Table 5.1).

As the learning algorithm might be biased towards the most frequently occurring vowel in the sample, care was taken that each target vowel was represented by an equal number of formant pairs. For this reason, the large number of formant pairs was subsampled such that for each mother, for each speech style, there were 1000 formant pairs per vowel. Hence for each mother and speech style there were 3000 data points in total.

5.3.3 *The learning algorithm*

In this experiment, an automatic learning algorithm tries to find the centres of the vowel categories that are present in the input data. It can

TABLE 5.1 *Number of tokens in data set (and formant pairs) per target word, register, and mother.*

	Adult-Directed			Infant-Directed		
mother	*sheep*	*sock*	*shoe*	*sheep*	*sock*	*shoe*
AG	4 (9412)	2 (9304)	5 (20 539)	6 (30 716)	4 (22 593)	3 (18 866)
AH	6 (14 029)	5 (15 643)	9 (37 117)	6 (24 967)	9 (35 723)	7 (22 543)
AL	8 (18 806)	3 (6921)	9 (32 997)	9 (38 126)	7 (40 196)	8 (27 384)
AO	4 (7941)	3 (12 414)	3 (6441)	9 (27 756)	6 (19 736)	3 (25 905)
AP	8 (29 513)	6 (22 767)	4 (10 110)	7 (30 869)	9 (41 406)	6 (40 018)
AS	7 (19 916)	8 (28 359)	7 (21 633)	7 (31 137)	7 (21 619)	6 (35 546)
AT	3 (9420)	3 (10 477)	3 (8499)	5 (12 121)	7 (54 130)	4 (27 386)
AW	8 (16 443)	4 (12 109)	4 (10 754)	8 (33 268)	6 (35 561)	5 (27 124)
AX	4 (15 838)	7 (34 152)	7 (20 083)	8 (41 969)	7 (29 949)	5 (17 057)
AZ	4 (11 965)	6 (22 971)	9 (20 450)	4 (16 890)	7 (35 663)	6 (34 239)

be assumed that the centres of vowel categories correspond to the places where the concentration of data points is highest. Given that vowels are never articulated perfectly, the vowel categories will cover a part of the available acoustic space. The learning algorithm therefore needs to get an idea of which parts of the space belong to which category. Here we assume that data points for each vowel are normally distributed over the acoustic space and we will also assume that there are three vowels. The means of the normal distributions are assumed to correspond to the centres of the vowel categories, while their covariances are assumed to represent the way the vowel categories are spread over the acoustic space. In mathematical terms, the data points will be assumed to follow a distribution that consists of a mixture of three Gaussian distributions. The learning task consists of finding the means and covariances that best cover the data set. The values of the means are then considered to be the positions of the learned vowels.

The learning algorithm used here is based on the expectation maximization of a mixture of Gaussian distributions (Dempster et al. 1977; Bilmes 1998). This is a standard technique from statistical machine learning. It finds a specified number of Gaussian distributions (or Gaussians for short) that fit best on a given data set. The number of Gaussians used has to be fixed beforehand. This is unrealistic if one wants to model learning by children, as they cannot be expected to know beforehand the number of vowels in the language they are learning. However, the aim of the research presented here was to compare the learnability of infant-directed speech and adult-directed speech. As the same learning procedure is used in both cases, and the same prior knowledge is assumed, the comparison remains fair. In the model, the number of Gaussians was fixed to three, one for each vowel in the data set.

Samples drawn from a Gaussian distribution follow the well-known bell curve. In a mixture of Gaussians, there are multiple Gaussian distributions, each with its own mean and standard deviation, and each occurring with a specified probability. If one draws a sample from a mixture of Gaussians, one first selects one of the individual Gaussian distributions using their given probabilities, and then takes a point from this distribution. The total distribution of the mixture is the weighted sum of the individual Gaussians. This is illustrated in Figure 5.2 for the one-dimensional case. Gaussian mixtures work equally well in more dimensions. Given enough Gaussians, any distribution can be approximated.

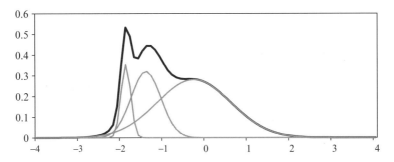

F<small>IG</small>. 5.2 Example of a mixture of three Gaussians. The thin grey lines indicate the individual Gaussians, the bold line indicates the total distribution (approximating a triangular distribution). Note that the surface of the total distribution sums to one, as the individual Gaussians are scaled with their respective probabilities.

The expectation maximization algorithm starts by initializing the mixture of three two-dimensional Gaussians to a starting value. In the experiments presented here, the means of the Gaussians were set approximately to the three corners of the acoustic space that is used for ordinary vowel articulations (see top left frame of Figure 5.3).

The corners were determined by making measurements of prototypical /i/, /a/, and /u/ produced by a female speaker. The covariances were set to circles with a radius of 30 Hz (unrealistically small for a vowel). The probabilities of the three Gaussians in the mixture were set to 1/3. These values were then iteratively re-estimated in order to maximize the likelihood that the given data set was taken from the Gaussian mixture. Details of the re-estimation can be found in Bilmes (1998). Ideally, the Gaussian mixture converges to a situation where the samples from each target vowel are covered by one and only one of the Gaussians in the mixture.

The expectation maximization algorithm is guaranteed to converge, but it is not guaranteed that it will find the optimal solution. There are two ways in which the outcome can be less than optimal. Firstly, if the vowels in the data set have too much overlap, the algorithm will converge to a solution where two Gaussians overlap. This might be the optimal solution, but the algorithm still hasn't learned the correct positions of the vowels. Secondly, if the structure of the data set is too confusing, it is likely that at least one of the Gaussians will 'get stuck' on an insignificant peak. The algorithm might then find three different vowels, but the positions of these vowels do not correspond to those of the original vowels in the data

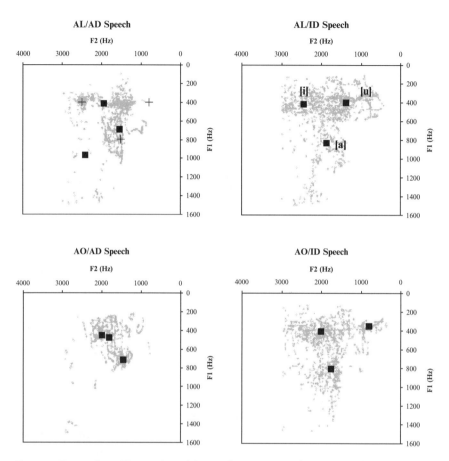

FIG. 5.3 Examples of learned positions of Gaussians. The results of two mothers (AL, top and AO, bottom) are shown for both adult-directed (AD) speech (left column) and infant-directed (ID) speech (right column). Centres of Gaussians are indicated as black squares, data points as grey points. Starting positions of Gaussians are indicated with crosses in the top left frame. Approximate positions of typical target vowels are indicated in the top right frame.

set. The possibility that the learning process can get stuck makes it more informative than a straightforward statistical analysis of the data set. Such an analysis tells us whether the structure that is expected to be found (i.e. three vowels) is present at all, but does not tell us how difficult it is to learn this structure from the data set.

5.3.4 *The results*

The learning algorithm was run on the utterances of each of the ten mothers for both the infant-directed speech and adult-directed speech data sets. Then a check was made for how well the three Gaussians that made up the mixture corresponded with the positions of the original vowels [a], [i], and [u]. Learned vowel systems were considered especially bad if two Gaussians overlapped, or if one of the Gaussians was stuck on outlier data points. An example of learned positions of Gaussians for two mothers and both types of speech is given in Figure 5.3.

For each mother, the learned positions of the Gaussians were compared between the infant-directed data set and the adult-directed data set. It turned out that without exception, the infant-directed data set resulted in better positions for the three Gaussians. Learning on the basis of the adult-directed data set resulted in outliers and overlapping Gaussians, indicating that only two out of three vowels were learnt. When both data sets resulted in three peaks, the centres of the Gaussians for the infant-directed data set were further apart (indicating more careful articulation, and hence better targets for learning). This means that infant-directed speech is more learnable than adult-directed speech with $p < 0.01$.

5.4 Investigating infant-directed speech and diachronic stability

The second computer model investigated the role that infant-directed speech plays in stabilizing vowel systems as they are transferred from one generation to the next. If children learned the prototypical positions of their vowels on the basis of rapid casual adult-to-adult speech, their vowel systems would become reduced with respect to the vowel systems of their parents. This would happen because vowel articulation is reduced in this type of speech. Here I investigate two possible scenarios that prevent this collapse from happening. The first scenario posits that infants compensate automatically for the reduction that occurs in adult speech. In other words, children learn vowel representations that are further apart from each other than the vowels that they actually hear. The second scenario is that children do not necessarily learn on the basis of the speech that occurs most frequently, but that they preferentially learn on the basis of clear speech. This clearer speech could be detected because it tends to occur in face-to-face interactions with adults, or because its intonation is exaggerated and its tempo is slower.

The model proposed here uses a statistical learning mechanism to learn vowels generated by an artificial vowel synthesizer. In the model, a population of agents can produce and learn vowels. Some of these agents are infants and others are adults. Adults produce speech sounds, and infants learn on the basis of these. After a while, adults die and infants become the new adults. The idea is to investigate how vowel systems change over time. In contrast with the previous experiment, no real data are used. Using real data would be impossible, as it is necessary to compare different vowel systems under controlled conditions.

5.4.1 *The population*

The computer model is based on a population of adult and infant agents. In all the experiments described here, at any instant there are twenty adult and twenty infant agents. Interactions in the population always occur between one randomly selected adult and one randomly selected infant agent. Adults have a repertoire of vowels that does not change during their life. In an interaction, they randomly select a vowel from their repertoire and produce it, while adding noise and reducing the articulation by a specified amount. How this happens exactly is explained in the next section. Infants do not yet have a repertoire of vowels, but learn this on the basis of the signals they perceive from the adults they interact with. The learning mechanism is described briefly in section 5.4.3.

After a fixed number of interactions, which was set to 10,000 in all simulations described here (giving on average 500 interactions per agent) all adults were removed from the population and all infants were transformed into adults. The vowels of the new adults were the ones they had learned on the basis of the signals they had heard during their interactions.

Because of the use of a population of interacting agents, the model is similar to language game models proposed by Luc Steels and co-workers (Steels 1998a; de Boer 2000, 2001b) and the iterated learning model proposed by James Hurford and Simon Kirby (e.g. Kirby 2002b).

5.4.2 *The production and perception mechanisms*

The production mechanism is the same formant synthesizer that I used in previous work (de Boer 2000, 2001a). This synthesizer produces the first four formants for any given vowel. The input to the synthesizer consists of the three major vowel parameters: tongue height, front–back position of the tongue, and lip rounding (see e.g. Ladefoged and Maddieson 1996: chapter 9 for details of how different settings of these parameters are used in the world's languages). These are represented by real numbers with values between zero and one. Noise in the articulations is modelled by adding a random value taken from the normal distribution with zero mean and standard deviation 0.05 to all articulatory parameters. In order to model reduction of articulation, all articulatory parameters are attracted to the centre (where all articulators have value 0.5) using the following formula: $x \leftarrow \alpha(x - 0.5) + 0.5$, where x is any articulatory parameter and α is a constant smaller than one. This constant is a parameter that is varied over the different simulations.

Perception is implemented using a distance function based on the first formant and the effective second formant of a vowel. This distance function was from Schwartz et al. (1997b). The effective second formant is a non-linear weighted sum of the second, third, and fourth formants and is based on the way humans perceive vowels. It allows for a convenient two-dimensional representation of vowel systems and for realistic distance calculations between vowels. Calculations are not performed on formant frequencies in Hertz, but on frequencies in Bark, a perceptually realistic, near-logarithmic scale. Detailed formulas can be found in Schwartz et al. (1997b). Whenever a signal, consisting of four formants, is perceived by an agent, it is converted into the more perceptually realistic pair of the first formant and the effective second formant.

An adult agent only stores the values of the articulatory parameters for each vowel in its repertoire. Whenever the vowel is pronounced, first of all noise is added, then it is reduced, and finally the values of the four formants for this noisy, reduced articulation are calculated. In an infant agent, the four formants it perceives are transformed into a first and effective second formant pair, and each example it hears is stored. When an infant agent changes into an adult, a statistical learning mechanism is used to convert the numerous stored examples into a small number of vowel categories.

5.4.3 *The learning mechanism*

The learning mechanism needs to detect how many vowels were present in the data set and where these vowels are located. It can be assumed that the centres of the vowel categories have the highest densities of data points. In contrast with the previous experiment, it cannot be assumed that the number of categories is known. Therefore a different learning algorithm was employed. This learning algorithm tries to locate the peaks in the data set using a certain degree of smoothing (otherwise each data point could be considered a small peak). It then tries to determine which data points belong to which peaks by finding the valleys that separate the peaks. It is therefore called iterative valley seeking (details can be found in Fukunaga 1990). On the basis of the peaks that are found, a new set of vowel articulations is determined.

Like expectation maximization, iterative valley seeking makes an initial estimate of the classification of the data set, and improves this iteratively. Unlike expectation maximization, it does not make assumptions about the shape of the distributions of data points, nor about the number of classes (peaks) in the data set. It is therefore called an unsupervised learning algorithm: it does not need any inputs other than the data set. After the algorithm finishes, only a small number of classes remain. These classes tend to correspond to the peaks in the distribution of data points, while the valleys between the peaks correspond to the boundaries between the different classes. Classes with complex shapes can be learned in this way.

The result was a number of sets of data points that each represented a vowel. The point in each class where the distribution of data points was densest (this corresponds to the highest point of the peak corresponding to this class) was taken to be representative of the data set. These points were taken to be the acoustic representations of the new vowels of the infant agent. The articulatory values corresponding to these acoustic representations were then determined and stored.

Finally, a compensation for reduced articulation could be performed. This was done by shifting articulator values away from the centre, using the following formula: $x \leftarrow \beta(x - 0.5) + 0.5$, where β is a constant larger than one and x is any articulatory parameter. Note the similarity between this function and the reduction function described above. In this way a new set of articulatory values for the vowels that corresponded to the observed signals was found.

5.4.4 *The experimental set-up*

The experiments consisted of initializing the adults in a population with a given repertoire of vowels, such that all adults initially had the same vowels (either five or seven, as indicated per experiment). The infants in a population always started out empty. I do not want to claim that real human infants come 'empty' to the task of learning language, but this was the easiest to model, and at the same time the most basic assumption possible. If transfer worked in this case, it would also work in the case where more knowledge was available beforehand.

After initialization, the interactions started, and after each 10,000 interactions, all adults were removed, all infants became adults (with the learned vowel repertoire) and a new generation of empty infants was added. This was repeated for 100 or for 250 generations. The vowel systems and the number of vowels per agent were logged for each generation. The conditions compared were (i) infant-directed speech, (ii) automatic compensation for reduction, and (iii) both. In the infant-directed condition, there was very little reduction of vowel articulations, and correspondingly, no automatic compensation.

5.4.5 *Preliminary results*

A number of experiments were performed to investigate how well vowel systems are preserved under different conditions. Three conditions were compared. In the first, vowel articulations were shrunk by 20 per cent ($\alpha = 0.8$) and in order to compensate for this, learned vowel systems were expanded by 25 per cent ($\beta = 1.25$). A reduction of 20 per cent is considered to be on the low side of realistic. It is likely that real rapid, casual speech has even more reduction, given the difference in acoustic space used in infant-directed speech and adult-directed speech (Kuhl et al. 1997). This condition modelled learning on the basis of adult-directed speech and subsequent automatic compensation. In the second condition, articulations were only shrunk by 2 per cent. Articulations were shrunk a little bit, as it is unrealistic to expect that infant-directed speech is articulated completely perfectly. No compensatory expansion was performed. This condition modelled use of infant-directed speech. In the third condition, articulations were shrunk 2 per cent and learned vowel systems were expanded 2.05 per cent. This modelled a combination of infant-directed speech and automatic compensation.

In the experiments described here, two sizes of vowel systems were used. These were five-vowel systems and seven-vowel systems. Only one type of five-vowel system was investigated: the one containing [i], [e], [a], [o], and [u]. This five-vowel system is the most frequently occurring vowel system in the world's languages. Three types of seven-vowel system were investigated. All contained the vowels [i], [e], [a], [o], and [u]. The remaining vowels were [ɛ] and [ɔ], [ɯ] and [ə], or [y] and [ø]. These, too, are all frequently occurring vowel systems.

When vowel systems are transferred from generation to generation, they are modified. Vowel categories shift place, and categories may be lost, or new categories may be added. How vowel systems change over time is illustrated in Figure 5.4.

The frames in this figure show, for each generation, the vowel system of one agent from the population. All vowels of this agent are plotted in the acoustic space of the first and effective second formant. The starting vowel system is shown with squares, and the final vowel system is shown with triangles. This is done for the five-vowel system and the first seven-vowel system, for the reduction/expansion condition and for the pure infant-directed speech condition. It can be seen how categories shift over time and how some of the vowel categories disappear. It can also be observed that the five-vowel systems are more stable over time than the seven-vowel systems, and that perhaps the five-vowel system is better preserved in the infant-directed speech condition. However, these plots are not well suited for a statistical comparison of how well the different vowel systems are preserved over time.

In order to compare multiple runs of the system, I decided to look at the number of vowels in the vowel systems in each generation. Judging from the way vowel systems change over the generations, the change in number of vowel categories is the most important factor in estimating how well agents could understand each other. As there was no change over time in the number of vowels in populations that started with five-vowel systems, these are not plotted over time. All conditions performed equally well in this case.

For seven-vowel systems, things are different. The way the number of vowels changed over time for populations that started with the first seven-vowel system is shown in Figure 5.5 for all three conditions.

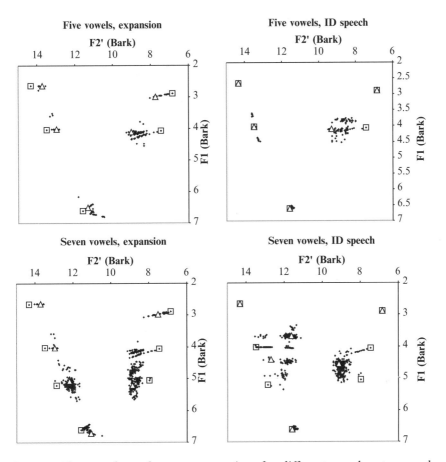

FIG. 5.4 Change of vowel systems over time for different vowel systems and different conditions. Note that for the five-vowel systems, only 100 generations were modelled, while for the seven-vowel systems, 250 generations were modelled.

It can be observed that there is no statistically significant difference in long-term behaviour between the compensation condition and the infant-directed speech condition. In the infant-directed speech condition, vowel systems seem to collapse slightly more slowly than in the compensation condition, but this changes dramatically when the reduction of articulation is increased from 2 per cent to 5 per cent. With 5 per cent contraction, the vowel system collapses within a few generations. However, if both infant-directed speech and compensation are combined, vowel systems are preserved significantly better, and the system also turns out to be more

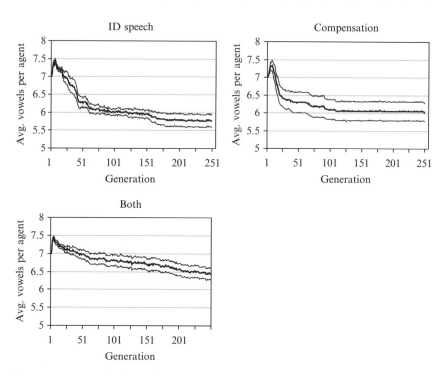

FIG. 5.5 Average number of vowels per agent for seven-vowel system for all conditions (bold lines). Also shown are the 90 per cent confidence intervals (thin lines).

robust in the face of higher reduction rates (of course, correspondingly larger expansion rates are needed). Similar results were found for the two other seven-vowel systems. It can also be observed that the seven-vowel systems collapse towards six-vowel systems within approximately fifty generations in the conditions where only infant-directed speech or only simple compensation is used. This is unrealistically fast. Seven-vowel systems of the type modelled occur frequently in the world's languages and tend to be stable over time.

5.5 Conclusions and discussion

Two conclusions can be drawn from the experiments presented here. First, infant-directed speech is more learnable than adult-directed speech, as far as the identification of vowel qualities is concerned. Second, infant-directed speech alone is not sufficient to guarantee stability of vowel systems over a large number of generations, but neither is simple compensation. Apparently both are needed to prevent collapse of larger vowel systems over time.

That infant-directed speech is more learnable than adult-directed speech comes as no great surprise. The properties of infant-directed speech (slower tempo, more exaggerated intonation, better articulation, and occurrence in face-to-face interactions) as well as its near-universal and automatic occurrence, would make it better input for extracting vowel categories than rapid, casual, and reduced adult-directed speech. However, this increased learnability has now been demonstrated directly with a computer model.

The preliminary results concerning the role of infant-directed speech in transfer of vowel systems from one generation to the next are perhaps harder to interpret. The model seems to indicate that both a form of automatic compensation for reduction and infant-directed speech are needed to transfer larger vowel systems successfully. Special infant-directed speech does not seem to be required for smaller five-vowel systems. This seems to indicate that infant-directed speech is not necessary for smaller vowel systems, but becomes increasingly important for larger vowel systems. This finding seems to be supported by empirical data. From the data presented by Kuhl et al. (1997) one can calculate the ratio between the surfaces in first formant/second formant space used for articulating vowels in adult-directed speech and infant-directed speech. This ratio increases with the number of vowels. Thus for Russian (six vowels) one finds a ratio of 1.73, for English, with a larger vowel system, one finds a ratio of 1.85, and for Swedish, with the largest vowel system, one finds a ratio of 1.96. Mandarin Chinese, with a five-vowel system, seems to fit the pattern with a ratio of 1.4 (Liu, personal communication; Liu et al. 2000). This indicates that infant-directed speech is more present in languages with more vowels.

What are the implications of this for our understanding of the evolution of language? Apparently, learning language is made easier by parental behaviour towards infants. This means that the evolution of language must partly be considered as co-evolution between infant learning behaviour on the one hand and parental behaviour on the other. A complete theory of language must therefore accommodate both the capacity for acquiring language and the ability to simplify speech and language when addressing infants.

This does not necessarily mean that such a theory of language evolution is more complex than a theory that doesn't take caregiver-child inter-actions into account. On the contrary, learning mechanisms can be simpler if the linguistic material to be learned is presented in a way that aids learning. It is difficult to imagine how adult-directed (rapid, casual, reduced, and context-dependent) language can be learned directly by a child. However, when it is assumed that the complexity of language which the infant is exposed to is gradually increased, one can imagine that a child can bootstrap its way into a language that is much more complex than one that needs to be learned all at once. In this sense, a special infant-directed speech register might be a prerequisite for more complex language to emerge.

Finally, we can imagine that the presence of infant-directed speech could generate an environment in which biological adaptations to more complex linguistic structures can evolve. Infant-directed speech helps to stabilize the cultural transmission of more complex linguistic structures (such as larger vowel systems) over many generations. Although in principle these more complex structures might be learnable, they might not remain stable over generations without infant-directed speech. Therefore they could not exert evolutionary pressure on the members of the population, and adaptations that are favourable for learning those structures would not be expected to occur. However, with infant-directed speech and bootstrapping of more complex linguistic structures, such structures might be stable over longer periods of time. This might cause extra evolutionary pressure on language users to increase the complexity of their (biological) adaptations for language.

The models used here are quite crude. Many important aspects of learning speech, such as how the number of vowel categories is determined and how sounds are imitated have not been modelled properly. Possibly, work on mirror neurons in relation to speech (e.g. Studdert-Kennedy 2002) can be useful here. Also, it is assumed that speakers and learners already know how to do many things: analyse discrete sounds, take turns, interact, etc. In this volume, some of these issues are addressed. Notably, Oudeyer (Chapter 4) and Studdert-Kennedy (Chapter 3) address the question of how speech came to consist of discrete units.

Also, I have only focused on the role of infant-directed speech, i.e. the acoustic-phonetic and phonological aspects of language. Although it has been suggested that the evolution of speech can be studied independently of language (Fitch 2000), it is clear that infant-directed language contains many syntactic and semantic modifications with respect to adult-directed speech. It is very likely that these too have an influence on learnability, and this should be investigated. However, the state-of-the-art of language modelling is not yet up to doing this with computer models.

Although much work on the role of infant-directed speech in the acquisition and evolution of language remains to be done, this chapter has shown that infant-directed speech can play an important role. The chapter has also shown that a combination of real language data and computer modelling can provide otherwise unobtainable insights into learnability and language change.

ACKNOWLEDGEMENTS

An important part of this work was performed at the Center for Mind, Brain and Learning at the University of Washington in Seattle. The author wishes to thank Pat Kuhl, Huei-Mei Liu and Willem Zuidema (now at the University of Edinburgh) for suggestions on the work described here.

FURTHER READINGS

The following provide relevant background on the evolutionary origins of vowel systems, and other types of speech, on modelling, and on infant-directed speech:
- de Boer (2001a)
- de Boer and Kuhl (2003)
- Fitch (2000)
- Kirby (2002b)
- Kuhl, Andruski, I. A. Chistovich, L. A. Chistovich, Kozhevikova, Rysinka, Stolyarova, Sundberg, and Lacerda (1997).

Evolution of grammar: How did syntax and morphology emerge?

Introduction to Part II: Protolanguage and the development of complexity

Maggie Tallerman

The five chapters in this section examine the emergence of various aspects of grammar: clause structure (Tallerman) and movement (McDaniel); morphology (Carstairs-McCarthy); and grammatical categories (Comrie and Kuteva). The fifth chapter (Franks and Rigby) has a somewhat different basis: this proposes a possible model for the emergence of grammatical complexity, in terms of mate selection.

The first two chapters examine the evolution of syntax in the broad sense, both being concerned with the properties of what is commonly known as protolanguage. Although this term is often associated primarily with the work of Derek Bickerton (e.g. Bickerton 1990, 1995), it has now gained a wider currency as any form of pre-modern, asyntactic linguistic structure: for instance, Arbib in Chapter 2 defines protolanguage as:

a system of utterances used by a particular hominid species (possibly including *Homo sapiens*) which we may recognize as a precursor to human language, but which is not itself a human language in the modern sense.

Specifically, writers who use the term 'protolanguage' envision a stage in which language lacked the syntactic structure found in all known languages today, including long extinct ones. The study of protolanguage, then, involves questions such as 'How did the syntax and morphology of attested languages come to be the way it is?' and 'How did linguistic features now known to be universal initially emerge?'.

Looking first at the development of clause structure, in Chapter 6 Maggie Tallerman examines some recent work by Andrew Carstairs-McCarthy on a 'syllabic model' of 'syntax-as-it-is'. This work (e.g. Carstairs-McCarthy 1999, 2000) makes the initially surprising (though bold and intriguing) claim that the basic structure of the clause was exapted from that of the syllable. Carstairs-McCarthy's idea is that the syllable literally forms the evolutionary model for the structure of modern syntax, meaning that its shape and structure were exapted for use as a template for the transitive clause. Thus, the onset of the syllable is claimed to appear in the clause as the subject of a sentence, the syllabic nucleus becomes the verb, the coda becomes the object, and the syllable rhyme becomes the verb phrase. Fundamental asymmetries in the clause—between the subject and the predicate, between the subject and the object, between the verb and the noun phrase arguments—then follow automatically, because these patterns are already instantiated in cognition: 'the neural organization underlying syllable structure was co-opted to provide a syntax for strings of "words" when the need became pressing' (Carstairs-McCarthy 1999: 148). Jackendoff (2002: 253, n. 11) comments favourably on this proposal, yet simultaneously suggests another possibility:

Although this asymmetry had good acoustic or articulatory reasons in phonology, in syntactic structure it is just one of those accidents of evolution. Whether or not one endorses this argument, I find it has the right sort of flavor. Another possibility, however, is that subject–predicate structure arose from Topic–Comment organization in information structure. It subsequently became grammaticalized and overlaid with lots of other grammatical phenomena, so that some languages (including English) came to reinvent another pre-subject topic position.

Clearly, other plausible hypotheses could also be proposed, but Carstairs-McCarthy is quite correct to note that few linguists have even posed the question as to why these asymmetries exist. In Chapter 6, Tallerman does not offer an alternative of her own, but dissects the central claims of the syllabic model. She examines the problems posed for it by verb-initial and by SOV (subject–object–verb word order) languages, and shows that the idea of subject as 'onset' is fraught with difficulties. She concludes that the apparent similarities in structure between the clause and the syllable are superficial, leaving the field open for other hypotheses to emerge concerning the shape of the clause.

The syllabic model stops short of proposing an answer to the question of why languages apparently all employ the property of syntactic displacement of constituents, or movement; Carstairs-McCarthy's view, in fact, is that this would have been a later development, coming well after the construction of the clause. However, this conclusion is by no means the only possibility, as we see in Chapter 7. Instances of movement are found in examples such as the following, where the constituent in brackets has been displaced from its canonical position, represented by the dash __ :

(1) [Which book] did she choose __ ?
(2) [This picture] was chosen __ as the first prize.
(3) [Can] we __ see the mountains from here?

So the verb *choose* is understood to have a direct object in (1) and (2), despite the fact that this phrase no longer follows the verb, and the auxiliary *can* is understood as belonging with *see*, although separated from it, in (3). Dana McDaniel's Chapter 7 considers how a protolanguage could have evolved the property of movement. Although theories of the evolution of movement often focus on comprehension, and how displacement could facilitate it (for instance by showing the topic of a sentence), McDaniel takes a different view: she suggests that the particular language *production* system existing in the protolanguage period was a prerequisite for the evolution of movement. A grammar including movement was advantageous, due to the nature of the production system that had developed up to that point: unstructured word strings containing copies of crucial content words. McDaniel suggests that protohumans had a system of 'quick lexical retrieval, but no syntax'; a typical protolanguage utterance, then, might have been something like *baby tree leopard baby baby kill* (in a situation in which a leopard in a tree was about to attack a baby). Note that the concept of protolanguage McDaniel assumes is again distinct from that of Bickerton: in Bickerton's model, word strings are very short, and repetition is not expected, whilst McDaniel suggests that presyntactic language could easily have developed to a stage where speakers employed fluent, repetitive strings of this kind.

In the utterance illustrated above, the speaker starts with *baby* because that is her main concern, and reiterates that word many times for just the same reason. Now imagine that movement creates a copy or 'trace' of the word *baby*, to give something like *baby leopard tree kill* [*trace/copy of 'baby'*]. This allows the speaker to carry on as before, producing words in whatever order they tumbled into her mind; the speaker, rather than the hearer, initially has the advantage, in that she doesn't have to constrain the order of her words to fit a single syntactic mould. So movement does not evolve in order to enhance communication, as is commonly assumed; instead, the established type of production, involving long word strings with much repetition, was more compatible with a newly emerging syntax that *did* include movement than one which did not. Here, McDaniel's proposals meet those of Chomskian minimalist syntactic theory (e.g. Chomsky 1995): movement is seen as a copying operation.

Carstairs-McCarthy's Chapter 8 also considers protolanguage, looking not at the syllabic model of syntax discussed in Tallerman's chapter, but instead examining the evolution of morphology, or more specifically the development of allomorphic variation. Allomorphy refers to the situation in which morphemes—the smallest meaningful units of a language—have more than one phonological shape; this can be illustrated in English with alternations such as *drive ~ drove*, or *mouse ~ mice*, as well as the three variants of the third person singular present tense <-*s*> suffix that occur, for instance, in *waits* [s], *wades* [z], and *lazes* [ɪz]. As Carstairs-McCarthy points out, this type of morphological variation, so familiar from (for instance) European languages is not a *necessary* part of language: an invented language such as Esperanto can function perfectly well without any allomorphic variation, and there are also real languages (such as Chinese) that function equally well without much morphology of any kind. Nonetheless, morphology is very prevalent in the world's languages: most languages do exhibit morphological alternations of the kind illustrated.

Once again, Carstairs-McCarthy considers questions that other linguists have not thought to ask. Why would languages have developed morphology, when they already have one level of complex organization, namely syntax? Why does morphology exhibit a different kind of organization, at word level, than syntax exhibits when it combines words into phrases and clauses? Although not all linguists are convinced that an independent morphological component of the grammar does exist outside syntax (see, for instance, Emonds 2002; Halle and Marantz 1993), there are, nonetheless, intractable phenomena in morphology which could otherwise not easily be accounted for.

The answer to the question of why morphology evolved, Carstairs-McCarthy argues, lies in the fact that adjacent 'words' in protolanguage must always have influenced each other phonologically, just as they do today. Especially given the kind of rapid-fire, word-after-word delivery envisaged by McDaniel, assimilation effects must necessarily have occurred—that is simply the nature of the way the vocal tract operates; the speech organs do not move independently, but interact in a complex symphony (see Studdert-Kennedy, Chapter 3). So, strange as it may seem, allomorphic variation would have come to exist even before there was morphology: to put this another way, 'words' would have had various pronunciations, depending on their linguistic environment, before those differences in pronunciation were exploited to do the work that they do in modern morphology, such as marking tense, number, gender, and so on.

In fact, Carstairs-McCarthy suggests that the kind of 'non-concatenative' morphology which is considered rather marked in modern languages (such as the *mouse* ~ *mice* distinction) is the evolutionary origin of all morphological variation. At some early stage, contiguous 'words' would influence the pronunciation of an item in different ways according to context, but speakers would be unaware of these low-level changes. This is exactly the kind of process that led to the *mouse* ~ *mice*, *goose* ~ *geese* kind of alternations in the Germanic languages. Even when the triggers for the change in pronunciation have been lost (as they have in these English examples) the work done by the allomorphy remains—in fact, the allomorphy alone does the work that was previously done by some long-lost linguistic element. So in this case we utilize the morphological distinction to give the 'singular' versus 'plural' distinction. And once the brain was primed to use differences in the pronunciation of a lexical item in this way, then other types of morphology could follow. The idea, Carstairs-McCarthy notes, is that all of the items in a linguistic paradigm are perceived as 'same-but-different': their fundamental meanings are unchanged even though they may have a different phonological shape. So *mouse* and *mice* are both word forms of an item meaning MOUSE, for instance. Once the notion of 'same-but-different' got established, it could also be exploited to yield what we now think of as the more natural, typical kind of morphology: the concatenative morphology seen in the simple affixal plural of *cat* ~ *cats*, for example. Small variations in the word form can now be regularly taken advantage of to do all sorts of linguistic work, registering the many morphosyntactic categories that natural languages utilize. But all of this variation has an evolutionary origin in the natural phonological changes that occur when words meet up in fast speech, and cause each other to change in pronunciation.

Comrie and Kuteva's Chapter 9 also considers protolanguage, but mainly examines what must surely have been a significantly later stage than that investigated by the first three chapters in this section: they look at the historical development of grammatical categories and construc-

tions. Specifically, they examine tense marking and relative clause formation. They argue that there is nothing adaptive in the development of
grammatical categories and constructions: these do not develop in order
to satisfy some 'gap' in the language, and nor do they respond to any
notion of 'functional need'. Certain kinds of grammaticalization occur
frequently whether or not a language happens to contain a gap; for
instance, the development of new auxiliaries such as English future *will*,
or far more recently, the *be going to* future. Furthermore, grammatical
categories such as tense need not be expressed by grammatical tense
morphemes, and if a language lacks (for instance) a future tense marker,
that does not entail that it lacks a notion of future time.

Turning to a detailed study of the relativization strategies found in the
languages of the world, Comrie and Kuteva go on to show that elaborate
strategies, using as many as three or four or even five markers of relativization within a single instance of the construction, do not confer any
communicative benefits in a language that has them. Once a language has
them, multiple markers of relativization are typically put to work encoding various grammatical distinctions, but these same distinctions are often
made in simpler ways in closely related languages which lack the multiple
markers. And of course, other languages just lack the grammatical distinctions altogether, yet function equally efficiently. Grammatical complexity is not there because a language needs it; it is typically there for
historical reasons, and residues of earlier constructions may linger on and
be given new uses, or they may simply be lost and not even missed.

Why, then, do some languages maintain systems of great grammatical
complexity, if the distinctions encoded are not linguistically indispensable? Comrie and Kuteva suggest that there are social and cultural reasons
for a society to keep its distinctive linguistic characteristics: these serve to
set a community apart from its neighbours, in the same way that customs
and costumes often do. The authors even compare this maintenance of
apparently dysfunctional and superfluous grammatical material with the
notion of costly signalling (Zahavi 1975). Something that is a positive
drawback in physical terms (the classic example is the peacock's tail)
requires so much stamina to maintain that only the fittest individuals
can achieve this: thus, the tail is a good indication to a potential mate that
the bird is healthy and fit to reproduce. For members of a speech community, it might well be 'simpler' in some sense to dispense with instances
of grammatical complexity, but preserving these (presumably at some

cognitive expense) proclaims individuals to be members of that community. So we might indeed see the use of complex grammatical systems as 'honest' signals (in this case, of group membership)—signals of the kind that can't be faked.

In the final chapter in this section, Chapter 10, Franks and Rigby also appeal to the notion of honest signalling. They propose that the creative use of language is a kind of sexual display, and could well have been employed by early hominids as a reliable method of honest signalling, and thus employed in mate selection. It is not only physical characteristics that are used by our species to select a mate: cognitive traits such as intelligence and creativity are important too, because in evolutionary terms the ability to solve problems efficiently can mean the difference between life and death. But since cognitive features are difficult to detect reliably (they can't be seen, unlike the peacock's tail) it becomes even more important for the individual making the selection to have a way of evaluating the evidence, in order to avoid deception. Semantic creativity in language use has just the required properties, according to the authors.

Experimental evidence presented by Franks and Rigby supports this proposal. Given novel noun–noun compounds such as *book bicycle*, the participants in an experiment are asked to provide a definition. Under 'display' conditions (males displaying to an attractive young female experimenter, for example) more creative definitions emerge. At the same time, the hearer can avoid being dazzled by the speaker's brilliant use of creative language (and thus deceived about his 'fitness') because she can successfully evaluate the linguistic forms he produces. So definitions that are too crazy may be perceived as creative, but if they are not semantically relevant, the attempt to impress will fail.

Although cognitive traits may be subject to sexual selection in this way, Franks and Rigby point out that prior to that, they are doubtless subject to natural selection: individuals who are good at problem solving are more likely to provide for themselves successfully, and avoid predation. So creativity could have been exapted for use in sexual selection subsequently. This feeds into the developing language system not by making linguistically creative individuals more likely to survive, but by making them more attractive to potential mates. In this way, semantic and syntactic systems of greater complexity might evolve not because they inherently conferred fitness, but because the possession of such complex forms indicated a mate of better worth. It seems, then, that here we might at last have a riposte to Lightfoot's barbed critique of the notion that important universal aspects of language could possibly have evolved by the usual Darwinian mechanisms: 'The subjacency condition has many virtues, but I am not sure that it could have increased the chances of having fruitful sex' (1991: 69).

To summarize, the themes that are dealt with in this section are quite varied, but what the authors have in common is their desire to uncover the evolutionary basis for the observed syntactic and morphological properties of attested languages. The properties investigated are clause structure, syntactic movement, the existence of morphology and allomorphy, the variation in ways of marking relative clauses, and semantic/syntactic creativity. All the authors assume, with Pinker and Bloom (1990), that language did evolve, and that linguistic complexity was progressive in its emergence, rather than instantaneously present (either from the start, or at some later stage). Some measure of consensus has, then, also emerged in this section.

6 Initial syntax and modern syntax: did the clause evolve from the syllable?

MAGGIE TALLERMAN

6.1 Introduction: a sketch of the syllabic model

In a monograph and two related papers, Andrew Carstairs-McCarthy (1998, 1999, 2000) has proposed that the syllable formed the evolutionary model for the structure of modern syntax, in the sense that its shape and structure were literally exapted for use as a template for the clause. This chapter undertakes an examination of certain of the pivotal claims made by the syllabic scenario (see also Tallerman forthcoming), and concludes that it does not form a convincing model for the evolution of a precursor to modern syntax.

The basic idea presented by Carstairs-McCarthy (henceforth CM) is sketched here; full details can be found in CM's own work, as cited. Anatomical changes to the oral and nasal cavities in ancestral homonids were the result of the exclusive adoption of bipedal locomotion; these physiological changes in turn gave rise to a greater range of vocalizations in *Homo erectus*. A larger vocabulary of 'calls' would then naturally be available, but until these calls could be strung together to form patterns, the expansion of vocabulary could not properly be exploited—even the largest animal 'vocabularies' of calls are restricted to a few dozen items at most. Clearly, advantages would accrue from having a combinatorial system—what we know as syntax. The obvious problem is how could syntax have arisen:

Where was syntax to come from, however? A handy source would be any already existing neural mechanism for imposing a regular pattern on speech. Such a pattern could indeed be found, namely in [...] syllabic frames [...] (CM 2000: 253).

One way to arrive at a syntax which mimics [the structure of the syllable] directly is to relabel 'syllable' as 'sentence'; 'onset' as 'NP-subject', 'coda' as NP; 'nucleus' as 'verb' or 'stative'; and 'rhyme' as 'VP' (CM 2000: 255).

Thus, according to CM (1999: chapter 5) we arrive at a template for the clause as seen in (1), which reflects a syllable structure like that in (2):

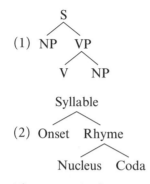

The syntactic frame can then be put to use for encoding predicate-argument structure (CM 2000: 255). Moreover, the prediction is that various *properties* of the syllable are carried over into clause structure. CM suggests (1999: 151) that structural asymmetries in the syllable (between its nuclei and margins, between the two kinds of margins, and between the syllable itself and its constituents)[1] are also observed in modern syntax. The following syntactic asymmetries are said to result:[2]

(3) a. ... [E]ach sentence obligatorily contains a nucleus-like position.
   b. This nucleus-like position is filled by a class or classes of words that are substantially but not completely distinct from the classes of words that fill constituents occupying margin-like positions.
   c. Substantially the same classes of words are found in all constituents occupying margin-like positions.
   d. Some non-nuclear constituent(s) are privileged in onset-like fashion.

It can immediately be noticed that the simplified structure in (1) might provide a crude match for the kind of SVO sentence structure seen in

---

[1] The third asymmetry, between the syllable itself and its constituents, manifests itself most crucially as a distinction between the syllable and the syllable margins; this CM proposes as the origins of the universal S/NP dichotomy in syntax: see section 6.4 below.
[2] Two further specific asymmetries are in fact proposed in the 1999 monograph: see CM (1999) and Tallerman (forthcoming) for further details.

English (and around 42 per cent of the rest of the currently known languages of the world; Tomlin 1986) but it does not appear to correspond to the word order found in SOV languages (which form another 45 per cent of the world's languages) or verb-initial languages, which form around 12 per cent of the current total. However, CM does not find this problematic, since the syllabic model is explicitly presented, not as a model of *modern* (i.e. attested) syntax, but rather as a model of what I will refer to as Initial Syntax (see section 6.4): '[T]he syllabic scenario does not purport to explain everything about how the grammar of contemporary languages works [...]. Rather, it purports to explain how syntax got started [...]' (CM 2000: 254). Nonetheless, CM does expect the syllabic model to be judged on the basis of the predictions it makes about attested syntax: pointing out that we cannot test directly the closeness of the match between syllable structure and the structure of Initial Syntax, he states: 'What we can do, however, is consider whether the kind of syntax that the asymmetries [in (3)] predict is a plausible candidate to be the ancestor of syntax-as-it-is' (1999: 151). The latter challenge—to examine whether the predictions made by the syllabic model add up to a plausible candidate for the ancestor of modern syntax—is taken up in this chapter.

Sections 6.2 and 6.3 present arguments concerning the structure of modern syntax which demonstrate various serious shortcomings of the syllabic scenario. In section 6.2 I outline the problems for the syllabic model posed by the existence of verb-initial languages, and argue that these cannot be explained away, but remain an intractable counterexample to the predictions of the model. In section 6.3 I examine one of the central proposals in the syllabic model, namely the idea that clauses have a maximized onset which is parallel to that found in the syllable. Section 6.4 turns to the structure of Initial Syntax, looking at some issues in the evolution of argument structure, and concludes that the syllable does not form a plausible pattern for this central facet of modern syntax.

6.2 The problem of verb-initial languages

One of the major putative parallelisms between syllable structure and clause structure proposed by CM concerns the principle of onset maximization (1999: 134–8). There is a universal tendency for consonants, especially consonant clusters, to appear in the syllable onset rather than its coda, giving for example the syllabification [ak$trəs] 'actress' rather than *[akt$rəs], despite—as 'act' shows—final -*kt* clusters being perfectly possible. In the syntax, 'onset maximization' is claimed to be manifested in various ways (see also section 6.3), but the basic premise is that non-verbal material (such as subjects) appears *before* the verb. Languages which do *not* have subjects as sentence 'onsets'—chiefly, verb-initial languages—appear problematic for the syllabic model, as noted by CM (1999: 157). Such languages manifest the exact opposite property to 'onset maximization', since all margin-like material (everything non-verbal) appears *after* the verb. CM maintains, though, that the problem of verb-initial languages is superficial, arguing on a number of different grounds (1999: 157–9) that this language type presents no challenge to the syllabic model. In this section I counter each of these arguments.

CM's first claim is that verb-initial languages are relatively infrequent. However, this is no argument at all. At least several hundred completely stable verb-initial languages exist, many of which are unrelated; verb-initial syntax therefore cannot be disregarded. And of course, we have no idea if the verb-initial pattern was more or less frequent in prehistory, or might even represent the word order of the earliest language(s).[3]

CM's second argument is that these languages are not consistently verb-initial, but typically either (a) allow a non-verbal element to be fronted 'for purposes of emphasis or topicalization' (1999: 158), or else (b) display a non-verbal functional element in fronted position, which prevents the verb from being truly initial. The first point here, that some constituent may be fronted, seems entirely irrelevant, since it is also true of most other language types, including SVO. The existence of an optional, and possibly marked, set of alternative word orders does not preclude an analysis of a language as basically verb-initial. Example (4) illustrates CM's second option, whereby the sentence has some initial functional element.[4] CM's

---

[3] Note that Newmeyer (2000) proposes an SOV word order for the earliest human language, a claim which might well be supported by the modern geographical preponderance of this word order type (Nichols 1992), as well as its frequency. If this were true, then the earliest syntax still could not be a homologue of the syllable structure in (2): see section 6.3.1.

[4] Examples such as (i) are also intended by CM to illustrate this second point:

(i) Fe   welodd   y   ddynes   ffilm (Welsh)
     PRT   see:PAST   the   woman   film
     'The woman saw a film.'

However, CM incorrectly glosses the Welsh particle *fe* as 'past' (1999: 158). In fact it is an affirmative particle and is not at all obligatory. Examples such as (i) do not then support

position is that languages which behave in this way are not genuinely verb-initial, since the initial functional element acts as the 'onset':

(4) E   kōrero ana   ngā   wāhine (Maori: CM 1999: 158)
     PROG   speak   the   women
     'The women are speaking.'

However, the tense/aspect markers that commonly occur in preverbal position in Maori and many other Polynesian languages are strictly part of the verbal complex, since they express the inherent morphosyntactic categories of verbs. The same applies to the Celtic affirmative markers (for instance Welsh *fe*, seen in n. 4 in this chapter) and their negative counterparts: they indicate the polarity of the following verb. In the terms of generative grammar, these categories are part of the extended projection of the verb. As such, the markers must surely be part of the sentence nucleus, as they are merely the free morpheme equivalents of bound (affixal) verbal morphology. These particles, then, are not parallel to the entirely separate onset position in the syllable, which is not a *category* of the nucleus, nor a *part* of the nucleus, nor even closely related to it.

The third argument proposed to deal with the complication which verb-initial languages pose for the syllabic model runs as follows: 'the initial "verbal" element may be an auxiliary, separated from the lexical verb by an NP that functions as subject and that is therefore privileged in relation to the lexical verb' (CM 1999: 158). Thus, many VSO languages have an Aux-SVO alternative word order, as for instance is the case for all the Celtic languages, illustrated by Welsh in (5):

(5) Aux   S   V   O
     Roedd y   ddynes yn   chwarae   tennis.
     was   the woman PROG   play:NONFIN   tennis
     'The woman was playing tennis.'

What I understand CM's claim to be here is that the subject acquires an onset-like special status by appearing immediately before the *lexical* verb, and that therefore what is truly at the margin of the sentence (an auxiliary in (5)) can be discounted. The problem with this argument is that auxiliaries absolutely have to 'count' as verbal elements in CM's system,

---

the idea that verb-initial languages have some non-verbal onset. Apart from Breton, which is verb-second, all the Celtic languages are truly verb-initial in the sense that what is obligatory in initial position in unmarked word order is the finite verb or auxiliary.

because one of the language types that he cites as illustrating the principle of privileged onsets, (3d), is the verb-second (V2) type (CM 1999: 159). V2 languages such as German are claimed to comply with the privileged onset principle because they have some single constituent—not necessarily the subject—in initial 'onset' position, with the finite verb (the 'nucleus') immediately following:

(6) [Gestern   abend]   **ist**   diese   Frau   gegangen. (German)
    yesterday evening   is   this   woman   gone
    'This woman went yesterday evening.'

But since that nucleus may actually be an auxiliary, as it is in (6), then auxiliaries must also be allowed to count as nuclei in the situation illustrated in (5). It appears, then, that the Aux-SVO pattern does have the sentence 'nucleus' in initial position, even in CM's own terms, and contrary to the predictions of the syllabic model.

Note that in (6), the lexical verb (the past participle of *gehen* 'go': *gegangen*) is separated from the auxiliary—in fact, its position is irrelevant to the calculation of verb-second placement. Furthermore, V2 languages differ in terms of the position of a non-finite lexical verb: the V2 language Breton, for instance, does not place the verb in clause-final position. So what is important cross-linguistically is clearly *not* the position of the lexical verb, but rather, the position of the inflected element, which may be a lexical verb or may be an auxiliary. What bearing does this have on the syllable/sentence parallel proposed in (3a), which states that sentences, like syllables, have a nucleus-like position which is basically obligatory? In the sentence, the nucleus is 'a verb or verb-like element' (CM 1999: 151). Since sentences generally do contain verbs, or at least finite elements, this item on the checklist is superficially unproblematic. However, CM assumes that in the case of verb-initial languages, the 'nucleus' that counts is the lexical verb, whereas the evidence from both verb-initial and V2 languages points to the fact that the true nucleus in terms of generalizations about word order is actually the *finite* element, which may or may not be a lexical verb.

On the other hand, of course, the lexical verb is indeed the nucleus of the sentence in another sense—in terms of the number and type of arguments it selects for. This suggests that the 'nuclear' property in the sentence is not monolithic, but rather, is potentially split between two of its components: the finite element and the lexical verb. Chomskyan generative syntax has in fact acknowledged this from its earliest inception, by postulating an element variously termed Aux, I(nfl) and, most recently, T (for Tense), as a functional head separate from the lexical V head. The problem for CM is, then, that there is no clearly identifiable sentence 'nucleus' in the way that there is a syllabic nucleus, but rather, the 'nuclear' properties of a sentence can be split between two of its constituents, so that the 'tense-marking' element is not necessarily the same as the 'argument-taking' element.

In part, CM seems to acknowledge this situation: he notes (1999: 166) that 'it should be possible for the syllabic nucleus to be emulated in two different ways in the same sentence, once by a verb with lexical content, and once by a member of the lexically empty verb-like class' (i.e. an auxiliary). He remarks that such is the case in German sentences like that in (6), which have both V2 syntax and a verb in final position. But his position is problematic in various ways. One: as noted in the text above, the role of the auxiliary only seems to be recognized in the case of V2, and not verb-initial languages. Two: there is no systematic method of deciding when the auxiliary 'counts' as nucleus, and when it does not. Three: there appears to be an unwanted prediction in the direction from syntax back to syllable structure: the clause can have two verbal elements but syllables cannot have two nuclei. Four: the syllable does not provide an evolutionary model for a two-nucleus sentence: a branching nucleus (such as a diphthong) in which one element is dependent on the other is not a possible model for auxiliary + lexical verb, since crucially, the two elements in a diphthong are not structured into anything like a 'tense-marking' and an 'argument-taking' element. And five: whilst auxiliaries and verbs are frequently separated, the elements within a branching nucleus cannot in any case be separated so that each would occur in a different constituent of the syllable.

The fourth and final argument adduced by CM to handle the problem of verb-initial languages is that they only acquire that word order as a result of syntactic movement: verb-initial orders are *derived* orders, whilst the underlying structure is SVO. This view is certainly consistent with most, though not all, transformational accounts of Celtic and other verb-initial languages over the last twenty-five years (see, for instance, the papers in Borsley and Roberts 1996, and Carnie and Guilfoyle 2000). CM regards this argument as support for the syllabic model because he assumes that syntactic displacement evolved considerably later than the emergence of the earliest form of (syllable-influenced) syntax. So verb-initial languages can be removed from the equation because in some sense they are not verb-initial at all, but SVO: 'modern VSO languages can be regarded as irrelevant for the purpose of testing the predictions of the syllabic model' (CM 1999: 159). We might object to the idea of choosing in this way which facts are relevant to the testing of a hypothesis and which are not, but there is also a more concrete problem.

It is likewise true of transformational accounts of V2 languages that they involve syntactic movement, so if we discount evidence from languages which acquire their surface word order by movement processes, then we must also discount V2 languages. Yet, as we have seen, CM considers V2 syntax to support his hypothesis, in that V2 constitutes one type of onset maximization. And just the same problem occurs with languages that have a particular focus position (see section 6.3.2) since generative accounts of these also characteristically assume movement of a constituent to the focus position: see, for example, É. Kiss (2002). Again, CM cites such languages as illustrating the syntactic principle of onset maximization, but if they rely on movement to attain onsets, then again, in CM's own terms, they must be discounted as possible evidence.

In sum, I have argued in this section that verb-initial languages (and, by extension, V2 languages and any languages with a privileged focus position) pose considerable difficulty for the syllabic model, and that the counter-arguments offered by CM cannot be upheld. In the following section I address problems raised by the notion of 'onset-like privileges' in syntax.

6.3 'Privileged onsets' and the relationships between constituents

I turn now in more detail to (3d) on the proposed checklist of parallel features between the syllable and the sentence: '[s]ome non-nuclear constituent or constituents are privileged in onset-like position' (CM 1999: 151). One of the main problems, I argue, is that relationships contracted in the syntax between 'onsets' and other parts of the sentence appear entirely unlike those contracted generally in phonology (see also Tallerman forthcoming). CM suggests four different ways in which 'onset-like privileges' can be manifested in syntax (1999: 156), which I examine in turn.

6.3.1 *SOV syntax: the constituency problem*

CM's first idea is that onset maximization in syllable structure is paralleled by a sentence structure in which all non-verbal parts of the sentence appear before the sentence nucleus, therefore in preverbal position—in other words, SOV syntax. Crucially, though, the onsets of syllables *are constituents*, as is clear from the fact that they act as a unit in spoonerisms, for instance. But there is no constituent consisting of the subject and the object in SOV languages. CM apparently forsees this criticism, since he says (1999: 157) that 'nothing in the model imposes an expectation' that the onset in syntax should be a single constituent, but this surely results in the proposed cross-structural generalization being so diluted as to be vacuous.

Furthermore, the whole point of CM's proposed parallelism in structures in (1) and (2) is presumably that the clause *has* somehow evolved to display constituent structure (giving in subject-initial languages a subject versus predicate split, the predicate consisting of a verb and its arguments). Yet if we can ignore the actual constituent structure in the case of SOV languages in order to promote the 'onset maximization' principle, then nothing at all is actually predicted by the syllabic model.

6.3.2 *The two-onsets problem*

A second manifestation of the principle of privileged onsets is claimed to appear in languages in which the constituent in immediate *preverbal* position is in some way special. CM illustrates (1999: 160) from Hungarian, in which a focalized constituent occupies this preverbal slot. It is not controversial that preverbal position can be privileged in various ways. However, the parallel with syllable structure is not maintained. The problem is that there is always only one onset to the syllable—an onset may be complex, but there is still only one per syllable. Therefore there is only one prenuclear constituent in the syllable. But a language with, say, a preverbal focus position (which may contain any constituent of the sentence) is likely to also have a subject with the usual privileged syntactic status, including the possibility of appearing in sentence-initial position. In other words, in CM's terms, the sentence in such a language appears to have two onsets.

Exactly the same problem applies to the third language type adduced by CM to illustrate 'onset-like privileges', namely V2. The constituent immediately preceding the finite element may or may not be the subject; see (6) for example, where an adverbial is in initial position. Nonetheless, since V2 languages also have subjects with a privileged syntactic status (manifested for instance in binding asymmetries, or the ability to control the covert subject position in an embedded infinitival clause) then once again there appear to be many sentences with two onsets, the subject being one and the prefinite constituent the other, in cases where this differs from the subject. Again, of course, this is entirely unlike the situation in the syllable, where there is always just one onset. As seen in section 6.2 with reference to the two nuclei issue, CM does note that 'onset-like privileges' may in fact be manifested in two different ways in the same sentence (1999: 166). But neither the two nuclei question nor the two onsets question apparently strikes him as problematic, despite the fact that neither situation is reflected in syllable structure, and is thus inconsistent with an account which proposes syllabic origins for syntax.

6.3.3 *Subjects as privileged onsets*

The fourth proposed manifestation of privileged onsets is the existence of NPs with special syntactic properties, such as subjects or topics. Here, I consider the notion of the subject as onset. It is hardly controversial that cross-linguistically, subjects do indeed have particular properties, even though there are no truly universal criterial properties relating to subjecthood (see Keenan 1976). However, a number of problematic issues arise from the predictions of the syllabic model. Specific syllable/sentence parallelisms from the list in (3) are not met, in part exactly because of the differences between subjects and other constituents in the sentence, and the relationships contracted between the subject and other constituents.

Recall firstly parallelism (3c), which states that '[s]ubstantially the same classes of words are found in all constituents occupying margin-like positions' (CM 1999: 151). It is true that a substantial class of NPs—the vast majority, by tens of thousands—can occur in both subject and object positions. But crucially, many languages exhibit a class of NPs that cannot occur in both positions: elements without independent reference can be objects, but cannot occur as subjects in simple sentences. Consider the familiar distribution of the English reciprocal *each other* and the reflexives, *herself, himself, themselves*, etc.:

(7) a. John and Mary hate each other.
    b. *Each other hate John and Mary.
    c. Pictures of each other disturb John and Mary.

(8) a. John hates himself
    b. *Himself hates John
    c. Pictures of himself disturb John

As (7c) and (8c) show, a reciprocal and a reflexive may be *part of* a subject constituent, but cannot *be* the subject, as in (7b), (8b). In the large class of languages which operate similarly, which NPs will be admissible in any given 'marginal' slot depends on the syntactic structure, and for these languages, the proposal in (3c) appears to be unsupported.

Secondly, the syntactic facts illustrated in (7) and (8) also fail to match one of the specific asymmetries which CM notes as occurring in the syllable, namely that 'the inventory of codas in a language tends to be smaller than that of possible onsets' (1999: 141). Since anaphors can only occur as bare NPs when they are objects in a simple sentence, this situation is in fact the complete converse to that predicted by the syllabic model: such NPs can occur in 'coda' position, but they cannot be onsets. Presumably, though, the binding asymmetries illustrated in (7) and (8) might nonetheless be argued by CM to constitute evidence of the 'privileged onset' in syntax in the sense that subjects *license* the anaphors. The problem, however, is that such data could equally well be seen as supporting a principle which is the exact antithesis of CM's, namely a privileged sentence *coda*, i.e. a position privileged because it can contain as bare NPs reciprocal and reflexive phrases.

A third problem is that no aspect of syllable organization appears to give rise to syntactic behaviour such as that illustrated in (7) and (8). There are no elements that systematically, across languages, can occur in the coda position of syllables but not the onset (or vice versa).[5] There are no ways in which onsets and codas within a syllable systematically interact:

---

[5] Of course, any language may have its own *ad hoc* restrictions, as illustrated by the distribution in English of [h] (onset only) and [ŋ] (coda only). This does not detract from the point made in the text.

a particular onset never affects or gives rise to what is licit in its own coda, entirely unlike the situation in (7) and (8). In other words, contrary to what is usual in syntax, there is no licensing contracted *within* the syllable between onset and coda.[6]

It is true, however, that not all language families exhibit the same kind of binding phenemona found in English. For instance, the Austronesian family contains many examples of languages in which binding relations operate in terms of thematic relations, rather than hierarchical structure; see, for instance, work on Balinese and Malagasy by Wechsler and Arka (1998) and Rackowski and Travis (2000). These languages allow various arguments of the verb to appear in what we can usefully term 'onset' position in the sentence (not merely to play devil's advocate, but also so as to abstract away from questions of the grammatical relation of this position). However, the binding conditions do *not* appear to refer to that onset position—nor, presumably, to such notions such as c-command. Instead, irrespective of the syntactic structure, an agent NP can bind a theme, but not vice versa, as these Balinese examples show:[7] consider the binding possibilities for the reflexive marker *awakne*:

(9) Awakne   tingalin-a.
    self   TT:see-3SG
    '(S)he saw himself/herself.'

(10) *Wayan   tingalin-a   teken   awakne.
     Wayan   TT:see   PREPOSITION   self
     ('Wayan was seen by himself.')

(11) Ia   ningalin   awakne.
     3SG   AT:see   self
     '(S)he saw himself/herself.'

In (9), the 3SG marker on the verb (the agent) binds the theme topic *awakne*; in (10), *Wayan* is the theme, and as themes can't bind agents, it

---

[6] On the other hand, phonotactic interactions between the coda of one syllable and the onset of the *next* are common (Harris 1994: 158), for instance in homorganic clusters as in <win$ter> versus <wim$per>. But this commonplace phonological interaction between coda and following onset has little counterpart in syntax: the only way in which the object of one sentence affects or licenses a following subject is by sometimes providing a full NP as a referent for a (covert or overt) pronominal subject in the next sentence.

[7] Examples (9) through (11) are taken from Rackowski and Travis (2000: 131); Wechsler and Arka (1998: 406). TT in the gloss indicates 'theme topic'—i.e. the NP with the role of theme is found in onset position in examples (9) and (10); in (11), AT indicates 'agent topic'—the 'onset' is filled by an agent NP.

cannot bind *awakne*, and the sentence is ungrammatical; on the other hand, in (11), the 3SG pronominal—which is an agent—is available to bind the theme *awakne*. Unlike in English, the 'self' NPs can indeed appear in either of the sentence margins, so clearly, there is a sense in which these data seem to reflect directly one of the predictions of the syllabic model—the one which states that '[s]ubstantially the same classes of words are found in all constituents occupying margin-like positions' (CM 1999: 151). But these data no more support the idea of a 'privileged onset' position than do the binding facts of English: from the contrasts in grammaticality between (9) and (11), which are grammatical, and (10), which is not, it is evident that there is nothing privileged about the onset at all, but rather, whatever NP bears the thematic role of agent is privileged over the theme NP.

We have looked, then, at the very different binding relations found in two distinct language types. Neither of them meets with the predictions of the syllabic model in terms of a privileged onset position. Both have something important in common, however: whether the relevant factors regulating binding concern hierarchical structure or thematic roles, both language types exhibit binding relations between NPs in 'onset' and 'coda' positions *within a single clause*, whereas, as noted above, there are no analogous relations within a single syllable between onset and coda.

Furthermore, both the Balinese and the English language types allow binding relationships to be formed *across* clause boundaries: the licensing of reciprocals and reflexives may also occur between two independent 'onset' positions, as follows:

(12) **Ia**   nawang   [**awakne** lakar tangkep   polisi].
     3SG   AT:know   self   FUT TT:arrest   police
     'He$_i$ knew that the police would arrest self$_i$.' (Lit. 'He$_i$ knew himself$_i$ to have been arrested by the police.')
     (Rackowski and Travis 2000: 132; Wechsler and Arka 1998: 437)

(13) **He$_i$** knew [**himself$_i$** to have been arrested by the police].

In these examples, the 'onset' of the main clause licenses the 'onset' of the embedded clause. But no comparable relationships appear to be contracted in the syllable. Even ignoring the fact that there is no embedding in the syllable, there is no interconstituent licensing in the syllable between two independent onset positions: see Harris (1994: 158). So again, the syllabic model does not provide a plausible evolutionary source for the binding relationships occurring across a typologically diverse set of languages.

A fourth problem with subjects as 'onsets' concerns the way subjects interact with the predicates of which they are an argument.[8] Subjects have selectional restrictions imposed by a predicate; onsets have no such relationship with the nucleus. In all languages, the predicate (typically headed by a verb) assigns a specific thematic role (e.g. AGENT, EXPERIENCER, etc.) to the subject as well as to its other arguments. In addition, often either the verb or the subject (or sometimes both) mark their close relationship via morphosyntactic markers of agreement/cross-referencing or of case. These are absolutely fundamental facts about syntax, but they are not reflected in the syllable. Harris (1994: 47, 168) lists various phonotactic domains which are universally established within and across syllables, involving licensing between two positions. Crucially, one of the potential relationships that is *not* on the list of typical phonotactic domains is that between onset and nucleus. As Harris remarks (1994: 47), the phonotactic independence of onset and nucleus is one of the very ways in which the onset/rhyme bifurcation is justified: '[a] single onset position in English displays a near-maximal inventory of consonantal contrasts, disregarding to a large extent the nature of the vowel that occurs in the following rhyme'. In other words, specific nuclei do not typically select specific onsets, nor vice versa.[9] The question is, if the onset and the nucleus in the syllable have such a loose relationship, seldom involving any selectional restrictions and with nothing analogous to morphosyntactic marking, then how under the syllabic model does the close relationship between subject and verb evolve?

A fifth problem with the idea of the subject as privileged onset again concerns word order. CM suggests (1999: 160) that the syntactic onset does not have to precede the verb in order to accord with the syllabic model, although of course, subjects do precede the verb in the vast majority of the world's languages. However, it is hard to see how the parallel is maintained in the case of subjects that do not precede the verb:

[8] Indeed, the very fact of *being* an argument of a predicate is not parallelled in the syllable by the relationship between onset and nucleus. See also the arguments put forward by Tallerman (forthcoming), and section 6.4 below.

[9] There are occasional cases of selection of the nucleus by the onset: in English, for instance, no other vowel except /u/ is possible in /Cju:/ syllables, as in *cute* and *astute*. But such cases are marked rather than the norm.

how are these nonetheless privileged onsets? Such subjects are almost certainly a privileged *argument* of the verb, but this appears to be straightforwardly true of nearly all languages, whatever the position of the subject. For instance, subject–object asymmetries are reported in the strongly verb-initial Celtic languages (see Hendrick 1990; McCloskey 1990). But cross-linguistically, subjects do not have to be in onset position, therefore 'onsets' do not appear to be uniquely privileged.

In considering the structural prominence of subjects, we also need to ask, what drives what? It seems likely that subjects are typically initial in the world's languages *because* they're a privileged argument, rather than subjects becoming a privileged argument *because* they're initial. This means that there is something special about subjects rather than something special about onsets, and it also means that it is unsurprising to find subjects often, but not solely, in initial position.

We have seen in this section that the notion of 'privileged onset' in syntax is highly problematic, and that even what might appear to be the least controversial 'onset', the subject, fails to parallel syllabic onsets in a number of crucial ways. Remaining problems concerning predicate/argument structure and further mismatches between syllable structure and sentence structure are the topic of the final section.

6.4 The evolution of argument structure: some remaining questions

Section 6.3.3 notes the problem of there being no parallel within the syllable to the property of selectional restrictions imposed on a subject by a predicate. In fact, the problem is more extensive. The syllable does not appear to provide a possible model for the evolution of argument structure. A fundamental property of verbs is that they subcategorize for a range of arguments, and can be classified according to the number, syntactic category, and thematic role(s) of the arguments that they require. This is not merely a question of the verb (nucleus) selecting a range of 'onsets' or 'codas', something which does happen sporadically within the syllable (see n. 9 in this chapter, and Tallerman forthcoming). A crucial difference is that in the syntax, the *entire* predicate phrase ('nucleus' and 'coda')—and not just the verbal 'nucleus'—is responsible for the specific thematic role taken by the subject 'onset': compare, for instance, the different narrow thematic roles taken by the subjects in *Kim hit Lee, Kim hit it off with Lee, Kim hit the nail on the head, Kim hit the bottle, Kim hit on Lee, Kim hit the sack,* and *Kim hit on the answer right away.* Nothing in the syllable leads us to expect this behaviour. Further, in general the syllabic nucleus clearly does not select anything analogous to complements; see also Carr (2000: 91–2, forthcoming).[10]

The development of argument structure has received a great deal of attention in recent work (see for instance Bickerton 1998, 2000; Calvin and Bickerton 2000; Jackendoff 1999, 2002) and the topic must surely be a prerequisite for any discussion of the relationship between arguments and predicates, which is what the syllabic model is fundamentally concerned with. CM is, however, critical of the prevailing emphasis on predicate/argument structure in the literature (see also Bickerton 1990; Pinker and Bloom 1990) on the grounds that the concept does not equate to the crucial S/NP distinction shared by all languages. He argues (1999: chapter 4.4) that predicate/argument structure can be expressed perfectly well by a number of hypothetical—but non-existent—languages lacking the S/NP distinction, including what he terms Nominalized English, which has NPs but not clauses:

(14) a. John gave the encyclopedia to Mary.
   b. John's gift to Mary of the encyclopedia. (=Nominalized English)

If we agree that the NP standing in for a clause in (14b) does have a predicate (*gift*) and arguments (*John, Mary, the encyclopedia*) then clearly, the existence of predicate/argument structure does not entail a distinction between S and NP. Within the syllabic model, CM's proposal is that the distinction is bought by bolting the structure of the syllable on to words to form a pattern for clauses: 'The syllable frame was [...] available to provide a model for a sentential frame, into which individual calls (we can now perhaps call them "words") could be fitted as "content", just as consonants and vowels supply the "content" of the syllable' (CM 2000: 253).

---

[10] In the Government Phonology model, the coda is seen as a 'rhymal adjunct' rather than a complement (see for instance Harris 1994). However, as Carr notes (2000: 92), the analogy between complement and adjunct in syntax is not a good one: it is not the case that 'complements' are obligatory and 'adjuncts' optional elements within the syllable.

However, if the predicate/argument distinction does not buy the S/NP distinction, the converse is also true. Let us assume for the sake of argument that the syllabic model accounts for the difference between S and NP, as proposed by CM. It still does not explain where syntactic 'nuclei' (verbs) and 'margins' (arguments) actually come from. CM suggests that verbs and arguments result essentially from humans' experience of the world: 'The classification of experience in terms of objects and actions [...] may be largely independent of syntax-as-it-is' (1999: 164). However, what really concerns evolutionary linguistics is how verbs and arguments evolved to have the particular *properties* they exhibit in modern syntax; on this, CM states: 'The noun/verb dichotomy [...] arises from a filtering of the object-action spectrum (or the thing-event space) through a kind of syntactic structure that emulates the nucleus-margin asymmetry within syllables' (1999: 164–5). But whilst nouns and verbs *may* have evolved as the two universal categories 'so as to copy the distinction' between consonants and vowels, as CM suggests (1999: 172), I have argued here and in Tallerman (forthcoming) that the structure of the syllable does *not* predict or in any way explain the kinds of properties that we see universally in argument structure.

Another crucial—but unaddressed—development in the evolution of syntactic structure has to have been the emergence of grammatical morphemes, as also noted by Bickerton (2000: 277–8) and Jackendoff (1999: 277). The syllabic scenario does not have anything to say about this, but this lacuna might be thought to be explicable if the model is seen (only) as a model of Initial Syntax. Interestingly, however, the kinds of utterances which CM supposes to have been possible for speakers of Initial Syntax are *not* free of either grammatical morphemes or of the kind of syntax which makes it possible to recover thematic relationships from the surface form. Throughout his work on the syllabic scenario, CM in fact gives little indication of what he supposes Initial Syntax to have been like. However, CM (2000: 257) does offer the following, as an example of recursion-free utterances which are restricted to nothing more complex than transitive clauses:

... [I]n a syntax strictly modelled on syllable structure [...], the best achievable [...] will be circumlocutions on the following lines: *Bill had fruit. Alice stole fruit. Mary stopped Alice. John helped Mary.*

Now of course, we should not take such 'examples' too literally. It is nonetheless noteworthy that CM appears to assume for Initial Syntax (a) the existence of tensed sequences, and (b) the existence of strategies for distinguishing the arguments of verbs. Although CM (1999) suggests that the syllabic model in some way accounts for the development of tense,[11] it is hard to see that the case is in any way made; moreover, the model certainly does not address the development of grammatical morphemes themselves, either in the form of independent particles or bound affixes. Without tense, though, it barely makes sense to think of a *sequence* of events such as that CM proposes in the fruit-stealing scenario.

Turning to methods of distinguishing the arguments of verbs, broadly speaking there are three (often overlapping) strategies in existence in modern syntax: verbal cross-referencing morphology; nominal case morphology; and linear order. Morphology is definitely not bought by the syllabic model, as I have noted (though see Carstairs-McCarthy, Chapter 8 in this volume) but CM's hypothetical examples from Initial Syntax do seem to display fixed linear order. However, if the earliest clauses are modelled on syllable structure, then there is no reason to think that they would (or could) neatly represent both arguments of a transitive verb in just the right places. The universally unmarked syllable type—and thus arguably the earliest to evolve—is CV. All languages have surface CV syllables (i.e. onset and nucleus), and tellingly, some 'modern' (i.e. attested) languages have no syllable type with codas (e.g. Hawaiian, Senufo). Harris (1994: 162–3) confirms that branching rhymes are marked options, and that non-branching structures are both more widely distributed cross-linguistically, and are acquired earlier by children. We can therefore assume that CV is the prototypical syllable, that it evolved first, and that other syllable types came later in some but not all languages. In the scenario proposed by CM, the prediction would seem to be that sentences with just onsets and nuclei should also have evolved first. Would it not then be more likely to find the utterances of Initial Syntax restricted to *Bill had, Alice stole, John helped* and so on?[12] How does argument

---

[11] See for instance CM's comments in the 1999 monograph: on page 85 he suggests that the syllabic model 'dispels some of the mystery surrounding the evolution of tense markers'; see also the remarks on pages 165–7 concerning the idea that auxiliaries/verbs developed to emulate the syllabic nucleus. But no details are given concerning the actual origins of tense.

[12] In fact, Bickerton's work suggests that ancestral protolanguage, which CM (1999: 174) assumes to be in existence *before* Initial Syntax, did indeed display utterances of this

structure evolve out of the syllable frame, if even the simplest verb-plus-two-arguments clause structure is not bought by it?

Even taking the best evidence we have for pre-modern syntax, which is protolanguage in Derek Bickerton's sense of the term (see Bickerton 1990, 1995, 1998, 2000; Calvin and Bickerton 2000), we find sporadic examples of transitive verbs used with both arguments, as the following examples from the appendix of Bickerton (1995) show:

(15) Pidgin English: *I try hard get good ones*
     Pidgin Hawaiian: *Oe kipu au* (You bribe I)
     Child language (Adam, 25 months): *I get that brush; I change diaper*

(However, see McDaniel, Chapter 7, for comments on why pidgins cannot be used to illustrate the way protolanguage might have been.) Note that in any case, what I am referring to as Initial Syntax is intended by CM to represent a *later* development than protolanguage: 'According to the syllabic scenario, there existed a clear-cut stage in syntactic evolution beyond protolanguage but before the fully modern stage' (1999: 174). Now, if existing protolanguage is at all representative of ancestral proto-language, we can assume that this too had occasional examples of verbs with two arguments; if Initial Syntax is more complex than protolanguage, then it is likely that it had many *more* examples of dyadic predicates. But the prototypical CV syllable does not form a model for such predicates, and thus appears to be a poor candidate for exaptation for clause structure.

Finally, as noted by Tallerman (forthcoming), Bickerton's work (1990, 1998) suggests that linear order is part of a package of syntactic effects which are interdependent, so that any one of them could not be selected without the concomitant features. We are left, then, with the question of where grammatical morphemes and the various systems for representing semantic relationships come from in the syllabic model, including a standardized linear order and the systematic expression of all the arguments of a verb. If these features are present, even in embryonic form, in

kind (see for instance Bickerton 1995), in which the arguments of a verb are not system-atically expressed. The problem is that nothing in the syllabic model indicates how that situation could have evolved into one in which all the arguments of a predicate are not only systematically expressed, but also have their thematic roles reliably recoverable from the surface form.

Initial Syntax, then any model of Initial Syntax ought to have something to say about their development.

The foregoing arguments suggest serious problems for the syllabic model. Given the discrepancies outlined, I conclude that the predictions made by the model do not constitute a credible representation of Initial Syntax, nor 'a plausible candidate to be the ancestor of syntax-as-it-is' (CM 1999: 151).

ACKNOWLEDGEMENTS

Many thanks to Derek Bickerton, Phil Carr, Mike Davenport, S. J. Hannahs, Patrick Honeybone, Anders Holmberg, Jim Hurford, April McMahon, Gary Miller, and Fritz Newmeyer, who all read previous drafts and were enormously constructive in their criticism. Any errors and misunderstandings are my own.

FURTHER READING

Carstairs-McCarthy (1998, 1999, 2000) is an intriguing and stimulating body of work which outlines in detail the proposal that the syllable formed the evolutionary model for the structure of the modern clause. Bickerton's work (1990, 1995, 1998, 2000; Calvin and Bickerton 2000) discusses the proposed development of protolanguage into full language; for a slightly different view, see Jackendoff (1999, 2002). The argument presented here against the syllabic model is developed further in Tallerman (forthcoming).

7 The potential role of production in the evolution of syntax

DANA MCDANIEL

7.1 Introduction

This account of the evolution of language is very much in line with accounts such as Bickerton (2000), Calvin and Bickerton (2000), and Jackendoff (2002) which posit a protolanguage with some of the characteristics of modern human language; see also Tallerman, Chapter 6. The primary contribution of the current chapter lies in the suggested role of the production mechanism. Simplicity is often thought of in terms of the comprehension mechanism, leading to accounts of a protolanguage containing sentences that are simple to comprehend. This chapter suggests a different type of simplicity, based on simplicity of production. This account, though no less speculative than the others, has the advantage of offering an explanation for the existence of long-distance dependencies (movement) in human syntax. The claim is that a certain type of language production system would have been a natural precursor to a syntax with movement.

7.2 Movement

One of the mysteries of the human linguistic system is why it allows syntactic movement. Berwick (1998) argues that the question becomes superfluous within the Minimalist Program (Chomsky 1995). This is because the operation Move can be subsumed under the operation Merge (Kitahara 1997). Merge is the operation that forms larger syntactic items out of two smaller syntactic items. That is, Merge selects two items from the numeration (set of lexical items) to form a larger constituent. The newly formed item can then merge with another item from the numeration. For example, the constituents 'the' and 'cat' could merge to form 'the cat'. According to the copy theory of movement, Move consists simply of merging a copy of an item to a constituent that already contains that item. For example, 'who' could merge with 'you saw who' to produce 'who you saw who' (deriving the sentence 'Who did you see?'). Only one of the copies is pronounced at the phonetic level. (See Nunes 1995 for an analysis determining which copy is pronounced.) Chomsky (1995: 251) suggests further that the copies be analysed as two occurrences of the same item rather than as two distinct duplicate items. In other words, a single syntactic item can have more than one occurrence, where an occurrence is the relationship between the item and a position on the tree (Fitzpatrick 2002). With this view of Move, the subsumption of Move under Merge is even more straightforward, since no copy operation needs to be stipulated. The same item can simply be merged more than once in the course of the derivation.[1]

Though this account of Move seems promising, it does not, in my view, solve the evolution question. The possibility of subsuming Move under Merge does not preclude a linguistic system with a version of Merge that does not allow Move. According to Chomsky (2002), such a system would require an extra stipulation to exclude Move. It is not difficult, however, to envision a system without the occurrence relationship (or a copying operation). In such a system, Merge would select items from the numeration and create larger items out of them. Once an item was selected, it would not be available for reselection; it would now be part of a larger item rather than being related to the larger item by an occurrence. It is not clear that either of the two systems is necessarily simpler than the other. Starting from either of the two systems, a stipulation would be necessary to derive a system (dis)allowing Move. Starting from a system with the occurrence relationship, a stipulation would be necessary to disallow Move by preventing an item from having more than one occurrence; starting from a system without the occurrence relationship, a stipulation would be necessary to allow a copying operation. Since either of these

---

[1] The question arises of how this system is constrained; that is, what keeps anything from moving anywhere? The question is actually about Merge: what prevents any item from merging with any other item? Once this question is answered, Move (whether achieved through a copy operation or through multiple occurrences) will be similarly constrained. Any syntactic theory that does not posit specific phrase structure and movement rules needs to address this question. The operation Merge is constrained by formal feature matching; only items from the numeration that match in features can merge.

systems could have evolved, the evolution question remains: what could be the evolutionary antecedents of a syntactic system that included a version of Merge that subsumes Move?

Chomsky (2000: 12-13) suggests that movement was motivated in part by the systems of language use, in particular by interpretive requirements:

> Why language should have this property [movement] is an interesting question, which has been discussed since the 1960s without resolution. My suspicion is that part of the reason has to do with phenomena that have been described in terms of surface structure interpretation; many of these are familiar from traditional grammar: topic-comment, specificity, new and old information, the agentive force that we find even in displaced position, and so on. If that is correct, then the displacement property is, indeed, forced by legibility conditions: it is motivated by interpretive requirements that are externally imposed by our systems of thought, which have these special properties (so the study of language use indicates).

The current chapter follows this suggestion, but explores the possibility that movement was motivated by properties of language production rather than language comprehension. Although movement structures can facilitate interpretation, for example by marking a topic, this facilitation is, according to this account, secondary. Interpretation, it seems, would work best if surface word order corresponded exactly to thematic structure. The kinds of functions often marked by movement can be marked through other means, as they often are in the world's languages (wh-*in-situ*, emphatic stress, etc.). According to this account, the evolutionary role of movement was to facilitate language production. In other words, movement responds to requirements imposed by our systems of thought, as Chomsky suggests, but it is the connection between thought processes and language production (not interpretation) that created the environment in which movement emerged.

7.3 The protolanguage

Assuming the existence of a protolanguage, it would have been natural for the production mechanism to develop during the period of its use. Following Bickerton (1998), I assume that the protolanguage had many of the properties of modern language except for syntax. It could have contained a large vocabulary (see Jackendoff 2002) and a phonological system. Also, following Bickerton, protohumans at this time had a notion of thematic structure in the sense that they understood how to assign roles to participants in an action. Without syntax, however, they were unable to express thematic structure using language.

The current account differs from the other accounts of protolanguage on the question of concatenation. In other accounts, protohumans produced short utterances containing only a few words. According to Jackendoff (2002), the ability to concatenate words into short strings would have been the first of a series of innovations leading to modern syntax. Protohumans in this period would have talked like children in the early stages of language production or like speakers of pidgins; see also Tallerman, Chapter 6. A string of words would have been interpreted as a combination of the meanings of the parts, leading to word-order requirements. A variety of factors would have prevented longer strings from occurring. Bickerton (1998) and Jackendoff (2002) claim that the utterances could not have been longer without syntax, since listeners would not have been able to interpret them. Bickerton (2000) and Calvin and Bickerton (2000) suggest that protohumans at this time would not have had the neural capacity to plan longer, more complex structures. The strings would have been short due to the protohumans' attempt to represent a thematic structure prior to utterance.

The following section explores how a speedier and more fluent production mechanism may have developed without any kind of syntactic system controlling concatenation.

7.4 The development of the production system

In order to produce even one word, a lexical retrieval system would have been necessary. It is possible that during the period of protolanguage use, the protohuman production mechanism included (in some form) all the non-syntactic parts of the modern production mechanism. Levelt's (1989) model of language production, for example, includes a conceptualizer, where the message is generated, a formulator, which retrieves items from the lexicon and encodes the message syntactically and phonologically, and an articulator. This model could have been the same for protolanguage, except that the formulator would not have done any syntactic encoding. In addition, lexical items would have included only phonological and basic semantic features. In Levelt's system, retrieval of lemmas (non-phonological lexical information) drives the creation of syntactic structure and occurs at a point before the actual forms are retrieved. In the protohuman system, lemma retrieval would similarly have been based on the preverbal message and could have taken place prior to form retrieval. However, lemma retrieval would not have resulted in syntactic structure, due to the absence of syntactic and morphological features.

Assuming that the lack of syntax prevented the linguistic representation of thematic structure, protohumans of this period would have only been able to express their thoughts as unstructured strings of words. For example, to express the fear that a leopard in a tree might kill a baby, a speaker might produce the utterance *leopard* or *baby leopard*, or a longer string, such as *baby leopard baby baby tree baby kill kill leopard tree tree leopard baby kill.* The process would have occurred in the following way. First the conceptualizer creates the preverbal message that a leopard might attack a baby. Then the formulator retrieves relevant lemmas and forms from the lexicon and creates a phonetic plan, which the articulator transforms into speech. Without syntax, there was no notion of 'sentence'. Concepts would have been transformed into a flow of unordered words. The ordering of the linear strings of words would have been determined by a haphazard assortment of factors, such as the relative prominence of various notions in the conceptual structures which the speaker entertained at the moment of speaking.

If this account is correct, it is likely that the lexical retrieval system became quicker over time. Initially, it may have been tedious to take one or two words through the elaborate production process. Protohumans may have used a hybrid system, such as the one described by Wray (2000, 2002), where words from the protolanguage were used together with holistic chunks (with meanings like 'Leave my territory') from an earlier period; and the holistic chunks may initially have far outnumbered the words from the protolanguage. It would have been advantageous to be able to utter words from the protolanguage and to utter them quickly, since this would have allowed for more information to be expressed in a given time span. (The issue of comprehension will be discussed below.) This advantage may have driven the development of the production mechanism to allow for the rapid production of successive words. It is possible that the lexical retrieval system underwent the same kind of shift, as part of language evolution, that Dapretto and Bjork (2000) suggest occurs in modern human children. They studied lexical retrieval in children before and after the vocabulary spurt, a sudden increase in vocabulary use that often occurs at around age two. Their study suggests that the pre-spurt lexical retrieval system requires an environmental stimulus. Children can produce a word if they see the corresponding object, but not if it is out of sight. The post-spurt retrieval system, on the other hand, functions without environmental stimuli. The result is that children produce words with greater ease and aren't restricted to the here and now.

It seems plausible that this same kind of shift in lexical retrieval occurred in the species. The holistic chunks remaining from an earlier repertory system would have consisted primarily of responses to environmental stimuli (for example, uttering *leave-my-territory* in response to an intruder). The retrieval process would differ for words due to their sub-propositional nature. It would not be enough for the speakers to generate a message and retrieve a corresponding signal; instead they would need to choose a set of items from their lexicon. It is likely, though, that the retrieval process for words initially required the same kind of environmental stimulus as was required for the production of holistic chunks. Lexical retrieval at this point would have been a slow, laborious process. A major development in the production system would have allowed lexical retrieval to operate independently of environmental stimuli, which would have resulted in a much greater degree of fluency.

7.5 Comparison with speech of other populations

Though this account (like others) lacks a source of supporting evidence, it would be encouraging to find cases of language production consisting of fluent, unstructured strings of words. To my knowledge, speech output of this type is not attested in modern humans. However, humans, including special human populations like children and pidgin speakers, are not good examples because humans may have an innate syntactic system.

Children's speech consists of structured strings from the outset. Even early one-word utterances have the prosodic pattern of a sentence, and early multiword utterances generally reflect word order and other constraints. However, the sentences are often missing morphemes—early on they consist of just one or two lexical items, and later on, they often still lack function morphemes. A plausible account of children's non-adult speech is that their production system is underdeveloped. Dapretto and Bjork's (2000) study, discussed above, indicates an immature lexical retrieval process. Other findings suggest that young children have grammatical knowledge long before it is clearly manifested in their speech (e.g. Gerken and McIntosh 1993; Shady 1996). It is likely that all of these discrepancies between children's knowledge and their speech can be accounted for in terms of the developing production system. Modern human children, therefore, seem to represent a case that is the exact reverse of the situation proposed here for proto-humans. The protohumans had a well-developed production system, consisting of quick lexical retrieval, but no syntax. They would have produced long, fluent, unstructured strings of words. Modern human children, on the other hand, plausibly have a syntactic system, but an underdeveloped production system. They therefore produce short, laboured, structured strings of words. This discrepancy between modern human children and protohumans is not problematic. The emergence of syntax fundamentally changed the human linguistic system. If modern human child language is constrained by human syntax from the outset, then the expectation is that their speech should be nothing like that of the protolanguage users.

Today's pidgin speakers also do not provide a good comparison group for the same reason; they have a modern human syntactic system. Aspects of their production will, therefore, be affected by this system. Pidgin speakers may speak slowly and haltingly due to an attempt to represent thematic structure with limited means and due to their knowledge (which is mostly unconscious, but possibly also conscious to some extent) that comprehension is guided by the syntactic system. If the protolanguage did not have a syntactic system, then the production system at that time would not have been restricted by the same considerations. In other words, protolanguage speakers would not have been disturbed by any sense of how language is 'supposed to' work.

Language-trained nonhuman primates may provide a better comparison group for protolanguage speech. As is claimed to be the case for protolanguage users, nonhuman primates have no syntactic system, but plausibly have a sense of thematic structure. Some of these primates have in fact displayed speech patterns similar to the one described here for protohumans. Nim Chimpsky (Terrace 1979) illustrates this particularly well, using unstructured strings with many repetitions, e.g. *Me banana you banana me you give.*

7.6 Comprehension

If protohumans were producing language by 'translating' their thoughts into words, stringing the words together as they were triggered, then the important question arises of how comprehension could have occurred. There would have been no syntax to guide comprehension and the order of the words did not correspond to thematic structure. Listeners would have had to process one word at a time and attend to their referents, making associations among the words by using context and world knowledge. Consider, again, the example of the leopard in the tree about to attack a baby. A speaker, hoping that the listener would save the baby, might achieve this by simply saying *baby*, causing the listener to notice and save the baby. Just saying *baby*, however, might not suffice; the listener might simply look at the baby. Saying *leopard baby*, on the other hand, might lead the listener to notice both the leopard and the baby. If the speaker says, *baby tree leopard*, the listener will also attend to the tree, which might be the place where the leopard is or where the baby is. The speaker would continuously produce words in an attempt to get the desired reaction from the listener. From a modern point of view, this system seems far from optimal. Since it doesn't include syntax, it depends heavily on the listener's knowledge of the world and works best for expressing the here and now. Much of what modern human language is capable of expressing using multiclause and other recursive structures would have been impossible to express in the protolanguage. However, in spite of these limitations, the system would have allowed for a much greater degree of communication than the predetermined repertory systems which would have preceded protolanguage. The pressure to achieve successful communication would have been the driving force behind the development of the production mechanism. As mentioned above, it would have been advantageous to utter as many words as possible corresponding to a given thought. A larger number of words would have led the listener to attend to more aspects of the situation, therefore making the listener more likely to give a desired response.

Note that the system described here, though possibly not always as successful as the two-to-four-word utterance systems described by Bickerton (2000) and Jackendoff (2002), would not have differed greatly from those in success rate. Without syntax, both types of system will result in communication failures and will have the severe expressive limitations discussed above. In fact, the possibility of producing a greater number of words corresponding to a given conceptual representation might in some cases lead to more effective communication than would a system which produces short strings of words in a set order.[2]

7.7 The onset of a syntactic system with movement

The account proposed here is compatible with various other accounts of the emergence of syntax. One possibility is Berwick's (1998) proposal that Merge was the single innovation responsible for syntax. (See also Bickerton's appendix in Calvin and Bickerton 2000, for an account along similar lines.) The operation Merge is what allows syntax to represent thematic structure and, according to Berwick's arguments, subsumes other properties of syntax. The innovation of Merge could have been catastrophic or gradual. Possibly, the actual innovation was not Merge itself, but the addition of formal features to the lexicon, which could have evolved gradually. Since Merge consists of combining words which match in features, Merge requires that lexical items have formal features.[3]

However syntax emerged, the innovation of syntax could have occurred at a point where the production system had developed into a speedy lexical retrieval and output system which translated concepts into words as they ran through the minds of the speakers. Any syntactic system would

---

[2] In my personal experience with children in the early stages of language production, comprehension of their speech is enhanced through their use of more words (as long as they are articulated clearly) relating to the thought they are expressing. One anecdote illustrates this particularly well. I was cooking meat for a one-year-old who was watching. He said, 'Meat burn'. I understood that he meant that the meat was burning and assured him that it wasn't. He repeated 'Meat burn' several times and our conversation went in circles. Finally he said, 'Dada. Meat burn. Smoke, smoke', which led me to understand (correctly) that his father had burned some meat on an earlier occasion. The point is that, although, as discussed above, young children's utterances are structured, they are initially so limited that the structure does not seem to aid much in our ability to interpret their utterances. When we do understand the utterances, it is usually because we have guessed correctly using context and world knowledge. The addition of content words, even single-word utterances, is helpful because it provides us with more clues.

[3] Cecile McKee (personal communication) suggests that formal features may have emerged in conjunction with theory of mind. (See also Dunbar 1998, and Worden 1998, for arguments that theory of mind was a precursor to language.) Given arguments that chimpanzees do not have theory of mind (e.g. Povinelli and Eddy 2000), it is possible that

have restricted the production mechanism; utterances would now need to conform to the principles of syntactic structure. A system without movement, however, would have required a more radical overhaul of the production mechanism to ensure that words were produced in an order determined by thematic structure. A system allowing movement, on the other hand, would have better accommodated the existing production mechanism. Mechanisms for syntactic and morphological planning would emerge, but these would add to the existing mechanism instead of replacing it. Returning to the example of the leopard about to kill the baby, prior to syntax a speaker might have said, *baby tree leopard baby baby kill.* This speaker might have begun with the word *baby* because the baby was his primary concern at that moment. A syntactic system without movement would force a certain sequence, such as: *Leopard tree kill baby.* A speaker whose attention was primarily focused on the baby would still have to begin with *leopard.* A system with movement would still allow the speaker to start with *baby,* saying, for example, *Baby leopard tree kill* [*trace/ copy of 'baby'*]. The existing lexical retrieval system which produced words rapidly as the corresponding concepts came into the mind of the speaker would, in this way, have been preserved to the greatest degree possible.

The issue of comprehension arises here again. The first speakers with syntax would have produced movement structures which conformed to the fundamental constraints of universal syntax. The Minimalist principle of Economy greatly constrains movement possibilities. Beyond this, however, speakers plausibly did not obey any language-specific constraints. Listeners would have had to use their knowledge of universal syntax combined with heavy reliance on world knowledge and context to match the moved elements with their traces. Eventually, the system would have developed in a way that facilitated comprehension, possibly leading to more specific morphological features which resulted in language-specific constraints on movement and overt morphological mark-

protohumans initially lacked it. Without theory of mind and without a linguistic system that represented thematic structure, a listener would not have tried to recover the speaker's message. Instead, the listener would have just retrieved the speaker's words from the mental lexicon, processing each word individually. Listeners would have made their own associations among the words, with no regard for the possible intents of the speakers. With the development of theory of mind, listeners would have begun to attempt to retrieve speakers' messages, which would have made the representation of thematic structure (through formal features) advantageous.

ing; see Carstairs-McCarthy, Chapter 8, for an account of the development of morphology.

7.8 Sole speaker problem

Every account of the emergence of syntax that is based on natural selection has the problem of explaining how an innovation supporting a syntactic system would have been an advantage initially. If the innovation occurred in one speaker, the new system might not have been advantageous without comparably equipped listeners. This problem may seem especially severe for the account proposed here, since the speaker with the innovation would be equipped with a comprehension system that would not correspond to the production system of others in any way. The innovation could have remained inert, however, until a community of speakers shared it. This community of people with syntax would have communicated more effectively with each other than would the group of people without syntax and would therefore be more successful. Furthermore, though they would misunderstand asyntactic speakers on many occasions (since the utterances of asyntactic speakers would not conform to the grammars of the syntactic speakers), they might actually understand asyntactic speakers better than asyntactic speakers understood each other. This is because listeners with syntax would attempt to parse the unstructured strings of words and would be in a position to relate the words to each other through features, whereas asyntactic listeners could only relate the words through association. Note that comprehension of asyntactic speakers by listeners with syntax would be difficult without movement. Any time an asyntactic speaker uttered a string of words that did not correspond to thematic structure, a listener with a syntactic system which did not include movement would misunderstand.

7.9 Relationship to modern language

If this account is correct, then movement would have allowed for the existing language production system to operate along some of its same principles. Specifically, movement would have given speakers some freedom in the order of the lexical retrieval process. As was discussed above, the first speakers would have ordered words as freely as the grammar allowed. This system would have been a precursor to some of the movement constructions in modern languages, where phrasal movement often marks topic, focus, and scope. However, the claim is not that movement evolved for the expression of these contrasts. Though these usages of movement may aid communication, the same effects are also achieved cross-linguistically without overt movement, as pointed out earlier. Furthermore, Minimalist analyses posit covert feature movement, which would not aid communication in any direct way. The connection this account makes between communication and the evolution of movement is indirect. Movement itself didn't aid communication (any more than a syntax without movement would have); rather, the production system that had developed prior to syntax responded to communication needs, and a syntactic system with movement was most compatible with that production system.

Later on, tensions between speakers and listeners would have added limitations, and, as the production system developed to more easily respond to the demands of morphology and syntax, these limitations would have become easier to deal with. Newmeyer (2000) argues, based on patterns exhibited by modern human languages and language change, that the earliest human language had rigid SOV word order. This claim, which is in part based on the assumption that thematic structure was expressable in the protolanguage, is incompatible with the account proposed here. However, it is plausible that, even if word order was initially free, the pressure to enhance comprehension would have led to a more rigid word order, which, if Newmeyer's argument is correct, would have been SOV. Today's languages therefore only loosely reflect the factors which drove a system with movement in the first place. Whereas some instances of overt movement might be described as representing the speaker's primary focus of attention (topicalization structures and wh-questions, for example), others cannot be. What can be said of modern human language—abstracting away from the grammars of specific languages—is that it allows for some flexibility on the part of the speaker; that is, to some extent, speakers can structure utterances in a way that corresponds to their thought process.

This account also does not claim that movement in the first syntax-governed languages served solely to facilitate production. In fact, if Minimalist accounts are correct, then this could not have been the case. The grammar requires Spec-head agreement, which involves at least covert feature movement. The claim is just that a grammar which included movement was advantageous over one that did not, due to the nature of the production system that had developed up to that point. This kind of a production system was a precursor to a syntactic system with movement, but this syntactic system also would have contributed novel constraints unrelated to any production issue.

7.10 Conclusion

The suggestion unique to this account is that the developing language production system was a prerequisite for the evolution of the syntactic property of movement. This leads to a very different picture of the protolanguage than is presented in other accounts. Instead of the simplicity of protolanguage utterances lying in their comprehensibility, it lies in ease of production. Protolanguage output would have consisted of utterances of any length with free word order. A syntactic system overlaid on such a production system would have been advantageous only if it included the property of movement. Like other accounts of the evolution of language, this one is only speculative. The more general point of this proposal is that language production should be kept in mind as a potential driving factor in the evolution of language.

ACKNOWLEDGEMENTS

I am grateful to Helen Cairns, Wayne Cowart, Cecile McKee, Michael Studdert-Kennedy, Maggie Tallerman, and two reviewers for suggestions and comments on earlier versions of this chapter.

FURTHER READINGS

On the emergence of a protolanguage, see Bickerton (1998, 2000). On the argument that Move can be subsumed under Merge, see Berwick (1998) and Kitahara (1997). On the language production system, see Levelt (1989).

8 The evolutionary origin of morphology

Andrew Carstairs-McCarthy

8.1 The puzzle: not one but two patterns of grammatical organization

The evolution of grammar is well established as a subfield within research on language evolution. One influential view is that of Bickerton (1990, 1995; Calvin and Bickerton 2000): there existed a presyntactic stage, 'protolanguage', in which the interpretation of strings of linguistic items (protowords, one might say) depended solely on pragmatics. For the transition to syntax, various widely divergent scenarios have been proposed; see also McDaniel, Chapter 7. But one question concerning grammatical evolution has been relatively neglected. Why is it that in most (though not all) contemporary languages, it is necessary to distinguish two kinds of grammatical organization: syntax and morphology? How and why did this distinction arise in linguistic prehistory?

There is no reason in principle why there should be more than one set of traffic rules for ensuring the reliable interpretation of strings of individually meaningful elements in language. A thought experiment will establish this. Imagine an alternative world in which the behaviour and distribution in sentences of all minimal linguistic items (all morphemes, one could say), both bound and free, can uncontroversially be described in terms of a single uniform set of grammatical principles (phrase structure and movement rules, 'Merge', or whatever). Would it occur to linguists in this world to wonder why no more than one set of principles was needed? That would be rather as if some linguist in our actual world were to wonder why (for example) left-handed and right-handed people are not mirror images of each other linguistically, so that corresponding to a right-handed person's rendering [ðə kæt sæt ɒn ðə mæt] for *The cat sat on the mat*, a left-handed person would say [tæm əð nɒ tæs tæk əð]. If some linguists in our actual world were to apply for a research grant to investigate this problem, it seems unlikely that any funding agency would oblige. In recommending refusal, the agency's referees would say something like this: 'It is hardly surprising that left- and right-handers' language does not differ in this way. One can scarcely imagine any advantages in the existence of two mirror-image language systems that would outweigh the massive extra burden of the dual processing mechanism that this would necessitate, assuming that left- and right-handed people could understand each other. The applicants should turn their attention to genuine problems!'. Similarly, no granting agency in the alternative world would be likely to fund research into why there were not two or more kinds of grammatical organization, given that the answer to that question would seem so obvious: the lack of any evident countervailing advantage to compensate for that extra complexity.

It is not surprising, therefore, that a number of grammatical theorists have tried to argue that there is indeed only one pattern of grammatical organization. Selkirk (1982) and Lieber (1992) suggested that morphology is simply syntax below the level of the word. More recently, the Distributed Morphology school (Halle and Marantz 1993) has taken a similar line: the analysis of morphological phenomena is 'distributed' among independently needed architectural components of language, namely the lexicon, phonology, and syntax. However, many morphologists would deny that these attempts have been successful in capturing all aspects of the behaviour of complex word forms. Even Distributed Morphologists posit analytical devices such as 'fusion', 'fission', and 'impoverishment' that have little or no application outside morphology. The morphology–syntax duality therefore remains as a genuine puzzle for anyone interested in language evolution.

The answer outlined here is novel in that, if it is correct, the earliest manifestations of morphology were of a kind that is widely regarded as relatively 'unnatural' in contemporary languages. I argue first, in section 8.2, that two superficially attractive alternative motivations for the morphology–syntax distinction are inadequate, so the problem is genuine and serious, whatever one thinks of my answer to it. My own suggested solution is deferred to section 8.5, where it is developed out of consideration of an issue that at first sight seems logically secondary: the origin of morphophonological alternation, or allomorphy. I point out in section 8.3 that this phenomenon has a motivation that lies outside morphology, namely in the blurring of the boundaries between neighbouring items in speech production. I then suggest in section 8.4 that this assimilatory blurring is likely to have been characteristic of speech well before fully modern grammar had come into existence. Allomorphy may thus have been prior to morphology, in a fundamental sense, and may provide the clue to how morphology became established as a distinct pattern of grammatical organization, in response to factors independent of those that gave rise to syntax. Finally, in section 8.6 I comment on some implications (superficially surprising ones) for the relationship between two kinds of morphological coding: concatenative (or affixal) and non-concatenative.

8.2   Two inadequate reasons for the existence of morphology

The title of this section seems to imply an asymmetry between syntax and morphology: it is the existence of morphology that needs to be explained, not that of syntax. This is more a terminological than a factual issue, however. If syntax deals with the structure of larger complex units and morphology deals with that of smaller ones, a natural way to express the question that concerns us is as follows: why are there relatively small complex grammatical units (let us call them 'complex words') within which the kind of organization observed in larger units does not apply? So the question 'Why is there morphology alongside syntax?' can be reformulated as 'Why are there complex words?'.

   In terms which are standard within generative grammar, we may define 'complex word' more precisely. It denotes a complex item which (a) is assignable to a syntactic category (word class) at the X^0 ('minimal projection') level, but (b) has an internal structure not explicable in terms of the usual syntax of the language in question. Both legs of this definition are necessary. Items with characteristic (a) but not (b) include nouns such as *forget-me-not* and *jack-in-the-box*, which I have elsewhere called 'phrasal words' (Carstairs-McCarthy 2002). Although these look like phrases (albeit with archaic syntax, in the case of *forget-me-not*), they behave grammatically like words, as is shown by their plurals *forget-me-nots* and *jack-*

in-the-boxes (not **jacks-in-the-box*). Items with characteristic (b) but not (a) include some proverbs and idiomatic expressions (*like father, like son; least said, soonest mended; by and large;* French *feu le roi* 'the late king'). Neither phrasal words nor syntactically peculiar idioms will be discussed further here.

Can we then conceive of a kind of language in which there are no complex words? The answer is yes. It would be a kind of language in which syntax alone determines compositionally the meaning of complex items. So the question becomes: 'Why does syntax alone not take care of all complex linguistic items?'.

One popular but bad answer to this question presupposes that word-hood has an intrinsic connection with lexical listing. It is often implied (though less often stated explicitly) that complex words, just by virtue of being words, must be idiosyncratic (especially in respect of their meaning), and hence require listing in the 'lexicon', that is the component in the description of a language that deals with all those characteristics that are not semantically, grammatically, or phonologically predictable. But this answer is bad for two reasons: there are many complex words or word forms that do not need to be listed in the lexicon, and there are many items that must be listed in the lexicon but that are not complex words.

Examples of words that are not in the lexicon are in (1):

(1) re-deurbanize un-Clintonish dioeciousness

I do not know whether any of these words has ever been used by anyone other than me, but, even if they have not, that is no obstacle to my using them now, in such a fashion as to be immediately understood. And this immediate comprehensibility indicates that none of these words, just in virtue of being used, must enter the lexicon. It is true that *dioeciousness* will not be understood except by the minority of English-speakers who are acquainted with the botanical term *dioecious* 'having male and female flowers on separate plants'. The point is, however, that, once a person has made acquaintance with the adjective *dioecious*, he or she gets the noun *dioeciousness* for free, so to speak, with no need for a separate entry in the lexicon.

Examples of non-words that are in the lexicon are idioms such as are contained in the items at (2). These contrast with the syntactically parallel but unlisted expressions at (3):

(2) a. They put the cat among the pigeons.
    b. The man in the street doesn't care.
    c. a red herring

(3) a. They put the cat among the doves.
    b. The person in the road doesn't care.
    c. a red lobster

The distinction between what is listed in the lexicon and what is not is thus independent of the distinction between syntactic and morphological structure. All four possible combinations of structure and listing status are exemplified.

The point that I am making here was made forcefully some years ago by Di Sciullo and Williams (1987), and was re-emphasized by Aronoff (1994). It ought to be common ground among grammatical theorists. The fact that it is not is probably due to a terminological confusion: 'lexical' is widely used to mean both 'relating to words' and 'relating to what is unpredictable and hence lexically listed'. This dual usage shows up in, for example, the 'Lexical Phonology' framework developed by Kiparsky (1982), in which morphological and phonological operations are interspersed among a variety of levels or strata. Kiparsky specifies that, on leaving a given stratum, a complex word form is associated with a 'lexical identity rule' that is item-specific in precisely the same way as the 'rules' that introduce simple, unanalysable items at stratum 1: monomorphemic words such as *dog, cat,* and *catamaran*. This specification is potentially misleading, however, in that only the rules for monomorphemic words are necessarily 'lexical' in the sense 'relating to what is unpredictable'. For example, the word *teachers* is formed (according to one version of Lexical Phonology) through suffixation of [z] at stratum 3 to an item *teacher*, or ['tiːtʃə], that has entered stratum 3 by way of a lexical identity rule '['tiːtʃə] → ['tiːtʃə]' on exiting stratum 2. However, that does not mean that *teacher* is unanalysable, and hence semantically unpredictable, in the way that *cat* or *catamaran* is. Clearly, *teacher* is made up of two components: *teach* and *-er*, the suffix that recurs in *writer, reader,* and many other words. I am not here expressing a view, either negative or positive, on the substance of Kiparsky's framework; I am merely drawing attention to a potential confusion latent in his terminology.

Another bad answer to the question 'Why is there morphology alongside syntax?' involves technical issues surrounding clitics (bound items that attach to phrases rather than to words). Before discussing these issues, I will illustrate two kinds of English clitic and some restrictions on their behaviour. The first kind are the clitic forms -'*ll*, -'*ve*, -'*s*, etc., corresponding to the auxiliaries *will*, *have*, *is*, etc. These clitic forms behave just like full auxiliaries, as illustrated in (4), except that they lean phonologically leftwards and they require an overt verb phrase to their right, as illustrated in (5), by contrast with (6) (Klavans 1985):

(4) a. I will come tomorrow.
    b. I'll come tomorrow.

(5) He won't come tomorrow but I will.

(6) *He won't come tomorrow but I'll.

The second kind is illustrated by the definite article *the*. This behaves just like a demonstrative (*this*, *that*) or possessive pronoun (*his*, *our(s)*), except that, unlike them, it is bound to an overt noun phrase, as shown in the contrast between (7) and (8):

(7) a. I've eaten that donut.   I've eaten that.
    b. I've eaten his donut.   I've eaten his.

(8) I've eaten the donut.   *I've eaten the.

The technical issue that arises is whether, just in virtue of being bound forms, clitics (or a subset of them) ought to be described in morphological rather than syntactic terms. Is cliticization not perhaps just a form of affixation, but to phrases rather than to words? This idea has been put forward by Anderson (1993, 2000). In effect, it turns the tables on those who would like to see morphology as 'the syntax of words', for it claims that there is such a thing as the morphology of phrases. However, we do not need to discuss the merits of this idea in detail here, because from the examples at (4) through (8) it is clear that it is not inevitable that all clitic behaviour must be described in morphological, as opposed to syntactic, terms. Indeed, clitics such as -'*ll* (at least), with full-word counterparts, are handled syntactically even by Anderson.

I know of no other argument current in the marketplace that bears on the issue of why morphology should exist alongside syntax. It was necessary to consider these arguments, however, to allay the misgivings of any readers who may have thought that there must be some solidly established explanation for a grammatical contrast that is so generally taken for granted. We can now consider another possibility, unencumbered by such misgivings.

8.3 A more tractable question: the origin of allomorphy

I propose to put on one side for the time being the question 'Why is there morphology?' in favour of the question 'Why is there allomorphy?'. That is: 'Why are there alternations of the kind we observe in the stems of *foot* and *feet*, and in *keep* and *kept*, and in the shapes [z∼s∼ɪz] of the English plural suffix -*(e)s*?'.

At first sight, this tactic may seem strange. Allomorphy is an aspect of morphology, but not necessarily (it may seem) its most central aspect. In some languages, many stems and affixes remain uniform in shape when they combine in different ways to yield complex word forms. Answering the question why allomorphy exists (or how it comes about) may therefore seem secondary to the question why morphology exists. Nevertheless, I will argue that the former question does indeed point towards an answer to the latter.

An example of a language with elaborate morphology but no allomorphy at all is Esperanto. Ludwig Zamenhof created Esperanto as a language with an essentially Indo-European vocabulary and European grammatical habits. It has a generous repertoire of derivational affixes, and inflectional affixes that realize number and number agreement on nouns and adjectives, case on nouns, and tense and mood on verbs. Verbs also have active and passive participles corresponding to each of three tenses (present, past, and future). However, one characteristic of western European languages is rigorously excluded, namely allomorphy. Every Esperanto morpheme has only one shape. There is nothing resembling any of the English patterns of alternation just mentioned. Zamenhof clearly thought that this sort of variation was an encumbrance that an artificial language could conveniently dispense with. Yet it is a feature of almost every natural language, to a greater or lesser degree. Why?

Shelfloads of books have been written in attempts to answer that seemingly innocent question. For present purposes, what is relevant is that, in speech production, individually meaningful units, or morphemes, are not diamond-hard and immutable, but are subject to influences (usually assimilatory) from their neighbours in the speech chain, and also to influences arising from their position (more or less prominent) within prosodic units such as feet and phonological words. That is, speech is 'analogue' rather than 'digital' in character. The same applies to the visual medium of sign languages, including the native sign languages of deaf communities. Much of the phonological description of both spoken and sign languages is concerned with the factors that give rise to alternations such as /z~s~ɪz/, and the historical phonology of English makes it clear that the *keep~kept* and *foot~feet* alternations have their origin in such factors also.

In emphasizing the analogue character of speech, I am not denying that there may be phonological units realized in speech ('phonemes') that are digital in character, as argued by Oudeyer (Chapter 4). But Studdert-Kennedy (Chapter 3) is right to emphasize that discrete-seeming units such as consonants and vowels are far from being acoustic or articulatory primitives. Rather, they are cognitive entities with only an indirect relation to articulatory gestures and the acoustic signal, as has been clear since the earliest days of acoustic phonetics. My concern here is with the implications for language evolution of the fact that, in the physical instantiation of these cognitive entities, their boundaries are blurred by what Oudeyer calls the 'low-level motor controller' of articulation (Chapter 4, n. 1).

There are thus phonological reasons why in natural languages, unlike Esperanto, many items have more than one phonological shape. If Esperanto ever acquired a substantial community of native speakers, transmitting the language naturally from one generation to the next, it would not take many generations (one is inclined to think) for morphological alternations to creep in. The strict pattern of 'one form, one meaning' imposed by Zamenhof, even if in the view of some morphologists it is a 'natural' pattern for natural languages too (Mayerthaler 1981; Dressler 1985a; Dressler et al. 1987), is subject to disruption because different ideals of naturalness may compete. The most obvious competing ideal is naturalness in phonology. The tug-of-war between well-behaved, Esperanto-style morphology on the one hand and phonological naturalness on the other is central to the approach of Optimality Theory, where constraints are classified into two broad families, relating to 'faithfulness' and 'markedness' (see, for example, Kager 1999). And obstacles to 'one form, one meaning' arise not only in phonology but within morphology too, such as pressure for a clear indexical relationship between an affix and the stem it attaches to (Dressler 1985b).

Let us however conduct a second thought experiment. Imagine a second alternative world in which all languages are like Esperanto: they may distinguish syntax and morphology, but their morphology exhibits no allomorphy. Imagine in this world a linguist who seeks funding for a research project on why allomorphy does not exist. Again, I suggest, the application would be turned down. 'It is too obvious!' the referees would say: 'Morphemes are signs whereas speech sounds are not. So, even granting that pressures exist to reshape word forms in a phonologically more natural direction, the semiotic priority of morphology over phonology ensures that, whenever a move towards phonological naturalness risks disrupting the relationship between morphological expression and content (or between *signifiants* and *signifiés*), either the phonological innovation is halted (at least in certain morphological contexts), or else it is generalized beyond its triggering environment. Thus, one way or the other, every morphological *signifié* continues to be expressed uniformly by only one *signifiant*. The search for some further explanation can hardly be regarded as a high priority, given that our budget is limited!'.

Plausible though that argument may seem in the alternative world, we know that in the actual world it is not valid. Phonological factors can indeed complicate morphology by introducing alternations. 'One form, one meaning', even though it may underlie 'analogical' changes that repair some of the depredations of rampant sound change, is not strong enough to prevent morphological alternations such as in *foot~feet* and *keep~kept* from arising. In the context of our present concern with the evolutionary origins of morphology, a crucial question now arises: for how long has this been so? The next section will be devoted to this question.

8.4 The relative priority of proto-'allomorphy' and protogrammar

Is the assimilatory character of phonology a recent feature in language evolution? That is, did it arise only in languages of the fully modern type with fully modern biological underpinnings in the brain and the vocal tract? Or is it likely to have been present earlier—say, at the stage of Bickerton's protolanguage, assuming that something like that existed? If the answer to the latter question is 'yes', allomorphy may conceivably shed light on the evolutionary origin of morphology. I will argue that the answer is indeed 'yes'.

Protolanguage is a hypothetical stage of linguistic evolution at which there was vocabulary but no grammar, or at least very little. Strings of juxtaposed protowords would have been interpreted pragmatically, with no systematic use of word order or grammatical particles, no expectation that all the arguments of a predicate should be overtly expressed and no method of reliably identifying an argument's role (as agent, patient, etc.) from the linguistic context. However, it might already be possible, perhaps, for interpretation to be guided by the principle of 'Grouping' (Givón 1995), according to which, other things being equal, modifiers are adjacent to what they modify. Thus, a protolanguage utterance that one might gloss as 'hunter kill three mammoth' could only report an event involving three mammoths, not three hunters, but would leave it to the non-linguistic context to determine whether it is the hunter or the mammoths that come out on top.

A somewhat different picture of a premodern stage of linguistic evolution is painted by Heine and Kuteva (2002b). They describe what they call 'Stage X', a stage of language before the operation of the various grammaticalization processes that, in historical times, have created out of what were originally full words many of the items that signal grammatical functions (clitics and affixes). At Stage X, unlike Bickerton's protolanguage, they suggest that there may already have been a systematic syntax relying solely on word order, with a distinction between nouns and verbs. Yet a third scenario for premodern grammar is Jackendoff's suggestion (2002) that it may have resembled the Basic Variety used by many adult second-language speakers (Klein and Perdue 1997), with characteristics such as 'Agent First' and 'Focus Last'. However, all these three versions of a premodern stage of language are alike in one respect: they posit for it no morphology, or at least no inflectional morphology. Furthermore, Heine and Kuteva cite with approval Comrie's (1992) postulation of a prehistoric time when language was in a variety of ways less 'complex' than it is now, and specifically lacked any morphological alternations such as in *foot~feet* and *keep~kept*.

All these writers, however, for understandable reasons, fail to draw an important distinction: between (a) morphology as a distinct pattern of grammatical organization from syntax, and (b) alternations of the kind that in contemporary languages are classified as 'morphophonological'.

The term that we use to label such alternations encourages us to assume that (b) presupposes (a). But we have already seen in section 8.3 that the connection between morphology and morphophonological alternation is loose. Morphology without morphophonological alternation is instantiated (at least in artificial languages such as Esperanto) and could conceivably be universal, as our second thought experiment showed. The basis of alternations that in contemporary languages are classified as morphophonological is not morphology itself but the fact that the speech chain (or the gesture chain, in sign languages) has an 'analogue' rather than a 'digital' character. Contiguous items in the chain can affect each other's expression. So, for 'morphophonological' alternations to have originated even before morphology had become established (at Stage X, for example), all that is necessary is that contiguous linguistic items, or 'words', should have been able to affect each other in something like the modern fashion. That, in turn, would depend largely on speed of utterance. Would all 'word'-strings have been produced in a slow, deliberate fashion, with pauses long enough to inhibit assimilatory affects, or would 'words' have followed close on each others' heels, as in modern speech, as suggested by McDaniel in Chapter 7?

A conclusive answer to that question will be as elusive as conclusive answers to nearly all questions about language evolution. It has been suggested that the Nariokotome boy, a representative of *Homo erectus* who died about 1.5 million years ago, would not have had the breath control necessary to sustain utterances as long as in contemporary speech (MacLarnon 1993). It also seems likely (assuming that speech was one of his mediums of communicative expression) that his articulatory agility was not as great as that of a modern human. But, against this, it seems unlikely that, right up until the appearance of the first elements of modern-style syntax, spoken or signed delivery remained so slow that phonological assimilatory effects were entirely absent. McDaniel (Chapter 7) suggests that rapid speech production preceded even the earliest stages of grammar. Whether or not that is so, at least some collocations of meaningful items seem likely to have become sufficiently frequent in proto-'discourse' for those items to affect one another phonologically. So there is good reason to think that proto-'allomorphy' existed before morphology did. That sounds paradoxical, because the term 'allomorphy' seems to imply the existence of morphology. But, once one appreciates that alternations of the kind that in contemporary languages are called 'morphophonological' are in principle independent of morphology as a component of grammar, the paradox disappears.

I will assume, then, that proto-'allomorphy' existed at a pre- or proto-grammatical stage like Bickerton's protolanguage (see also Tallerman, Chapter 6) or Heine and Kuteva's Stage X. The task of the next section will be to trace some of the implications of that, and in particular to investigate which characteristics of contemporary morphology (if any) can plausibly be derived from it.

8.5 Consequences of proto-'allomorphy'

Let us assume that, with something approaching the present vocal tract, early humans had at their disposal a vocabulary of simple meaningful items which could be combined in strings, even without any established syntax, as in Bickerton's 'protolanguage'. (I will address in due course the possibility that the earliest medium of language or protolanguage was gestural.) These simple meaningful items might all be free, or some of them might already be bound (that is, incapable of occurring in isolation). In either case, mutual phonological influence between contiguous items could yield a kind of alternation. This kind of alternation would at first lack 'grammatical' or semantic function, and it is doubtful whether at any level the brain would treat the alternants as 'different'. A contemporary example of what I have in mind is the alternation between the form [ʔeit] in *eight apples* and the form [(j)eiṯʔ] in *the eighth apple*. The contrast between the presence and the absence of an initial glottal stop, and between the plain alveolar and the glottalized dental renderings of the final coronal plosive, is a matter of low-level allophony—a kind of alternation that will naturally occur even in Esperanto when spoken, but also a kind that would hardly strike the inventor of Esperanto as problematic.

An alternation of this kind would retain its low-level character, however, only as long as its phonological triggers in adjacent meaningful items remained. Suppose, however, that these assimilatory triggers came to be lost or reduced through phonological change. A likely effect would be to render the alternation communicatively salient in a new way. I do not mean that the speakers of this early form of language would become consciously aware of it, any more than the average speaker of English is consciously aware of the voicing of the stem-final fricative in the plural form *houses* ['haʊzɪz] of the English noun *house* [haʊs]. What I mean is that the brain would ascribe to the alternation at least part of the semantic work that was previously done by its trigger. The result would be a relationship of contrast with a semantic or 'grammatical' function. A contemporary example of what I have in mind is the well-known process whereby a Proto-Germanic plural suffix *-i* triggered umlaut, i.e. a fronting of back vowels in the stem, as in *[fo:t-i] > *[fø:t-i] 'feet'. In modern German, umlaut combines with the suffix *-e* to signal plural in this word (*Fuß* 'foot', plural *Füß-e*), but in modern English it signals plural on its own (*foot*, plural *feet*). Unlike the alternants [ʔeit] and [(j)eiṭ?], the alternants *Fuß* ~ *Füß-* (and *foot* ~ *feet*) are 'different' in a communicatively salient fashion, while at the same time being recognizably forms of the same linguistic item.

Just now, I called the relationship between [haʊs] and [haʊz] a relationship of contrast. A more technical term that is appropriate here is 'paradigmatic'. Saussure (1973) (first published in 1916) emphasized a distinction that has been central in linguistic theory ever since: the distinction between sequential relationships, on the one hand, such as that of *house* and *-s* in *houses*, and of *John* and *ran* in *John ran*, and on the other hand relationships of choice or contrast, such as that between *-s*, *-ed*, and *-ing* in *waits*, *waited*, and *waiting*, or between *ran* and *walked* in *John ran* and *John walked*. The former relationships he called 'syntagmatic' and the latter 'associative' (although the term 'paradigmatic' has now supplanted 'associative'). Since the early twentieth century, linguists have in general paid more attention to syntagmatic relationships than to paradigmatic ones. But a better understanding of language in general, as well as language evolution in particular (I believe), will require this imbalance to be redressed.

I also pointed out that *Fuß* and *Füß-* are, in some sense, the same but different. This notion 'same-but-different' plays a crucial role in the scenario I am sketching. The form in which the lexeme HAND appears in singular and plural contexts (that is, in the word forms *hand* and *hands*) is the same. The suffixation of *-s* to form the plural here (an instance of affixal or concatenative morphology) does not automatically create a paradigmatic relationship between two 'different' forms of 'the same' item: rather, we can say that 'the same' form *hand* appears in both contexts. By contrast, the forms in which the lexeme FOOT appears in singular and plural contexts (that is, the word forms *foot* and *feet*) are in an obvious fashion 'the same but different'. This kind of sameness-but-difference, once it became a feature of pre- or protolanguage, introduced a new kind of relationship between linguistic items. In addition to syntagmatic (or, less technically, sequential) relationships between successive items in the speech or gesture chain, there were now also paradigmatic relationships between 'same-but-different' items.

The kind of morphology exhibited in the alternation between *Fuß* and *Füß-* and between *foot* and *feet* is technically labelled 'non-concatenative' or 'modulatory'. It is thus the ancestor of non-concatenative morphology, rather than of concatenative or affixal morphology, that was crucial in establishing 'sameness-but-difference' as a pattern of linguistic relationship. But, in principle, it is not solely through stem-internal alternations that forms of the same item can differ. Once a pattern of relationship of the kind illustrated by *foot* and *feet* had got established, there would be scope to analyse in the same way relationships such as that between *hand* and *hands*. That is, there would be scope to analyse in the same way relationships involving the meaningful presence versus absence of edge-most segments and segment-clusters (proto-'affixes'). It would not matter whether these 'affixes' originated as bound items in a syntagmatic or (proto)syntactic relationship to the stem, or as parts of the stem itself that, through phonological developments, had been dropped from other alternants. Either way, an item such as *hands* (or its prehistoric analogues) would be open to analysis not solely in syntagmatic fashion, as a concatenation of elements (*hand* and *-s*), but instead in paradigmatic fashion, as a form that belongs to the same item as *hand*, while differing from *hand* in its meaning or function.

At first sight, it may seem as if there is a contradiction here. I said earlier that the suffixation of *-s* to form the plural *hands* from *hand* did not automatically create a paradigmatic relationship between two 'different' forms of 'the same' stem. What entitles me then to say that *hand* and *hands* came to be treatable as paradigmatically related? The qualification 'automatically' is important here. If phonological assimilation did not operate, so that alternations of the *foot~feet* kind never arose, no precedent would ever arise for treating *hand* and *hands* any differently from, for example, *hand* and *that hand*: as syntagmatic units that are indeed partially similar, but no more fundamentally related to each other than, say, *that hand* is to *that*. But assimilatory processes of the kind that in recent linguistic history have yielded *Fuß~Füße* and *foot~feet* played a prehistoric role too, in making crucial for speech processing the recognition of paradigmatic relationships as well as syntagmatic ones. And once the brain was prepared in this way, there would have been no reason for it not to apply the same kind of paradigmatic analysis also to pairs of items analogous to *hand* and *hands*, that is to items which (in contemporary terms) display solely affixal morphology.

I promised to deal in due course with the possibility that the earliest medium of linguistic expression was gesture rather than speech. What difference would that make to the scenario presented here? Very little, as it happens. The individual signs of sign language are just as susceptible of 'phonological' influence from preceding and following signs as are the individual 'morphemes' of spoken language. Assimilation is just as much a feature of sign language as it is of speech. Therefore there is just as much scope for the paradigmatic implications of 'sameness-but-difference' to emerge in an evolving gestural language as in an evolving spoken one. Arguably, indeed, there is more scope for this with gesture; for, with gesture, signs can be superimposed or overlap more freely than in speech (Klima and Bellugi 1979), so as to provide an independent route through which 'different forms of the same sign' can come to be recognized.

Gesture and speech thus turn out to be similar in the respect that currently concerns us: the possibility of assimilatory influences between syntagmatically neighbouring items. Let's imagine, by contrast, a world in which the only communicative medium is visual, something like printing, using an 'alphabet' much like the printed Roman one, in which neighbouring letters have no effect on each others' shape (and thus unlike the Arabic alphabet, whether handwritten or printed). In such a world it could well be that language develops many of the same characteristics as actual human language: syntactic marking of thematic roles by devices such as order and grammatical morphemes, subordination, use of displacement to signal discourse factors ('topic' versus 'comment'), and so on. One thing that would not develop, however, would be morphophonology. It is hard therefore to see how phenomena such as inflection class distinctions could arise, involving different ways of expressing morphologically the same grammatical content. There would be nothing that these distinctions could evolve out of: no alternative to phonological assimilation that might render salient the crucial paradigmatic relationship of sameness-with-difference. In such a world, as in ours, languages

could have bound forms, and some complex items could become semantically opaque, yielding idioms, just as in our own languages. But there
seems to be no reason why the languages of that world would develop
morphology.

8.6. Some unexpected (but not necessarily unwelcome) implications

The most obvious implication of this scenario is that non-affixal (non-
concatenative or modulatory) morphology preceded affixal (or additive)
morphology in language evolution. This may seem startling, in that it
implies that so-called 'natural' morphological encoding—that is, encoding that is uniform, transparent, and constructionally iconic, as in the
superlative adjective form *short-est vis-à-vis* the positive *short,* or the
progressive verb form *sing-ing vis-à-vis* the base form *sing* (Dressler et al.
1987; Kilani-Schoch 1988)—exploits a kind of structure that originated in
relatively 'unnatural' coding, as in superlative *furth-est vis-à-vis* positive
far, or in the past participle *sung vis-à-vis* the base form *sing.*

This points to what may seem an obvious objection. If morphology
originated in this way, why is it that affixal, relatively 'natural', morphological encoding seems to predominate over non-affixal encoding in
contemporary languages? After all, there are many languages whose
morphology is overwhelmingly agglutinative, with relatively little allomorphy or stem alternation. But this objection can be answered. The fact
that morphology originated in relationships such as that between *Fuß* and
Füß-, the by-products of phonological assimilation, does not mean that a
type of morphology that mimics the by-products of phonological assimilation is the easiest to learn or to use. There is a sense in which Zamenhof's
decision to permit no allomorphy in Esperanto reflects a correct intuition.
A kind of morphology in which each morpheme has a constant shape, and
in which differences between word forms are purely affixal, is almost
bound to impose a smaller burden on the language learner and user in
the realm of grammatical structure, even if the accompanying phonology
is relatively 'marked'. (I say 'almost' because there are languages in which
some patterns of non-concatenative morphological encoding are absolutely regular, and therefore perhaps just as easy to learn as patterns of
regular affixation.) Equally, there may be some advantages in a kind of

morphology in which all or nearly all the individual morphemes within complex word forms are free and invariant, even though this kind of morphology is furthest removed from morphology's phylogenetic origin. It will not be a surprise, therefore, if it turns out that in some languages, such as perhaps Vietnamese, compounding is virtually the only morphological process (Nguyen 1987). At the same time, the brain is biologically equipped to handle much more 'unnatural' and complex patterns of relationship between word forms, so when phonology begets allomorphy, this allomorphy is not necessarily tidied away, but may be seized upon for derivational and inflectional purposes (Lass 1990).

A second implication has to do with the etymology of individual affixes in the reconstructable history of contemporary languages. There is a tendency among historical linguists to assume that most if not all affixes are descended from free morphemes that have become progressively more firmly linked to some class of forms with which they typically appear in a syntagmatic collocation, leading to phonological reduction and semantic bleaching. Thus, Givón (1971) talks of morphology being an 'archaeologist's field trip' for historical syntacticians, and there is a considerable recent literature on the development of morphology through 'grammaticalization' (e.g. Hopper and Traugott 1993). Similarly, Bybee (1985: 211), even when discussing synchronic morphological theory, cites 'the length of time an affix has been attached to a stem' as a factor influencing morphological 'fusion'—as if taking it for granted that every affix originated historically in something that was not attached to a stem.

Let us assume that nearly every affix could be shown to have such an origin, if one could delve deep enough into their history. (I say 'nearly every' rather than 'every', because there are a few clear examples of bound morphemes that have no free ancestor, such as -*thon* in *telethon*, prised off *marathon*.) Even so, the creation of bound morphemes by this route does not entail the creation of a whole new pattern of grammatical organization for the complex items that these bound morphemes form part of. The discussion in section 8.1 of the lack of any obvious need for two patterns of grammatical organization shows that there is no reason to think that the ontogeny of individual affixes will shed light on the phylogeny of morphology in language evolution.

Anyone who is uneasy with this conclusion may, I suggest, be making a covert uniformitarian assumption about language, to the effect that it must always have been much as it is now—an assumption that is inappropriate in respect of early prehistoric stages of linguistic evolution, and perhaps recent prehistoric stages too (Newmeyer 2002). The historical development of a free word form into an affix need not be merely a shift on the syntagmatic dimension, from the domain of phrasal syntax to that of 'word syntax'. Rather, I suggest, it is a shift from a domain of grammar in which the syntagmatic dimension is dominant to one in which the paradigmatic dimension has at least equal importance, motivated originally by patterns of relationship that are quite independent of affixation.

The central role that I attribute to the paradigmatic dimension in the evolutionary origin of morphology derives some support from evidence that paradigmatic relationships are still central to inflectional morphology (e.g. Carstairs-McCarthy 1994; Cameron-Faulkner and Carstairs-McCarthy 2000). The centrality of paradigms is indeed recognized by some morphologists (Anderson 1992; Stump 2001). Even they, however, tend to emphasize relationships between morphosyntactic categories (the sets of grammatical meanings that can be expressed morphologically in words of a given class) rather than between the word forms that express those categories—relationships that involve such matters as inflection-class organization and interactions between affixal and non-affixal morphology. Meanwhile, for other morphologists, including most of those working in the framework of 'Distributed Morphology' (Halle and Marantz 1993), morphological paradigms have no theoretical significance. To some extent this reflects their predominant interest in the syntagmatic dimension within morphology, which is undeniably important. But to some extent, too, I think it reflects the quite reasonable intuition that for language to have at its disposal two patterns of grammatical organization, morphology and syntax, is superfluous. These morphologists are therefore dedicated to exploring ways in which responsibility for various morphological phenomena can be 'distributed' among grammatical domains that are independently necessary, particularly syntax and phonology.

In linguistic theorizing, morphology often suffers a fate rather like that endured by Poland for several centuries: it is carved up between phonology, the lexicon, and syntax, so as to vanish from the linguistic map. A more profitable attitude, I suggest, is to consider how, despite its superfluousness, morphology came into existence, and what light its origin may shed on its current characteristics and vice versa. This is part of the larger question of why language is as it is—not nearly so well designed as it may at first seem (Carstairs-McCarthy 1999; for an opposing view, see Tallerman, Chapter 6). Whether or not readers are convinced by the answer sketched here, these questions deserve attention.

ACKNOWLEDGEMENTS

For comments on earlier versions I am grateful to John McWhorter, Maggie Tallerman, audiences at Canterbury and Manchester Universities, and three referees. Faults that remain are my responsibility.

FURTHER READING

For the purpose of tracing the evolutionary history of an organism, those aspects of its physiology and behaviour that seem particularly well designed for its survival in its present environment are likely to be the least informative, because it is these aspects that can most readily be explained by its present circumstances. Rather, it is poor design features that are likely to be historically most illuminating, since these are more likely to be inherited from some ancestral situation. This point is made persuasively by the evolutionary biologist Williams (1992). In this chapter and in Carstairs-McCarthy (1999) I apply Williams's style of reasoning to language, asking which aspects of it seem least well designed, with a view to exploring what light these aspects may shed on its history.

For further reading on morphological structure, I recommend Haspelmath (2002) (an introductory treatment) and Aronoff (1994) (more advanced). Aronoff's emphasis on aspects of morphology that are not explicable in terms of other domains of language structure such as syntax and phonology is in tune with the approach taken here. However, no linguist (so far as I know) has in recent years broached the issue of why morphology exists in the first place.

9 The evolution of grammatical structures and 'functional need' explanations

BERNARD COMRIE AND TANIA KUTEVA

9.1 Introduction

When speaking about the way language evolved in human prehistory, it is highly implausible to assume that humans developed language because they *needed* it in order to adapt better, and faster, to their environment.

We do, indeed, have adaptive theories of language evolution but, as will become clear from the following section, the view of language underlying all adaptive Darwinian theories of language evolution does not ascribe any meaningful role to 'need' as a driving force. When it comes to the genesis and evolution of individual grammatical categories, however, the factor of 'need' often assumes the very conspicuous status of a driving force for the rise of grammatical categories. A number of explanations for grammatical categories proposed in the literature do just this: they assume that individual grammatical categories arise in order to fulfil a functional need, to fill a gap in the grammatical system, so that the system becomes better adapted to communicative needs.

Our goal in this chapter is to show that just as the adaptive Darwinian explanation of the origins and evolution of human language as an overall communicative system does not entail need as a triggering factor, so, too, it is unwarranted to posit (functional) need as the crucial factor either in the explanation for the evolution of individual grammatical categories or in their formal expression.

For this purpose we briefly consider grammatical categories such as the durative/continuative/progressive. We lay emphasis, however, on the formal expression of a particular syntactic category, the relative clause, basing our argumentation on an investigation of how relativization is encoded in the languages of the world. We conclude that grammatical categories—

and their encoding—are not designed to 'fit' functional needs; they evolve historically rather than because they were 'needed'.

The chapter is organized as follows. In the next section, we argue that, while most theories of the evolution of language presuppose that language, once it evolved, gave selective advantages to the species that made use of it, this does not entail that language emerged in order to supply a need. In section 9.3, we take a look at 'functional need' explanations proposed in the literature for the rise and development of individual grammatical categories. Our main results are presented in section 9.4, where on the basis of a study on the encoding of relativization in the languages of the world, we build a case against the validity of 'functional need' explanations with regard to the elaborateness of formal expression of grammatical categories.

9.2 Darwinian explanations of the origins and evolution of language

Most of the theories proposed for the origins and evolution of language are Darwinian, and involve the notion of adaptation: the human ability to acquire language enables organisms that have it to adapt better to their changing environment. Thus, according to the so-called 'hunting' theory (*'there's a herd of bison down by the lake'*), primitive man was a great hunter. Acquiring language enabled him to hunt better: he was now capable of communicating plans for herding prey or trapping them in particular places.

Similarly, on the 'foraging' theory, the acquisition of language had a high adaptive value: it enabled early humans to communicate about locations, as well as the nutritional value and safety of available foodstuff.

According to another theory—the 'Machiavellian intelligence' theory— having evolved, language made it possible to sustain the complexity of social life. It enabled those organisms that could acquire it to understand matters such as alliances, familial relationships, dominance hierarchies, trustworthiness of individual members of the group. Hence, language had a high adaptive value with regard to the needs of social life (on theories of language evolution, see Jespersen 1933; Dunbar 1996; Hurford, Studdert-Kennedy, and Knight 1998; Carstairs-McCarthy 1999;

Knight, Studdert-Kennedy, and Hurford 2000; Blackmore 1999; and Wray 2002, among many others).

Common to the majority of theories on the evolution of human language is the idea that having evolved, language gave an adaptive advantage to those organisms that were capable of acquiring it. It is highly implausible, however, to assume that human language evolved *because* it was needed. As an anonymous referee points out, contemporary with our ancestors among whom language evolved were the ancestors of present-day chimps and gorillas, among whom language did *not* evolve. Is that because their 'need' for language was less?

While the notion of need is kept separate from the issue of the genesis and evolution of language, this same notion has been often coupled with issues of the evolution of individual grammatical structures, and this is what we briefly address in the following section.

9.3 'Functional need' explanations of the evolution of grammatical categories

The linguistic literature is rife with 'functional need' explanations of the rise and development of individual grammatical categories, according to which a grammatical category evolves because it is needed to fill a gap in the grammatical structure of a language (see Danchev and Kytö 1994 on the *going to*-future in English; Hewson and Bubenik 1997 on the durative/continuative/progressive in Germanic languages; and Molencki 2000 on the *modal + have + past participle* counterfactual in English, to name just a few recent examples). Let us illustrate this by taking a closer look at Hewson and Bubenik's (1997) proposal for the development of the durative/continuative/progressive in a number of languages (for a discussion of the implications of Hewson and Bubenik's proposal, see also Kuteva 2001: 44–8).

Hewson and Bubenik (1997) note that in some Indo-European languages, in particular the Romance, Indic, and Slavic languages, the verb system is based on semantic oppositions including aspect (imperfect versus aorist, or perfective versus imperfective), and therefore has no need of additional, imperfectivity-denoting expressions like the progressive. Germanic languages, by contrast, have a verb system based purely on tense (past versus non-past), and therefore they have a 'functional need' to develop verb forms explicitly expressing imperfectivity, such as the durative/continuative/progressive. Uncontroversially, these develop from the grammaticalization of structures of the *be + preposition + main verb* type.

Such a 'functional need' view of this grammaticalization of the progressive, however, loses a lot of its credibility in light of the following fact. The structure *be + preposition + main verb* grammaticalizes into a durative/continuative/progressive marker not only in languages whose verb system happens to have a functional 'gap' here (such as Germanic languages), but also in languages which do not have this 'gap'; that is, in languages with an inherent, consistently expressed perfective:imperfective contrast, for instance Romance languages such as Portuguese (with the durative/continuative/progressive *estar + a + infinitive*), and the Kru languages Godie and Neyo (with *kU 'be at' + main verb*, see Marchese 1986: 60–66).

In other words, there is no reason to assume a 'functional need' explanation of the auxiliation development *be + preposition + main verb > durative/continuative/progressive*. Rather, this development is the result of a natural conceptual-semantic extension of a particular conceptual pattern to a particular functional domain of language[1] (for an analysis of the locative-to-durative/continuous/progressive auxiliation as the result of a particular—and cross-linguistically very pervasive—extension of a basic conceptual pattern, see Heine et al. 1991; Heine 1993; Heine and Kuteva 2002a).

9.4 'Functional need' explanations and the formal expression of grammatical categories

So far we have considered the (in)adequacy of 'functional need' explanations of how and why grammatical categories arise and develop. In this section we are concerned with the validity of 'functional need' explanations with respect to the material used to encode grammatical categories.

---

[1] As an anonymous reviewer remarks, it is not possible to tell 'why this extension happens in some languages but not in others'. Note that this development is recognizable *post hoc*, but not predictable.

9.4.1   *On formal distinctions and 'functional need'*

It is particularly tempting to accept a 'functional need' explanation for the formal expression of a grammatical category in situations where a given formal distinction has been lost, and then new phonological material has come to encode the same grammatical category. In spoken French, for instance, the old formal distinction between singular and plural has been lost (Aitchison 1995). Thus the sequences *chat* [ʃa] 'cat' and *chats* [ʃa] 'cats' are now indistinguishable: both the final [t] and the [s] which used to mark the plural are no longer pronounced. The grammatical category of number (singular versus plural), however, has not disappeared. It has now come to be marked by means of the article *le, la, les* 'the', which is placed in front of the word in question. Note that the use of an article is obligatory in French. Thus in order to say 'Cats are stupid' one must use the article:

(1)   French (Indo-European)
      Les   chats   sont   stupides.
      the.PL   cats   are   stupid.PL
      'Cats are stupid.'

In other words, plurality in French has come to have new formal expression, which occupies the beginning of the noun phrase. In cases like this, it is tempting to think that the new formal expression came into existence *because* it was needed. One may presume that any disruption in formal expression results in a gap in the overall system, which later—necessarily—gets filled; that is, language restores its patterns and maintains its equilibrium. Such an approach is in fact entailed in the popular view of language and language change. Language is seen as a healthy organism with a remarkable instinct for self-preservation, whereby every disruption of a pattern is remedied: 'In response to disruptions, therapeutic changes are likely to intervene and restore the broken patterns' (Aitchison 1995: 161), and language change in general 'is triggered by social factors, but these social factors make use of existing cracks and gaps in the language structure' (Aitchison 1995: 210).

Such a conception of language as a neat and healthy phenomenon is intellectually very appealing. Note, however, that there is no way for us to prove it valid. We can never know whether particular phonological material appeared because it was 'needed' or not. It is a truism that any language can express any notion; the interesting issue is whether a language has to express a particular notion obligatorily by means of (a) grammatical morpheme(s). That is, if a language lacks a grammatical morpheme to express something, it can then use lexical means to do so. (It is well known that even notions such as temporality do not necessarily have to be encoded by grammatical morphemes, for instance in Chinese). Crucially, this truism runs counter to 'functional need' explanations of the appearance of formal expression for a grammatical category: if a particular notional category, e.g. pastness, does not have a grammaticalized expression in a particular language, this functional 'need' does not necessarily have to be satisfied by the development of a grammatical category 'past'; adverbials with specific past meaning ('yesterday', 'last year', 'a long time ago', etc.) can be employed for the same purpose.[2]

While we cannot test directly the validity of 'functional need' explanations, we can try and falsify the logical implications following from them. This is what we do in the remainder of the present chapter. We base our argument on an investigation of the formal expression of a particular syntactic construction, the relative clause, in the languages of the world. In what follows we first describe the empirical aspect of our study. We then present a particular type of scale—which we have termed the elaborateness-of-expression scale—along which natural languages can be placed with regard to the way they encode relativization. The final subsection addresses the validity of a 'functional need' explanation for the formal elaborateness with which natural languages may encode relativization.

9.4.2 *The empirical basis*

Our language sample is geographically and genetically balanced, and encompasses 157 languages (see Appendix 9.1 at the end of this chapter; for references on the sample languages, see Comrie and Kuteva, forthcoming). These languages have been examined for the way they relativize on the subject (as opposed to the direct object or oblique case roles such as the instrument, etc.).

---

[2] In fact, it is more common for the content of grammatical morphemes not to be expressed at all in the languages that lack them (with thanks to an anonymous reviewer).

We decided to take relativization on the subject of a clause as the representative case because, as is well established (Keenan and Comrie 1977; Comrie 1989), it is easier to relativize on the subject than the direct object, or the indirect object, or the possessor, as can be seen in the fact that there are a number of languages where relativization on the subject is possible but relativization on obliques is not.

9.4.3 *The elaborateness-of-expression scale*

Relative clauses have been the focus of interest for a number of linguists during recent decades, and a sizable body of knowledge about the relative clause construction has been accumulated already. A number of classifications of relative clauses have been proposed in the specialist literature. All of these classifications depend on *where* (that is, positioning with respect to the head noun), and *how* (that is, by means of what kind of element, e.g. relative pronoun, resumptive element, general subordinator, gap, etc.) relativization is expressed.

Here we also propose a particular type of classification of relative clauses. Our criterion, however, is different from the criteria used in previous studies. Instead of *where* and *how,* the question we ask is *how many times*—that is, by means of how many elements or relativization markers—relativization is marked in a complex sentence containing a relative clause. Depending on the number of relativization markers,[3] we can speak of different degrees of *elaborateness of expression,* e.g. one-(relativization)-marker language, two-marker language, etc.

On the basis of a genetically and geographically balanced sample of 157 languages representing the languages of the world (see Appendix 9.1), we propose the following elaborateness-of-expression scale:

| Covert | 1 marker | 2 markers | 3 markers | 4 markers | 5 markers |

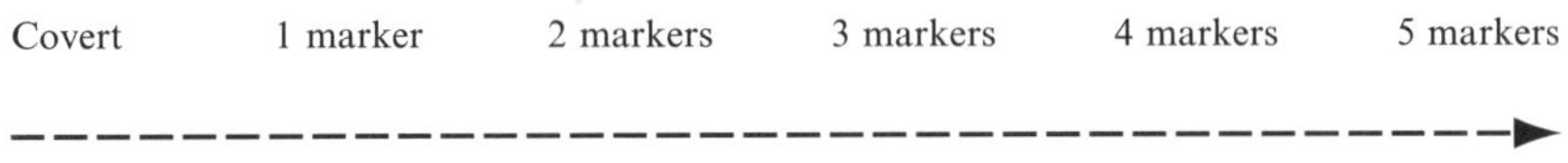

Fig. 9.1 The elaborateness-of-expression scale.

---

[3] Note that not only markers specific to relative clauses count but also general subordination markers. Besides this, in addition to morphosegmental markers, non-segmental marking (e.g. prosody) is also taken into account.

At the starting point of this scale, we can place languages where relativization is covert. In such languages, there is no formal marking whatsoever of the relative construction, i.e. we have a situation with zero relativization markers. We can distinguish between two subcases here. First, the language may have a unified, noun-modifying construction which, depending on context, may be interpreted as a particular type of subordinate clause (temporal, conditional, relative, etc.):

(2) Khmer (Mon-Khmer, Austro-Asiatic, spoken in Cambodia; John Haiman, p.c.)
Baan,   took;   ruəc,   viə   thom
catch   small   escape   it   big
a. 'When you catch it, it is small; when it escapes, then it is big.'
b. 'If you catch it, it is small; if it escapes, it is big.'
c. 'The one you catch is (always) small; the one that escapes is (always) big.'

Second, the language may have a specific relative construction—even though using it involves zero relativization marking—to signal relativization. An example of this comes from Maale (Omotic, Afro-Asiatic, spoken in Ethiopia):

(3) Maale (Azeb 2001: 160)
ʔííní   [[ziginó   mukk-é]   ʔatsi]   za-é-ne
3MS.NOM   yesterday   come-PF   person:M.ABS   see-PF-A.DCL
'He saw the man who came yesterday.'

Here, the relative clause precedes the head noun and it contains no pronominal element coreferential to the relativized noun. The relative clause in Maale can be regarded as a specific relative construction because it differs from other subordinate clauses in having no affix indicating the dependent status of the clause. And it also differs from independent sentences. Independent sentences are characterized by clause-final illocutionary force morphemes which classify the utterance as an assertion, interrogative, manipulative, etc.:

(4) Maale (Azeb 2001: 160)
ʔatsi   ziginó   mukk-é-ne
person.M.NOM   yesterday   come-PF-A.DCL
'The man came yesterday.'

On the other hand, the (restrictive) relative clause ends in one of the aspect and/or polarity suffixes, *-é-, -á-, -uwá-,* or *-ibá-*(see the innermost bracketed phrase in (3) above) and cannot be marked by the illocutionary force morphemes, so that it cannot form a complete utterance on its own.

At the other end of the scale, there are languages with no less than five morphosyntactic segments serving as markers of the relativization strategy. Ngemba (Bantoid, Niger-Congo, spoken in Cameroon), for instance, marks relative clauses by means of:

- a relative conjunction/determiner (varying for number and nominal class)
- a complementizer marker *-bah*
- pronoun retention
- a verbal suffix *-ne* (a multi-purpose marker for topicalization, nominalization, and relativization)
- a sentential definitizer *-la* (related to the determiner system), see Chumbow (1977: 296–7, 302).

This spectacular abundance of marking is illustrated in the following example:

(5) Ngemba (Chumbow 1977: 290)
nyung wá   bah a-keshung-ne   mung wa   la   a
man   REL BAH he-TNS.beat-NE child DET LA   he
kung   atsang
enter.into prison
'The man who beat the child went to prison.'

The complementizer *-bah* is optional, whereas the other four relativization markers are obligatory:

(6) Ngemba (Chumbow 1977: 291)
mbap zá   e-kung-ne   menda   la   makying ako
mouse REL it-enter-NE into.house LA   trap   caught
'The mouse which entered the house, a trap caught it.'

Note also that the obligatory markers do not occur in the corresponding simple declarative sentence, apart from the subject pronominal element, which, however, is only *optionally* used after demonstrative/definite determiners (Chumbow 1977: 290):

(7) Ngemba (Chumbow 1977: 291)

   a. Mbap   za   kung   menda
      mouse DET   enter   into.house
      'The mouse entered the house'

   b. Mbap   za   e-kung   menda
      mouse DET   it-enter   into.house
      'The mouse entered the house.'

In between the two extremes of the elaborateness scale, there are a number of intermediate situations. Next to the covert situation, we can place languages where the relative clause construction contains one relativization marker. A pertinent example is Russian, where relativization is marked by means of a special relative pronoun deriving from the interrogative pronoun and marking the case role of the head noun with respect to the relative clause:

(8) Russian

   Devuška,   kotoraja   priexala včera,   uexala segodnja
   girl.NOM   who.NOM   arrived   yesterday left   today
   utrom.
   morning
   'The girl who arrived yesterday left this morning.'

Thus the relativization marker in the above sentence is *kotoraja*, and its inflectional ending, -*aja*, carries the information that the head noun 'girl' functions as the subject of the relative clause.

A more elaborate situation of marking relativization is the use of two relativization markers. Kilivila (the language of the Trobriand Islanders) illustrates this:

(9) Kilivila (Oceanic, Austronesian, spoken in the Trobriand Islands; Senft 1986: 66)

   Bokawana   bi-la   bi-gisi   ina-la
   Bokawana(she) will-go(she) will-see mother-her
   mi-na-na   i-sisu   Labai.
   this-woman-this she-live   Labai
   'Bokawana will go to see her mother, who lives in Labai.'

The relative clause here is marked by means of both the morpheme *mi* and the morpheme *na*; these are the full forms of demonstrative pronouns for third person, and they serve as pronouns marking the relative clause.

The next intermediate situation along the elaborateness-of-expression scale involves three markers of the relativization strategy. A typical example here is Northern Sotho, a Bantu language spoken in South Africa. The relative construction in Northern Sotho consists of (a) a relativizer, (b) a relative subject concord, and (c) the relative suffix *-go*:

(10) Northern Sotho (Poulos 1994: 103)

Batho	ba	ba	šoma-go
people	RELATIVIZER	REL.SUBJ.CONCORD	work-REL.SUFFIX
ba		gôla	tšhêlêtê.
BASIC.SUBJ.CONCORD		earn	money

'People who work earn money.'

A situation which comes close to the rightmost end of the elaborateness-of-expression scale marks relativization by means of four elements. In subject relativization in Kɔɔzime (Bantu, Niger-Congo, spoken in Cameroon), for instance, the subject is sometimes an erstwhile instrument (i.e. the initial instrument has been advanced to a subject), which leads to no less than four markers of the relativization strategy, as in (11). This combination seems to be unique to some languages spoken on the African continent, and involves double pronoun retention:

(11) Kɔɔzime (Beavon 1985: 38)

e-bák	['+	l'-e	á	cík-ɔ	tíd	e
C5-knife	SUB	c5-3rd	PST	cut-PASS	meat	with
l'-e]	l-ɨ					
c5-3rd	c5-this:REL					

'The knife which was used to cut meat with.'

Here, the first relativization marker is a subordinator which consists of a high replacive tonal morpheme (represented by '+'). This tone, which is glossed as SUB, causes an immediately following low tone to become high. The last marker, *ɨ*, is a relative determiner (deriving from a demonstrative), and is placed after the relative clause; see Beavon (1985: 32, 34). Within the relative clause itself, the head noun, *e-bák* (C5-knife), is referred to twice, by the pronominal element *l'*-e (C5-3rd), hence we can speak of a double pronoun-retention strategy, and of a four-marker language.

9.4.4 A 'functional need' explanation for elaborateness of expression?

The crucial question that arises at this point is: why do some languages exhibit such an abundance of formal 'packaging' in their encoding of relativization strategies (as in Kɔɔzime and Ngemba)? Is all this phonological material just 'garbage' (Lass 1990), or is it functionally motivated?

At first sight, a look at some Chadic languages would rather suggest a 'functional need' explanation. In these languages, the contexts of use of the relative construction, that is, the discourse pragmatic specificities of relative clauses, show that what we refer to as high elaborateness of expression is not necessarily just decorative linguistic 'garbage'; rather, it is possible to observe—on a synchronic level—that the garbage can actually perform very subtle functions. Thus, in a comprehensive study of Chadic languages, Frajzyngier (1996) shows that the additional marking of the relativization strategy by a post-relative marker (along with a relative marker) has a specific function with regard to the existential status of the head noun. Frajzyngier (1996: 433) calls this the *de re* existential status function of post-relative markers. The *de re* function involves discourse world knowledge shared between speaker and hearer, that is, it involves contexts where the head noun is either (a) known to the hearer, or (b) has been mentioned in previous conversation, or (c) was present in some previous event, or (d) is present during the conversation. (The *de re* function is contrasted with the *de dicto* existential status function, involving contexts where the hearer is no longer 'a participant in the event' and there is no previous discourse world knowledge shared by speaker and hearer.) Examples of post-relative marking—which often consists of demonstrative pronouns[4]—come from Mupun (Chadic, Afro-Asiatic, spoken in Cameroon), where the post-relative *nə* marks the *de re* existential status of the head noun, and is used in addition to the relative marker *ðə/ðe:*

(12) Mupun (Frajzyngier 1996: 435)
      head noun mentioned earlier in discourse:
      kuma   naat   ðə   get   wu   maŋ   an
      also   boss   REL   PAST   3M   take   1SG
      nə   səm   wur   a   F.
      POSTREL   name   3M   COP   F.
      'The boss who employed me was called F.'

---

[4] Note, however, that—as Frajzyngier (1996: 433) argues—post-relative markers belong to a system of coding of relative markers, and not of demonstrative/definite determiners.

(13) Mupun (Frajzyngier 1996: 435)

head noun present in the environment of speech:

kat	an	mbə	raŋ	puo	ðe	mun
when	1SG	FUT	write	words	REL	1PL

pə	sat	nə	sə
PREP	say	POSTREL	here

'when I write the words that we are saying here...'

If, however, the head noun has not been mentioned before and if it is not present in the environment of the conversation, the post-relative marker will be omitted in Mupun. Thus, in the example below, the heads of the relative clauses, *dalili* 'reason' and *lek* 'war' are mentioned for the first time in discourse:

(14) Mupun (Frajzyngier 1996: 434)

to,	a	nə	a	dalili	ðe	nə	le
well	COP	it	COP	reason (H.)	REL	ANAPH	cause

ðaŋ	mo
COMP	3PL

ji	n-Mupun	a	lek	ðe	nə	cen
come	PREP-Mupun	COP	war	REL	it	drive.away

nen	nan	fun
people	old	1PL

'Well, the reason why they came to Mupun was because of war, which drove our fathers away'.

It looks then as if we are justified in speaking of the elaborateness of expressing relativization as something which is there in order to mark the subtle intertwining of the semantics of the relative clause construction with additional, discourse-pragmatic distinctions.

Such a conclusion, however, turns out to be less than convincing, if we look around for other languages even within the same group and region. It turns out that languages can find another—no less efficient—solution for encoding exactly the same distinction, the *de re* versus the *de dicto* existential status of the head noun, whereby no additional, post-relative marker is required. Thus, instead of employing the presence versus the absence of post-relative markers, other Chadic languages such as Gidar (spoken in Cameroon and Chad) and Pero (spoken in Nigeria) have employed a contrast between two types of relative markers. In Gidar, for instance, the relative marker *màs* indicates that the head noun phrase has

not been mentioned before, is not known, is not present in the environment of speech, i.e. has *de dicto* status, and *án* indicates that the head noun
phrase has been mentioned before, is known, or is present in the environment of speech, i.e. has *de re* status (Frajzyngier 1996: 427):

>(15) Gidar (Frajzyngier 1996: 427)
>
>dəf   tá-ì   **məs** də́   dáw   kái-t   ɓà
>man   be-3M   REL   3M   HAB   want-3F   NEG
>'She has no suitors.' (lit. 'There is no man who wants her.')

>(16) Gidar (Frajzyngier 1996: 427)
>
>dəf   **án**   də́   dáw   kái-tá
>man   REL   3M   HAB   want-3F
>'the man who courts her'

In other words, there is nothing particularly indispensable about the
use of additional formal expression for encoding the *de re* versus the
de dicto distinction, since the same distinction can be encoded
perfectly well without stacking both relative and post-relative markers in
the same sentence. Moreover, many languages fail to make this distinction
at all.

Thus it appears that elaborate expression does not necessarily have to
encode some specific and subtle grammatical distinction. The question
remains then: why is this elaborateness of expression there at all?

Observations on some of the languages for which we have attested
history may, we propose, be helpful to answer this question. In such
languages it turns out that the 'frills' of material are there due to historical
residue or rather fossilizations of earlier uses; and if in addition to the
previous, historically earlier marking there emerges new relative marking,
there will then be the possibility for an overlap—or coexistence—of the
two. Thus, in present-day Swahili (Bantu, Niger-Congo) there are two
main forms relative clauses can take, the *amba-* form as in (17a), and the
infix form (*-o-* in the example below) related to the so-called 'relative
pronoun', as in (17b) (Liner 1977: 269):

>(17) Swahili (Liner 1977: 269)
>
>a. Wa-kikuyu   **amba-o**   wa-na-fanya   kazi   kwa
>   c2-kikuyu   REL-RELPRON   SUBJ-PRES-do   work   with
>   bidii   wa-na-fanikiwa
>   diligence   SUBJ-PRES-successful
>   'The Kikuyus who work hard are successful.'

b. Wa-kikuyu   wa-na-o-fanya   kazi   kwa
c2-kikuyu   SUBJ-PRES-RELPRON-do   work   with
bidii   wa-na-fanikiwa
diligence   SUBJ-PRES-successful
'The Kikuyus who work hard are successful.'

Diachronic investigations show that there were no *amba-* relatives up to the middle of the twentieth century. It is as late as the 1950s that the first occurrences of *amba-* markers are attested. Liner (1977: 272) reports that in these first attestations from the middle of the twentieth century, there are double relative forms too, i.e. relative clauses containing relative markers in both *amba-* and the verb (infix). Liner (1977: 272–3) proposes that in these cases, *amba-* was used with the infix relative to emphasize the restrictive meaning, and later it specialized as the marker for restrictive (but not non-restrictive) clauses.

Furthermore, there exists a very strong typological argument against a 'functional need' explanation of the elaborate expression of relative clauses. This argument involves the overwhelming prevalence of a single relativization marker for the encoding of the relative clause construction in the languages of the world. Thus, as can be seen from the Appendix to this chapter, most languages employ one relativization marker, which may be:

- a participial form of the verb (sometimes a multipurpose marker of relativization, *the fact-S* construction, and so on, e.g. Karachay-Balkar)
- a general subordinator (e.g. Mangarayi)
- a relative tense marker (e.g. Amharic)
- a complementizer (usually a multifunctional one, e.g. Chalcatongo Mixtec)
- a relative pronoun (e.g. Russian), etc.

That is, the results of our investigation into relative clause formation indicate that there are few languages that employ two, or three, or four, or five relativization markers. Moreover, Appendix 9.1 shows that in many cases where there is more than one relativization marker, we are dealing with one *obligatory* marker, plus one or more optional markers, the latter shown in brackets.

Now, what is the theoretical strength of this typological argument? What does it mean if most of the world's languages have opted for one particular way of encoding a given grammatical distinction rather than another?

Our contention here is that if lack of elaborateness is typologically 'fit'—that is, most frequent cross-linguistically—then it is difficult to make a case for elaborateness being functionally motivated. Elaborate formal expression of the relative clause construction does not evolve because it is functionally needed. Rather, it happens to 'be there'—in some languages—as a result of their historical development. In some cases, this may involve historical inertia, or historical 'junk' (Lass 1990). In other cases, language contact may be the crucial factor: a contact situation may result in elaborate double marking of relative clauses (see Heine and Kuteva, forthcoming, on double marking in post-nominal relative clauses in certain parts of the Basque-speaking area under the influence of Spanish).

At this point, it is worth considering explicitly how our claims about elaboration relate to functionalism in linguistics. We do not deny that functionalism has a role to play in language. Indeed, it is striking that in our data on elaborateness of relative clause marking across the world's languages, the vast majority of languages have one and exactly one marker of relative clause status, essentially the variant that would be predicted by functional considerations: failure to mark relative clause status is at least potentially lacking in expressiveness (since this may lead to relative clauses being misinterpreted as some other construction), while more than one marker is redundant. But what is not consistent with a strong functionalist position that is restricted to considerations of economy and expressiveness is the fact that some languages have more elaborate, in some cases considerably more elaborate ways of marking relative clauses. How could such elaboration have come about?

In part, this could be simply the result of random historical changes. There is clear evidence from other areas, such as morphophonemics and morphology, that, for instance, relatively straightforward and phonetically natural sound changes can give rise to morphophonemic and eventually morphological complexity (see Carstairs-McCarthy, Chapter 8); such complexity is simply an automatic result of changes that in themselves do not have complexification as an aim—indeed, their aim may even be to simplify other areas of the grammar, in this instance in particular the phonetics.

In part, the development of elaboration can be the result of more systematic processes, including reasonably well-understood cognitive processes such as grammaticalization. Grammaticalization is a natural process that leads, *inter alia*, to the development of more abstract semantic units and to the development of more complex morphology.[5]

But there is perhaps another aspect of language change that needs to be taken into account in considering reasons for elaboration of particular parts of the grammar of a language, namely the social factor that language has an emblematic function, as one of the symbols—often a very potent symbol—of a particular social group. Perhaps the clearest examples come from phonology, where, although there is a cross-linguistic tendency to prefer simple kinds of phonetic segments and sequences, there are nonetheless languages (and language groups, and dialects of languages) that depart strikingly from these norms in one or more areas of their phonology; examples are the development of click consonants in the Khoisan languages of southwestern Africa or of rich vowel systems in the Austronesian (Micronesian) language Nauruan or in several Mon-Khmer languages—or indeed some varieties of English. While such developments can often be initiated by random sound changes, even by the interaction of a number of quite natural sound changes, once an unusual phenomenon of this kind arises it can be seized upon by the speech community as an emblem of that speech community, differentiating it from all other speech communities and likely to be emphasized even further, just as can a particular pattern in dress or ritual; such a phenomenon can thus be maintained quite tenaciously despite its apparent dysfunctionality. In terms of general thinking on evolution, it might be compared with the notion of costly signalling; in terms of more traditional pre-scientific concepts, with that of shibboleth.

We are of course aware that in a broader sense even the emblematic function of language could be regarded as 'functional', in the sense that developing unusual, emblematic characteristics serves the function of characterizing the speech community in question. But first, such a general concept of functionalism is in danger of voiding the term of all empirical content. Perhaps more importantly, the term 'functionalism' in linguistics, including studies of the evolution of language, is usually given a narrower interpretation, along the lines of 'utility of existing structure', and it is this narrower concept that we particularly want to address here. In other

---

[5] An anonymous reviewer points out, however, that a grammaticalization development 'might also lead to a decrease in elaborateness, e.g. *going to* > *gonna*'.

words, functional considerations, in this narrower interpretation, will always have to compete with other considerations, and these other considerations will sometimes win out and lead to systems where not all existing structure is functionally loaded. What we mean by functionality, in this sense, is very relevant to simplicity (as contrasted with complexity and elaborateness).

Our approach thus predicts that human language must originally have been much simpler, and highly functional, but that over the millennia since that time, various kinds of elaboration have developed. More precisely, following Comrie (1992: 205), we assume that certain complexities of all or many currently attested languages were not present in early human language. This standpoint is reinforced also by recent findings about the grammaticalization processes in the languages of the world (Heine and Kuteva 2002a; Heine and Kuteva 2002b: 394); note that, from a different, UG-theoretical background, Wunderlich (ms.) holds a similar position. An anonymous referee observes that 'the fact that many grammatical elements arise through the bleaching and fusion of what were once free morphemes does not presuppose that there was once a stage in language evolution when all morphemes were free and exhibited no allomorphic variation', the reason for this being the premise that 'contiguous items in the speech chain must always have tended to exercise assimilatory and dissimilatory influences on each other'; see also Carstairs-McCarthy, Chapter 8. Our response to this is that it is possible to argue that at the earliest conceivable stage, human language(s) might have been much simpler and highly functional, and might have lacked grammatical forms such as case inflections, agreement, voice markers, etc. In addition to the arguments given in Heine and Kuteva (2002b), an argument in support of such a standpoint comes from what we can observe in historic time: some languages, e.g. isolating languages (that is, without inflectional morphology), may stay isolating over time despite ongoing grammaticalization.

In other words, language in prehistoric time appears to have had entities that were highly functional/polyfunctional—and simple—in formal expression rather than elaborate, a situation which does not appear to have a parallel in modern language forms. Of course, once elaboration set in, there was also the possibility of simplification, so that we are not claiming that language has since its inception been on a continual cline of greater and greater complexification. But given that all languages with millennia of history—for creole languages, see the next paragraph—have some degree of elaboration somewhere in their grammars, it is clear that the forces leading to elaboration have overall had an edge over those leading to greater simplicity.

Although we believe that our approach to the elaboration of language between its initial evolution and the present day stands on its own, one might nonetheless consider another area of language change where similar ideas have been propounded. McWhorter (2001a) argues that creole languages have the world's simplest grammars because these grammars are recent creations, while grammars of other languages have had at least millennia to develop and have therefore become considerably more elaborated. (The other papers in issue 5, 2/3 of *Linguistic Typology* are reactions, ranging from sympathetic to highly critical, to McWhorter's ideas.) It would be interesting in this respect to investigate whether creole languages regularly have simply-marked relative clause constructions; unfortunately, relative clauses are not one of the constructions investigated by McWhorter.

ACKNOWLEDGEMENTS

We thank Ted Briscoe, Terrence Deacon, John Haiman, Bernd Heine, Maggie Tallerman, and two anonymous referees for helpful comments. The second-named author also thanks the German Research Foundation for its support.

FURTHER READING

The following are relevant recent works on typology and relative clauses by the authors of the current chapter:

- Comrie and Kuteva (2004)
- Comrie (1998)
- Kuteva and Comrie (forthcoming)

Appendix 9.1

Language	Number of relativization markers[6]
Abkhaz	1
Alamblak	0
Amele	0 + (1)

[6] The first (or only) numeral gives the number of obligatory markers; the numeral in parentheses gives the number of additional optional markers.

Language	Number of relativization markers
Amharic	1
Anywa	1
Arabic (Cairene Egyptian)	1
Babungo	3
Bagirmi	2
Baka	3
Bambara	2
Barasano	1
Bari	1 + (1)
Bawm	1
Big Nambas	1
Bole	1
Bulgarian	1
Brahui	1
Bukiyip	1
Burmese	1
Burushaski	1
Canela-Kraho	1
Chamorro	1
Chibak	1
Chinantec Lealao	1
Chinese (Mandarin)	1
Dagbani	1
Dani (Lower Grand Valley)	1
Dawuro	1
Dholuo	1
Diyari	1
English	1
Epena Pedee	1
Ewe	2
Evenki	1
Fijian (Boumaa)	0
Finnish	1
French	1
Fur	1
Fyem	1
Georgian	1
German	1
Gidar	1
Giziga	2
Gooniyandi	0

Greek	2
Greenlandic (West)	1
Hausa	2
Guaraní	1
Hebrew	1
Hindi	1
Hmong Njua	1
Hungarian	1
Ik	1
Ika	0
Imbabura Quechua	1
Imonda	1
Indonesian	1 + (1)
Ingush	1
Irish	1
Italian	1
Jacaltec	1
Japanese	0
Kambera	1 + (1)
Kannada	1
Karachay-Balkar	1
Karo-Batak	1
Kayah Li (Eastern)	0 + (1)
Kayardild	1
Kewa	1
Kilivila	2
Khmer	0
Kisi	2
Kiowa	1 + (2)
Kobon	0 + (1)
Koasati	0
Koranko	2
Korean	1
Koromfe	1 + (1)
Koyra	1
Koyraboro Senni	1
Krongo	1
Kxoe	2
Kwaio	0
Lango	1
Latvian	1
Lavukaleve	1

Language	Number of relativization markers
Lele	1
Lezgian	1
Lingala	0 + (1)
Luvale	1
Maale	0
Maasai	1
Mamvu	2
Mangarayi	1
Manipuri	1 + (1)
Maori	1 + (2)
Mapuche	1
Maranungku	0
Maricopa	2
Marthuthunira	1
Maung	1
Maybrat	1
Mbay	2
Miya	2
Mixtec (Chalcatongo)	1
Muna	1
Mupun	2
Nama	0
Nandi	1
Ndyuka	1
Ngemba	4 + (1)
Ngiyambaa	1
Nkore-Giga	1
Nubian (Dongolese)	1
Nunggubuyu	1
Oromo (Harar)	0 + (1)
Paamese	1
Paiwan	1
Pero	2
Persian	2
Piraha	1 + (1)
Pitjantjatjara	1
Rama	0
Rapanui	0
Russian	1
Sango	1
Sanuma	2

Seediq	0
Slave	1
So	1
Sotho (Northern)	3
Spanish	1
Sonrai	2
Supyire	2
Swahili	2
Svan	1
Tagalog	0
Tamazight	0 + (1)
Thai	1 + (1)
Tukang Besi	1
Turkish	1
Ungarinjin	1
Usan	1
Wambaya	0
Warao	1
Wardaman	1
Warí	0 + (2)
Warndarang	1
Wichita	1
Yagaria	1
Yagua	2
Yaqui	1 + (1)
Yidiny	1
Yimas	2
Yoruba	2
Yukaghir, Kolyma	2
Zulu	2

10 Deception and mate selection: some implications for relevance and the evolution of language

BRADLEY FRANKS AND KATE RIGBY

10.1 Introduction

A major question in the evolution of language concerns the balance between honest communication and deception. We suggest that the capacity to differentiate honest from dishonest communications may be one of the prerequisites for the evolution of sophisticated linguistic communicative faculties. We consider the role of this capacity in the arena of mate selection. Once established in mate selection, we suggest that a co-evolutionary process supports increasingly sophisticated language use in creative displays, which feeds into further development of language as a tool for deception in mate selection, and this inspires a more sophisticated deception detection capacity.

The propensity to attempt to deceive in communication may be hypothesized to increase in interactions that have significant costs and benefits. Mate selection is such a case: there are significant benefits to a displayer who deceives successfully (in attracting an otherwise unavailable mate), and significant costs to a selector failing to detect deception. Miller (2000) suggests that human mate selection often involves display of cognitive traits such as intelligence, which can be signalled by creativity in language use. However, since cognitive traits are less transparent than physical traits (in that they cannot be read directly off behaviour or appearance), the detection of deception is rendered more complex (Rigby and Franks 2001).

We argue that the Relevance Theory of pragmatics developed by Sperber and Wilson (1986) can provide a way of conceptualizing the distinction between some honest and deceptive displays in mate selection. Relevance Theory is based on the relative calculation of costs and benefits in the interpretation of utterances. We suggest that this calculation can provide a criterion for detecting deception and a limit on its extent. However, we need to investigate deception in a way that takes into account possible adaptive functions of communication beyond those normally discussed by Relevance Theory. One such function arises from sexual selection.

We also sketch the results from a series of experiments that investigated the role of mate selection in generating a sex-based difference in creativity in language use. Participants were presented with non-lexicalized, novel two-word concept combinations (e.g. *steam thorn, fork scarf*) and asked to produce a brief definition for each. These definitions were then categorized by interpretation type—relation-linking or property-mapping, where property-mapping interpretations are more creative (Gagné 2000). A baseline condition was compared to experimental conditions in which participants were motivated to display by the presence of experimenters of different sexes. These experimenters were either a young, attractive male or a young, attractive female. The results indicate that males produce significantly more property interpretations than females, as a result of the motivation to display themselves to the experimenter. A criterion for differentiating honest displays of creativity from deceptive attempts arises from the latter not fitting into the interpretation types or bearing no semantic link to the two concepts in the combination.

In section 10.2, we sketch some aspects of a Relevance approach to pragmatics, discussing connections with deception and indication, suggesting a consideration of deception beyond the question of semantic truthfulness. This is reflected in the discussion in section 10.3 on the connections between sexual selection and indication, with a focus on the role of creativity as a genetic fitness indicator. Section 10.4 integrates the issues thus far and presents the empirical findings concerning the impact of sex differences on understanding novel concept combinations. Section 10.5 notes some suggestions for further research.

10.2 Relevance Theory, deception, and indication

Relevance Theory is a 'post-Gricean' approach to pragmatics (Sperber and Wilson 1986). It characterizes interpretation as a cognitive process that implicitly balances the cognitive effort that a hearer needs to use during interpretation against the informativeness (or 'cognitive effects') that this effort yields. In most circumstances, the hearer processes a speaker's utterance according to the assumption that the effort expended is worth the effects yielded.

According to Relevance Theory, much communication is 'ostensive', in that the mere fact of communicating the information implies that the information is worth the processing effort. Ostension thus provides two levels of information to be detected by the recipient: (i) the information that has been communicated as the overt subject matter of the communication; (ii) the information that the overt subject matter has itself been deliberately pointed out. The first level of information could be processed without the second, but the claim is that efficient processing of the overt subject matter is enhanced by detecting that the communicative act is ostensive. This is because acts of ostensive communication communicate the presupposition of their own optimal relevance. This means not only that the effects yielded are worth the effort to interpret them, but also that the communicative act (phrase, sentence, utterance, etc.) used in the communication is itself the most relevant to those effects. The process of interpretation involves fleshing out a fragmentary sentence meaning into a full interpretation of speaker's meaning, by pursuing a path of least effort that stops when an expectation of relevance is satisfied.

Several aspects of this position are pertinent. The claim is *not* that people always actually produce optimally relevant communications; rather that *ceteris paribus*, they intend their hearer to believe that they do. So hearers are entitled to process communications on the assumption that the speaker has produced an utterance that is optimally relevant—one that is worth the effort of processing because it will yield sufficient information. Additionally, relevance—and therefore optimality—is not a fixed quantum. Rather, both the effort required and the resulting effects will depend on a range of parameters: for example, the knowledge of the speaker and hearer and their understanding of each other's knowledge, the type of communication, such as whether it has formalized expectations of informativeness or not (a university lecture versus a used-car salesman's verbiage), etc. So the degree of effort expected or justified will vary between contexts. The situation becomes more complicated given the possibility for multiple interpretations of an utterance. Sperber (1994) discusses three different interpretation strategies a hearer might adopt in understanding an utterance, in ascending order of sophistication. The first is 'naive optimism', which amounts to accepting the first interpretation that *seems relevant enough* to the hearer; the first that seems to offer a reasonable balance of effort to effects is then considered to constitute the speaker's meaning. The second is 'cautious optimism', where the hearer accepts the first interpretation that *the speaker might have thought* would be relevant enough—this involves additional complexity since it requires attempting to discern the communicative intentions of the speaker. There are two circumstances where this strategy can yield more appropriate interpretations than naive optimism: one where the most easily generated interpretation is not one that the speaker could plausibly have intended, such as an obvious risqué interpretation arising from a lecturer inadvertently producing a *double entendre* (accidental relevance), and one where the speaker makes a slip of the tongue (accidental irrelevance). The third interpretation strategy is 'sophisticated understanding', where the hearer accepts the first interpretation *the speaker might have thought the hearer would think* was relevant enough. This strategy adds a third level of complexity since it requires attempting to discern what the speaker believes about what the hearer believes about the communicative intentions of the speaker. As a result, the third strategy opens up the possibility of deception. Note that none of these three strategies presumes that there is an explicit or conscious awareness of the effort and effects of processing, or of the intentions of the speaker.

Now, hearer effort is usually justified on a broad assumption of the speaker telling the truth. Origgi and Sperber (2000) suggest that hearers 'sift' the content of communications for truthfulness. Given the widespread possibilities for deception, this is a crucial aspect of any pragmatic theory, though the specific position of Relevance Theory on this issue is thus far underdeveloped. The main suggestion (Sperber 2000) is that the hearer checks the information that is communicated for internal consistency (i.e. with past information communicated by that speaker), and for external consistency (i.e. with non-linguistic facts). This principally takes place via the hearer's assessment of the appropriateness of the speaker's use of logical connectives and rhetorical constructions that carry the argument structure and persuasiveness. Rather than merely appearing honest or consistent in information content, speakers deploy argument structures (such as conditionals, quantifiers) to indicate that the information they are communicating is internally coherent and persuasive.

Sperber's claim is that hearers also pay attention to these structures and employ questions about the adequacy of their use in order to 'sift' the information communicated.

Concerning this sifting mechanism, it is firstly a semantically driven mechanism, whose focus is on the truth of statements and the soundness of inferences and argument structures. It is therefore concerned with the 'surface' purpose of the communication—one that is known to, and can be deliberately manipulated by the speaker. However, this is only one kind of deception, and concerns language as a simple semantic descriptive–communicative device. A further important kind of deception concerns language that may also indicate something non-semantic—a feature of the speaker that isn't directly described by the semantic statement. A key possibility is of language as a device to display to potential mates: for example, as an indicator of the genetic fitness of the displayer. We return to the characterization of fitness indicators below; the intuitive notion is of a phenotypic property of an individual (such as a morphological or behavioural characteristic) caused by qualities of their genotype, which can be *interpreted* as indicating the presence of this genetic cause by another individual. There is no supposition that either the indication or its interpretation is under the conscious control of the agents involved. There can be a chain of such causal dependencies from the genes through different aspects of the phenotype, so that indication can be indirect. Our suggestion is that surface semantics may express a communicative act that indirectly indicates the genetic qualities of the male, though the semantics does not describe those genetic qualities. Here, any deception does not concern the truthfulness of the message's semantics, but the connection between the semantics and the indicated genetic fitness. Hence, deception may arise through the semantics expressing a use that appears to indicate high fitness, when the communicator does not possess such fitness. For example, suppose that creativity in language use serves as an indirect indicator of genetic fitness in mate selection (for instance, via intelligence and problem-solving capacity). Then deception would involve someone manifesting creativity even though they lacked the associated intelligence and underlying genetic qualities. Whether such 'faking' is open to, or requires, deliberate deception on the part of the speaker, is an empirical matter. Since these two types of deception are orthogonal, four possible scenarios emerge, three of which involve deception (see Table 10.1).

TABLE 10.1 *Varieties of deception based on indication and semantics.*

	Indication	
	True	False
Semantics		
True	No deception	Deception
False	Deception	Deception

Now, it is possible for an indicator to be false, but still employ truthful statements—a speaker's utterance could 'pass' Sperber's logico-rhetorical sifting mechanism but nonetheless deceive the hearer about their genetic fitness. A speaker could also 'fail' the sifting test but still be giving accurate information about their genetic fitness. And so on. The main implication is that communicating as a descriptive device is only one of the potential evolved functions of language: language use as an indicator of genetic fitness in mate display is a further possibility. If this is the case then a full picture would need to consider other arenas for deception, and a complicated picture of representation and meta-representation ensues.

A second point about sifting is that it operates over structural semantics only—assessing the argument structures employed in persuasion, and therefore the connections between different lexical, phrasal, or conceptual contents, but not the specific nature or details of those contents. Now, broadening the types of deception as above allows us to consider the possibility of indicator (as opposed to semantic) deception at levels 'inside' the sentence or argument structure. For example, interpretations of concept combination may act as an indicator of genetic fitness, regardless of their connections to sound argument structures. However, since the structural criterion for deception used by sifting does not apply inside those structures, an alternative characterization is required. For sifting, the criterion is truth or soundness of argument. For concept combinations we will, following Miller (2000), take a criterion of accurate indication to be creativity, and a criterion for false indication would then be a failed creative effort. Creativity receives a specific operationalization in terms of concept combination that admits of clear empirical measurement.

And the final point about sifting is that the mechanism is separate from the Relevance Theory account of interpretation. Sperber moots an additional 'logical' module to handle the logico-rhetorical sifting: the interpretation is first generated according to relevance theoretic precepts, but then, before accepting this interpretation, the content is sifted for honesty. Presumably the result of sifting is then itself checked against knowledge about the speaker, before deciding whether it is an acceptable characterization of speaker-meaning. The upshot is that sifting for deception in this approach does not in any way serve to limit the amount of effort that the hearer is required to expend in generating an interpretation. Our contention is that, for the level of concept combinations, we should be able to articulate a mechanism for detecting deception that is continuous with or part of the normal calibration of interpretive effort and effects, rather than requiring a further mechanism or level of checking.

10.3 Sexual selection, indication, and creativity

As suggested, some communicative acts function as displays in mate selection. Traditionally, mate selection has emphasized display via physical traits, such as the peacock's tail (Darwin 1871/1971). However, there is increasing research on the potential of *cognitive* traits as display (Donald 1991; Miller 2000). Concerning the long-term genetic survival of an individual, by which we mean the perpetuation of some of that individual's genes over generations, there are many reasons why cognitive traits can indicate a potential mate's fitness.

The mechanisms of sexual selection have been established through the model of display via physical traits. Physical morphological or behavioural traits can indicate a male's genetic fitness and health, and therefore their quality as a mate. Above-average examples of key, species-specific attributes, for instance symmetry, colouring, antlers, tails, may all be means of detecting a male's worth as a mate. This may be because the features indicate high genetic fitness (e.g. symmetry) or health and strength (e.g. condition of coat, plumage, antlers, etc.). In this account, we are employing a standard notion of genetic fitness, namely the relative survival potential of an individual, measurable via species-specific adaptive traits. Whilst there remain concerns in broader theory relating to this notion's potential for circularity, its role as an empirical predictor is well established (see, for instance, Rose and Lauder 1996). Hence a genetic indicator can be characterized as a trait (or collection of traits) that allows an individual to be assessed in terms of its own survival potential and thus that of its genes (Wilson 1978; Ridley 1997). These indicators are species-specific and readily measurable, and comparable within species (e.g. colouring, birdsong). So fitness indication is a relational concept—concerning the properties of one individual that can be detected by another individual as indicative of the former's genetic quality. It requires the manifestation of a property that is reliably caused by gene quality in the male, and further requires that females can detect such a property and preferentially employ it as a criterion in their selection of a mate. We should note that there is no supposition here that females have an explicit or conscious motivation to select mates with the highest genetic fitness. Just as the overall tendency in natural selection towards survival is not 'programmed' as an explicit aim to perpetuate the genetic line, so the overall tendency in sexual selection towards selecting a genetically fit mate is not expressed as a single adaptation or conscious decision (Symons 1992).

The survival of an individual is affected by more than their physical health or fitness—cognitive strengths and weaknesses are also important. A candidate for a cognitive trait that aids survival is intelligence, since it is the basis for successful problem solving. In general, a male that fulfils physical requirements for selection would have an increased chance of selection by the female if they also possessed critical cognitive selection traits. In the mate selection literature, differential investment in the mating process has generally led the male to be characterized as the displayer, and the female as the selector. One of the key problems for females is to recognize reliably these desirable cognitive traits. How can they detect whether a male has high intelligence or high problem-solving ability? This requires there to be a specific behavioural or morphological indicator of the hidden cognitive trait that is recognizable and assessable by the female, and producible by the male (though not so easily produced as to be readily faked in deceptive communication).

Creativity is a cognitive ability that has high positive correlations with intelligence (Sternberg 1999; Miller 2000). It is also a fundamental aspect of problem solving—effective solutions to problems often incorporate creative recombination of aspects of the original problem, and/or the potential solutions that are available. If an individual's prolonged survival is aided by the ability to adapt to changing circumstances via successful problem solving, then creativity (as a key to problem solving) may be a major contributor to such adaptability. Moreover, since creativity is often associated with publicly visible products (either actions or objects), this association can be exploited in mate selection, allowing creative outputs to act as publicly assessable indicators of intelligence. In this way it can provide a mode of display for males and a selection criterion for females.

Any display requires a medium, and one central way of expressing creativity is through language. Research on human conversation indicates that language is often used as a flirting device, both in terms of explicit propositioning and in more subtle displays. For example, male conversation tends towards increased intellectualism when there is a female present (Dunbar 1996). The choice of linguistic expression can also be used as a cognitive indicator of fitness in mate display. Given that creativity provides a suitable trait for indicating fitness, we would argue that males would utilize creative linguistic expressions to display to females, and females would assess utterances for creativity (attractiveness), in the way that females of other species assess physical traits.

However, can a view of cognitive traits as sexually selected attributes respond to the problems that have beset sexually selected physical traits? In particular, how can the issue of faking and deception in mate display and selection be addressed? Zahavi (1975) developed the Handicap Principle to illustrate how physical traits could be reliable as fitness indicators even though some individuals could 'fake' fitness. He argued that traits used by males for display (and females to select) made high physical demands, such that they could only be maintained in a desirable state by appropriately fit males. The traits were in themselves a handicap, requiring a premium of fitness in the male to flourish to the better-than-average level at which a female will select them. For example, stags' antlers can grow to a size that can be a practical impediment in ordinary activity, and can be increasingly difficult to maintain intact—they become a handicap to the possessor. Only the most healthy and strong individuals will be able to maintain such above-average-sized antlers, so that their possession indicates high genetic fitness. And it is precisely such above-average-size antlers that female deer employ as a mate-selection criterion. Within the sphere of cognitive traits, the problem of faking fitness, and consequent deception of the selector by the displayer, is just as great. The parallel possibility is that some cognitive traits that act as fitness indicators in human males may be subject to the handicap principle, in that their production carries high cognitive costs; as a result, faking them is also costly. The female must have a way of verifying with tolerable success that the male's display is honest, otherwise the use of that indicator for mate selection becomes unreliable.

The assessment of cognitive indicators has two different aspects (which echo the related constructs in assessing mental states in psychological theory): *validity* and *reliability*. The validity of creativity as a cognitive indicator must be assessed, concerning whether the communication or expression really is creative—this relates to the semantic properties of the communication or expression and their relation to other possible or competing expressions. The reliability of the display as a fitness display must also be considered—this relates to its non-semantic properties, and in particular whether it does, in fact, truly indicate mate fitness, rather than being an instance of dishonesty. Although these two aspects of creativity as an indicator are analytically distinct, there is no supposition that they are assessed independently or by different processes.

Concerning validity of displays, a problem pertaining to creativity is that it allows for exaggeration. There is an oft-cited link between creativity, genius, and madness (Nettle 2001). Indeed, some creative acts can be taken to extremes in which they become simply dangerous. A male who, due to a mental disorder, produces unpredictable acts that could be construed as creative is not a good example of a reproductively fit male. This suggests that *constraints* on creativity are required if it is to function as a display mechanism. Thus, rather than using random acts of unbridled creativity, a male displays via the fulfilment of a creativity that lies within parameters. This allows females to select those males that are reproductively fitter, it allows clearer comparison between males, and it reduces the likelihood of fakers by introducing creativity criteria that need to be respected. Constraints also ensure that displays are recognizable and interpretable as being displays. Examples that could fall outside these constraints might include utterances that are not interpretable, or totally irrelevant communications that do not follow the conversational or pragmatic lines of the communicative interaction, or utterances that fall outside of the topic or style of communication.

Since indication is a relational construct, in order for creativity to succeed as a display trait females need to be responsive to creativity. They are therefore hypothesized to have a degree of neophilia (liking for novelty and creativity). However, there is also a requirement for a parallel level of constraint on female neophilia. This ensures that the female is *not* attracted to random behaviour resulting, for example, from mental disorder rather than deliberate display. Such neophilia suggests a co-evolutionary process in which males' disposition to creativity is matched by females' preference for creativity. Such evolutionary interdependence has the possibility of resulting in a runaway process (Fisher 1930), in which increasingly extreme creative products by males are matched by female demand for increasingly extreme products. In such cases, the need for constraints on acceptable creativity to limit runaway processes is magnified. How such a co-evolutionary process might get off the ground to begin with is uncertain. One possibility can be derived from Ryan's (1990) 'sensory exploitation' theory. He suggests that a sexual selection process might take over (or exapt) tendencies already established via natural selection. For example, species that use primarily visual information to forage also tend to use visual information as a key mode of display and selection, where the visual sense has been finely honed by natural selection. Similarly, human creativity in solving problems—such as in predator evasion and hunting—is a likely instance of a naturally selected trait, which might later have been exapted by sexual selection to provide a cognitive display trait.

A display's reliability as an indicator of fitness also needs to be evaluated. Differential parental investment means that in humans, as in many other species, females typically invest far more in an offspring than do males. This has produced a pattern of the male as the displayer and the more parsimonious female as the selector, because the female pays more for her choice: the costs of a wrong choice are high for the female but almost negligible for the male. This results in a differential pattern of potential deception in mate display in which the male is, on average, keen to mate with as many females as possible. However, the female is more limited in the frequency with which she can reproduce and is therefore more 'choosy' in her mate selection. Thus, males attain a high benefit and low risk in using deception in mate display, whereas females must detect this deception or pay a much higher cost. A handicap is therefore required that will reduce the possibility of fakers successfully displaying and that will thereby also increase the reliability of creativity as an indicator for female selection.

The semantic complexity of language lends itself to achieving this handicapping requirement and therefore to being used in male displays as a fitness indicator via creativity. Notice that such display is an example of ostensive communication. The displayer wishes to communicate some information, but also wants the selector to recognize that the information is being communicated. Moreover, display involves a further level in communicating not only the content of the communication ostensively, but also its purpose. At least by default, display seems to involve the displayer in communications that are intended to be received as displays. The sophistication of human language allows several concurrent levels of creativity. For example, in semantic terms creativity occurs in what individuals discuss, how they describe it, and in the specific form of descriptions that support reference, such as noun phrases. Pragmatically, individuals could be creative in terms of overall message-level communicative intentions (including invited inferences or implicatures), or in terms of component referential intentions that are encoded in noun phrases (including ways of referring to entities for discussion). We consider the assessment of creativity at the level of the interpretation of noun phrases, thus indicating their referential intentions. Relevance Theory is central to our account of how the creative productions of males can be constrained into reliable and assessable displays.

Before proceeding, we should note an alternative possibility for oral communication in mate selection. We have focused on the general equation: if a linguistic display is deemed creative by the female, then it is an honest indication of underlying good quality in the male, where the criterion for creativity is a semantic one. An alternative would be to consider the possible role of a *syntactic* basis for creativity, with syntactically complex expressions being deemed more creative. Given that, by assumption, syntactic complexity is more easily assessed than semantic creativity, this might suggest a simpler mechanism for mate selection. Such a possibility provides an insight into potential evolutionary sequences. It may suggest—as noted above—that the utilization of semantics in sexual selection was not an original cause of the evolution of linguistic communication, but rather that sexual selection exapted and extended a capacity already established by natural selection. Moreover, this exaptation may have arisen from the drive to go beyond a simple indicator of fitness provided by syntax, which (given easy assessibility, and the absence of a need to make sense *per se*) would have been relatively easy to fake by humans. The drive towards more complex indicators may have been supported by the co-evolutionary process in which females select above-average examples of displays, and in which the ability to produce such displays occurs at a cost to the male. Such indicators need to provide more finely grained differentiations between potential mates, and this opens the way for semantic display (see Zuberbühler, Chapter 12, for a related discussion of the important role of semantics in sexual selection and the evolution of complex linguistic capacities).

10.4 Concept combination, creativity, and sexual selection

Concepts have been argued to act as building blocks of thought and communication, since they can be combined to form the contents of complex thoughts and utterances. Creativity can be readily expressed via the novel combination of pairs of concepts that rarely co-occur. Concept combinations, by which we mean the mental representations of meanings associated with two-word noun phrases (comprising a pair of nouns or a noun and adjective) thus provide an empirically tractable method of researching the possible display role of creativity in language.

10.4.1 *Experimental investigations*

To provide insight into whether sexual selection has had an effect on cognitive evolution, we carried out a series of experiments (Rigby 2002). The specific question was whether males would produce more creative interpretations of concept combinations in settings where they were motivated to display. The experiments presented participants with a series of novel concept combinations. The combinations were novel in that the two constituent concepts co-occur highly infrequently in everyday discourse (as verified by participants' assessment of familiarity), and have not been lexicalized into common phrasal units. The role of pragmatics in interpreting such noun phrases has been widely discussed elsewhere (for instance, Costello and Keane 2000; Franks 1995; Nemeth and Bibok 2001).

The experiments followed a standard procedure. Participants were shown the concept combinations and asked to produce brief interpretations of them. These interpretations were then categorized via content analysis into different interpretation types. Two key types of interpretations are based on 'relation linking' and 'property mapping'. These types are well established in the cognitive psychological literature on concepts (Gagné 2000, 2001; Wisniewski and Love 1998; Costello and Keane 2000). The former connects two concepts by forming a context-appropriate relation between the entities. For example, interpreting *sponge table* might employ the relation of an entity described by one concept as 'being for' the entity described by the other—hence, 'table *for* holding sponges'. Levi (1978) identified nine determiners of relation-linking interpretations, in which the interpretations either explicitly include the relation term itself, or implicitly include its sense; they include *on, with, is, causes, has,* etc. Property-mapping interpretations differ in that they understand the whole by mapping a property of one of the concepts (usually, the modifier concept) onto the other (the head concept). So for *sponge table*, if *sponge* is the modifier and *table* is the head, a property interpretation might be 'table that is soft and absorbs a lot of water' (resulting from mapping the property of 'absorbency' from the modifier onto the head). Some different interpretation types are shown in Table 10.2.

A recurring empirical quality of the interpretation types is that they tend to be produced with different regularity and frequency. Gagné (2000) has shown that individuals generate relation interpretations faster, more easily, and more frequently than property interpretations. These qualities of property interpretations parallel key criteria for creative products: creative products are rarer and harder to produce, and this originality is important to their being creative. Thus property interpretations may be seen as more creative than relation interpretations. Independent assessments of the level of creativity of a random sample of property and relation interpretations verified that participants considered property interpretations to be more creative. In particular, female participants

TABLE 10.2 *Property-mapping and relation-linking interpretations for concept combinations.*

concept combination	property-mapping interpretation	relation-linking interpretation
book bicycle	*a book with two wheels*	*a bicycle <u>used</u> to deliver books*
steam thorn	*hot, smoky thorn*	*a thorn <u>made of</u> steam*
mourner musician	*a sad musician wearing black*	*a musician performing <u>for</u> mourners*

Note: the items determining the relations in relation-linking interpretations are underlined.

assessed property interpretations to be more creative and interesting than relation interpretations, as required by the general indication hypothesis.

Given that property interpretations are more creative, our data analysis considered the relative production of property and relation interpretations by males and by females. Since males are hypothesized as the displayers and females as the selectors, we predicted that males would produce more property interpretations than females, when they were displaying. A pre-test removed concept combinations that participants assessed as more closely associated with either sex; this was to ensure that the combinations did not lend themselves to greater creativity by either sex as a result of cultural gender roles. Note also that we do not suggest that males would display higher creativity across *all* contexts, but only in *display* contexts. The predicted sexual dimorphism would thereby be an instance of a *facultative* trait, the operation of which depends on appropriate eliciting circumstances (Williams 1966). In this case, the eliciting circumstances are conditions under which a sexually attractive member of the opposite sex is present, and there is a reason to communicate with them. Thus we analysed the relative production of interpretation types across the sexes in a baseline (non-display) condition versus display conditions.

The baseline condition was compared to two test conditions in which participants were motivated to display in their production of interpretations of concept combinations. This motivation was hypothesized to be induced by the presence of particular experimenters, whom participants were informed would be assessing their interpretations for 'interest value'. Hence participants were given a simple motivation to 'display' to the experimenters, but one whose explicit nature did not differentiate between male or female experimenters. In the baseline condition, predicted to induce no display motivation, the experiment was carried out by a mature female, since menopause in the later stages of female maturity causes the cessation of reproductive potential, meaning that such individuals technically have the lowest reproductive value as compared to young males, young females, and mature males. A separate pre-test had already determined the young experimenters to be perceived as attractive. The two display conditions—using a young male and a young female experimenter respectively—were included for different reasons. Including a male experimenter aimed to assess whether female participants would display to an attractive male by producing more property interpretations, and whether male participants would compete with a male. Including a female experimenter sought to examine the mirror questions: whether females would compete with a female experimenter and males would display to a female experimenter. The competition possibility aimed to assess the suggestion of Kodric-Brown and Brown (1984) that intra-male competition, as well as inter-sex display, might form a part of display behaviour in sexual selection.

We predicted that there would be no significant difference between the sexes in production of property and relation interpretations in the baseline condition. However, for the test conditions we predicted that male participants would be motivated to display to the female experimenter and to compete with the male experimenter. This would result in male participants in the test conditions producing more property interpretations either than females from the test conditions or participants in the baseline condition. Having different sexes of experimenters was posited to have less of an effect on female participants, as a result of differential parental investment and the decreased role of display and competition in female behaviour. The results supported these predictions (see Table 10.3).

Males produced significantly more property interpretations than females, in both test conditions, though not in the baseline condition. In situations where the motivation to compete or display was active, males increased their production of property interpretations. Female production of property interpretations remained relatively constant over the three conditions, suggesting that they were not affected by these motivational factors in the same way. The discovery of a sexual dimorphism in the interpretation of noun phrases is a striking finding, which has not been

TABLE 10.3 *Experiment 1 results.*

Experimental condition	Mean (maximum = 5) production of property interpretations by:	
	Male participants	Female participants
Baseline	1.815	1.804
Male experimenter	2.773[*]	1.787
Female experimenter	2.592[*]	1.567

Note: Comparisons between male and female participants within test conditions (i.e. between columns): [*] indicates a significant difference between males and females at the 1% level.

countenanced in the literature on concepts in the past. We also found, in line with Gagné's position, that property interpretations were less frequently produced overall than relation interpretations.

A second series of experiments was carried out to consider the effect of competition on creative concept combination interpretation. This was necessary since, in the first experiment, the female experimenter could arguably have motivated the male subjects to either display *or* to compete. The experiment was designed to allow comparison of the effects of competition under different conditions. As with experiment one, participants generated interpretations for novel concept combinations. In experiment two, they were motivated to compete by first being shown one property interpretation and one relation interpretation as example combinations which they were told had previously been generated by one of three different kinds of individual. These three different competition conditions were: competition with a sexually unspecified individual, competition with a female individual, and competition with a male individual; participants were informed that the individuals were in the same age group as themselves. A final, control condition was included for comparison purposes. Participants were randomly assigned to one of these four conditions. The prediction was that, if the males in experiment one had been displaying to the female experimenter, then in experiment two, males would produce more property interpretations in the male competition condition than in the female and neutral competition conditions; however, if the males in experiment one had been competing with the female, then in experiment two we would expect males to produce the same number of property interpretations in the male and female competition conditions. The results supported the prediction based on male display to the female but not competition with her (Table 10.4).

The results showed that whereas males did indeed compete with another male, there was significantly less competition with a female and no difference between competition with a female and the control condition, as shown by the mean number of property interpretations. The results suggest that both display and competition are important aspects of sexual selection, as argued by Kodric-Brown and Brown (1984). Both motivations led males to display themselves, in generating a higher number of creative, property interpretations. Thus, the set of experiments provided empirical support for the theoretical position that sexual selection has acted on cognitive traits; and for the specific hypothesis that males are

TABLE 10.4 *Experiment 2 results.*

Competition condition	Mean (maximum = 15) production of property interpretations by:	
	Male participants	Female participants
Competition with a male	8.156[*]	5.733
Competition with a female	6.725	5.200
Neutral competition	6.450	4.933
Control	6.200	5.667

Note: Comparisons between competition conditions within male and female participants (i.e. between rows):[*] indicates a significant difference between competition with a male and other competition conditions, for male participants, at the 5% level.

more creative in appropriate sexual-selection contexts—in this case, display and competition-for-display contexts.

Let us return to a key quality of the dimorphism that we have empirically demonstrated—its context-specificity. We have argued and found that the dimorphism holds only in circumstances pertaining to mate selection (that is, display and competition). There is no implication that there would be an overall dimorphism were we to consider the use of language (or concept combinations) in all contexts. The empirical import of this result lies not in the number of contexts in which it holds, but in its being specific to contexts that are of crucial evolutionary significance— those that involve selection of a mate.

10.4.2 *Implications for deception*

How do these findings relate to deception? A constraint on deception arises via a constraint on creativity: a creative interpretation is a property interpretation, and a less or non-creative interpretation is a relation interpretation. An attempted—though failed—creative interpretation would be one that was either a relation interpretation or a different type altogether, possibly a 'clever' interpretation that was too extreme or tangentially related to the combination's constituents or context. An example of a 'clever' interpretation for *sponge table* is 'squishy, fashionable designer product' for which the receiver has to work hard to form a definition linking this interpretation to its original stimulus. And the interpretation types are characterizable in terms of the effort/effects ratio suggested by

Relevance Theory. For property interpretations the hearer, in order to understand the connection between the noun phrase and the interpretation, has to engage in a greater amount of processing effort than for relation interpretations. This is a reasonable inference from our findings and those of Gagné. However, the informational yields of the two kinds of interpretation are arguably not dissimilar—they both make sense in being transparently traceable to the constituents of the noun phrase itself, and both permit the determination of a referent for the phrase. Since the phrases were presented with no sentential context, the difference cannot lie in a better 'fit' for property interpretations to the sentential or narrative context. The question is, what justifies the acceptability to participants of engaging in the higher cognitive effort required for property interpretations? Relevance Theory would suggest that extra effort is justified by a change in some quality of the task. In this case, the information-processing task is identical; all that changes is the sex of the person by whom males are expecting their interpretations to be judged. Our suggestion, therefore, is that the extra effort is justified by the strategic nature of the communication as a display. We noted above that display communications may be ostensive communications, in that they not only communicate their overt semantic content but also communicate the claim that their overt content is worth the processing effort; we suggest that it is worth the extra effort to process precisely *because* it is a display. Since the long-term costs of selecting a poor mate are, for a female, very high indeed, there is an incentive to engage in the extra short-term effort to process a creative display communication as one means of gathering information about a potential mate. And, feeding into the co-evolutionary process, females would be correspondingly more likely to select males who have engaged in the extra cognitive effort to produce creative interpretations, since this is a less risky choice. The implication is that a display context involves a particular variant of the 'sophisticated interpretation' heuristic, which produces expectations of relevance that differ from non-display conditions: display conditions motivate the acceptance of additional effort for no obvious gain in *semantic* effects. For non-display conditions, the acceptability of the extra effort required to process a property interpretation will likely depend on specific details of the communication itself, as opposed to a generic quality of the type of communication.

The criterion for deception in creative noun phrase interpretation therefore parallels that of semantic deception. Semantic deception strictly—in Sperber's view—involves making false statements. The analogue at the level of noun phrases would likely be either reference to nonexistent entities, failure to achieve reference at all, or failure to achieve reference to a referent that plausibly falls under the denotation of the noun phrase. We have noted extreme or 'clever' instances of interpretations as falling outside of the criterion of acceptable creativity, but nonetheless appearing to be in some sense creative; such instances, as a result of their extremeness, may fail in one of the above three ways as regards establishing reference, or in bearing no reasonably transparent relation to the noun phrase itself. These are therefore interpretations for which even more extra effort is required. However, a key difference from the sentential/message level concerns the connections between display and semantic acceptability (see Table 10.1). The 'clever' cases we have considered would be a failed attempt at creativity, since the hearer's interpretive efforts would be prohibitive. Such cases parallel false semantics at the sentential level, but differ from the sentential level in the result that due to their semantic 'failure' they may thereby fail to function as an indicator of fitness. So at this sub-sentence level, there may be a closer connection between failed semantics and failed indication.

This interpretation has suggested that display may be a strategic form of communication that alters the expectations of relevance. A further question concerns the nature of the 'effects' that are derived from communications in a display context. We have noted that property and relation interpretations may not differ significantly in important semantic qualities that they communicate. However, in display settings, property interpretations may additionally communicate the creativity of the displayer; they thus carry additional non-semantic information about the communicator as indicators of mate fitness. It is not obvious precisely how such effects might relate to the characterization of effects as cognitive only, in Relevance Theory. It may be that in order to fully understand the nature of communication, a broader view of effects (and therefore the possibilities for deception) is required—one that takes account of the possibilities raised here. Another option is to consider the assessment of the costs and benefits of possible mates as proceeding in parallel with the cognitive costs and benefits of interpretation, with the latter feeding into the former; such a separate mate-choice evaluation echoes Sperber's positing of a separate logico-rhetorical checking device.

10.5 Implications and conclusions

We have suggested a role for sexual selection in influencing the creative linguistic productions of males and their assessment by females in display contexts. The metarepresentational capacities involved in deception and its detection appear to be quite general cognitive abilities, whose existence may have been a prerequisite for the evolution of language (see Whiten and Byrne 1997), and may be one of the general skills that interacted with protolanguage in the evolution of more sophisticated language skills (see Briscoe, Chapter 14). One speculation is that basic linguistic-cognitive capacities (including interpretation of noun phrases) arose via such processes of natural selection. However, the polysemy of many expressions in natural language (which itself deserves attention from an evolutionary perspective) provides an invitation to creativity. And this possibility might then have been exapted by sexual selection processes, in establishing more sophisticated and harder-to-fake displays of fitness.

We are aware, however, that we have raised many more questions than we have answered. One question arises from the likelihood that criteria for creativity vary across cultures. Our empirical results indicate a dimorphism in participants tested in Western Europe; future research would be needed to assess its extent and basis in other cultures. A second question concerns the extent to which the ideas developed here can be applied to other aspects of language and its evolution. For example, would a role for failed creativity as an indicator of deception extend beyond the phrasal level to the level of whole utterances? If so, then there is the possibility of employing the effects/effort trade-off as an empirical criterion for indicator deception at the utterance level, even if truth-telling remains the criterion for semantic deception. Third, we have focused on one type of (strategic) communication—mate display—in which the purported adaptive function differs from the widely assumed adaptive function of accurate description or truth-telling (or at least, of appearing to truth-tell). The question then is, can we isolate other such strategic communication types deriving from different adaptive functions. For example, might one postulate such a strategic adaptive function in communication with superiors and inferiors in social hierarchies (see, for instance, Mealey, Daood, and Krage 1996)? Again, might the general approach be applied to communications in a strictly competitive setting—whether intra-sex or inter-sex, and whether for material or social resources, or for mates? Would it generalize to communications in group-based interactions relating to social categories or coalition-based groupings? Each of these possibilities would involve refining or changing the expectation or criterion for relevance, as appropriate to the different types of strategic communication. These questions all relate to a broader issue which concerns the relations between the descriptive function of language and communication and other possible adaptive functions. Given that these different functions may give rise to different characterizations of deception, each with different criteria for its deployment by a speaker and its assessment by a hearer, there is the suggestion of a very complex pattern both in terms of evolutionary sequence and current processing, which we have only begun to investigate.

ACKNOWLEDGEMENTS

We are very grateful to Maggie Tallerman and two reviewers for very constructive comments on an earlier version of this chapter.

FURTHER READING

On concepts and concept combination, see Franks (1995). On relation-based versus property-based combinations, see Gagné (2000). On sexual selection, see Kodric-Brown and Brown (1984) and Miller (2000). For views of semantic deception and evolution, see Sperber (2000).

PART III

Analogous and homologous traits: What can we learn from other species?

Introduction to Part III: The broadening scope of animal communication research

ALISON WRAY

Pinning down precisely what it is that makes human language special has never been so difficult. It's not that we no longer regard it as special, but almost every time you think you have a feature that helps define the real essence of language, or that provides a necessary context for its emergence, you seem to find some other animal that has it as well. It's happened with sequential planning (e.g. Terrace 2002), aspects of Theory of Mind (Dunbar 2004; Tomasello and Camaioni 1997), naming (Savage-Rumbaugh, Shanker, and Taylor 1998; Kaminski, Call, and Fischer 2004), displaced reference (von Frisch 1993), structural recursion (Okanoya 2002), and, in the chapters in this section, arbitrariness and 'grammar'—in the limited sense of one signal modifying the meaning of another (Zuberbühler), and speech and semantics (Pepperberg). Overall, the broadening of the scope of animal communication research away from what Beck (1982) termed *chimpocentrism* is making a considerable impact on how we perceive our own communication relative to that in other species.

Nevertheless, as far as we can tell, human language is (still) the most sophisticated and flexible natural mode of communication found on the planet. What is changing is the basis upon which the assertion is made. Historically, it was built upon a 'tick list' approach (e.g. Hockett 1960: 10–11) that pinpointed major qualitative differences between animal systems and our own. One of these differences, productivity—that is, our capacity to use a finite system to create an infinite number of new meaningful messages—remains resilient (Hauser, Chomsky, and Fitch 2002; Fitch and Hauser 2004.). More generally, however, the idea that human language primarily displays differences in *type* is increasingly counterbalanced by two rather more messy notions.

One is that of differences in the *quantity* and *complexity* of design features. Darwin (1871/1971) said of the mind that 'the difference ... between man and the higher animals, great as it is, certainly is one of degree and not of kind' (p. 126). The same seems to be true of aspects of the language package: an animal species may be found to do a version of something that we do, but to a lesser extent, or without combining it with something else that we do.

The other departure from tidy taxonomies relates to the capacity for a species to achieve a particular function that we also achieve, but using quite different mechanisms from our own. Different species facing the same communicative challenges—expressing solidarity, or informing others about a threat, say—may find different solutions, equally effective but sometimes so unlike our own that we take a while to notice what they are. Lest this seem irrelevant to the question of whether or not a given species has something that is at all language-like, it is worth considering that language-like solutions are often the expensive option, and might reasonably be dispreferred where something cheaper will do just as well. If so, we might find that not all animal species are wearing their full 'linguistic' potential on their sleeves: some may actually possess rather more of the prerequisites for language than they have cause to use in their natural environment.

Ascertaining whether this is the case can only be partly achieved by observing animals communicating with each other, and so it is that there are now two major branches of research into animal communication. One, illustrated by Zuberbühler's chapter, focuses on how a species achieves certain communicative functions in the wild. The other, illustrated by Pepperberg's chapter, explores the potential for a species to display additional capabilities when challenged to communicate with humans.

Twenty years ago, every undergraduate knew that however impressively a parrot may be able to recite a nursery rhyme or call itself a pretty boy, this was mere parroting. Owners who insisted that their bird was not quite such a birdbrain were treated with the indulgent scorn that is reserved for all who anthropomorphize their pets. There are some, still, who doubt that parrots are engaged in anything at all sophisticated or language-like, but the evidence from Pepperberg, in particular, deserves to be fully evaluated before it is written off so lightly. The feats of Alex and Griffin are reported to include 'label acquisition, categorization, numerical competence, relative size, conjunction [and] recursion' (Pepperberg, Chapter 11; see also the more speculative N'kisi project, <http://www.sheldrake.org/nkisi/nkisi1_text.html>. Parrots cannot pick up any of these skills without a lot of training, but, of course, training can only harness a natural potential, and this potential is usually unknown in a species until training is attempted and found to work.

Faced with the somewhat unnatural task of attempting to exchange messages with humans, species seem to vary in the balance that they can achieve between comprehension and production. Pepperberg appears to offer only relatively simple input to her parrots, to which they can respond appropriately, suggesting that there is not too much of a gap between what they understand and what they can say. In contrast, there is a huge disparity in Savage-Rumbaugh's bonobos. Bonobos appear—though again only after training (Williams, Brakke, and Savage-Rumbaugh 1997)—to be capable of understanding, in tests, a large number of nouns within an array of grammatical structures (Brakke and Savage-Rumbaugh 1995), plus, if the anecdotal and television evidence is to believed, casual spoken utterances of a much wider variety (Savage-Rumbaugh et al. 1998). Yet they produce very few word combinations of any kind, let alone grammatical configurations (e.g. Brakke and Savage-Rumbaugh 1996).

Human language is a particularly flexible tool for communication, but at times it seems to be too productive for the good of its users: when it is a question of pure survival, we strip away much of what makes it most different from other communication systems. There are two possible explanations for why humans might have evolved a communication system that is as disadvantageous in some circumstances as it is advantageous in others (e.g. Lightfoot 2000: 244). One is that natural and/or sexual selection do in fact favour those with the 'advanced' skills of eloquence and novel expression (see Franks and Rigby, Chapter 10), because they permit a range of social behaviours that are discriminatory in non-emergency situations. The other is that natural and sexual selection simply do not *dis*prefer those skills: so long as we know when to elaborate and when to stick to the basics—that is, so long as our general and pragmatic intelligence can guide our use of language; and so long as we can balance our complex grammatical processing with less effortful alternatives when necessary—we can avoid the worst effects of a suite of abilities that we inherited by accident, as a by-product of something else (Lightfoot 2000: 245).

Insights that could help us to choose between these two possibilities might come from many sources, including Zuberbühler's chapter (Chapter 12). Campbell's and Diana monkeys appear to engage in a measure of what might be generously termed 'grammatical processing'. It is considerably simpler than human grammar: one sound, a pair of low-pitched 'booms', modifies another sound, an alarm call, resulting in a reduction in the potency of the latter as a warning. However, even such a simple 'grammar' crosses the Rubicon: the inherent structure of the system imposes potential limitations on the efficacy of the messages it generates. Specifically, unlike the alarm calls of other species, which always mean something like 'beware of the (particular) predator', in a call system in which boom-alarm is also possible, the meaning of the alarm call is no longer fixed: you cannot determine its meaning without taking into account the presence or absence of another signal. How does a species come to cross this Rubicon? It is not at all evident just what advantage there is to adopting such 'grammar'. It does not apparently furnish any opportunity for novelty, for instance.

Meanwhile, if the boom-alarm sequence is a low-level warning about a particular predator or other danger, we can surmise that it necessarily creates uncertainty: during the thirty second wait between the two components, the hearer does not know what sort of danger it is that is only moderately present. Furthermore, the boom-alarm does not allow for there to be a change in the threat level in the middle of the message. If you have just made a public announcement that you are going to test the fire alarm, it is not a good time to discover a real fire. If the Campbell's alarm call were modified by pitch or volume instead, then the modified message would be delivered as a single event, avoiding the serial expectation. Indeed, why use a boom to modify a necessarily potent signal at all, rather than developing a separate 'yellow alert' call?

The boom-alarm call does not seem to be a particularly elegant solution to the problem of how to warn of a low-level threat. Other animals use less sophisticated means, which seem at least as effective, if not more so. The issue is complicated by the existence of different possible interpretations of the calls, in isolation and together. Zuberbühler identifies two different functions for the isolated alarm calls: they warn conspecifics (and Diana monkeys) about the predator, and they inform the predator that it has been seen. It is impossible to determine which is the primary function of the call (Zuberbühler, personal communication), but if it is the latter, then it is not only the Diana monkeys that are eavesdropping on the male

Campbell's monkey's alarm call: the other Campbell's monkeys, when they react with their own alarm call, are also responding to something that was not intended primarily for their ears, but for those of the predator. This may seem an unnecessarily nice point, but it is of some potential relevance when interpreting the boom-alarm sequence.

Zuberbühler offers three interpretations of the boom-alarm message: (a) the boom informs conspecifics that there is a distant threat, and then specifies its nature; (b) the boom informs conspecifics that the caller is about to warn off a predator but that the predator is distant; (c) the boom informs conspecifics that the caller is engaging in sexual display behaviour that includes an alarm call that is not a response to a predator. The potential difficulties of scenario (a) have already been noted. In scenario (b) the two calls are actually addressed to different species: the boom to the conspecifics and the alarm call to the predator. This makes it somewhat more difficult to depict the relationship as 'grammatical' at the primary level. The modification resides at the secondary level: the boom is telling the conspecifics not to pay attention to the coming message to the predator. Scenario (c), almost certainly a later exaptation (Zuberbühler, personal communication), is the clearest case of real modification, because the alarm call is entirely bleached of meaning. But here, as in (a), the strategy is a risky one, relative to other potential options that never give an alarm call without really meaning it.

Pepperberg (Chapter 11) proposes that the boom-alarm compound is not a modifying relation at all, and the monkeys are simply 'respond[ing] associatively to the compound as an unanalysed whole, without learning rules of formation'. Interpreting the boom-alarm as holistic essentially relegates it to the status of an etymological relic: some particularly clever individual must have invented the 'grammar' but everyone since then has just learned the combinations without understanding why they have the form they do. Despite the appeal of a holistic explanation, there is something rather perverse about it here. A holistic message that just happens to contain a component that is identical to a primary predator alarm call is going to be rather problematic if you *don't* understand what the boom is doing to the meaning. The point of an alarm call is to incite an immediate reaction, so it is not going to be helpful to have it featuring in something else unless you are engaged in the active processing necessary to suppress the normal response. It would be rather like naming your child *Harry FIRE! Jones*.

Perhaps complexity develops in communication as an annexe, to be drawn on in particular environmental conditions but suppressed in others. If so, then the capacity of any species for complex communication needs to be defined not as an absolute, but as a range that spans all environments capable of challenging that species in different ways. The same applies to humans. We may be mistaken in measuring our linguistic capabilities *only* with reference to the ways that language is used in literate westernized societies.

The exploration of any species' communicative abilities needs to be multifaceted. Two approaches have been discussed here: communication in the natural environment, and the potential for enhanced communication in an inter-species communicative environment. Increasingly now, however, there is scope for new developments in a third direction: comparisons across species. Such comparisons are already encouraged in relation to straight studies of social cognition, but some interesting challenges exist in comparing different species attempting to communicate with humans (e.g. Brakke and Savage-Rumbaugh 1995, 1996). Are there features of language that are consistently mastered, while others are not? Or are the achievements of any given species a unique combination of different subcomponents of the human language package? A more difficult question might be whether we prejudice the answers to the first two questions by virtue of assumptions that we make about what constitutes a feature or subcomponent of language.

The apparent differences between parrots and bonobos in matching production complexity to comprehension complexity have already been noted. Other issues that might usefully be explored include:

1. Which animals can and cannot engage in turn-taking, that first and apparently most basic achievement of the human infant? Many pet-owners believe that their dogs, cats, and budgerigars can play the game of alternate noise exchange. If so, is it a trait selected for in domesticated creatures, as a potent marker of 'genuine' communication? How extensive is the capacity for turn-taking in undomesticated creatures when they attempt to communicate with humans, and why?

2. Which animals other than dogs, the large primates, dolphins, and parrots can learn to associate a thing or action with a word? Whether or not this skill is considered to constitute a 'naming insight', is it simply an

index of general intelligence? Why does it keep cropping up in species that don't apparently need to name anything for themselves?

3. Is it generally true that, naming notwithstanding, accumulating a large vocabulary is not all that easy for an animal? If so, why? Are we right to compare the training and practice entailed in teaching animals new words with that required by a human infant rather than, for instance, by a human adult in a second-language classroom?

There has always been a long way to go in learning about how other animals communicate, but recent research has opened up new horizons. We may not ever attain a full picture of what is going on, but there is certainly plenty of scope for deepening our understanding.

11 An avian perspective on language evolution: implications of simultaneous development of vocal and physical object combinations by a Grey parrot (*Psittacus erithacus*)

IRENE MAXINE PEPPERBERG

11.1 Introduction

Although direct connections between avian and human communication systems are unlikely—other than for the Bwiti tribe, who claim Grey parrots brought language to humans as a gift from the gods (Fernandez 1982)—language evolution studies previously included avian models. Parallels between birdsong and human language (for instance, issues of adequate input, presence of babbling or practice periods, learning appropriate context for specific vocalizations; Byers and Kroodsma 1992; Marler 1970, 1973; Nottebohm 1970), however, are no longer considered central to such studies; similarly, laboratory-based avian communicatory achievements (e.g. Pepperberg 1999) may be considered artifactual. But, given our knowledge of avian vocal learning, how social interaction affects such learning, and of birds' advanced cognition (see Pepperberg 1999, 2001), we should not ignore *Aves* in determining the evolutionary pressures that affected how complex communication—particularly vocal learning—arose, and in developing testable theories and models.

Given that parrots' referential use of English speech and complex cognitive capacities likely represent traits that are analogous rather than homologous to those of humans, I argue not that avian abilities are precursors to human language, but rather that certain linguistically relevant cognitive abilities common to humans and parrots are significant for the evolution of complex communication, and that necessary neural substrates for behavioural precursors to language can evolve in any reasonably complex vertebrate brain, given the right socio-ecological selection pressures. Specifically, parrots likely acquire elements of human communication that can be mapped or adapted to their code; by observing what is (or is not) acquired, how certain elements are acquired, and by looking for commonalities in human and avian evolutionary histories, we may uncover the very basic building blocks of language.

11.2 Background: Grey parrot cognitive and communicative abilities

Although phylogenetically remote, Grey parrots and humans share several cognitive and communicative abilities. Greys learn simple vocal syntactic patterns and referential elements of human communication; and, despite walnut-sized brains organized differently from those of primates and even songbirds (Jarvis and Mello 2000; Striedter 1994; but see Jarvis 2004), their processing abilities and learning strategies on certain tasks (e.g. label acquisition, categorization, numerical competence, relative size, conjunction, recursion) may parallel those of children (Pepperberg 1999; Pepperberg and Shive 2001; Pepperberg and Wilcox 2000). Our oldest subject, Alex, labels over fifty objects and has functional use of 'no' and phrases such as 'come here', 'I want X' and 'Wanna go Y' (X and Y are appropriate object or location labels; Pepperberg 1999). Trainers' incorrect responses to his requests (e.g. substituting something other than that requested) generally result in his saying 'No' and repeating the request (Pepperberg 1987a, 1988a). He identifies seven colours, five shapes (as 'two-', 'three-', 'four-', 'five-', or 'six-corner'; Pepperberg 1983), and uses labels 'two', 'three', 'four', 'five', and 'six' to distinguish quantities of objects, including collections made of novel, randomly placed items and heterogeneous sets (Pepperberg 1987b, 1994). He comprehends the concept of 'category', responding to 'What colour?' or 'What shape?' in addition to 'What matter?' for objects having both colour and shape (Pepperberg 1983). Alex understands abstract concepts of *same/different*, and responds to the *absence* of information about these concepts. Thus, given two objects that vary with respect to none, some, or all of the attributes of colour, shape, and material, he responds with the appropriate *category* label as to which attribute is *same* or *different*, or 'none' if nothing is same or different (Pepperberg 1987c, 1988b). He responds accurately for novel objects, colours, shapes, and materials, including those he cannot label. Using attribute labels, he designates which of two objects is bigger or smaller, and without training, indicates when exemplars did not differ in size by responding 'none' (Pepperberg and Brezinsky 1991). He understands recursive, conjunctive questions: given various collections of coloured, shaped objects of different materials, he can answer a series of queries such as 'What object is green and three-corner?', 'What shape is blue and wood?', and 'What colour is wool and four-corner?' (Pepperberg 1990, 1992). Because all question types are equally likely and each requires sequential processing, such data demonstrate at least comprehension of concepts previously thought limited to humans (Hauser et al. 2002). Alex combines vocal labels to identify proficiently, request, refuse, categorize, and quantify over 100 objects, including those varying somewhat from training exemplars; his accuracy is ~80 per cent. Additional parrots have now demonstrated some of these capacities (Pepperberg 1999).

Other Grey parrot vocal behaviour intriguingly parallels that of humans. Like humans, Grey parrots use sound play (phonetic 'babbling' and recombination) to produce new speech patterns from existent ones (Pepperberg 1999), implying that their acoustic representations of labels are similar to those of humans, and also implying that they develop phonetic categories. Alex's spontaneous novel phonemic combinations often occurred socially outside of testing and training (Pepperberg 1990); juvenile Greys behave similarly (e.g. Neal 1996). These vocalizations were rarely, if ever, used by trainers but resembled both existing labels and separate human vocalizations—for example, 'grain' from 'grey'. Here trainers mapped the novel utterance to an existent item by giving Alex seed (not normally available), talking about and identifying 'grain' for one another; later we used sprouted legumes. Alex received joined paper clips for 'chain', appropriate fruit for 'grape', and wire mesh (later a nutmeg grater) after uttering 'grate'. 'Cup' (from 'up') was mapped to metal cups and plastic mugs, 'copper' (first produced as 'cupper') to pennies, and 'block' to cubical wooden beads. 'Chalk' (from 'talk') was mapped to coloured blackboard chalk; 'truck' to toy cars and trucks. Thus, when we *referentially mapped* spontaneous utterances, Alex rapidly integrated these labels into his repertoire, subsequently using them routinely to identify or request appropriate items (Pepperberg 1990). Other behaviour suggests that parrots view their labels as made of elements that can be recombined in novel ways, independent of meaning, to respond to novel situations, and that they transfer such use across contexts (Pepperberg 1999). Thus, although parrots usually need about twenty training sessions to acquire a new label, those such as 'carrot' that combine elements already in their repertoire (/k/ from 'key', '-arrot' from 'parrot') can arise after one session (Pepperberg 1999). Recently, Alex's first 'spool' attempts were 's-wool' (/s/ from work on phonemes, 'wool' for woollen materials), from which he later developed 'spool'. A younger parrot, Griffin (the main subject of this chapter), still produces 's-wool'.

Importantly, Alex's combinations suggest that he abstracts rules for the beginnings and endings of utterances. Analyses of over 22,000 English vocalizations yielded no 'backwards' combinations (e.g. 'percup' rather than 'cupper', Pepperberg et al. 1991, although our transcriptions are subjective). His behaviour, and that of our other parrots, thus implies (but cannot prove) that these birds parse human sound streams in human-like ways, acoustically represent labels as do humans, and have similar phonetic categories (Patterson and Pepperberg 1994, 1998). Such behaviour did not likely arise from instruction, suggesting a cognitive architecture analogous to that of humans. Such performance may be integral to development and, because it occurs across species, suggests an evolutionary theory of language play (Kuczaj 1998).

Additional data (e.g. from X-ray video, Warren et al. 1996) suggest that our birds use 'anticipatory coarticulation', setting the vocal tract for the next speech sound as the previous one is completed. Thus, Alex apparently separates specific phonemes from speech flow *and* produces them so as to facilitate production of upcoming phonemes (for example, his /k/ in 'key' differs from that in 'cork', Patterson and Pepperberg 1998). In humans, these abilities together with sound play are considered evidence for *top-down processing* (Ladefoged 1982).

Grey parrot social behaviour also is interesting. Captive Grey parrots learn from each other (Pepperberg et al. 2000), and although extrapolating natural behaviour from New World and Asian to Old World species is risky, if Greys resemble other parrots, they likely establish strong pair-bonds, recognize individuals, have vocal sentinel behaviour, complex pair-bond duets, dialects, and alter calls when changing dialect areas (see Pepperberg forthcoming a). Long-lived animals, they reside in large groups whose social complexity may match that of primates.

The above data suggest that parrots can provide insights into the evolution of cognition and communication. Parallels with human children's sound play, referential mapping, learning strategies, and cognitive competence have been presented previously (see Pepperberg 1999) and summarized above; here I will emphasize the simultaneous emergence of both vocal and physical hierarchical combinations in Grey parrots, behaviour once considered exclusive to primates and central to human language evolution (e.g. Greenfield 1991; Johnson-Pynn et al. 1999). I also present some neurobiological data and suppositions related to the issues involved.

11.3 Combinatory behaviour: an issue in language evolution and development

11.3.1 *Rationale*

Researchers emphasize the development of present-day non-human primate social and cognitive skills which could be precursors of human abilities—including language—as their basis for evolutionary theories. A common ancestor for non-human primates and humans is undeniable, as are many neurological, anatomical, and resultant behavioural parallels (e.g. Deacon 1997), but such an argument has limitations. Various evolutionary pressures and exploitation of different ecological niches may cause similar abilities to evolve differently; some lineages may have lost some abilities. I question researchers' emphases on primate-centric neurology and neuroanatomy as the bases for certain abilities, because comparable skills and patterns exist in avian and cetacean lines (e.g. Bednarz 1988; Evans 1987; Forestell and Herman 1988; Hulse et al. 1984; Stoddard et al. 1991), that is, in creatures with different evolutionary histories and brains wired differently from those of humans (e.g. McFarland and Morgane 1966; Morgane et al. 1986; Nottebohm 1980; Striedter 1994). Thus, we may miss insights into the evolutionary pressures exerted in the development of complex cognitive and communicative processes—particularly vocal behaviour—by focusing on primates. The study of combinatory behaviour provides one such caution.

Young children almost simultaneously acquire the ability to combine objects (e.g. spoon-into-cup) and phonological/grammatical units (for instance, the 'more+X' type of emergent syntax; Greenfield et al. 1972).

Greenfield (1991) posited that control of such parallel development initially resides in a single neural structure (roughly Broca's area) that differentiates, as a child's brain matures, into specialized areas for, respectively, language versus physical combinations; she also at first suggested that such competence was a critical issue in language (i.e. human) development. Subsequent research on both physical combinatorial behaviour in non-human primates (Johnson-Pynn et al. 1999) and combinatorial communicative acts by 'language'-trained chimpanzees (*Pan paniscus, P. troglodytes*) (Greenfield and Savage-Rumbaugh 1990, 1991) showed that apes' combinations of physical objects, as well as their labels (e.g. 'more tickle') are similar to, if simpler than, those of young children. Greenfield (1991) then proposed that non-human primate behaviour derives from a homologous structure predating the evolutionary divergence of apes and hominids (see Deacon 1992).

Greenfield (1991) further argued for uniquely primate cognitive connections among seriation (hierarchical) tasks, all rule-governed behaviour, and possibly language. Simple seriation—putting smaller into bigger objects—demonstrates elementary knowledge of ordinality and may relate to grammatical constructs (e.g. 'Want X'; Greenfield 1991). More complex forms—e.g. putting C into B, then manipulating the unit into A, showing knowledge that B is smaller than A and larger than C—requires awareness of multiple, two-way relationships underlying other advanced abilities (e.g. transitive inference, Delius and Siemann 1998). Greenfield (1991) claimed that such advanced knowledge is required for appropriate phoneme or word combinations (e.g. respectively, 'd' plus 'a' for 'da' then 'dada'; 'Want more X')—rudiments of language and, ultimately, syntax. Such arguments support proposals (e.g. Hewes 1973) that spoken language derived from gestural forms without major neural restructuring. One might conclude that parallel development of communicative/physical combinatorial acts controlled by a purported single neural centre, if not unique to humans, is unique to primates.

Interestingly, although monkeys do not demonstrate spontaneous hierarchical manual combinations (Greenfield 1991), evidence for the posited requisite brain structures first came from monkeys (brain area F5: Deacon 1992; Rizzolatti and Arbib 1998), and limited hierarchical combinatory activity, both physical and vocal (e.g. $A_i + B_j$), has been observed or trained in rhesus and capuchins (Johnson-Pynn et al. 1999; Robinson 1984; Shaofu et al. 1997; Westergaard and Suomi 1993, 1994). Hierarchical combinatorial activity thus might be evolutionarily older than first posited, but the fact that monkeys need training in human-based actions (serial cup insertion, Johnson-Pynn et al. 1999) could mean that their behaviour involves different mechanisms and/or neural centres from those of apes or humans. But are vocal and physical hierarchical abilities—and responsible neural substrates—limited to creatures phylogenetically close to humans? Demonstration of spontaneously co-occurring vocal and physical combinatory behaviour in *Aves* would be evolutionarily interesting: if similar actions arose in birds, with minimal or no training, researchers might posit convergent brain evolution (i.e. that similar socio-ecological pressures shaped different brains in similar ways), or an unexpected ancestral common neural structure, or that such structures were indeed requisite for complex communication—not just language.

Few investigations of spontaneous object manipulation include birds (e.g. Huber et al. 1997), and only one study (Pepperberg and Shive 2001) examines co-occurrence of avian vocal and physical hierarchical combinations. Our project began after observing spontaneous two-object combinations by a Grey parrot, Griffin, when he was routinely combining two human vocal labels. During initial label acquisition, our parrots act like very young children, moving through analogous early stages of sound and label production and combination (Pepperberg 1999; Pepperberg and Wilcox 2000). Thus, whatever neural structures are involved, simple (two-item) parallel physical and vocal combinatory behaviour is not limited to primates. Moreover, if certain avian and mammalian brain structures are homologous, not analogous (Medina and Reiner 2000; Jarvis 2004), brain areas underlying combinatory actions might predate the primate line. Although unable to examine neural mechanisms, we began, in June 1999, to examine the nature, extent, and time lines for Griffin's development of advanced physical and vocal combinations.

11.3.2 *Subject and procedures for examining parrot combinatory behaviour (from Pepperberg and Shive 2001)*

Griffin, a male Grey parrot, had never been trained on object or label combinations, nor had he observed humans stacking items used in the study. He was being taught single labels (for objects, colours), and also to clarify existing labels. He heard 'want X' and 'wanna go Y' (X and Y, respectively, were item or location labels) from another Grey parrot, Alex (e.g. Pepperberg 1999) and in students' queries, but received no formal drills or tests on such phrases. He routinely uttered 'want X' and 'wanna go-back' (*go back* sounded like 'g-back') and also some untrained colour-object combinations. Observations occurred on a laboratory counter-top where he spent most of each day; food and water were available at one end. In July 1999, a month after his first (and for sometime thereafter only) successful three-object combination, we began training shape labels 'x-corner' (x = two and five for regular polygons) along with material labels; a pine pentagon thus was 'five-corner wood'. The live-tutoring Model/ Rival (M/R) procedure for label acquisition, in which two humans demonstrate functional and referential use of the targeted label, was adapted from Todt (1975). In this procedure, the parrot initially observes two humans interacting, handling and speaking about one or more objects in which the bird has previously demonstrated interest. As the parrot watches and listens, one trainer presents objects and queries the other trainer about them, with such expressions as 'What's here?', 'What colour?', giving praise and transferring the named object to the human partner to reward correct answers. Incorrect responses are punished by scolding and by temporarily removing items from sight. Thus the second human is both a model for the parrot's responses and its rival for the trainer's attention, and illustrates consequences of errors. Humans reverse roles, and parrots are included in interactions (details in Pepperberg 1999).

Given appropriate opportunity, would Griffin simultaneously exhibit more complex vocal combinations and spontaneous physical object combinations? We recorded Griffin's vocal combinations outside of training[1] (while alone or in the presence of another parrot) so as to document spontaneous use (Pepperberg and Shive 2001).We calculated percentages of two- and three-label combinations from each recorded session; we report highest and lowest values overall. Griffin generally performed object combinations silently; thus, utterances occurred outside such sessions although physical combinatory sessions and vocal taping sessions could occur on the same day.

---

[1] All our Greys engage in sound play (review in Pepperberg 1999), most often when solitary (monologue speech) but sometimes when humans are present.

To examine combinatory object behaviour, we used coloured plastic or metal bottle caps and jar lids which could be nested and which Griffin had previously manipulated (Pepperberg and Shive 2001). During a trial, objects were designated small, medium, and large, but what was, for example, medium-sized in one trial could be large-sized in another. Initially Griffin received three objects; seven later trials (one per test session) involved four items. We randomly placed items simultaneously on his counter, then recorded his behaviour. Unlike subjects in previous studies (e.g. Johnson-Pynn et al. 1999), he never observed humans combine or manipulate items and never received rewards for his actions; we observed spontaneous behaviour. If he tossed items off the counter we ended the trial; we continued replacing items and recording behaviour until he engaged in another activity (e.g. eating, preening). If substituting new items at that point did not cause him to re-engage, we ended the session. Thus his interest dictated the number of trials, and the length of each trial and of each session. He received fifty sessions so he would not habituate to the items or view the task as a chore. We manually recorded all actions on all trials; we videotaped a proportion of trials, transcribed them, and tested for inter-observer reliability.

Following Greenfield et al.'s (1972) and Johnson-Pynn et al.'s (1999) studies on, respectively, children and non-human primates, we noted whether and how many times Griffin used various combinatorial strategies: (a) paired two objects (pair), (b) put two items successively into the third or placed a third onto a pair (pot assembly), and (c) put two objects as a unit into a third (subassembly). We separately classified picking up versus further manipulating paired items as a unit. 'Attempts' were any combinatory efforts. An assembly staying together was a success; an unstable assembly (pieces did not fit or stay together) was a failure. We tallied several of Griffin's behaviour patterns: (a) when he, like apes and *Cebus*, but unlike children in Greenfield's (1991) study, dismantled paired units during a trial or tossed units off his counter; (b) whether he combined units out-of-order (i.e. tried putting middle-sized caps onto or into combinations of large and small ones); and (c) any other multiple object manipulations. These data, including actions which Greenfield (1991) did not directly discuss for either children or non-human primates, highlight Griffin's dexterity with objects and his approach to object combination.

11.3.3 *Results of object and label combinations*

Using his beak, Griffin consistently combined two out of three objects (e.g. placed one inside or over another; put two side-by-side and lifted them together), but rarely three (Pepperberg and Shive 2001; Table 11.1). In 233 attempts, he had 217 successful pairings (93 per cent; binomial test, $p \ll .001$). In ~65 per cent of trials (141 trials, binomial test, $p < .05$), he picked pairs up in his beak, carried them around, threw them off the counter, or, with his beak, flipped the internal object over. Only 38 per cent of successful pairings were not serial. Successful potting was rare (seven times; 3 per cent of total attempts, 58 per cent of potting attempts), but his first (and for several months only) success was in the first month of the study. He did not succeed at subassembly, but attempts occurred as he began spontaneously uttering three-label combinations (late February–early March 2000, Figure 11.1). Some subassembly efforts are described in Pepperberg and Shive (2001).

On seven trials with four items, he always combined two (e.g. put smallest in biggest or next-to-biggest) and tried but failed at four further combinations; he picked up and threw each of these units or took them apart to recombine them successively (e.g. removed and replaced the internal object, or removed the internal object then covered it with a larger one, a physically easier task). Failures seemed to occur not

TABLE 11.1 *Griffin's data for combining objects (6/99-5/00).*

Method	Attempts[a]	Successes[b]	Pick up as unit only[c]	Unit thrown[d]	Unit manipulated[e]
Pairing	233	217	74	38	29
Pot	12	7			
Subassembly	6	0			

[a]We scored an attempt as any effort made to place one object on top of or in another; thus Griffin had sixteen failures. His overall number of trials was 251; 244 of these were with three objects.
[b]We scored a success as a stable assembly, i.e. in which pieces fitted and stayed together.
[c]Here Griffin picked up and put down a successful assembly; he then did not further manipulate the assembly.
[d]Here Griffin tossed the successful assembly off the counter.
[e]Any manipulation of the assembly not described in the other two categories such as destruction of the assembly; includes seven trials in which he lifted and set down a two-unit construction without throwing it after additional manipulations (e.g. flipping the internal cap over while it was inside the external cap).

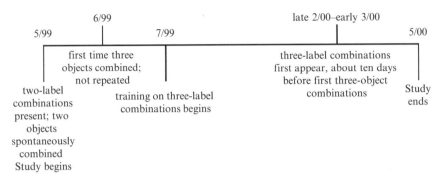

Fɪɢ. 11.1 Timeline for vocal and object combinations (source: Pepperberg and Shive 2001).

because he lacked an understanding of seriation, but because he lacked dexterity in manipulating the objects: most attempts were correct but unsuccessful.[2]

Other object manipulations (Table 11.2) replicated those which Greenfield (1991) described for children and non-human primates. Griffin moved objects together, banged them against his perch, or placed two objects sequentially or simultaneously (i.e. as a pair) inside a plastic ring. Applying the same action to successive objects (e.g. banging two caps sequentially, an act seen in six-month-old children; Langer 1986) occurred every session. Many acts observed in children (e.g. simultaneously picking up two objects independently) are either prohibited or made difficult by parrot anatomy, but Griffin often simultaneously picked up two objects with sides touching. He demonstrated transformational acts (e.g. placing a cap into a ring transforms the latter into a receptacle) and combinatorial acts (e.g. fitting a ring inside a cap) which parallel the behaviour of somewhat older children (Langer 1986) and relate to specific combinations of caps and lids that we studied.

Griffin's frequency of spontaneous label combinations paralleled his physical combinations (Table 11.3). Two-label combinations occurred more often (61–93 per cent of the time) than single labels; three-label

---

[2] Note that Griffin is like most Grey parrots, though unlike other psittacids, in not generally using his feet to manipulate objects. Grey parrots will use their feet to hold an item they are eating or chewing, but will first pick the item up with their beaks, then transfer it to their feet. Whether foot use would have imparted additional physical dexterity is unclear.

TABLE 11.2 *Combinations involving other objects (6/99-5/00).*

Objects	Description of action
Large cap, perch	Cap fitted over perch end
Small and medium caps	Picked up side-by-side
Small and large caps	Picked up side-by-side
Small cap, piece of food	Cap placed over food
Ring, large cap	Ring placed in large cap, picked up, manipulated
Medium cap, paper bag	Cap removed from bag by tilting end upward
Ring, medium cap	Ring fitted inside cap
Small cap, spoon	Cap and spoon picked up as unit
Water bottle top with spout	Spout removed, attempted to rejoin
Ring, medium cap	Cap wedged sideways in centre of ring
Large cap, soda bottle	Balancing cap on soda bottle

combinations were rare (6–10 per cent of the time).[3] Most two-label combinations (91–93 per cent) were clearly hierarchical (e.g. 'want+X', 'wanna+X'); others (e.g. 'green+X') might be termed so. Inter-observer reliability was ~85 per cent; most disagreements involved phonetically similar single labels, not the level of combination (Pepperberg and Shive 2001). Of two-label combinations, only two (8.7 per cent), 'walnut grape' and 'wanna chair', could be termed nonsensical, although the first might be a request for two items (NB: our birds lack 'and') and the second, a failed 'wanna go chair'. Of three-label combinations, again only two (13 per cent), 'cork nut shower' and 'do you wanna nut grape?' might be termed nonsensical, but only by assuming these are not multiple-item requests. Three-label combinations began late February 2000, after eight months of exposure, and were rarely those trained.

Greenfield (1991) also considered children's phonemic combinations as relevant to seriation and syntactic development. She argues that, for example, 'kye-bye' (which she interprets as 'car bye-bye') is pot-like—two different consonants combined with a common vowel—and that 'ball' is a

---

[3] The number of vocalizations varied dramatically across sessions; thus an absolute number of pairings would not provide relevant information.

TABLE 11.3 *Examples of label combinations (6/99-5/00); each was transcribed at least once.*

Two-label combinations	Three- or more label combinations
want pa[a]	want pop corn[b]
want walnut	want corn nut
want cork	want grain nut
want ring	want cork nut
want grape	want a nut
want grain	wanna cork nut
want corner	wanna corn nut
wanna come-here?[c]	want some corn(er)
wanna go-back[c]	two-corner wood
wanna chair	cork nut shower
go back	go back chair
go chair	do you wanna grate?[d]
here corn	do you want grape?
cork nut (an almond)	you wanna go-back?[c]
walnut grape	you wanna nut grape
what's here?	
five corner	
green corner	
green nut	
green beeper	
green water	
green wool	
green birdie	

[a]'Pa' is Griffin's term for pasta.

[b]Griffin was likely to have heard this utterance from Alex, but was not trained to produce it. Although we cannot prove that the parrot understands that popcorn is a form of corn, the similarity in taste between the two items would suggest that such is the case. An additional utterance like 'want pop cork', which would provide additional linguistic evidence for three-item combinations, would make little referential sense and thus its absence is not surprising. We provided particular different foods for 'corn nut' and 'cork nut'.

[c]'Come-here' and 'go-back' seem to function as single units, i.e. unanalysed wholes.

[d]'Grate' is a nutmeg grater.

TABLE 11.4 *Examples of phoneme recombinations (6/99–5/00).*

green/bean (also related to beeper)
paper/baper/beeper/neeper/greeper
corn/cork
here/chair (pronounced 'chere')/cor-neer
hello/yellow
walnut/walcork
grape/grate/grain (also related to green)
rock/brock

Note: These are examples of combinations that Griffin spontaneously produced when not in training or testing situations, and in the absence of his human companions. Some of these (e.g. 'brock') may have arisen as a consequence of training a related label (e.g. 'block'). Others, if repeated in the presence of a trainer, were referentially mapped to an appropriate object (e.g. 'grain'). Some, like 'greeper', were tallied but ignored if subsequently repeated.

subassembly of 'ba' ('b'+'a') and the consonant 'l'. (NB: Cheremic combinations in signing apes must be examined for comparison with other primates.) Griffin's common phonemic recombinations (e.g. cork/corn) predated this study, but others (e.g. 'beeper' from paper, green, and /b/) occurred in early 2000 (Table 11.4). Given the above examples, Greenfield (1991) would likely consider 'Want corn', 'Want cork' as three-element combinations (want+cor+n/k) involving serial knowledge. Even if phonemic combinations are less important than those involving labels with respect to seriation and syntactic development, such combinations represent serial knowledge, because we never encountered misorderings (e.g. 'perbee' from 'beeper') by Griffin (or any other parrot, see above). That is, Griffin, like Alex, appeared to understand appropriate and inappropriate phoneme order. Note that, just as for Alex, labels formed from phonemes or other utterances already in Griffin's repertoire were learned far more quickly than those containing novel sounds, and initially meaningless combinations could efficiently be referentially mapped.

11.4 Discussion: the relevance of combinatory behaviour

Correlated emergence of physical object and label combination is not restricted to primates. Two-item and -label combinations predated this study, but we documented a parrot's almost simultaneous three-item and

-label combinations. Note that: (a) percentages of physical and vocal combinations roughly match; (b) despite months of training on *x-corner wood/paper*, vocal three-item combinations emerged only when Griffin began combining three objects; (c) vocal combinations were rarely those trained; and (d) physical combinations were performed with his beak/ tongue, not feet. Thus, mammalian brain structure is not uniquely responsible for such behaviour, and co-occurrent combinations need not involve manual actions. Additional data (discussed below) suggest that experience in object manipulation appears necessary for physical hierarchical development.

11.4.1 *Manipulative combinations*

At present, Griffin predominantly pairs; he pots less than apes do. His potting was approximately 58 per cent successful but he is still acquiring this strategy; likewise for subassembly. Although he hasn't mastered complex seriation, potting failures probably occur because he lacks physical dexterity, not because his combinations were impossible. He ignored smaller objects which we subsequently provided to address physical dexterity issues. Subassembly failures, in contrast, sometimes did involve impossible combinations. The frequency with which he picks up and manipulates paired caps/lids, together with his manipulations of other items, suggests intermediate or transitory stages leading to more difficult combinations.

11.4.2 *Vocal combinations*

Only one in fourteen of spontaneous three-label combination types that Griffin repeatedly produced was trained ('two-corner wood'). Phrases were generally novel, involving 'want+object' or reproducing what was heard from, but not taught by, trainers (e.g. 'Do you wanna go back?'). Some utterances were unlikely to originate with trainers (e.g. 'walnut grape'). Samples of three-label combinations are limited and a few lack obvious syntactic, hierarchical form (e.g. 'cork nut shower'; 'cork nut', however, is his label for an almond); others exhibit such form (e.g. 'you wanna go-back?'). I claim not that Griffin exhibits human syntax, but that he uses rule-governed order equivalent to that of a child at the same early stage of language acquisition. Clearly, a child acquires full-blown grammar and syntax, and even our most advanced subject, Alex, does not go much beyond simple sentence frames. The point is that parrots (and apes and even marine mammals) acquire these frames, which are early elements of and building blocks for language, and that such behaviour thus is, in and of itself, of considerable note in a creature so phylogenetically removed from humans. In any case, whether seriation improves as Griffin's three-label combinations develop must be tracked in future work. Will he, like some children and non-human primates (see below), need training to advance further?

Data from another parrot in our lab (Pepperberg 1999) demonstrate that Griffin's vocal combinations are not unique and that future three-label combinations are likely. Soon after acquiring individual labels, Alex spontaneously produced untrained two-label combinations (e.g. 'key chain', 'rock corn' [dried corn kernels]). He also spontaneously combined syllable subassemblies into higher order units. As noted earlier, 'grey', which occurred without formal training, led to 'grain', 'grate', 'grape'; 'grain' led to 'cane' and 'chain'; 'chalk' derived from 'talk'; 'key' and 'parrot' led to 'carrot'. After learning to label pine polygons 'x-corner wood', Alex, without training, combined 'corner' with all number labels (two to six) and object labels to identify other items (e.g. 'two-corner cork'). Shown a nut covered by a heavy metal mug he could not lift, he spontaneously combined terms in his repertoire to produce 'Go pick up cup'. After learning 'want X' and 'wanna go Y' for some referents, he spontaneously produced appropriate combinations for other Xs or Ys; Griffin has already begun demonstrating this ability, as has a third, younger parrot, Arthur.

Co-occurrence of physical and vocal combinations was probably not a fortuitous accident. Normally, parrots attempt new labels after around twenty model/rival training sessions (4–8 weeks; Pepperberg 1999) but Griffin needed eight months of training before combining three labels, and combinations produced were rarely those trained. Such data suggest that combinatorial behaviour could not occur until some developmental stage was reached; occurrence of that stage by chance just as he routinely began three-object combinations seems far-fetched. A coincidental hypothesis is also weakened by documentation of another developmental co-occurrence: Griffin's Piagetian Stage 4 object permanence (the first stage of understanding that a fully hidden object still exists and remembering where it exists) co-occurred with flight (Pepperberg et al. 1997)—the point at which memory for, for example, a nest hole no longer in view or a predator that 'disappears' into a tree becomes critically important.

11.4.3 *Other similarities between birds and non-human primates*

1. Ecological aspects

Griffin, like *Cebus* and *Pan* (Johnson-Pynn et al. 1999), formed and then dismantled structures. Like these non-human primates (e.g. Goodall 1986; Parker and Gibson 1977), Grey parrots are extractive, destructive foragers who open objects (e.g. nuts) to remove edible parts, and excavate tree trunks for nest sites (May and Lynn, personal observation 1999). Thus similar behavioural traits and ecological environments, even in divergent species, can lead to comparable behaviour patterns that may have involved evolution of analogous neural structures.

2. Other avian species

Co-occurrences of hierarchical vocal and physical combinations also occur in non-psittacids. Male marsh wrens, *Cistothorus palustris*, for example, form complicated woven nests (Leonard and Picman 1987) as they construct/memorize hierarchies of neighbours' song repertoires so they can serially order their own responses (i.e. reorder or recombine their songs in new ways) to best defend their territories (Kroodsma 1979). Possibly similar patterns exist in other oscines.

3. Neural implications

Recent data on mirror neuron (MN) systems in monkey F5 and human Broca's areas (Rizzolatti and Arbib 1998; Fadiga et al. 1995; Fogassi 2000; Arbib, Chapter 2) suggest a mechanism for primate co-development of gestural and vocal combinations; hard data for birds (see below) do not yet exist. Monkeys' F5 are activated by both action and observation of gestures made by hand or mouth;[4] such data reactivates interest in a gestural origin of speech because a similar system exists in the human Broca's area, including gestural function (e.g. Parsons et al. 1995). For monkeys, however, unlike humans, observed actions must already be in the repertoire and must be goal-oriented (Chaminade et al. 2001; Chaminade et al. 2002; Rizzolatti et al. 2001); apes have not been examined. These data could explain Greenfield's experimental results and, eventually, the data from Griffin.

---

[4] The exact same neurons and neural pathways are not used for hand and mouth actions; rather these pathways reside in the same brain structure/area.

A plausible scenario is the following: monkeys do not imitate; their MN system, however, may recruit innate grasping motions of hand and mouth to replicate goal-directed actions (for a review see Pepperberg forthcoming b). Thus they can be *taught* individual seriation actions; their natural combinatorial behaviour, whether vocal or physical, is probably either innate also, or else involves some level of emulation. Tamarins (*Saguinus oedipus*) which, for example, learned the relative serial order of simple speech elements (Hauser et al. 2001) had eight years of exposure to human speech and probably recruited innate systems, initially used to process their own elements, to process speech; whether they process other serial patternings is unclear. And although Campbell's monkeys (*Cerco-pithecus campbelli*) may use boom calls as introductory elements to their alarm calls to indicate a lesser threat than that indicated by the alarm call itself, and Diana monkeys (*C. diana*) may understand this modification, the data do not prove that these combinatory calls are syntactically complex (Zuberbühler 2002b; Chapter 12 below). Rather, monkeys appear to respond associatively to the compound as an unanalysed whole, without learning rules of formation. The human MN system, in contrast, probably evolved to analyse and *developmentally* recreate exactly those actions to which they are exposed, even those such as speech, in which neurons that are reacting activate muscles which are not directly observed (Sundara et al. 2001). I propose that *exposure* to complex speech patterns and everyday combinatorial acts in humans (and possibly in apes) initiates recruitment of neurological paths (involving MN systems) that are critical for simultaneous complex combinatorial behaviour; emergence is then a matter of intention and achieving physical competence. Although such behaviour apparently occurs without *ostensible* training, 'training' has been occurring for the life of the organism. Note that the human system allows more flexibility than a monkey's, so different syntactic and phonemic patterns can arise based on input. Interestingly, autistic children, whose MN system is functional at the motor cortex level (Avikainen et al. 1999)—like that of the monkey—appear unable to integrate MN information into higher-level cognitive processes, and thus lack—as do monkeys—the ability to imitate, to understand 'theory of mind' problems (Heavey et al. 2000), and most important for the current research, to solve seriation problems at the level of normal human individuals (Yirmiya and Shulman 1996).

How might the parrots' system work? Does exposure to human speech and behaviour initiate patterns in parrot brains that are analogous to or homologous with human patterns? We know little about the natural vocal systems of parrots, but our birds recognize phonemic differences—minimal pairs (e.g. 'pea' versus 'tea', 'cork' versus 'corn')—that constitute English speech (Pepperberg 1999). Interestingly, such sensitivity is found even in birds that lack vocal learning (e.g. quail: Kluender 1991; Kluender and Lotto 1994; Kluender et al. 1987), suggesting that the ability is unrelated to speech.

Further research must determine if the same (or closely connected) neural substrates mediate concurrent vocal and physical combinatory behaviour in any given avian species and whether a single substrate, if found, differs across avian species. Neural structures of vocal control pathways differ between oscine songbirds and psittacids, and although vocal learning supposedly arose independently in these groups (Nottebohm 1980; Striedter 1994; cf. Jarvis and Mello 2000), responsible structures may have been inherited from a common ancestor and lost in some descendants. If one single structure is responsible for both object-based and vocal combinations (see Fogassi 2000) and even if this structure differentiates as animals mature, then psittacine and oscine combinatory behaviour either arose independently or both evolved from a much earlier brain structure. Interestingly, physical and vocal combinations in both wrens and parrots involve beaks and tongues—closer vocal–physical ties than for primates. Such data, and arguments that spoken language derived from gestural forms without major neural restructuring (see above), add credence to a motor control theory of song origin (Nottebohm 1991) and involvement of a single neural substrate, similar to that proposed for primates. Arguably, emphasis should not be on a specific neural substrate, but on types of coordinated, neuronal activity linking brain areas (Deacon 1997)—and how alternative neurological means achieve the same end (Jarvis and Mello 2000).

So, might a parrot—a creature that cannot recreate human vocalizations or actions in exactly the same manner as humans (even if it achieves the same results)—have a neuronal system corresponding to primates' MN? Electrophysiological studies on the frontal neostriatum of awake budgerigars (*Melopsittacus undulatus*) show activity both in production of and response to calls (Plumer and Striedter 2000); evidence exists for additional budgerigar auditory–vocal pathways (e.g. Brauth et al. 2002). Although not yet technically feasible, fMRI recordings of awake parrots, comparable to human studies, would enable researchers to determine the possible existence of psittacine MNs.

4. Effect of experience and enculturation

Does enculturation affect combinatory behaviour? Might the enculturation of great apes and the training of monkeys enable otherwise improbable behaviour? In studies on other topics, enculturation sometimes did, but sometimes did not, affect apes' outcomes (reviewed in Pepperberg and Shive 2001). For monkeys, training needed to complete combination tasks (Johnson-Pynn et al. 1999) could be considered enculturation. In human societies (e.g. Zinacanteco; see Greenfield 1972) where object manipulation is not emphasized and children thus do not experience tasks such as nesting cups, the youngest children who observed the most complicated strategy immediately proceeded to use the simplest strategy, at an age similar to American counterparts. Somewhat older Zinacanteco children, again age-matched to their American counterparts, used an intermediate strategy, but most of the oldest, unlike Americans, needed additional demonstrations and all needed additional experience to proceed to the most advanced physical assembly stages (Greenfield et al. 1989). Such data suggest that the purported neural structure may be necessary but not sufficient for full emergence of combinatory behaviour, that maturation affects choice of combinatorial strategy, and that development is arrested without appropriate experience.

Early general experience of manipulation may have assisted Griffin (Pepperberg and Shive 2001). He was never trained on combinatorial tasks, but from 7.5 weeks of age had simultaneous access to several items he could manipulate (Pepperberg et. al. 1997). In contrast, our oldest subject, Alex, discussed above, who referentially uses three-label combinations (e.g. 'three-corner wood') and contextually uses longer phrases ('You be good, I'll see you tomorrow', Pepperberg 1999), was 8.5 years old before gaining such experience (Pepperberg and Kozak 1986). Possibly as a consequence, he never spontaneously combines items (Pepperberg, personal observation). The behaviour of our other Greys suggests the possibility of advanced combinations similar to those described for children (Greenfield 1991). Kyaaro, given manipulative occasions as a juvenile, scoops water from a dish with a bottle cap and then drinks from the cap; such behaviour is 'subassembly' (Greenfield 1991: 540); he also uses vocal combinations (e.g. 'What toy?', 'What's this?'). Arthur (aka Wart), at eighteen months, began to utter 'Tickle Wart' and 'Hi Wart' while producing 'Hi', 'Wart', and 'tickle' separately; at the same time he put toys into his food dish to stabilize them during play. Arthur received simultaneous experience with multiple items before observations began. Just as for monkeys and children, such exposure could affect our birds' behaviour in combinatorial tasks.

Griffin has also always spent considerable time on countertops, which afford more stable surfaces for combining items than, for example, a T-stand, a tree branch, or a cage top, through which objects easily fall. Alex, unlike Griffin, lacked equivalent countertop experience until twelve years old. Grey parrots are partial ground-feeders in nature (May 1996) and thus might be expected to perform manipulations while on flat surfaces, but early experience with stable surfaces might still be necessary to develop physical combinatory behaviour.[5]

11.5 Implications

How does the fact of co-occurrent emergence of physical and vocal serial combinations in our parrot, with its relation to similar simultaneous emergence in humans and language-trained apes, affect the idea that anything language-like in non-human primates must be a function of their common ancestry with humans and, alternatively, that human language evolution must be phylogeny-based? Greenfield's studies on the simultaneous development of physical and vocal serial combinations in humans, and physical and verbal (whether vocal, signed, or via computer symbols) combinations in apes (see Greenfield et al. 1972; Greenfield 1991; Johnson-Pynn et al. 1999) give credence to arguments for a gestural origin of language; that is, that necessary neural substrates for all combinatory behaviour originated in the primate line and required only minor evolutionary neural reorganization to account for the shift from manual–manual to manual–vocal modalities. For parrots (and probably other birds such as wrens), however, the same structures (beaks/tongues) perform both physical and vocal combinatory acts. In the avian line, then, we see what might be a shift not to another modality but rather to add function to existing morphological structures. Might this system lead us to

[5] The extent to which Grey parrot vocalizations and physical manipulations are combinatory in the wild is unknown; thus we cannot argue either for or against enculturation effects of a laboratory versus a natural rearing environment, or (specifically) the effects of observational combinatorial learning in nature.

examine additional issues concerning the evolution of speech within language evolution?

In sum, our data are intriguing given the initial hypothesis of Greenfield (1991), later suppositions of Johnson-Pynn et al. (1999), and MN studies (Arbib 2002; Chapter 2 above), all concerning the evolutionary bases of language. Clearly, Griffin's behaviour—or even that of our most advanced subject, Alex (Pepperberg 1999)—is isomorphic neither with human language nor with the complex combinatory behaviour of two- to three-year-old humans. We have, however, documented co-occurrence of vocal and physical-object combinatorial behaviour not previously described in parrots. Thus, (a) the behaviour of our Greys compares to that of non-human primates, (b) parallel communicatory and physical development is not limited to primates, and (c) such data argue that the neural structures involved in such behaviour are not unique to primates. Avian neuroanatomy and its relation to the mammalian line is, however, not yet well enough understood to determine specific parallels among oscine, psittacine, and mammalian structures. The responsible substrates are probably analogous and arose independently under similar evolutionary pressures, although recent arguments (e.g. Medina and Reiner 2000; Jarvis 2004) suggest that additional study is needed before making definite conclusions. Nevertheless, given the evolutionary distance between parrots and primates, the search for and arguments concerning responsible neural substrates and common behaviour should be approached with care and not be restricted to the primate line. Data presented here, plus our knowledge of avian vocal learning, of how social interaction affects such learning, and of birds' advanced cognition, all suggest *Aves* as an important model both for determining the evolutionary pressures responsible for complex communication systems, and for developing testable theories about such systems, particularly those involving vocal learning.

ACKNOWLEDGEMENTS

Data were collected by Heather Shive, an undergraduate at the University of Arizona, now a graduate of the veterinary college at North Carolina State University. Research was supported by NSF Grants IBN 96-03803 and REU supplements, Kenneth A. Scott Charitable Trust, Pet Care Trust, the University of Arizona Undergraduate Biology Research Program, and numerous donors to *The Alex Foundation*. I thank Jeanne Slaughter and Clare Ellsworth for helping to train Griffin, Terry Clyne (Apalachee River Aviary) for donating Griffin, the Harrison family for Harrison's Bird Diet, and Fowl Play and Corky's Organics for treats. Manuscript preparation was supported by the MIT School of Architecture and Planning and donations to *The Alex Foundation* (particularly *The American Foundation*, the Eleanor Dees Foundation, the Andrew De Mar Family Foundation, West Surburban Cage Bird Society (IL), Rainbow Feathers Bird Club (MI), and South Bay Bird Society (LA)). I gratefully acknowledge the permission of the American Psychological Association to use copyright material which was originally published in the *Journal of Comparative Psychology* (Pepperberg and Shive 2001).

FURTHER READING

Greenfield (1991) outlines the importance of combinatory behaviour, whilst Johnson-Pynn, Fragaszy, Hirsh, Brakke, and Greenfield (1999) describes cross-species primate comparisons of combinatory behaviour. Details of parrot cognition and communication are given in Pepperberg (1999), whilst Pepperberg and Shive (2001) give details of the experiment described in this chapter; all tables are from Pepperberg and Shive (2001).

12 Linguistic prerequisites in the primate lineage

KLAUS ZUBERBÜHLER

12.1 Language evolution

Language is perhaps the single most important feature that distinguishes humans from the rest of the living world. Human language is an open-ended system of communication in which syntactic rules encode information of great complexity, and it is therefore of particular interest how this capacity has evolved. Theories of language origins are all faced with one problem: how to explain the evolution of a highly complex and sophisticated cognitive capacity in an extremely short period of time. Humans probably did not have the anatomical and neural prerequisites to produce the full range of modern speech until very recently (Lieberman 2000: 136). A recent comparative genetic analysis has provided additional empirical support, showing that non-human primates differ genetically from modern humans in a region on chromosome 7, which codes for the FOXP2 protein (Enard et al. 2002). Other work has shown that the FOXP2 gene is crucially involved in the development of normal speech abilities in humans (Fisher et al. 1998). The genetic differences in this region distinguishing us from our closest living relatives are the result of a few mutations, which have not become stabilized in the human population until very recently, about 200,000 years ago. Overall, this has led to the hypothesis that the human-specific form of the FOXP2 protein is essentially involved in brain development, affecting the ability to fine-control orofacial movements and thus the capacity to develop proficient speech (Enard et al. 2002). Yet a time period of 200,000 years, which equals about 7,000 generations, could be too short to evolve the entire necessary cognitive apparatus underlying the language capacity. In addition, neuro-biological work suggests that the brain regions most heavily involved in language processes in humans did not arise de novo, but evolved from older structures already present in the primate lineage (e.g. Cantalupo and Hopkins 2001; Hopkins et al. 1998). During language evolution these regions became substrates for language processing because the previous functions made them especially suitable for the new problems posed by language (Deacon 1997).

The hypothesis is, therefore, that many of the cognitive capacities that are prerequisite for language are phylogenetically much older, and evolved in the primate lineage long before the advent of modern humans. A systematic investigation of the linguistic capacities of non-human primates, therefore, is likely to shed light on the evolutionary history of the cognitive capacities necessary for language. Of particular interest are abilities that resemble the semantic and syntactic abilities of modern humans, as these two are central to virtually all definitions of language.

12.2 Semanticity in primate vocal communication

12.2.1 *The function and meaning of primate alarm calls*

It has been known for some time that in some non-human primates, particular vocalizations provide nearby listeners with information about some object or event that is physically separate from the calling individual, such as the appearance of a predator, the discovery of particular food, or the occurrence of a unique social event. The best-known example of natural semantic communication comes from studies of the alarm call behaviour of East African vervet monkeys, *Cercopithecus aethiops*. These monkeys produce acoustically distinct alarm calls to leopards, eagles, and snakes (Struhsaker 1967). When exemplars of these calls are played in the absence of actual predators, individuals respond as if they have seen the corresponding predator themselves (Seyfarth et al. 1980). These and other studies (e.g. Gouzoules et al. 1984; Hauser 1998; Macedonia 1990; Eckardt and Zuberbühler 2004; Crockford and Boesch 2003; Slocombe and Zuber-bühler 2005) have shown that primates are in fact able to produce acoustically distinct vocalizations in response to discrete external events. The suggestion is that these are examples of true semantic communication, since recipients treat these vocalizations as indicators of the actual object or event (Seyfarth et al. 1980).

A potential problem with this conclusion has always been that some species with a considerably less complicated nervous system than primates also produce specific signals in response to objects that are physically separate from them. For example, honeybees (*Apis melifera*) are able to inform each other about the presence and location of distant food sources (von Frisch 1973). Here, signallers produce a visual signal (a specific dance motion) in response to an event (the location of a food source) which describes the event sufficiently accurately for recipients to find it using only the signal. From a functional perspective, therefore, there does not seem to be a difference between the vervet monkey alarm calls and the honeybees' dance language, although the underlying mental mechanisms could be profoundly different. In both cases an external object and a corresponding signal elicit the same behaviour, thus satisfying the functional criterion for semanticity (Macedonia and Evans 1993). Bee language and monkey alarm calls, in other words, could be examples of mere *perceptual processing* and thus be fundamentally different from the kind of semanticity observed in human language. Signallers might simply produce a signal in response to a physical stimulus, such as the solar angle, whereas recipients might simply attend to physical dimensions of the signal, rather than its associated meaning. Human semanticity, however, is of a different kind. Here, the physical properties of speech sounds are only relevant insofar as they refer to an associated cognitive structure, the mental representation or concept shared by both the signaller and the recipient (see, for instance, Yates and Tule 1979). According to this dichotomy, human language is based on a conceptual semanticity, while bee language is based on a mere perceptual, or functional, semanticity. Research on animal semantic communication has traditionally not distinguished between perceptual and conceptual semanticity. Instead, examples of animals producing discrete signals to discrete external events have been called *functionally* referential (e.g. Evans et al. 1993; Hauser 1996: 508), thereby evading further debate about the underlying cognitive structures.

Two recent experiments with Diana monkeys and Campbell's monkeys living in the Taï forest of Western Ivory Coast have addressed this issue, and results suggest that primates process their calls on a conceptual level and therefore exceed the definition of functional referentiality. The following findings derived from long-term observations concerning the natural history of these two species are relevant. Both species live in small groups with one adult male and several adult females with their offspring. The females remain in their natal group in both species, and young males leave their native group and sometimes associate with other monkey species before trying to take over a group of females themselves (Uster and Zuberbühler 2001; Wolters and Zuberbühler 2003). In the Taï forest, both Diana monkeys and Campbell's monkeys are hunted by leopards, *Panthera pardus*, crowned eagles, *Stephanoaetus coronatus*, and chimpanzees, *Pan troglodytes* (Zuberbühler and Jenny 2002; Shultz 2001; Boesch and Boesch 1989). Because of the high predation pressure, both species frequently form mixed-species associations, and some groups spend up to 90 per cent of their time in association with each other (Wolters and Zuberbühler 2003). In both species, individuals produce acoustically distinct alarm calls in response to crowned eagles and leopards, and there is a sexual dimorphism in the call structure of the adult males and females (Zuberbühler et al. 1997; Zuberbühler 2001). Figure 12.1 depicts spectrographic illustrations of the male alarm calls of the

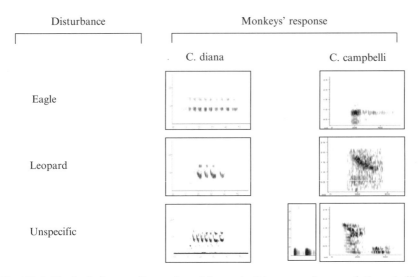

FIG. 12.1 Typical alarm calls produced by male Diana monkeys and Campbell's monkeys in response to leopards, crowned eagles, and unspecific disturbances, such as falling trees. Campbell's monkeys usually utter pairs of booms before an alarm-call series in response to unspecific disturbances. In both species, the female alarm calls are acoustically different from those of the males; spectrograms are published elsewhere (Zuberbühler et al. 1997).

Campbell's and Diana monkeys, exemplars of which served in the play-back experiments discussed below.

To investigate whether the acoustically different alarm calls of these monkeys in fact denoted different predator types, a series of playback experiments was conducted. Wild groups of Campbell's or Diana monkeys were sought throughout a roughly 100km^2 large study area surrounding the CRE research station in the western part of the Taï National Park, about 25 km east of the Liberian border (5° 50'N, 7° 20'W). The Taï Forest is classified as a tropical moist forest, with a protected area of about 4000 km^2, the largest remaining block of primary forest in West Africa (Martin 1991). Once a monkey group was located, typically by hearing their contact calls from a distance, the experimenter slowly and silently approached to about 50 m from the group and set up the playback and recording equipment without being detected by the monkeys. Then a short recording was played back to simulate the presence of either a leopard or a crowned eagle. Playback stimuli were chosen from among the following types: (a) a fifteen-second recording of leopard growls; (b) five male Diana monkey leopard alarm calls; (c) five male Campbell's monkey leopard alarm calls; (d) a fifteen-second recording of crowned eagle shrieks; (e) five male Diana monkey eagle alarm calls; or (f) five male Campbell's monkey eagle alarm calls.

Female Diana monkeys responded to predator vocalizations and to male Diana monkey or Campbell's monkey alarm calls by giving their own acoustically distinct alarm calls. These vocal responses were highly selective in the sense that playbacks of eagle shrieks, male Diana monkey eagle alarm calls, or male Campbell's monkey eagle alarm calls all elicited only one type of predator-specific alarm call from females— the females' eagle alarm call. In contrast, playback of leopard growls, Diana males' leopard alarm calls, or Campbell's males' leopard alarm calls all elicited an acoustically different alarm call—the females' leopard alarm call. Figure 12.2 summarizes the vocal responses of female Diana monkeys to these playbacks as stacked columns, comprising of the number of predator-specific eagle or leopard alarm calls given in the first minute, in addition to a number of other unspecific call types.

Results suggest that the main organizing principle in the responses of the female Diana monkeys to the six different playback stimuli were the meaning, or predator type, indicated by the playback stimuli, rather than

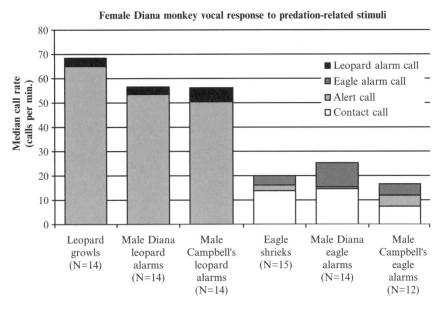

Female Diana monkey vocal response to predation-related stimuli

FIG. 12.2 Vocal responses of female Diana monkeys to playbacks of predator vocalizations or alarm call series of male Diana or Campbell's monkeys (data from Zuberbühler et al. 1997; Zuberbühler 2000a). Stacked bars depict median alarm call responses of female Diana monkeys from different groups in response to the different playback conditions during the first minute after beginning of a playback. Sample sizes refer to the number of different Diana monkey groups tested with a particular playback stimulus type.

the more proximate stimulus properties, such as the acoustic features of the signal or the biological species of the signaller.

These results raised a number of questions. In particular, why did male and female Diana monkeys evolve acoustically different alarm calls for the same predators? Note that the alarm calls of the female Campbell's monkeys are also acoustically different from the males', but no systematic investigation has yet been conducted. Clearly, the male calls described in Figure 12.1 function as alarm calls: they advertise to predators that they have been recognized and so further hunting will be futile (Zuberbühler, Jenny, and Bshary 1999), a function also described for some bird alarm calls (e.g. Perrins 1968). At the same time, they warn recipients about the presence of specific predators (Zuberbühler et al. 1997), suggesting that they have evolved through ordinary natural selection (Maynard Smith 1965). However, a recent analysis suggested that sexual selection had exerted additional selection pressure on the evolution of these calls (Zuberbühler 2002a). The polygynous mating system of these forest monkeys leads to intense competition of males for access over a group of females, and this mating system is a notorious target of sexual selection, typically resulting in the evolution of conspicuous male traits (Anderson 1994). Sexual selection, in other words, appears to have acted on male alarm calls and transformed them into structurally distinct loud calls, by selectively affecting the calls' transmission features and by favouring call usage to indicate male quality.

12.2.2   *Cognitive processes underlying call production*

What mental processes underlie call production in these monkeys? Studies of a number of non-primate species, such as California ground squirrels, *Spermophilus beecheyi*, and domestic chickens, *Gallus domesticus*, indicate that callers may simply respond to degrees of threat, rather than predator class (e.g. Owings and Hennessy 1984; Gyger et al. 1987). For example, ground squirrels appear to respond to a predator's distance, rather than its biological class. To investigate which aspects the monkeys responded to when giving alarm calls, the presence of a predator was simulated in various ways. The playback speaker was positioned in the vicinity of Diana monkey groups, such that (a) the distance to the group was either 'close' or 'far' (about 25 m or 75 m), (b) the elevation of the speaker was either 'below' or 'above' the group (about 2 m or 30 m off the ground), and (c) the predator was either a 'leopard' or an 'eagle' (fifteen-second playback of leopard growls or eagle shrieks).

Results of both male and female alarm call behaviour in response to these variations clearly showed that Diana monkeys consistently responded to predator type, regardless of distance or direction of predator attack (Figure 12.3). The same experiment was also conducted with Campbell's monkeys, confirming that predator type was the main determinant of alarm calling behaviour in this species as well (Zuberbühler 2001). Primate alarm calls, in sum, appear to label the predator type and not the degree of perceived threat.

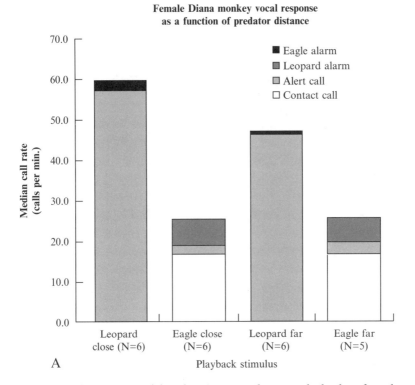

FIG. 12.3a Vocal responses of female Diana monkeys to playbacks of predator vocalizations presented with varying degrees of threat caused by different predator distances (data from Zuberbühler 2000c). Sample sizes refer to the number of different Diana monkey groups tested with a particular playback condition. Stacked bars depict median vocal responses from different groups during the first minute after beginning of a playback.

12.2.3 *Cognitive processes underlying call perception*

Complex cognitive processes reveal themselves through evidence of 'flexible behavioural adaptations in which individual organisms make informed choices based on mental representations', according to Tomasello and Call (1997: 12). As discussed earlier the bee language example has raised questions about the underlying cognitive processes of alarm call perception in non-human primates. Two basic models of call perception can be distinguished. First, monkeys might respond to alarm calls in a rather inflexible manner by simply attending to the calls' physical features

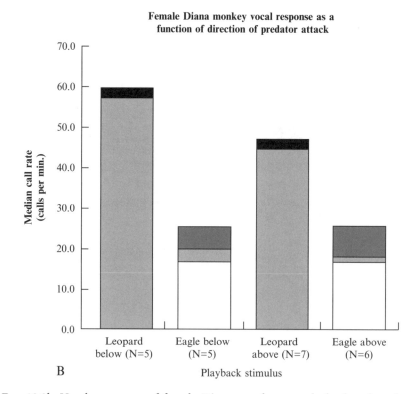

FIG. 12.3b Vocal responses of female Diana monkeys to playbacks of predator vocalizations presented with varying degrees of threat caused by different directions of probable predator attack (data from Zuberbühler 2000c). Sample sizes refer to the number of different Diana monkey groups tested with a particular playback condition. Stacked bars depict median vocal responses from different groups during the first minute after beginning of a playback.

rather than an associated mental representation of the predator class. This model is sufficient to explain communication about food sources in honeybees. Alternatively, the monkeys' processing of their own alarm calls could be of the kind that presumably underlies language perception. Here, the acoustic properties of a vocal stimulus are only relevant insofar as they refer to an associated mental structure (e.g. Yates and Tule 1979). A playback experiment was designed to distinguish between these two hypotheses.

Under field conditions, the choice of experimental techniques useful for investigating cognitive processes is limited and typically restricted to some variant of the habituation–dishabituation technique originally developed for prelinguistic children (Eimas et al. 1971). In a typical experimental design, the subject is exposed to a first set of stimuli, which are presented repeatedly until the subject loses interest (i.e. until it habituates). In the second test phase, the experimenter presents a second set of stimuli, which differ in some important feature from the first one. If the subject is able to perceive the difference between the two sets of stimuli, then it is expected to show renewed interest (i.e. it dishabituates). Zuberbühler, Cheney, and Seyfarth (1999) and Zuberbühler (2000a) have applied one form of this technique, the prime–probe procedure, to primates living in undisturbed natural conditions, in order to investigate the cognitive processes underlying their alarm-call behaviour. The prime–probe technique differs from a standard habituation–dishabituation protocol because it does not have a long habituation phase, in which stimuli are presented over and over again until the subject ceases to respond. Instead, it simply provides the animal with a one-off exposure to some critical information and then tests the effect of this manipulation on the animal's subsequent response to an experimental probe stimulus. Figure 12.4 illustrates the experimental design of a prime–probe experiment.

In each trial, the playback speaker was positioned in the vicinity of one of several wild Diana monkey groups to play two stimuli, a prime and a probe, which were separated by five minutes of silence. Monkeys were primed with either predator vocalizations (baseline condition) or monkey alarm calls given in response to the predators (test and control conditions). After a short (five minute) period of silence, the probe stimulus was presented, again from the same hidden speaker position. Baseline, test, and control condition differed in the acoustic and the semantic similarity between the prime and probe stimuli. In the baseline condition, both the acoustic and semantic features were alike: for example, subjects heard a fifteen-second recording of eagle shrieks (indicating the presence of a crowned eagle) followed by a second recording of eagle shrieks five minutes later. The prediction was that monkeys would produce many eagle alarm calls to the first set of eagle shrieks (the prime stimulus), but only few eagle alarm calls to the second set of eagle shrieks (the probe stimulus). This was expected because the information of the probe stimulus was redundant, both acoustically and semantically. In the test condition, subjects heard a Diana monkey's alarm calls (e.g. to an eagle) followed by vocalizations of the corresponding predator (e.g. eagle

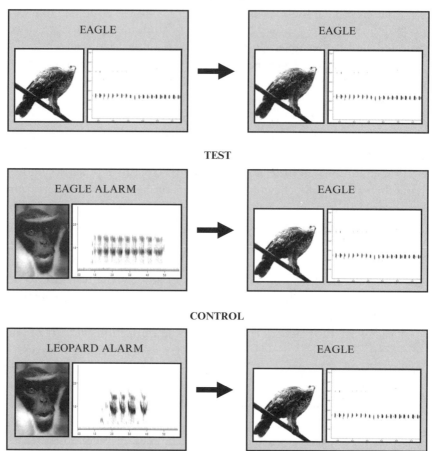

FIG. 12.4 Experimental design of a prime–probe experiment: Different Diana monkey groups were tested on two stimuli, the prime and the probe, separated by five minutes of silence. The prime–probe pairs test differed in similarity of the acoustic and semantic features across conditions as follows: (a) baseline condition—both the acoustic and the semantic features remain the same; (b) test condition—the acoustic features change but the semantic features remain the same; (c) control condition—both the acoustic and the semantic features change. If subjects are able to take the semantic features into account, they should transfer habituation between prime and probe stimuli in the baseline and test condition, but not in the control condition.

shrieks). In this condition, the semantic features remained the same across prime and probe stimuli, whereas the acoustic features changed. The prediction was that if the monkeys were able to attend to the semantic features of the alarm calls, then they were expected to produce only few (eagle) alarm calls in response to the probe. Alternatively, if they were unable to process the semantic features of the prime stimulus, then they were expected to produce many eagle alarm calls to the probe, because the acoustic features of the probe stimulus were novel to them. In the control condition, finally, both the acoustic and the semantic features changed between prime and probe, and therefore subjects were expected to produce many predator-specific alarm calls to both stimuli.

Data showed that the semantic content of the prime stimuli, not their acoustic features alone, explained the response patterns of the monkeys. That is, both eagle shrieks and leopard growls, two very powerful stimuli, lost their effectiveness in eliciting alarm calls as probe stimuli, if subjects were primed first with the corresponding male alarm calls. Figure 12.5 illustrates the response.

Results further showed that it did not matter whether the alarm calls used as prime stimuli were given by a conspecific Diana monkey male or by a heterospecific Campbell's monkey male. Although the alarm calls differed strongly in their acoustic structure, the priming effects remained the same: the monkeys ceased to respond to a predator if they were previously warned of its presence by a semantically corresponding alarm call, regardless of its species origin. These data showed that, although both the acoustic and the semantic properties of the stimuli varied between prime and probe stimuli, only variation in the semantic properties explained the monkeys' vocal response pattern. Data are consistent with the interpretation that recipients formed a mental representation of the predator type when hearing conspecific alarm calls and then were not surprised to detect the corresponding predator a few minutes later.

In sum, (1) the experiments reviewed so far show that primates are able to produce acoustically distinct vocalizations in response to discrete external events, in this case the presence of a particular predator type (Zuberbühler et al. 1997; Zuberbühler 2001). (2) Primate alarm calls do not appear to be the product of differences in the caller's perceived threat, but they label the biological class of a predator (Zuberbühler 2000a). (3) Primate alarm calls are meaningful to recipients because they elicit the same overall behaviour as do the corresponding predators

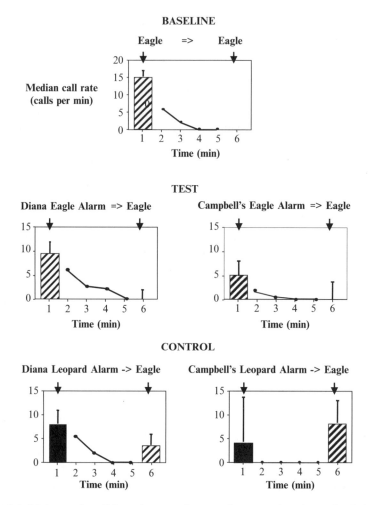

Fig. 12.5 Main results of the prime–probe experiments using the eagle shrieks as probe stimuli (data from Zuberbühler, Cheney, and Seyfarth 1999; Zuberbühler 2000a). Solid bars represent the median number of female leopard alarm calls; hatched bars represent the median number of female eagle alarm calls; error bars represent the third quartile. The connecting sloping lines represent the median alarm-call rates two, three, and four minutes after beginning of the experiment. As predicted by the semanticity hypothesis, the monkeys responded weakly to probe stimuli if they previously heard the same predator vocalization or the corresponding monkey alarm calls, suggesting that the semantic content of the stimuli drove the Diana monkeys' vocal response.

(Zuberbühler 2000b). (4) Call processing appears to take place on a conceptual level involving mental representations of the predator class, since monkeys do not simply respond to the acoustic features of these calls, but behave as if the calls invoke mental representations of the associated external events (Zuberbühler, Cheney, and Seyfarth 1999).

12.3 Syntactic abilities

12.3.1 *Generative systems*

Pinker (1994: 83) identifies two 'tricks', or principles, that underlie human language. The first one concerns the arbitrariness of the sound–meaning combinations. There is nothing about the word *dog* that tells a non-native speaker what this sound pattern could mean. Instead, the meaning of each word has to be learned individually, a defining aspect of human development. The previously discussed experiments outline the remarkable similarities between monkey alarm-call behaviour and Pinker's first trick of language. There is nothing about a Campbell's monkey eagle alarm call that indicates to a Diana monkey that the caller has spotted a crowned eagle, and there is empirical evidence that monkeys have to learn the exact meaning of alarm calls individually (Zuberbühler 2000c). More recent work suggests that comparable abilities are also present in some bird species (Rainey et al. 2004a; Rainey et al. 2004b; Pepperberg, Chapter 11).

Pinker's second trick refers to what von Humboldt (1836) has termed the ability of languages to 'make infinite use of finite means'. All languages possess a set of syntactic rules, which generate combined structures from a discrete set of elements, the lexicon; compare also the discussion of the parallel phenomenon in the sound system, in Chapter 3 (Studdert-Kennedy). According to Pinker, 'generative' (or 'discrete') combinatorial systems are rare in the natural world, one noteworthy exception being language, and another the genetic code, where four nucleotides combine to generate a vast number of genes. A crucial feature of generative combinatorial systems is that the property of the combination is distinct from the properties of its components. Generative combinatorial systems thus contrast with the more common *blending* combinatorial systems where the property of the combination lies between the properties of the components. Generative combinatorial systems exhibit two distinct behaviours. First, they possess enormous creative power and generate vast amounts of output. Second, although in the case of language this output is usually meaningful, this does not have to be the case. Generative combinatorial systems can just as easily produce rule-governed nonsense, if abandoned by the semantic system, for instance because of particular brain lesions (e.g. Wernicke 1874; see Pepperberg, Chapter 11).

12.3.2 *The evolution of syntactic abilities*

The evolution of the human syntactic capacity is widely seen as the central challenge for theories of language evolution (e.g. Hurford 1998). Although linguists typically stress the great structural complexity of language, the underlying cognitive skills do not necessarily have to be very complex. Moreover, there is considerable disagreement about the nature and evolution of the underlying cognitive mechanism responsible for generative combinatorial behaviour. Lightfoot (2000), for example, reviews Chomsky's claim that the grammar of a particular language is the derivate of a species-specific mental capacity, the universal grammar, which can take numerous forms, depending on the linguistic experience of the individual. According to this idea, universal grammar determines and constrains the range of possible hypotheses an individual can generate about linguistic structure, which ultimately enables young children to acquire their native language with relative ease. However, the evolutionary history of this mental capacity is controversial (Newmeyer 1998b). Some have argued that universal grammar has evolved in response to an ever-increasing repertoire (Nowak et al. 2000). Others have remained sceptical about the idea of universal grammar as a direct product of natural selection, mentioning alternative evolutionary accounts based on biological constraints or by-products of other adaptive processes (Lightfoot 2000). Unfortunately, this debate is plagued by an almost complete lack of empirical data.

12.3.3 *Primate precursors to syntactic abilities*

A recent study suggests that, as recipients, non-human primates possess some of the cognitive prerequisites required to deduce meaning from combinatorial rules (Zuberbühler 2002b). The study, again conducted with Diana and Campbell's monkeys, is based on a combinatorial rule present in the alarm-calling behaviour of the male Campbell's monkey: in some circumstances males produce a specific call, a brief and low-pitched 'boom' vocalization, in addition to the alarm calls described before (Figure 12.1). The boom calls are given in pairs separated by some seconds of silence, and typically precede an alarm call series by about thirty seconds. These call combinations are given in response to a number of discrete external events, such as a falling tree or large breaking branch, the far-away alarm calls of a neighbouring group, or a distant predator. Common to these contexts is the lack of an immediate danger, unlike situations in which callers are surprised by a close predator. When hearing 'boom'-introduced alarm-call combinations, Diana monkeys do not respond with their own alarm calls, which contrasts sharply to their vocal response to normal—that is, 'boom'-free—Campbell's monkey alarm calls (Figure 12.2). These observations have led to the hypothesis that the booms act as a modifier, selectively affecting the meaning of subsequent alarm calls.

To investigate whether this was the case and whether monkeys were in fact capable of understanding the semantic changes caused by the presence of 'boom' calls, the following playback experiment was conducted. In two baseline conditions, different Diana monkey groups heard a series of five male Campbell's monkey alarm calls given in response to a crowned eagle or a leopard. Subjects were expected to respond strongly, i.e. to produce many eagle or leopard alarm calls, as in the previous experiments (Figure 12.2). In the two test conditions, different Diana monkey groups heard playbacks of exactly the same Campbell's alarm call series, but this time two 'booms' were artificially added twenty-five seconds before the alarm calls to match the natural alarm-call pattern. If Diana monkeys understood that the 'booms' acted as modifiers (similar to hedges in language; see Lakoff 1972) to affect the semantic specificity of subsequent alarm calls, then they should give significantly fewer predator-specific alarm calls in the test conditions compared to the baseline conditions. Figure 12.6 illustrates the experimental design.

Results of this experiment replicated the natural observations. Playbacks of Campbell's eagle alarm calls caused the Diana monkeys to produce their own eagle alarm calls, while playbacks of Campbell's leopard alarm calls caused them to give leopard alarm calls (Figure 12.7). Playback of booms alone did not cause any noticeable change in Diana monkey vocal behaviour, but had a significant effect on how the monkeys responded to subsequent Campbell's alarm calls. Boom-introduced Campbell's leopard alarms elicited significantly fewer leopard alarm calls

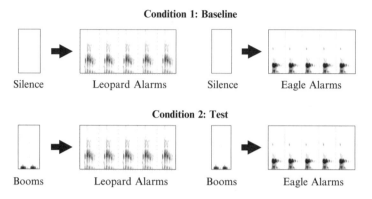

FIG. 12.6 Experimental design of the playback study representing the four different playback conditions (Zuberbühler 2002a)

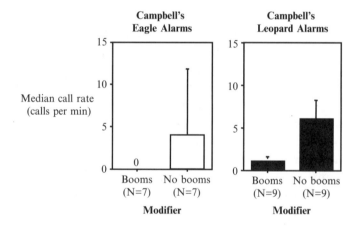

FIG. 12.7 Median alarm-call responses of female Diana monkeys from different groups to the different playback conditions. Black bars represent the median number of female Diana monkey leopard alarm calls; white bars represent the median number of female eagle alarm calls during the first minute after beginning of a playback (data from Zuberbühler 2002a). Vertical lines represent the third quartile. Playback of Campbell's monkey booms had a significant effect on how Diana monkeys responded to subsequent Campbell's eagle or leopard alarm calls, suggesting that the booms modified the meaning of the alarm calls.

in Diana monkeys, while boom-introduced Campbell's eagle alarms elicited significantly fewer eagle alarm calls than Campbell's alarm calls alone (Figure 12.7).

The booms, in other words, affected the way the Diana monkeys interpreted the meaning of subsequent Campbell's alarm calls. In particular, they seemed to indicate to nearby listeners that whatever message followed about half a minute later did not require any anti-predator response. Judging from the Diana monkeys' response to these playback stimuli, therefore, the booms modified the meaning of the subsequent alarm-call series and transformed them from highly specific predator labels, requiring immediate anti-predator responses, into more general signals of disturbance that did not require any direct responses.

12.3.4 *Is primate communication syntactic?*

The previous experiments showed that adding 'booms' before the alarm-call series of a Campbell's monkey created a structurally more complex utterance with a different meaning than that of alarm calls alone. But does this now qualify as an example of a syntactic rule? Recipients are clearly able to adjust to the meaning assigned to a particular call type and this adjustment is guided by an underlying rule imposed by the booms, which act as a modifier. Nevertheless, the behaviour of the signaller casts doubt on the statement that this is truly analogous to a syntactic rule in a human language: call production appears to be the product of a rather rigid calling behaviour with little flexibility. Alternatively, it appears that males make accurate judgements of the predatory threat of a situation and it is this assessment that appears to guide their decision as to whether or not to initiate an alarm-call sequence with a pair of booms. Further research will be necessary to determine the cognitive processes underlying the production of call combinations in these monkeys. As recipients, however, the monkeys have demonstrated significant cognitive flexibility. Rather than responding to individual calls they appear to take into account their functional role and importance as modifiers of semantic content.

Recently, Hauser and colleagues have argued that amongst the various syntactic rules, the capacity to implement recursion is the most crucial one, a defining feature of human language (Hauser et al. 2002; Fitch and Hauser 2004). According to this proposal, it is no longer the ability to deal with generative combinatorial systems in general, as suggested by Pinker (1994), but to master one particular one, recursion, that make us truly human. Although the Campbell's monkey example suggests that non-human primates can deal with combinatorial information, this is clearly not an example of a recursive rule. However, it is not entirely clear how indispensable recursion is in everyday spoken language (for instance, see Tomasello 2003). For example, textbooks often portray relative clauses as prototypical linguistic constructions to specify the reference of the subject. However, in spontaneous spoken speech people rarely employ relative clauses for this purpose (Fox and Thompson 1990). In general, relative clauses appear fairly late during language acquisition (Diessel and Tomasello 2000), suggesting that fully functional linguistic communication is possible without them. However, other authors have stressed that syntactic abilities are more likely to have evolved in the social domain, for example by aiding non-human primates to deal with hierarchical information inherent in their groups' social structure (Bergman et al. 2003).

How might the Campbell's monkey combinatorial communication system have evolved? As mentioned before, boom-introduced alarm calls are uttered when no direct danger is present and no anti-predator responses are required. Possibly, boom-introduced alarm calls serve as acoustic long-distance signals addressed to nearby rivals in search of a group of females, advertising the presence and vigour of the resident male. The ability of the recipients to deal with combinatorial information allows the male to produce acoustically conspicuous alarm calls in his dealings with competitors without causing semantic confusions in other group members. The male, in other words, is free to use an acoustically conspicuous signal, his alarm calls, to advertise his presence and vigour to other males without causing unnecessary anti-predator responses in other group members, such as costly escape responses or alarm-call behaviour.

12.4 Primate prerequisites to human linguistic abilities

As recipients, non-human primates have revealed highly sophisticated understanding of the semantic content associated with various of their calls, apparently involving mental representations of the referential situation (Tomasello and Zuberbühler 2002). These representations may include information on the possible causes of a call, rather than just a working knowledge on how best to respond to a particular call. This is further illustrated by the fact that the monkeys can respond differently to ground predator alarm calls of a familiar bird, the crested guinea fowls, *Guttera pucherani*, depending on whether the birds' alarm calls were caused by a leopard or by human poachers (Zuberbühler 2000d). This study suggested that primates attended to the likely cause of a call, rather than the call itself.

Despite a remarkable cognitive flexibility in call comprehension, in which vocal signals are responded to as outcomes of specific external events, non-human primates seem far less flexible as signallers than as recipients of calls. To date there is no evidence that they are able to invent and incorporate new call types into their repertoires or to combine calls creatively to produce novel meanings (see Franks and Rigby, Chapter 10), apart from the example discussed above. One possible explanation for this difference between human and non-human vocal communication has been linked to a lack of social intelligence in the latter case: non-human primates seem to have great difficulties understanding each other as mental agents and taking each other's mental states into account (Tomasello and Call 1997: 384; Cheney and Seyfarth 1998). It is perhaps this cognitive limitation that prevents non-human primates from using vocalizations intentionally in order to affect each other's knowledge in the way humans do. Alternatively, non-human primates might be hindered in their vocal expressive abilities, comparable to linguistically impaired humans suffering from a defective FOXP2 gene. Genetic defects in that region cause a severe form of speech and language impairment: individuals not only suffer from a striking articulatory impairment, but also from impaired syntactic abilities (Vargha-Khadem et al. 1995). Non-human primates similarly lack the ability to fine-control the larynx and mouth the way normal humans can (but see Riede and Zuberbühler 2003a, 2003b). Numerous attempts to teach non-human primates spoken language or to get them to imitate vocal signals have failed, suggesting that non-human primates do not possess the neural capacities required for speech production (but see Marshall et al. 1999; Taglialatela et al. 2003 for some evidence of vocal plasticity). Enard et al. (2002) suggest that the human version of the FOXP2 gene led to increased fine control of the larynx and mouth, ultimately enabling more sophisticated vocalization. If this scenario is correct, then early humans entered this new round of evolution well prepared, because they already possessed a large number of communicative prelinguistic skills, which had evolved in the primate lineage long before to deal with a range of evolutionarily important events.

12.5 Conclusion

The studies reviewed in this chapter provide empirical evidence that two of the most basic linguistic capacities, i.e. the ability to assign meaning to acoustic units and the ability to adjust meaning as a function of a combinatorial rule, are present in non-human primates, at least as precursors. These cognitive abilities could be homologous to the ones utilized by humans to deal with semantic and syntactic problems in language processing. In monkeys, they are most vividly expressed in the behaviour of call recipients, but they might also drive some aspects of call production. If future work is able to confirm that these abilities are phylogenetically related (for example, because they are dealt with by homologous brain structures), then these abilities must be phylogenetically old, having emerged in the primate lineage before the Old World monkey clade split off from the great ape/human clade some thirty million years ago.

ACKNOWLEDGEMENTS

Field research was funded by the University of Pennsylvania, the US National Science Foundation, the Leakey Foundation, the National Geographic Society, the Max-Planck Society, the Swiss National Science Foundation, the European Science Foundation (OMLL), and the British Academy. I am grateful to Jennifer McClung, Maggie Tallerman, and two anonymous reviewers for comments on the manuscript.

FURTHER READING

On primate cognition, see Cheney and Seyfarth (1990) and Tomasello and Call (1997). See also Hauser (1996) on the evolution of communication, and the chapters in the volume edited by Tomasello (2003).

PART IV

Learnability and diversity: How did languages emerge and diverge?

Introduction to Part IV: Computer modelling widens the focus of language study

JAMES R. HURFORD

The chapters in Part IV demonstrate a remarkably unified and coherent vision of a newly emerging approach to the study of language, despite being somewhat diverse in their investigative styles and specific target problems. There have been hints and socially isolated pockets of this vision around for decades, probably even for centuries, but the advent of powerful high-speed computing has given it the boost it needed to raise it above a hopeful ideology. The vision is that Language (deliberately conceived broadly, hence the capitalization) is a complex dynamic system resulting from the interplay of biological evolution of the species, ontogenetic development of individuals, and cultural processes shaping the histories of societies. The truth of this vision has been recognized even by those who have deliberately steered their scientific methodology away from its daunting implications. This is evident in such passages as the following:

[W]hat a particular person has inside his head [i.e. an idiolect] is an artifact resulting from the interplay of many idiosyncratic factors, as contrasted with the more significant reality of UG. ... [E]ach actual 'language' will incorporate a periphery of borrowings, historical residues, inventions, and so on which we can hardly expect to—and indeed would not want to—incorporate within a prin-cipled theory of UG (Chomsky 1981: 8).

The chosen research strategy of generative grammar has been to narrow the domain of enquiry as far as possible, excluding considerations from performance, irregularity, and 'periphery of grammar'. This narrow view-point is aptly characterized in Chapter 13 here, by Henry Brighton et al., as a 'Principle of Detachment'. They argue that there are good reasons to reject this Principle of Detachment, thus opening the doors (some might say floodgates) to consideration of how factors other than innate individual psychological biases could influence the shape of languages. Orthodox generative linguists have also, to the puzzlement of many observers, typically refused to speculate about the evolutionary biological pressures shaping the hypothesized domain-specific Language Acquisition Device. In Chapter 14, Ted Briscoe boldly faces up to the theoretical problem of the possibility of interaction between biological evolution and the histories of languages in populations, with interesting results. Chapter 15, by Matthew Roberts et al., also breaks away from the narrow research approach, in arguing, very plausibly, that a striking feature of languages, their stubborn proneness to irregularity, actually result from the historical process of social transmission by learning, through a tight bottleneck (i.e. from an impoverished stimulus) over many generations. And Chapter 16, by Zach Solan et al., also addresses an inevitably social question, namely the existence of so many languages. A research program only concerned with how a single individual acquires her linguistic competence cannot provide an explanation for why languages differ. Postulating that the Language Acquisition Device sets parameters merely describes the problem. Finally, Chapter 17, by Andrew Smith, probes another vital area which is typically not the concern of generative linguists, though it does exercise developmental psychologists, namely the growth of conceptual structures and corresponding lexicons in response to signals from other users and experience of the context of communication. Smith shows that a certain (presumably innate) learning bias, the Principle of Mutual Exclusivity, allows the growth of successful shared communication.

Both narrow and broad research strategies have their advantages and disadvantages. Dissecting a dead animal in a sterile lab can't tell you much about its social life, and watching it roam the savannah can't tell you much about its cells. Narrow and broad approaches should complement and learn from each other. A heartening aspect of the chapters in this section is the maturity with which they do not throw out the baby with the bath water. Promising insights from generative linguistics have been kept.

Thus, at a very general level, all contributors agree that there are significant learning biases which contribute (but do not wholly account for) the shape of languages. This is a welcome change from some early adverse reactions to generative grammar, which often did not seem to realize that all learning is inevitably biased in some more or less complex way. The idea of UG is not dismissed; rather, it is situated in a wider context. As

Brighton and his co-authors put it, UG is more opaque to the facts of languages than was thought, due to the interposition of historico-cultural processes. Briscoe, too, explicitly adopts a central theoretical device of (one phase of) generative grammar, namely the idea of invariable principles and settable parameters, though he gives these a (more plausible?) statistical interpretation. And Roberts and his co-authors accept as their starting point a conception central to generative theorizing, the 'logical problem of language acquisition', in particular how a learner can withdraw from overgeneralizations in the absence of negative evidence. Note that Roberts and his colleagues accept the generative insistence that children learn from positive instances only, but their approach to the standard acquisition problem is, like Briscoe's, statistical and based on Bayesian learning.

Four of the five chapters introduced here report on specific series of computational simulations carried out by the authors, and the first chapter (Chapter 13) serves as a theoretical introduction to such studies. All these studies adopt the methodology of simulating populations of agents which communicate with other agents and learn from their behaviour, thus collectively constructing a language. Of course, all computational simulation involves massive idealization. Thus Roberts et al. in Chapter 15 make a simplification similar to Chomsky's idealization to an individual speaker–hearer when they postulate a 'population' consisting of only one individual per generation. The crucial new feature is the transmission of language over many generations, and they show a very natural mechanism by which irregular gaps in grammar can arise as a result of this process. The existence of such irregular gaps cannot be explained by a more narrow theory which focuses on the prototypically exceptionless generalizations made by language learners. If an innate generalizing device were all that shaped languages, there should be no exceptions to generalizations, no irregularities.

Only one chapter, Briscoe's, Chapter 14, discusses the co-evolutionary interaction between biogenetic evolution and the cultural transmission of language. Most generative linguists have accepted the biological basis for the human language capacity, but not got to grips with the evolutionary mechanisms which could have shaped it. It has been a commonplace that the relationship between the language faculty and genes is very complex. Certainly there is no single 'gene for grammar', or even a very small number of such genes. This has generally been taken as an indication that it is premature to theorize about specific possible relationships between genes and language. Without committing himself to any particular propositions about chromosomes or loci, Briscoe models a range of possible relationships between genes and the language capacity. In his terminology, the relationship can be more or less 'decorrelated'. To the extent that it is impossible to allocate a small group of genes to certain specific features of the language capacity, the relationship between genotype and phenotype (the LAD) is decorrelated. Briscoe shows that it is in principle possible to build models of such complex interaction, and more specifically comes up with the rather surprising result that parameters with default settings would be, under his assumptions, expected to increase in the course of biological evolution. Thus another question which we can give generative linguistics credit for posing, but not answering, namely 'Why are there principles and parameters?' begins to get an answer. Of course, Briscoe's modelling of the gene–language relationship is idealized and simplified, but it does establish certain basic principled results about this relationship, seen in the context of a train of simultaneous biological (via DNA) and cultural (via learning) evolution of language.

Chapter 16, by Zach Solan and colleagues, also models the shifting fortunes of languages over time, accounting for the diversity of languages through a mechanism that resembles, but crucially is not, biological evolution. As in Briscoe's work, in their model individuals who communicate better have more offspring. (This is a very common, but not unchallenged, assumption of work in this vein in general.) But Solan et al.'s model has no genes for language learning transmitted biologically. The kind of fitness that they discuss has consequences in the proportions of certain kinds of individuals in the next generation, but the characterizing features of these various kinds are not encoded in a genome. This contrasts with Briscoe's model, in which agents vary in their innate language acquisition capacity. In Solan et al.'s model, any agent can migrate to another group in the population and have the same chances of learning its language as an agent native to that group. Thus this model, like that of Roberts et al., is a model of cultural evolution.

The final chapter, Chapter 17, by Andrew Smith, also has a simulated population of agents, but here there is no iterated learning, that is no simulation of a community's history. Smith's model is one-generational. Like the other studies, this study seriously considers factors external to narrow language competence, in particular the structure of the external world, which can be modelled to be more or less 'clumpy'. Smith also makes the same assumption of no negative evidence (or feedback) as is made by generative theorists and by the other modellers writing here. An interesting result is that agents do not need to acquire identical competences, that is identical structures representing concepts, to be able to communicate with each other effectively. Again, considering factors external to competence, in this case the context of an utterance and the referents of signals in a simple simulated world, sheds light on a property of language previously unquestioned within the linguistic community. It has generally been taken for granted that having (near-)identical internal representations of the meanings of utterances would be a prerequisite for successful communication.

These studies are made possible by massive computing power. Modelling a single agent acquiring an internal representation on exposure to experience can be complicated enough. Multiply that by as many agents in the population as your computer can manage. Also introduce possible variation in their language-learning strategies. Further, if that is what you want to investigate, define a genome and some hypothetical more or less complex relationship between the genome and the language-learning strategy. Now define an external world, with whatever ontology you choose, and let the agents loose in this world according to some defined routines, communicating with each other perhaps entirely at random, or perhaps in ways determined by some hypothetical social structuring of the population. Now give each individual a life history, including a critical period in which it is susceptible to language learning, and a period of maturity when it behaves according to its internalized rules. Finally add population history, letting these individuals be born, live, and die, and influence each other in the process. Maybe it all sounds too much like a computer game, where the programmer gets to play God and watch the consequences. It can be done for fun, but the only point in doing it is to derive results from modelling the interaction of carefully defined parameters, and not too many at a time. If your model is too complex, you are unlikely to understand it. The computer models in this collection are thus necessarily simplified. But as the subject develops, and more practitioners become acquainted with previous studies, it becomes possible to build somewhat more complex models on simpler earlier models, without losing understanding. The models described in this collection are part of that growing movement in the study of language. Such modelling studies do not replace, but complement, empirical research on language acquisition, language change, and the genetic basis for language.

13 Cultural selection for learnability: three principles underlying the view that language adapts to be learnable

HENRY BRIGHTON, SIMON KIRBY,
AND KENNY SMITH

> If some aspects of linguistic behaviour can be predicted from more general considerations of the dynamics of communication in a community, rather than from the linguistic capacities of individual speakers, then they should be.
>
> (Jackendoff (2002: 101))

13.1 Introduction

Here is a far-reaching and vitally important question for those seeking to understand the evolution of language: given a thorough understanding of whatever cognitive processes are relevant to learning, understanding, and producing language, would such an understanding enable us to predict the universal features of language? This question is important because, if met with an affirmative answer, then an explanation for why language evolved to exhibit certain forms and not others must be understood in terms of the biological evolution of the cognitive basis for language. After all, such an account pivots on the assumption that properties of the cognitive mechanisms supporting language map *directly* onto the universal features of language that we observe. We argue against this position, and note that the relation between language universals and any cognitive basis for language is opaque. Certain hallmarks of language are adaptive in the context of cultural transmission; that is, *languages themselves* adapt to survive by adapting to be learnable. This phenomenon is termed *linguistic evolution*. Now, when seeking to understand the evolutionary prerequisites for language, this observation requires us to reconsider exactly *what* has evolved. For example, if significant aspects of linguistic structure can emerge through the evolution of languages themselves, then any theory of the biological evolution of language must seek to explain the basis, or prerequisites, for linguistic evolution. In short, by proposing that significant linguistic evolution can occur in the absence of biological change, we are suggesting that the question of the evolutionary prerequisites for language needs to be recast to account for the opaqueness between the cognitive basis for language and the structural tendencies we observe in language.

Linguistics should explain why languages exhibit certain hallmarks and not others. In relation to this objective, the notion of cultural selection for learnability is far-reaching because, traditionally, cognitive science seeks a detached account of cognitive processes and their behaviour. The prevailing assumption is that cultural processes must be factored out as much as possible: the locus of study is the individual, with the relationship between observed input–output conditions explained by internal acts of cognition alone. Despite supporting this discussion with insights gained from several computational models, we aim to arrive at three principles that are independent of any particular model. In doing so, we attempt to frame in a wider context demonstrative results gained from computational evolutionary linguistics: the notion of selection for learnability.

First, in section 13.2, we set the scene by characterizing a principle of detachment: the position that an explanation for language universals can be gained through an exploration of the cognitive mechanisms underlying language. We discuss the motivation for deviating from this position, and sketch parallels between computational evolutionary linguistics and situated cognitive science. Next, in section 13.3, we outline some key results that support our argument. The main thrust of our argument is presented in section 13.4, where we consider three underlying principles. First, we propose an *innateness hypothesis*: to what degree are features of language explicitly coded in our biological machinery? Second, the *principle of situatedness*: how much of the characteristic structure of language can we explain without considering side-effects arising from cultural transmission? Finally, in the *function independence principle*, we make clear that our position is not rooted in any notion of language function: we seek a non-functional explanation for certain aspects of linguistic structure.

13.2 Explaining universal features of language

13.2.1 *Language universals*

Take all the world's languages and note the structural features they have in common. On the basis of these universal features of language, we can propose a *Universal Grammar*, a hypothesis circumscribing the core features of all possible human languages (Chomsky 1965). On its own, this hypothesis acts only as a description. But far from being an inert taxonomy, Universal Grammar (UG) sets the target for an explanatory theory. The kind of entities contained in UG that we will allude to consist of *absolute* and *statistical* language universals (Matthews 1997; O'Grady, Dobrovolsky, and Katamba 1997). Absolute universals are properties present in all languages. Statistical universals are properties present in a significant number of languages. Several further distinctions naturally arise when describing constraints in cross-linguistic variation, but in the interests of clarity we will restrict this discussion to one of absolute and statistical universals.

On accepting UG as a natural object, we can move beyond a descriptive theory by asking why linguistic form is subject to this set of universal properties. More precisely, we seek an explanation for how and where this restricted set of linguistic features is specified. The discussion that follows will analyse the possible routes we can take when forming such an explanation. The hunt for an explanation of universal features is traditionally mounted by arguing that Universal Grammar is an innate biological predisposition that defines the manner in which language is learned by a child. The linguistic stimulus a child faces, whatever language it is drawn from, through the process of learning, results in a knowledge of language. For example, Chomsky states that this learning process is 'better understood as the growth of cognitive structures along an internally directed course under the triggering and partially shaping effect of the environment' (Chomsky 1980: 34).

So an innate basis for language, along with the ability to learn, permits the child to arrive at a knowledge of language. Just how influential the learning process is in arriving at knowledge of language is frustratingly unclear. At one extreme, we can imagine a highly specialized 'language instinct' (Pinker 1994) where learning only 'partially shapes' the yield of the language acquisition process: the assumption here is that linguistic evidence faced by a child underdetermines the knowledge they end up with. At the other extreme, we can imagine a domain-general learning competence which serves language as well other cognitive tasks. Here, the suggestion is that knowledge of language can be induced from primary linguistic data with little or no language-specific constraints (Elman et al. 1996).

13.2.2 *Isolating the object of study*

Recall the conundrum we are considering: how and where are universal features of language specified? The explanatory framework discussed in the previous section concerns itself with the degree to which language-specific constraints guide language acquisition, and it is assumed that these constraints determine language universals. Nowhere in this analysis is the role of the linguistic population considered: an explanation for the universal features of a population-level phenomenon—language—has been reduced to the problem of the knowledge of language acquired by individuals. In short, the traditional route to understanding linguistic universals, to a greater or lesser extent, assumes that these universals are specified innately in each human, or at least, explainable in terms of detached linguistic agents. This de-emphasis of context, culture, and history is a recurring theme in the cognitive sciences, as Howard Gardner notes:

> Though mainstream cognitive scientists do not necessarily bear any animus [. . .] against historical or cultural analyses, in practice they attempt to factor out these elements to the maximum extent possible (Gardner 1985: 41).

Taking this standpoint is understandable and perhaps necessary when embarking on any practical investigation into cognition. The result of this line of explanation is that we consider universal features of language to be strongly correlated with an individual's act of cognition, which is taken to be biologically determined. Now we have isolated the object of study. Understanding the innate linguistic knowledge of humans will lead us to an understanding of why language is the way it is. For the purposes of this study, let us characterize this position:

Definition 1 (Principle of detachment). A thorough explanation of the cognitive processes relevant to language, coupled with an understanding of how these processes mediate between input (primary linguistic data) and output (knowledge of language), would be sufficient for a thorough explanation of the universal properties of language.

Now, when considering knowledge of language, the problem is to account for a device that relates input (linguistic stimulus) to output (knowledge of language). For example, Chomsky discusses a language acquisition device (LAD) in which the output takes the form of a system of grammatical rules. He states that:

An engineer faced with the problem of designing a device for meeting the given input-output conditions would naturally conclude that the basic properties of the output are a consequence of the design of the device. Nor is there any plausible alternative to this assumption, so far as I can see (Chomsky 1967).

In other words, if we want to know how and where the universal features of language are specified, we need look no further than an individual's competence, derived from primary linguistic data via the LAD. This position, which we have termed the principle of detachment, runs right through cognitive science and amounts to a general approach to studying cognitive processes. For example, in his classic work on vision, Marr makes a convincing case for examining visual processing as a competence understood entirely by considering a series of transformations of visual stimulus (Marr 1977, 1982). We will now consider two bodies of work that suggest that the principle of detachment is questionable.

13.2.3 *Explanation via synthetic construction*

One of the aims of cognitive science, and in particular, artificial intelligence (AI), is to explain human and animal cognition by building working computational models. Those working in the field of AI often isolate a single competence, such as reasoning, planning, learning, or natural language processing. This competence is then investigated in accordance with the principle of detachment, more often than not in conjunction with a simplified model of the environment (a micro-world). These simplifying assumptions, given the difficulty of the task, are quite understandable. So the traditional approach is centred around the belief that investigating a competence with respect to a simplified micro-world will yield results that, by and large, hold true when that agent is placed in the real world. General theories that underlie intelligent action can therefore be proposed by treating the agent as a detached entity operating with respect to an environment. Crucially, this environment is presumed to contain the intrinsic properties found in the environment that 'real' agents encounter.

This is a very broad characterization of cognitive science and AI. Nevertheless, many within cognitive science see this approach as misguided and divisive, for a number of reasons. For example, we could draw on the wealth of problems and lack of progress which traditional AI is accused of (Pfeifer and Scheier 1999: 59–78). Some within AI have drawn on this history of perceived failure to justify a new set of principles collectively termed *Embodied Cognitive Science* (Pfeifer and Scheier 1999), and occasionally *New AI* (Brooks 1999). Many of these principles can be traced back to Hubert Dreyfus's critique of AI, twenty years earlier (Dreyfus 1972). The stance put forward by advocates of embodied cognitive science is important: its proponents refine Dreyfus's stance, build on it, and crucially cite examples of successful engineering projects. This recasting of the problem proposes, among others, *situatedness* as a theoretical maxim (Clancey 1997). Taking the principle of situatedness to its extreme, the exact nature of the environment is to be taken as primary and theoretically significant. For example, the environment may be partly constructed by the participation of other agents (Bullock and Todd 1999). In other words, certain aspects of cognition can only be fully explained when viewed in the context of participation (Winograd and Flores 1986; Brooks 1999). It is important to note that this 'new orientation' is seen by many as opposing mainstream AI, or at least the branches of AI that claim to explain cognition.

Advocates of embodied cognitive science tell us that any explanation for a cognitive capacity must be tightly coupled with a precise understanding of the interaction between environment and cognitive agent. What impact does this discussion have on our questions about language universals? First, it provides a source of insights into investigating cognition through building computational models: a theory faces a different set of constraints when implemented as a computational model. Second, this discussion should lead us to consider that an analysis of cognitive processes without assuming the principle of detachment can be fruitful. In the context of language and communication, the work of Luc Steels is an example of this approach. Steels investigates the construction of perceptual distinctions and signal lexicons in visually grounded communicating robots (Steels 1997, 1998b). In this work, signals and the meanings associated with these signals emerge as a result of self-organization. This phenomenon can only be understood with respect to an environment constructed by the participation of others.

13.2.4 *The evolutionary explanation*

Only humans have language. The communication systems used by animals do not even approach the sophistication of human language, so the evolution of language must concern the evolution of humans over the past five million years, since our last common ancestor with a non-linguistic species (Jones, Martin, and Pilbeam 1992). Consequently, examining fossil evidence offers a source of insights into the evolution of language in humans. For example, we can analyse the evolution of the vocal tract, or examine skulls and trace a path through the skeletal evolution of hominids, but the kind of conclusions we can draw from such evidence can only go so far (Lieberman 1984; Wilkins and Wakefield 1995).

One route to explaining the evolution of language in humans, which we can dub *functional nativism*, turns on the idea that language evolved in humans due to the functional advantages gained by linguistically competent humans. Language, therefore, was a trait selected for by biological evolution (Pinker and Bloom 1990; Nowak and Komarova 2001). Here, we can imagine an evolutionary trajectory starting from some biological predisposition present in protohumans for using some set of communication systems C_{proto}. From this starting point, biological evolution led to the occurrence of the set of communication systems C_{UG}, which includes all human languages. The story of language evolution can then unfold by claiming that the biological machinery supporting C_{proto} evolved to support C_{UG} due to functional pressures (see Figure 13.1). Implicit in this account is the principle of detachment. The biological evolution of cognitive capacities supporting language are equated with the evolution of languages themselves.

Over the past fifteen years, computational evolutionary linguistics has emerged as a source for testing such hypotheses. This approach employs computational models to try and shed light on the problem of the evolution of language in humans (Hurford 1989; Briscoe 2000a; Kirby 2002b). One source of complexity in understanding the evolution of language is the interaction between three complex adaptive systems, each one operating on a different timescale. More precisely, linguistic

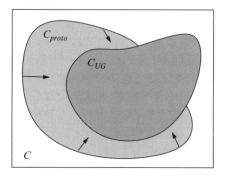

Fɪɢ. 13.1 Functional nativism. From the set of all communication systems C, the communication systems of protohumans, C_{proto}, evolved under some functional pressure towards C_{UG}.

information is transmitted on two evolutionary substrates: the biological and the cultural. For example, you are born with some innate predisposition for language which evolved over millions of years. The linguistic forms you inherit from your culture have evolved over hundreds of years. In addition to these evolutionary systems, your linguistic competence emerges over tens of years. Much of the work in computational modelling has analysed this interaction. By modelling linguistic agents as learners and producers of language, and then investigating how communication systems evolve in the presence of both biological and cultural transmission, computational evolutionary linguistics attempts to shed light on how language can evolve in initially non-linguistic communities. This approach draws on disciplines such as cognitive science, artificial life, complexity, and theoretical biology.

Recent work in this field has focused on developing models in which certain hallmarks of human language can emerge in populations of biologically identical linguistic agents. That is, characteristics of language emerge in the absence of biological change, where language is transmitted from generation to generation entirely through the cultural substrate. We detail this work in section 13.3, but mention it here as it impacts on the current discussion. In explaining how and why language has its characteristic structure, the evolutionary approach, by investigating the interaction between biological and cultural substrates, is in line with the claims made by proponents of embodied cognitive science. Because languages themselves can adapt, independent of the biological substrate, certain features of language cannot be explained in terms of detached cognitive mechanisms alone.

13.2.5 *Summary: should we breach the principle of detachment?*

This discussion has outlined the basis for asking three questions. First, what kind of explanatory framework should be invoked when explaining universal features of language? Secondly, are any of the principles underlying situated cognitive science relevant to understanding the characteristic structure of language?[1] Thirdly, what kind of explanatory leverage can be gained by breaching the principle of detachment, and exploring issues of language evolution via computational modelling and simulation? On the validity of artificial intelligence, Chomsky notes 'in principle simulation certainly can provide much insight' (Chomsky 1993b: 30). Perhaps more relevant is the quotation located at the beginning of this chapter from another prominent linguist, Ray Jackendoff. Taking these two observations together, we should at least consider the role of the cultural transmission of language in explaining the universal features of language. The next section outlines recent work on exploring precisely this question.

13.3 Modelling cultural transmission

13.3.1 *Iterated learning models*

An iterated learning model (ILM) is a framework for testing theories of linguistic transmission. Within an ILM, agents act as a conduit for an evolving language—language itself changes or evolves rather than the agents themselves. An ILM is a generational model: after members of one generation learn a language, their production becomes the input to learning in the next generation. This model of linguistic transmission, providing that the transfer of knowledge of language from one generation to the next is not entirely accurate or reliable, will result in diachronic change. Importantly, certain linguistic structures will survive transmission, while other forms may disappear.

---

[1] We should make clear that when we refer to situatedness, we mean nothing more than a full consideration of the environmental context of cognition.

The range of linguistic structures that can be explained using an iterated learning model can vary substantially. There are two broad categories of model: those of *language change* and *language evolution*. An investigation into language change will often assume a model in which hallmarks of language are already present. Models of language change cannot, therefore, impact on our discussion of the principle of detachment. If the hallmarks of language are pre-programmed into the model, then the model cannot inform us how these hallmarks came about. Instead, models of language change can explain aspects of change within fully developed languages, and therefore aim to shed light on issues such as, for example, statistical universals—those properties present in many but not all languages. In contrast, iterated learning models of language evolution model the transition to language from non-linguistic communication systems, and can therefore shed light on how hallmarks of language came to be. For this reason, iterated learning models of language evolution are particularly relevant to our discussion of the principle of detachment.

13.3.2 *Language change*

In studying language change we often consider the trajectory of language through possible grammars. Any resulting explanation is therefore orientated neutrally with respect to explaining absolute linguistic universals. From one grammar to the next, we presume hallmarks of language are ever present (see Figure 13.2). Models of language change must invoke a situated component. A model must tackle the problem of language acquisition: a learner will deviate from the grammar of its teachers when the primary linguistic data fails to unambiguously represent the grammar from which it is derived. Knowledge of language is therefore not transmitted directly from mind to mind, but instead some external correlate—linguistic performance—must stand proxy for knowledge of language. Modelling language change must therefore consider some environment allowing the transmission of language competence via language performance. This environment, importantly, is constructed by other individuals in the culture.

Using iterated learning, we can construct computational models of language change. These studies are motivated by the observation that language change is driven by considerations arising from language acquisition (Clark and Roberts 1993; Niyogi and Berwick 1997; Briscoe 2002). For example, using a principles and parameters approach to language

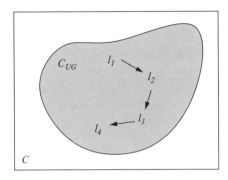

Fɪɢ. 13.2 Language change. An example trajectory of language change through languages l_1, l_2, l_3, and l_4.

specification, Niyogi and Berwick (1997) develop a population model with which they investigate the dynamics of language change. In particular, they use a probabilistic model of grammar induction to focus on the loss of verb second position in the transition from Old French to Modern French, which results directly, they claim, from misconvergences arising during language acquisition. In contrast, Hare and Elman (1995) address the problem of morphological change by examining connectionist simulations of language learning, which, when placed in the context of iterated learning, can be used to explain morphological changes, such as verb inflection in Modern English arising from the past tense system of Old English. Importantly, the linguistic phenomenon these models attempt to explain is relatively well documented: the historical accuracy of models of language change can be tested.

13.3.3 *Language evolution*

These studies of language change tell us that the learnability of languages, over the course of cultural transmission, has a bearing on the distribution of languages we observe. Now we will discuss extending the range of explanation offered by models of iterated learning to include the possibility of explaining hallmarks of language. The dynamics of iterated learning can make certain properties of communication systems ubiquitous. This must lead us to consider the fact that, just as the dimensions of variation can be explored via iterated learning, the undeviating features of language may also depend on issues of learnability.

Importantly, the possibility that iterated learning models can shed light on an explanation of these properties will make a convincing case for questioning the principle of detachment. If the unvarying features of language can be explained in the same way as those that vary, then issues of innateness become problematic and less clear cut. For example, Christiansen, Deacon, and Kirby have each claimed previously that universals should, at least in part, be seen as arising from repeated transmission through learning:

In short, my view amounts to the claim that most—if not all—linguistic universals will turn out to be terminological artifacts referring to mere side-effects of the processing and learning of language in humans (Christiansen 1994: 127).

Grammatical universals exist, but I want to suggest that their existence does not imply that they are prefigured in the brain like frozen evolutionary accidents. In fact, I suspect that universal rules or implicit axioms of grammar aren't really stored or located anywhere, and in an important sense, they are not *determined* at all. Instead, I want to suggest the radical possibility that they have emerged spontaneously and independently in each evolving language, in response to universal biases in the selection processes affecting language transmission (Deacon 1997: 115–16).

The problem is that there are now two candidate explanations for the same observed fit between universals and processing—a glossogenetic one in which languages themselves adapt to the pressures of transmission through the arena of use, and a phylogenetic one in which the LAD adapts to the pressures of survival in an environment where successful communication is advantageous. (Kirby 1999: 132).

These arguments place an explanation for the universal features of language well and truly outside the vocabulary of explanation suggested by the principle of detachment. In the context of cultural transmission, we term the process by which certain linguistic forms are adaptive and therefore evolve and persist *cultural selection for learnability*. More precisely:

> **Definition 2 (Cultural adaptation).** By cultural adaptation, we mean the occurrence of changes in the language due to the effects of cultural transmission.

We should contrast the notion of cultural adaptation to that of genetic adaptation, where genetic changes occur as a result of natural selection. Importantly, our notion of cultural adaptation refers to the *language* adapting, rather than the users of language. Next, we define cultural selection for learnability:

Definition 3 (Cultural selection for learnability). In order for linguistic forms to persist from one generation to the next, they must repeatedly survive the processes of expression and induction. That is, the output of one generation must be successfully learned by the next if these linguistic forms are to survive. We say that those forms that repeatedly survive cultural transmission are adaptive in the context of cultural transmission: they will be selected for due to the combined pressures of cultural transmission and learning.

In this context, the terms *adaptive* and *selection* only loosely relate to the equivalent terms used in the theory of biological evolution. Importantly, the idea that languages themselves adapt to be learnable, and in doing so organize themselves subject to a set of recurring structural properties, has been the subject of computational models that make explicit these assumptions. In particular, the experiments of Kirby (2002a) and Batali (2002) demonstrate that a collection of learners with the ability to perform grammar induction will, from an initially holistic communication system, spontaneously arrive at compositional and recursive communication systems. Because language is ostensibly infinite, and cultural transmission can only result in the production of a finite series of utterances, only generalizable forms will survive. These experiments suggest that certain hallmarks of language are culturally adaptive: pressures arising from transmission from one agent to another cause these hallmarks to emerge and persist. For example, adaptive properties such as compositionality and recursion, which we can consider absolute language universals, are defining characteristics of stable systems.

Breaching the principle of detachment requires us to adopt a conceptual framework in which the details of the environment of adaptation become crucial. The details form part of the focus of further work in this area. After all, if the precise nature of the environment of adaptation is to play a pivotal role, as suggested by situated theories of cognition, then the hope is that a wider range of linguistic forms can be explained within the iterated learning framework. For example, Kirby (2001) demonstrates that by elaborating the environment by imposing a non-uniform probability distribution over the set of communicatively relevant situations, regular/ irregular forms emerge. Why is this? By skewing the relative frequency of utterances, irregular forms can exist by virtue of the fact they are frequently used, and therefore are subject to a reduced pressure to be structured; see Chapter 15, Roberts, Onnis, and Chater. Similarly, Smith, Brighton, and Kirby (2003) show how clustering effects in the space of communicatively relevant situations leads to a stronger pressure for compositionality. These studies demonstrate that the precise nature of the environment of adaptation impacts on the resulting language structure. By understanding the impact of environmental considerations on the evolved languages, in tandem with an investigation into plausible models of language acquisition, we hope to shed further light on the relationship between cultural selection and the structure of evolved languages.

In this section we have discussed how models of language evolution and change based on a cultural, situated model of linguistic transmission can shed light on the occurrence of hallmarks of language. For a more thorough discussion and the modelling details we refer the reader to material cited, as well as a recent overview article (Kirby 2002b).

13.4   Underlying principles

We began this discussion by considering the manner in which language universals should be explained. We now present three principles that underlie the view that language universals are, at least in part, the result of cultural selection for learnability. We start by noting that any conclusions we draw will be contingent on an innateness hypothesis:

Principle 1 (Innateness hypothesis). Humans must have a biologically determined set of predispositions that impact on our ability to learn and produce language. The degree to which these capacities are specific to language is not known.

Here we are stating the obvious: the ability to process language must have a biological basis. However, the degree to which this basis is specific to language is unclear. Linguistics lacks a solid theory, based on empirical findings, that identifies those aspects of language that can be learned, and those which must be innate (Pullum and Scholz 2002). Next, we must consider the innateness hypothesis with respect to two positions. First, assuming the principle of detachment, the innateness hypothesis must lead us to believe that there is a clear relation between patterns we observe in language and some biological correlate. If we extend the vocabulary of explanation by rejecting the principle of detachment, then the question of innateness is less clear cut. We can now talk of a biological basis for a feature of language, but with respect to a cultural dynamic. Here, a cultural process will mediate between a biological basis and the occurrence of that feature in language. This discussion therefore centres around recasting the question of innateness. Furthermore, this observation, because it relates to a cultural dynamic, leads us to accepting that situatedness plays a role:

> **Principle 2 (Situatedness).** A thorough understanding of the cognitive basis for language would not amount to a total explanation of language structure. However, a thorough understanding of the cognitive basis for language in conjunction with an understanding of the trajectory of language adaptation through cultural transmission would amount to a total explanation of language structure.

Of course, the degree of correlation between a piece of biological machinery supporting some aspect of language and the resulting language universal is hard to quantify. But in general, given some biological basis for processing language, some set of communication systems $C_{possible}$ will be possible. A detached understanding of language can tell us little about which members of $C_{possible}$ will be culturally adaptive and therefore observed. The principle of situatedness changes the state of play by considering those communication systems that are adaptive, $C_{adaptive}$, on a cultural substrate, and therefore observed. In short, cultural selection for learnability occurs with respect to constraints on cultural transmission. These constraints determine which members of $C_{possible}$ are culturally adaptive, observed, and therefore become members of the set $C_{adaptive}$.

By conjecturing an opaque relationship between some biological basis for language and some observed language universal, the notion of UG becomes problematic. Universal Grammar is often taken to mean one of two things. First, the term UG is sometimes used to refer to the set of features that all languages have in common (Chomsky 1965). Secondly, and perhaps more frequently, UG has been defined as the initial state of the language-learning child (Chomsky 1975). Figure 13.3 depicts how these two definitions relate to our discussion of the biological basis for language, the set of possible communication systems, and the set of observed communication systems.

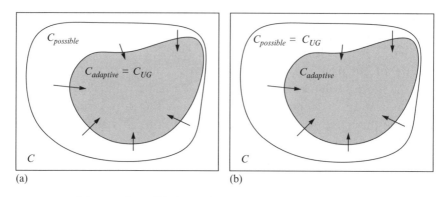

(a)   (b)

Fɪɢ. 13.3 Of the set of possible human communication systems $C_{possible}$, some set $C_{adaptive}$ are adaptive in the context of cultural transmission, and therefore observed. Depending on how we define UG, the set of communication systems characterized by UG, C_{UG}, are either precisely those we observe ($C_{adaptive}$), or those that are possible, but not necessarily observed ($C_{possible}$).

The set of communication systems that conform to the definition of UG are denoted as C_{UG}. Depending on which definition of UG we adopt, this set will be equivalent to either $C_{possible}$ or $C_{adaptive}$. These two alternatives are now explored:

1. *UG as the set of features common to all languages.* If we take UG as the set of features common to all observed languages, then C_{UG}, the set of communication systems conforming to UG, is identical to our set of culturally adaptive communication systems, $C_{adaptive}$. This must be the case, as only members of $C_{adaptive}$ are observed and can therefore contribute to a theory of UG under this reading. This position is represented in Figure 13.3(a).

2. *UG as the initial state of the language-learning child.* The alternative definition of UG, where UG defines the initial state of the learner, must encompass those communication systems which are possible, but not necessarily adaptive: $C_{possible}$. Because humans are equipped with the biological basis for using members of $C_{possible}$, their initial state must account for them. Hence, under this second reading of UG, $C_{possible} = C_{UG}$. As before, only some members of $C_{possible}$ will be culturally adaptive and therefore observed. Figure 13.3(b) reflects this relationship.

Irrespective of our definition of UG, an acceptance of the principle of situatedness allows us to explain a feature of language in terms of a biological trait realized as a bias which, in combination with the adaptive properties of this bias over repeated cultural transmission, leads to that feature being observed. However, if one accepts that cultural transmission plays a pivotal role in determining language structure, then one must also consider the impact of other factors which might result in the emergence of adaptive properties—for example, issues relating to communication and effective signalling. But as a first cut, we need to understand how much can be explained without appealing to any functional properties of language:

> **Principle 3 (Function independence).** Some aspects of language structure can be explained independently of language function.

A defence of this principle is less clear cut. Without doubt language is used for communication, but whether issues of communication determine all forms of language structure is by no means clear. The picture we are developing here suggests that constraints on learning and repeated cultural transmission play an important part in determining linguistic structure: the models we have discussed make no claims about, nor explicitly account for, any notion of language function. In short, the fact that, for example, compositional structure results without any model of language function suggests that this is a fruitful line of enquiry to pursue.

13.5 Conclusions

Universal features of languages, by definition, are adhered to by every user of language. We might then take the individual as the locus of study when seeking an explanation for why language universals take the form that they do. In line with this intuition, practitioners of cognitive science will often make the simplifying assumption that the behaviour of individuals can be understood by examining internal cognitive processes of detached agents. The principle of detachment characterizes this position.

In attempting to understand how and where language universals are specified, this discussion has focused on questioning the principle of detachment. We have explored two sources of ideas that suggest that an explanation of the characteristic structure of language could benefit from breaching the principle of detachment. Firstly, advocates of situated cognitive science claim that the property of situatedness, a full understanding of the interaction between agent and environment, is theoretically significant. Secondly, recent work in the field of computational evolutionary linguistics suggests that cultural dynamics are fundamental to understanding why linguistic structure evolves and persists. We should stress here that in one respect languages are not stable because they are constantly changing. But in contrast, absolute linguistic universals are entirely stable, or at least they have been over the duration of modern linguistic inquiry.[2]

Taking these two sources as evidence, we outlined recent computational models that explore the relation between language universals and those linguistic features that are adaptive in the context of cultural transmission. On the basis of these experiments, we claim that cultural selection for learnability must form part of any explanation relating to how and where language universals are specified. We claim that, due to constraints on cultural transmission, languages adapt to reflect the biases present in language learners and producers. The relationship between these biases and the observed universal features of language is therefore opaque: a cultural dynamic mediates between the two.

Here is the message we wish to convey: selection for learnability is an important determinant of language universals, and as such should be understood independently of any particular computational model. Our aim is to outline the theoretical foundations of cultural selection for learnability. We do this by proposing three principles. First, the Innateness Hypothesis (Principle 1) states that there must be a biological basis for our language-learning abilities, but the degree to which these abilities are specific to language is unclear. The second principle, the principle of Situatedness (Principle 2), states that language universals cannot be explained through an understanding of the cognitive basis for language alone. Importantly, we claim that certain properties of language are adaptive in the context of cultural transmission. The third principle, that of Function Independence (Principle 3), makes clear that any functional properties of language are not necessarily determinants of language structure. We note that an explanation for certain universals, such as

---

[2] See Newmeyer (2002) for discussion of this and other issues that relate to uniformitarianism in linguistics.

compositional syntax, need not appeal to any notion of language function. In short, we seek a non-functional explanation for certain aspects of linguistic structure.

By questioning the principle of detachment and pursuing a line of enquiry guided by Principles 1–3 we have argued that the concept of cultural selection for learnability can provide important insights into some fundamental questions in linguistics and cognitive science. The work presented here should be seen as the first steps towards a more thorough explanation of the evolution of linguistic structure.

ACKNOWLEDGEMENTS

Henry Brighton was supported by ESRC Postdoctoral Research Fellowship T026271445. Kenny Smith was supported by ESRC Research Grant No. R000223969 and ESRC Postdoctoral Research Fellowship PTA-026-27-0321.

FURTHER READING

Christiansen and Kirby (2003) provide a selection of articles by influential thinkers covering a broad sweep of topics relevant to evolutionary linguistics. For those interested in the debate on cognitive science and embodiment, Pfeifer and Scheier (1999) constitutes an excellent source of further reading. Whereas in this chapter we have avoided appealing to language function when attempting to explain linguistic structure (in accordance with our principle of function independence), Newmeyer (1998a) provides a thorough and thoughtful consideration of the place of such functionalist approaches in linguistics. Finally, computational models have played a key role in driving the development of the position that we present here. Briscoe (2002) provides a collection of articles describing recent research involving such models, and can be recommended to those seeking further insight into the topics, issues, and techniques of the field.

14 Co-evolution of the language faculty and language(s) with decorrelated encodings

TED BRISCOE

14.1 Introduction

Renewed interest in studying human language from an evolutionary perspective stems in large part from a growing understanding that not only the language faculty but also languages themselves can be profitably modelled as evolving systems. Deacon (1997) offers persuasive arguments for, and an extended introduction to, this approach. Working within this framework, a number of researchers have proposed that the language faculty evolved via genetic assimilation (sometimes referred to as the Baldwin Effect) in response to the emergence of (proto)languages—see Briscoe (2003) for a detailed review of these proposals and counterarguments.

Yamauchi (2000, 2001) argues that accounts of the fit between the language faculty and languages which invoke genetic assimilation are suspect because they assume correlation between the genetic encoding of the language faculty and the phenotypic encoding of nativized linguistic constraints. He describes a simulation in which he shows that progressively decorrelating the encodings slows, and finally prevents, genetic assimilation of linguistic information. In this chapter, I argue that the decorrelation argument does not undermine the account of the evolution of the language faculty via genetic assimilation, nor the extended co-evolutionary account in which the evolving language faculty in turn exerts linguistic selection pressure on languages.

Briscoe (1999, 2000a, 2002) describes a correlated simulation model in which co-evolution of the language faculty and language(s) reliably occurs, shortening the learning period and exerting linguistic selection pressure on language change. Here I report the results of new experiments using the extant simulation in which the genotypic encoding of the language faculty and the phenotypic encoding of the starting point for language learning are progressively decorrelated. The results show that decorrelation generally increases the probability of pre-emptive rather than assimilative evolution of the language faculty. However, because languages co-evolve rapidly, pre-emptive mutations which spread genetically lead to rapid compensatory linguistic changes, so that the 'fit' between language and the language faculty remains close. As it is only the detailed timing of genetic and linguistic changes which can discriminate pre-emptive from assimilative genetic change, it is likely that these two scenarios will never be discriminated empirically. However, high degrees of decorrelation lead to overall higher failure rates in language acquisition, and eventually either to breakdown in communication or to highly restricted linguistic systems which are largely genetically encoded. In reality, language acquisition and communication are very robust aspects of human behaviour, and languages appear, if anything, to accrue complexity rather than lose expressiveness (e.g. McWhorter 2001b), making the predicted evolutionary dynamic implausible.

Section 14.2 describes genetic assimilation and its putative role in the evolution of the language faculty, arguing for a co-evolutionary model in which languages themselves both influence and are influenced by the evolution of the language faculty. Section 14.3 describes my correlated simulation model and section 14.4 summarizes results demonstrating genetic assimilation of grammatical information and analyses the critical assumptions behind these results. Section 14.5 evaluates extant work on decorrelation, describes modifications to my model to allow for progressive decorrelation, and details how this affects the original results. Section 14.6 argues that consideration of decorrelation strengthens the case for a co-evolutionary account of the emergence and evolution of the language faculty based primarily on genetic assimilation.

14.2 From genetic assimilation to co-evolution

Genetic assimilation is a neo-Darwinian mechanism supporting apparent 'inheritance of acquired characteristics' (e.g. Waddington 1942, 1975).

The fundamental insights are that: (a) plasticity in the relationship between phenotype and genotype is under genetic control, (b) novel environments create selection pressures which favour organisms with the plasticity to allow within-lifetime (so-called epigenetic) developmental adaptations to the new environment, and (c) natural selection will function to 'canalize' these developmental adaptations by favouring genotypic variants in which the relevant trait develops reliably on the basis of minimal environmental stimulus, providing that the environment, and consequent selection pressure, remains constant over enough generations. For example, humans are unique amongst mammals in their ability to digest milk in adulthood. Durham (1991) argues that the development of animal husbandry created an environment in which this ability conferred fitness, as milk now became a particularly reliable source of nutrition. This created selection pressure for individuals with a genetic make-up for increased ability to digest milk later in life. The apparent 'feedback' from environment to genotype is nothing more (nor less) than natural selection for a hitherto neutral variant within the human genotype which became advantageous as a consequence of cultural innovation.

Waddington (1975: 305–6) suggests that genetic assimilation provided a possible mechanism for the evolution of a language faculty:

If there were selection for the ability to use language, then there would be selection for the capacity to acquire the use of language, in an interaction with a language-using environment; and the result of selection for epigenetic responses can be, as we have seen, a gradual accumulation of so many genes with effects tending in this direction that the character gradually becomes genetically assimilated.

In other words, the ability to learn is a genetic endowment with slight variation between individuals, and individuals with hitherto neutral variants allowing more rapid and/or reliable language acquisition would be selected for in the novel language-using environment.

Briscoe (1999, 2000a) speculates that an initial language acquisition procedure emerged via recruitment (exaptation) of pre-existing (preadapted), general-purpose learning mechanisms to a specifically linguistic, cognitive representation capable of expressing mappings from decomposable meaning representations to realizable, essentially linearized, encodings of such representations (see also Bickerton 1998; Worden 1998). The selective pressure favouring such a development, and its subsequent maintenance and refinement, is only possible if some protolanguage(s) had already emerged within a hominid population, supporting successful communication and capable of cultural transmission, that is, learnable without a language-specific faculty (e.g. Deacon 1997; Kirby and Hurford 1997).

Protolanguage(s) may have been initially similar to those advocated by Wray (2000) in which complete, propositional messages are conveyed by undecomposable signals. However, to create selection pressure for the emergence of grammar, and thus for a faculty incorporating language-specific grammatical bias, protolanguage(s) must have evolved at some point into decomposable utterances, broadly of the kind envisaged by Bickerton (1998). Several models of the emergence of syntax have been developed (e.g. Kirby 2001, 2002a; Nowak et al. 2000). At the point when the environment contains language(s) with minimal syntax, genetic assimilation of grammatical information becomes adaptive, under the assumption that mastery of language confers a fitness advantage on its users, since genetic assimilation will make grammatical acquisition more rapid and reliable.

Given that genetic assimilation only makes sense in a scenario in which evolving (proto)languages create selection pressure, Waddington's notion of genetic assimilation should be embedded in the more general one of co-evolution (e.g. Kauffman 1993: 242–3). Waddington himself notes (1975: 307) that if there is an adaptive advantage to shortening the acquisition period, then we might expect genetic assimilation to continue to the point where no learning would be needed, because a fully specified grammar had been encoded. In this case, acquisition would be instantaneous and fitness would be maximized in a language-using population. However, given a co-evolutionary scenario, in which languages themselves are complex adaptive systems (e.g. Kirby 1998; Briscoe 2000b), a plausible explanation for continuing grammatical diversity is that social factors favouring innovation and diversity create conflicting linguistic selection pressures (e.g. Nettle 1999; see also Chapter 16 in this volume, Solan et al.). Genetic transmission, and thus assimilation, are much slower than cultural transmission. Therefore, continued plasticity in grammatical acquisition is probable, because assimilation will not be able to 'keep up with' all grammatical change. Furthermore, too much genetic assimilation, or canalization to use Waddington's term, will reduce individuals' fitness, if linguistic change subsequently makes it hard or impossible for them to acquire an innovative grammatical (sub)system.

14.3 The co-evolutionary simulation model

The model is a stochastic computational simulation consisting of an evolving population of language agents (LAgts). LAgts are endowed with the ability to acquire a grammar by learning. However, the starting point for learning, and thus LAgts' consequent success, is determined to an extent by an inherited genotype. Furthermore, the fitness of a LAgt (that is, the likelihood with which LAgts will produce offspring) is determined by their communicative success. Offspring inherit starting points for learning (genotypes) which are based on those of their parents. Inheritance of *starting* points for learning prevents any form of actual (Lamarckian) inheritance of acquired characteristics, but allows for genetic assimilation, in principle. Inheritance either takes the form of crossover of the genotypes of the parents, resulting in a shared, mixed inheritance from each parent, and overall loss of variation in genotypes over generations, and/or random mutation of the inherited genotype, introducing new variation.

14.3.1 *Language agents*

A language agent (LAgt) is a model of a language learner and user consisting of (a) a learning procedure, *LP*, which takes a definition of a universal grammar, *UG*, and a surface-form:logical-form (*LF*) pair or 'trigger', *t*, and returns a specific grammar, *g*; (b) a parser, *P*, which takes a grammar and a trigger, *t*, and returns a logical form, *LF*, for *t*, if *t* is parsable with *g*, and otherwise reports failure; and (c) a generator, *G*, which given a grammar, *g*, and a randomly selected *LF* produces a trigger compatible with this *LF*.

I have developed several accounts of *LP* based on a theory of *UG* utilizing a generalized categorial grammar and an associated parsing algorithm *P* (Briscoe 2000a). In what follows, I assume the Bayesian account of parametric learning developed in Briscoe (1999, 2002) with minor modifications. Grammatical acquisition consists of incrementally adopting the most probable grammar defined by *UG* compatible with the *n*th trigger in the sequence seen so far:

$$g = argmax_{g \in UG} p(g) p(t_n | g)$$

Briscoe (1999, 2002) shows how this formula (where p is probability) can be derived from Bayes' theorem and how prior probability distributions can be placed on $g \in UG$ in terms of the number and type of parameters required to define g, broadly favouring smaller grammars and greater linguistic regularity. The probability of t given g is defined in terms of the posterior probabilities of the grammatical categories required to parse t and recover the correct *LF*. These posterior probabilities are updated according to Bayes' theorem after each new trigger is parsed and *LP* has searched a local space or neighbourhood around g, defined parametrically, to find a parse for t, if necessary. Although the evidence in favour of a given parameter setting is thus statistical, all parameters have finite, discrete values. So at any point, LAgts use a single grammar, though learning LAgts incrementally reassess the evidence in favour of all possible parameter settings.

In the experiments reported below, *LP* does not vary—however, the starting point for learning and the hypothesis space are varied. This starting point consists of twenty binary-valued individual p-settings, representing principles or parameters, which define possible grammars and the exact prior probability distribution over them. *P-setting(UG)* encodes both prior and posterior probabilities for p-setting values during LAgt learning and thus defines both the starting point for learning (initial p-settings) and which grammar, if any, a LAgt has currently internalized. Each individual p-setting is represented by a fraction: $\frac{1}{2}$ maps to an unset parameter with no prior bias on its value; $\frac{1}{5}$ and $\frac{4}{5}$ represent default parameters with a prior bias in favour of one or other specific setting. However, this bias is low enough that consistent evidence for the alternative setting during learning will allow *LP* to move the posterior probability of this parameter through the $\frac{1}{2}$ (unset) point to take on its other setting. Principles, which, by definition, have been nativized, have prior probabilities sufficiently close to 1 or 0, typically $\frac{1}{50}$ or $\frac{49}{50}$, that *LP* will not see enough evidence during learning to alter their (absolute) settings.

How a p-setting is initialized for specific LAgts determines their exact learning bias and hypothesis space. The 'weakest' language faculty variant is one in which all p-settings are unset parameters, so there is no prior bias or constraint in favour of any specific grammar. If all p-settings are principles, either a single grammar is already internalized or no grammar is learnable (as some 'off' settings preclude any form of sentence decomposition or are mutually incompatible). Mutation and one-point crossover operators are defined over p-settings and designed not to bias evolution towards adoption of any one of the three types of p-setting. However, if default settings or principles evolve this clearly constitutes genetic assimilation of grammatical information because it creates either learning biases or constraints in favour of subclasses of grammars with specific grammatical properties. This is additional to a general and do-main-independent bias in favour of small grammars, and thus linguistic generalization and regularity, which is a consequence of the Bayesian formulation of *LP* (see Briscoe 1999, 2002).

The space of possible grammars in *UG* is defined in terms of canonical constituent order, possible non-canonical ordering, and categorial com-plexity. The account of *UG* and associated p-settings is based on the typological literature on attested variation (e.g. Croft 1990) and treats most variation as, in principle, independent (as each individual default or unset p-setting can be (re)set independently during learning). *UG* defines seventy full languages and a further 200 subset languages of these full languages, generated by subset grammars which have some parameters unset or off so that some triggers from the corresponding full language cannot be generated or parsed. Further details of these grammars and language fragments are given in Briscoe (2000a). Default or absolute p-settings therefore create clear and concrete forms of specifically gram-matical learning bias or constraint in favour of specific constituent orders, and so forth. Simulation of *LP* on samples of the full languages confirms that there are many prior distributions which allow successful acquisition given sufficient triggers, where success is defined as convergence to the target grammar $g^t \in UG$ with high probability $P-\epsilon$, given an arbitrary sequence of n triggers drawn randomly from a fair sample for the target language (see Briscoe 2002 for more details of the learning framework).

In addition, each LAgt has an age, between one and ten, and a fitness, between zero and one. LAgts can learn until they exceed age four and pairs of LAgts can linguistically interact (INT i.e. parse or generate) with whatever grammar they have internalized between one and ten. The simplest version of fitness measures LAgts' communicative success as a ratio of *successful* to *all* interactions, but other factors can be included in the fitness function, such as the degree of expressiveness of the grammar acquired. A successful interaction (SUCC-INT) occurs when the trigger generated by one LAgt can be parsed by the other LAgt to yield the same

LF. This does not necessarily require that the LAgts share identical grammars. In summary, a language agent has the following components:

LAgt:
LP(UG,t)	= *g*
P(g,t)	= *LF*
G(g,LF)	= *t*
Age:	[1 – 10]
Fitness:	[0 – 1]

14.3.2 *Populations and speech communities*

The operations which define the simulation model for an evolving population of linguistically interacting LAgts, such as INT and SUCC-INT above, and the other (capitalized) ones described below, are summarized at the end of this section.

A population (POP) is a changing set of LAgts. Time steps of the simulation consist of interaction cycles (INT-CYCLE) during which each LAgt participates in a prespecified number of interactions. On average each LAgt generates (parses) for half of these interactions. LAgts from the entire population interact randomly without bias. After each cycle of interactions, the age of each LAgt is incremented and those over age ten are removed, the fitness of each LAgt over that interaction cycle is computed, and LAgts aged four or over who have greater than mean fitness reproduce (REPRO) a new LAgt by single-point crossover of their *P-setting* with another such LAgt with whom they have successfully interacted at least once. The resulting p-setting may also optionally undergo random unbiased single-point mutation creating new p-setting values at specific loci. The number of new LAgts per time step is capped to prevent the proportion of learning LAgts exceeding one-third of the overall population. Capping is implemented by random selection from the pool of offspring created from the fitter, interacting LAgts. Alternatively, in order to simulate the situation in which there is no natural selection for LAgts based on communicative success, a prespecified number of new LAgts can be created by unbiased random selection of parent LAgts.

The mean number of interactions (INT) per interaction cycle is set (typically, at thirty INT per LAgt per INT-CYCLE) so that, despite stochastic sampling variation, accurate grammatical acquisition by all learning LAgts is highly probable from many of the possible initializations of *UG*, including the 'weakest' language faculty in which all p-settings are unset parameters.

If a simulation run is initialized with no mutation and a mixed age population of adult LAgts sharing the same initial p-setting and the same internalized full grammar, then grammatical acquisition by subsequent generations of learning LAgts will be >99 per cent accurate, and communicative success (i.e. the proportion of successful interactions) will average 98 per cent, the 2 per cent accounting for learners who have temporarily internalized a subset grammar. Under these conditions, the population constitutes a stable homogeneous speech community, in which no significant grammatical variation is present and no grammatical change takes place.

If grammatical variation is introduced into such a speech community, then linguistic drift, analogous to genetic drift, means that the population will reconverge on one variant within around $2N$ time steps (where N is population size) due to sampling effects on LAgts' input during learning (Briscoe 2000b). Grammatical variation can be introduced by initializing the simulation with LAgts who have internalized different grammars or by periodic migrations (MIGRATE) of groups of such adult LAgts. Such migrations (crudely) model contact between speech communities. However, the dynamic of the simulation is always to recreate a single homogeneous speech community with a high overall communicative success because all LAgts in the current population interact with each other with equal probability, regardless of the grammar they have internalized, their provenance, or their age.

Linguistic selection, as opposed to drift, occurs whenever any factor, other than the proportion of LAgts who have internalized a grammatical variant, plays a role in this variant's ability to be passed on to successive generations of learning LAgts. Such factors might be the relative parsability of variants and their consequent learnability, the probability with which they are generated, the degree to which any learning bias or constraint militates for or against them, their expressiveness, social prestige, and so forth. In simple cases of linguistic selection (Briscoe 2000a), the population typically converges on the more adaptive variant within N time steps (where N is population size). In this simulation model, once linguistic variation is present there is a tendency for populations to converge on subset grammars and the languages associated with them.

These grammars require fewer parameters to be set and thus can be learnt faster. However, if all LAgts utilize the same subset language, then communicative success will remain high. This tendency can be countered by introducing a further factor into LAgt fitness which adds an extra cost for utilizing a subset grammar each time a LAgt generates a sentence, as in the fitness function defined below. This creates selection for grammars able to economically express the widest range of *LFs* (see Briscoe 2000a for more detailed discussion).

Linguistic selection can occur without natural selection for, or any genetic evolution of, LAgts so long as their initial *P-setting* contains principles or default parameters and thus creates learning constraint or bias. If genetic mutation is enabled and reproduction is random, then simulation runs inevitably end with populations losing the ability to communicate because accumulated genetic drift in p-settings eventually prevents learning LAgts acquiring any compatible grammars. However, if LAgt reproduction is fitness-guided and genetic evolution is possible via crossover with or without mutation, then there is (a) modest natural selection for p-settings which shorten the learning process and increase fitness at age four, since LAgts who have yet to acquire a full grammar are unlikely to have higher-than-average fitness and thus to reproduce at the end of this interaction cycle; and (b) more severe natural selection for p-settings which allow reliable, accurate grammatical acquisition by the end of the learning period at age five, since non-communicators will not reproduce at all and subset language speakers are likely to have below-average fitness for the remainder of their lives.

Figure 14.1 illustrates how the model incorporates both biological evolution of LAgt p-settings and linguistic evolution of languages, represented as sets of triggers which form the data for successive generations of learners.

The model's principal components, operations, and parameters are defined more succinctly below:

LAgt: <P-setting(*UG*),Parser, Generator, Age, Fitness>
AGE: 1–4 LAgt = Learning LAgt / 4–10 = adult reproducing a LAgt
POP_n: {$LAgt_1$, $LAgt_2$, ... $LAgt_n$}
INT: ($LAgt_i$, $LAgt_j$), $i \neq j$, Gen($LAgt_i$, t_k), Parse($LAgt_j$, t_k)
SUCC-INT: Gen($LAgt_i$, t_k)$\mapsto LF_k \wedge$ Parse($LAgt_j$, t_k)$\mapsto LF_k$
INT-CYCLE: $\approx$ 30 ints./LAgt

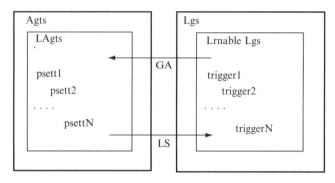

F<small>IG</small>. 14.1 Simulation model: Linguistic Selection (LS), Genetic Assimilation (GA), Initial P-settings (psettN), Trigger sentence types (triggerN).

REPRO: (aLAgt$_i$, aLAgt$_j$), $i \neq j$,
   Create-1LAgt(Mutate(Crossover(P-setting(aLAgt$_i$,P-setting(aLAgt$_j$)))))
MIGRATE: (POP$_n$), For i = 0 to n/3
   Create-aLAgt(Flip(P-setting(Dominant-Lg-LAgt(POP$_n$))))

LAgt Fitness (Costs/Benefits per INT):
   1. Generate cost: 1 (GC)
   2. Generate subset cost: 1 (GSC)
   3. Parse cost: 1 (PC)
   4. Success benefit: 1 (SI)
   5. Fitness function: $\frac{SI}{GSC+GC+PC}$

14.4 Results and critical assumptions

Previous experiments (Briscoe 1999, 2000a, 2002) with a variety of different initial *P-setting* configurations and several variants of *LP* have demonstrated that genetic assimilation occurs with natural selection for communicative success and that populations continue to utilize full grammars and associated languages if there is also natural selection for expressiveness. Inducing rapid linguistic change through repeated migrations does not prevent genetic assimilation, though it does cause it to asymptote rather than reach a point where the entire population fixates on a *P-setting* defining a single nativized grammar. Rapid linguistic change also creates a preference for the genetic assimilation of default parameters over principles, since the latter are potentially more damaging when subsequent linguistic change renders a principle maladaptive for learners. If the population were exposed to the entire space of grammatical variation within the time taken for a variant p-setting to go to fixation, then assimilation would not occur. However, for this to happen, the rate of linguistic change would be so great that communication would break down and the population would not constitute a speech community in which the majority of interactions are successful. Below, I describe one such experiment using the *LP* and simulation model outlined above, first reported in Briscoe (1999).

Populations of adult LAgts were created with initial p-settings consisting of three principles and seventeen unset parameters. In each simulation run, the first generation of LAgts all utilized one of seven typologically attested full grammars (see Briscoe 2000a for the linguistic details). Seventy runs were performed—ten under each condition. Simulation runs lasted for 2000 interaction cycles (about 500 generations of LAgts). Constant linguistic heterogeneity was ensured by migrations of adult LAgts speaking a distinct full language at any point where the dominant (full) language utilized by the population accounted for over 90 per cent of interactions in the preceding interaction cycle. Migrating adults accounted for approximately one-third of the adult population and were set up to have an initial *P-setting* consistent with the dominant settings already extant in the population; that is, migrations were designed to increase linguistic, and decrease genetic, variation.

Over all these runs, the mean increase in the proportion of default parameters was 46.7 per cent. The mean increase in principles was 3.8 per cent. Together these accounted for an overall decrease of 50.6 per cent in the proportion of unset parameters in the initial p-settings of LAgts. Qualitative behaviour in all runs showed increases in default parameters and either maintenance of or increase in principles. Figure 14.2 shows the relative proportions of default parameters, unset parameters, and principles in the overall population and also mean fitness for one such run. Overall fitness increases as the learning period is truncated, though there are fluctuations caused by migrations and/or by higher proportions of learners.

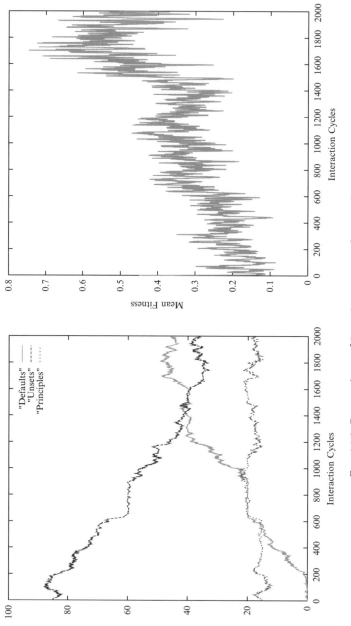

Fig. 14.2 Proportions of P-setting types and mean fitness.

In these experiments, linguistic change (defined as the number of interaction cycles taken for a new parameter setting to be acquired by all adult LAgts in the population) is about an order of magnitude faster than the speed with which a genetic change (i.e. a new initial p-setting) can go to fixation. Typically, 2–3 grammatical changes occur during the time taken for a principle or default parameter to go to fixation. Genetic assimilation remains likely, however, because the space of grammatical variation (even in this simulation) is great enough that typically the population is only sampling about 5 per cent of possible variations in the time taken for a single p-setting variant to go to fixation (or in other words, 95 per cent of the environmental pressure is constant during this period).

Many contingent details of the simulation model are arbitrary and unverifiable, such as the size of the evolving population, the number of learnable grammars, and relative speed at which LAgts and languages can change. These have been varied as far as possible to explore whether they affect the results. Importantly, it seems likely that the simulation model massively *underestimates* the true space of grammatical possibilities. Thus, there would very probably have been more opportunity to restrict the hypothesis space by genetic assimilation than is predicted by the simulation model as more of this space would have gone unsampled during the period of adaptation for the language faculty. Nevertheless, there is a limit to genetic assimilation in the face of ongoing linguistic change: in simulation runs with LAgts initialized with all default parameters, populations evolve away from this 'fully assimilated' *P-setting* when linguistic variation is maintained. Briscoe (2000a) reports variant experiments and discusses these issues in more detail.

14.5 Decorrelation

The relationship between genes and traits is rarely one-to-one, so epistasis (or 'linkage' of several genes to a single trait) and pleiotropy (or 'linkage' of a single gene to several traits) are the norm. In general, one effect of epistasis and pleiotropy will be to make the pathways more indirect from selection pressure acting on phenotypic traits to genetic modifications increasing the adaptiveness of those traits. Therefore, in general terms, we would expect a more indirect and less correlated genetic encoding of a trait to impede, slow, or perhaps even prevent genetic assimilation. Mayley (1996) explores the effects of manipulating the correlation between genotype (operations) and phenotype (operations) on genetic assimilation. In his model, individuals are able to acquire better phenotypes through 'learning' (or another form of within-lifetime plasticity), thus increasing their fitness. However, Mayley demonstrates that in his model the degree to which the acquired phenotype can be assimilated into the genotype of future generations, thus increasing overall fitness, depends critically on the degree of correlation.

Yamauchi (2000, 2001) replicates Turkel's (2002) simulation demonstrating genetic assimilation of grammatical principles. However, he then manipulates the degree of correlation in the encoding of genotype and phenotype. He represents grammar space as a sequence of N principles or parameters but determines the initial setting at each locus of the phenotype from a look-up table which uses K 0/1s (where K can range from 1 to $N - 1$) to encode each setting (one of two binary values or unset, i.e. a parameter), and to ensure that all possible phenotypes can be encoded. A genotype is represented as a sequence of N 0/1s. A translator reads the first K genes from the genotype and uses the look-up table to compute the setting of the first locus of the phenotype. To compute the setting of the second locus of the phenotype, the K genes starting at the second locus of the genotype are read and looked up in the table, and so on. The translator 'wraps around' the genotype and continues from the first gene locus when K exceeds the remaining bits of the genotype sequence.

Yamauchi claims, following Kauffman (1993), that increases in K model increases in pleiotropy and epistasis. Increased K means that a change to one locus in the genotype will have potentially more widespread and less predictable effects on the resulting phenotype (as the translator will 'wrap around' more frequently). It also means that there is less correspondence between a learning operation, altering the value of single phenotypic locus, and a genetic operation. The latter may potentially alter many phenotypic loci in differing ways, or perhaps alter none, depending on the look-up table. For low values of K, genetic assimilation occurs, as in Turkel's and my model; for values of K around $N/2$ genetic assimilation is considerably slowed, and for very high values ($K = N - 1$) it is stopped.

Yamauchi does not consider how the progressive decorrelation of phenotype from genotype impacts on the language-acquisition process, the degree of communicative success achieved, or how linguistic systems might be affected. In part, the problem here is that the abstract nature of Turkel's simulation model does not support any inference from configurations of the phenotype to concrete linguistic systems. Yamauchi, however, simply does not report whether increasing decorrelation, that is higher values of K, affects the ability of the evolving population to match phenotypes via learning. The implication, though, is that for high values of K, the population cannot evolve to a state able to match phenotypes and thus to support reliable communication.

Kauffman's original work with the *NK* model was undertaken to find optimal values of K for given N to quantify the degree of epistasis and pleiotropy likely to be found in systems able to evolve most effectively. Both theoretical analysis and experiments which allow K itself to evolve suggest that intermediate values of K are optimal (where the exact value can depend on N and other experimental factors). To stop assimilation, Yamauchi decorrelates his model to an extent to which Kaufmann's (1993) results suggest will yield a dynamically chaotic and evolutionarily highly suboptimal system. But despite these caveats, Yamauchi's simulation suggests that (lack of) correlation of genotype and phenotype with respect to the language faculty is as important an issue for accounts of genetic assimilation of grammatical information as it is for accounts of genetic assimilation generally.

My modified model supporting decorrelation does not distinguish genotype and phenotype; instead it utilizes a single *P-setting* which encodes both the initial and subsequent states of the learning process. Initial p-settings (i.e. those encoded by the genotype) are defined by a sequence of fractions which define the prior probability of each of three possible p-setting types: unset parameter, default parameter, and absolute principle. Arbitrary manipulation of the denominators and numerators of these fractions is very likely to result in values outside the range 0–1. For example, an *NK*-like scheme based on a binary sequential 'genetic' encoding of these fractions with single-point mutation by bit flipping will nearly always produce new absolute principles (under the fairly natural assumption that values outside the range 0–1 are interpreted this way).

Instead, the mutation operator was modified to create unbiased movement of parameters between default and unset settings at *multiple* random points in a *P-setting*. The maximum number of p-settings that could be modified in a single mutational event is the *decorrelation factor* which was varied in these simulation runs. The fractional values defining prior probabilities remained prespecified, as defined in section 14.3.1 above, but the exact number modified, the points in the p-setting modified, and the resultant settings are all independent stochastic variables of each such event. Just as increasing K in Yamauchi's model increases the maximum number of possible changes to the phenotype given a genetic mutation, so does increasing the decorrelation factor. Similarly, the possible *values* of phenotypic loci are not biased or otherwise altered by decorrelation in either scheme. The actual number of loci altered by any given mutation depends on the look-up table in stochastic interaction with the mutated gene in Yamauchi's simulation and on stochastic variables in mine. However, in both cases this number cannot exceed the absolute value of K or of the decorrelation factor.

New simulation runs were performed, identical to those reported in section 14.4 except that the degree of decorrelation between mutation of p-settings and parameter (re)setting was varied. Half the runs did not include migrations, as their general effect is to add greater linguistic variation and therefore to increase the potential for linguistic selection. Linguistic selection will also occur in a population in which the language faculty is evolving, because different p-setting variants can force even a homogeneous speech community to shift to a new language. For example, if a new LAgt inherits a mutated p-setting which alters a default parameter setting, that learner may acquire a variant grammar compatible with the new default setting if the input sample does not exemplify the non-default setting reliably enough to override it. If that LAgt and some of its descendents achieve better than mean fitness, because the new setting is only relevant for a small subset of possible triggers, or because these LAgts reset it successfully during learning, then the default initial setting may spread through the population. The likelihood of such LAgts achieving better than mean fitness is lower in an environment where members of the remaining population are learning accurately and efficiently, but is increased in one in which other LAgts are also inheriting mutated p-settings, some of which disadvantage them more seriously.

The main effect of progressively decorrelating the mutation operator is to increase the rate of linguistic selection and, despite natural selection on the basis of expressiveness, to cause populations to converge on successively less expressive subset languages. Often, linguistic change is coextensive with a few LAgts appearing who fail to learn any language. However, swift shifts to other (often less expressive) languages mean that other genetically similar LAgts do acquire a language. Thus, although decorrelation modestly increases the number of subset learning, mislearning, and non-learning LAgts, this, in turn, creates linguistic selection for other more learnable languages. When the decorrelation rate is very high, potentially affecting all of the p-settings during one mutational event, then the number of non-learners appears to go through a phase transition increasing about a thousandfold over the previous increment. The mean percentage of mislearning LAgts who do not acquire a full grammar or any grammar manifest in the environment is under 1 per cent for low rates of decorrelation, rising to 4.5 per cent for intermediate rates and to 24 per cent for the highest rate. In 100 per cent of the high decorrelation runs, populations converge on a minimal subset language, which is acquired by setting three p-settings, and in most cases, the population has fixated on correct default parameters for several of these settings. For intermediate rates of decorrelation, less than 5 per cent of runs end with the majority of the population acquiring a subset language, and for low rates none do.

Tracking the rate at which default parameters replace unset ones over these runs reveals that this rate *increases* by about 5 per cent over runs with correlated encodings, as measured by the number of default parameters in the population at the end of each run. This increase is broadly constant across all the runs regardless of the level of decorrelation and the presence or absence of migrations. However, as the decorrelation rate increases, the standard deviation of the mean also increases, reflecting the randomness of the potential changes induced by the increasingly dramatic mutational events. That is, for higher rates of decorrelation, distinct runs diverge more as the stochastic factors in the mutational operator affect the exact behaviour of individual runs to a greater extent. Similarly, even without migration, and starting from a homogeneous linguistic environment, the mean number of distinct languages acquired by LAgts across a run increases with decorrelation from a mean of twenty for lower rates to forty for intermediate rates, to sixty-three for the highest rate.

An increase in the number of default parameters in the language faculty only counts as genetic assimilation if the mutated defaults are compatible with the language(s) in the environment. Examining the timing of changes in the initial p-setting with linguistic changes reveals that decorrelated mutation is often the *cause* of a linguistic change, rather than assimilatory. These pre-emptive, non-assimilative mutations which spread and become adaptive are ones which drive rapid linguistic change, so that they rapidly become indistinguishable from assimilative ones. A default setting which is correct, and thus assimilative, in the current linguistic environment reduces the number of parameter settings required to learn the language, shortening the acquisition period and making it more robust against sampling variation in learner input.

If a correct default setting emerges via mutation, then it is likely to spread through the population, creating added linguistic selection pressure for subsequent linguistic change to remain compatible with the default setting. If a mutated default is incompatible with the current linguistic environment but manages to spread to other LAgts, either because grammatical acquisition is generally less accurate or because sampling variation allows enough learners to override the default without significant fitness cost, then it will exert increasing linguistic selection pressure, both because more learners will have the default setting and because fewer LAgts will generate the counterexamples that would cause the default setting to be overridden. For low rates of decorrelation, a mean 20 per cent of mutations going to fixation are pre-emptive, so 80 per cent remain assimilatory. The mean percentage of pre-emptive mutations going to fixation rises to 45 per cent for intermediate rates and to 99 per cent for the highest rate of decorrelation.

The left-hand plot in Figure 14.3 shows the rate of increase of default parameter settings within the population for a low and high degree of decorrelation in two runs with no migrations and otherwise identical initializations. The right-hand plot shows the corresponding decrease in the number of parameters which are (re)set by learners in the same two runs. Although the overall increase in defaults is consistently higher, and the number of (re)sets is mostly correspondingly lower with more de-correlation, in these runs the number of resets converges towards the end, because the 'fit' between the languages of the speech community and the language faculty tends to become less close with higher degrees of decorr-elation. This is also a tendency in other runs with no migrations. However,

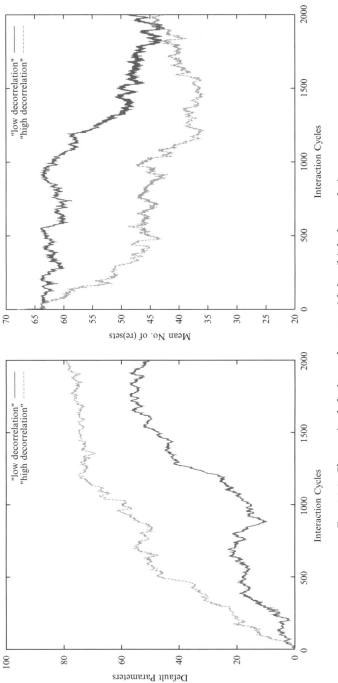

Fig. 14.3 Change in defaults and resets with low/high decorrelation.

the effect is removed and to some extent even reversed in runs with migrations, presumably because migrations provide linguistic variation supporting more rapid linguistic selection of variants more compatible with the continuously mutating language faculty.

One conclusion that can be drawn from these experiments is that if non-assimilatory random mutations were a factor in the evolution of the language faculty, then these mutations would rapidly mesh with linguistic systems, because of the greater speed and responsiveness of linguistic selection. Subsequently, such mutations will appear to be cases of genetic assimilation of grammatical information, unless one has access to the precise nature and timing of the mutational event, linguistic environment, and any subsequent linguistic change—something one cannot realistically hope to have access to outside the simulation 'laboratory'. Pre-emptive mutations are quite compatible with the co-evolutionary approach to the evolution of the language faculty and languages presented here. However, the experiments also suggest that high degrees of decorrelation (and thus non-assimilatory mutations) are unlikely, in line with the more general results of Kauffman (1993). The predicted consequence of such changes is that linguistic (pre)history would be punctuated by the periodic emergence of mislearners and non-learners, sometimes coupled with bursts of rapid linguistic change, often in the direction of less expressive languages. This is contrary to what most non-assimilationists have argued (see Briscoe 2003) and certainly not supported by the available evidence, which suggests that languages, if anything, accrue expressiveness and hence complexity, and that acquisition remains robust.

A simulation model in which greater expressiveness, or acquisition of innovative grammatical variants, outweighed learnability in LAgt fitness might predict natural selection for a less restrictive language faculty. A model which integrated some of the social pressures maintaining linguistic diversity that were discussed, for example, by Nettle (1999), might counterbalance the tendency for learnability to outweigh expressiveness. However, given the inalienable relationship between the size of the hypothesis space and the amount of data required to reliably acquire a specific grammar (e.g. Nowak et al. 2001), a model in which expressiveness regularly overcame learnability would predict that the learning period would increase over time or, if a critical period had been nativized, that the reliability of grammatical acquisition would degrade. The existence of a critical period for grammatical acquisition, the accuracy of grammatical acquisition, and its selectivity in the face of variant input (e.g. Lightfoot 1999) all suggest that this is an implausible evolutionary dynamic. Nevertheless, integration of a more realistic account of expressiveness into the simulation model would certainly be a worthwhile extension of these experiments.

A further set of similar experiments was undertaken in which the mutational operator was modified so that the fractional values defining initially unset parameters mutated randomly by increasingly large amounts. The increasing bias of this operator is to create more principles as the base of the fractions increases and as they exceed the 0–1 range (see discussion above), so that *LP* becomes unable to move them through the $\frac{1}{2}$ threshold which alters a setting. Unsurprisingly, in these experiments, there were many more cases of non-learners, since principles rather than just default settings were acquired. This mutation operator is exceedingly unlikely to create new unset parameters, and increasingly likely to only create principles with greater degrees of decorrelation. Overall, the rate of increase in defaults and principles was slightly higher in these experiments. However, just as in the previous ones, many of the mutational events are pre-emptive rather than assimilative, and where the pre-emption results in principles incompatible with the linguistic environment, a learning LAgt has less chance of reproducing, unless the overall accuracy of grammatical acquisition in the population has degraded significantly. Thus, as in the previous experiments, the trend in linguistic change is towards successive reconvergence on subset languages, until the population is speaking a minimal subset language compatible with the principles or with any remaining default parameter settings on which the population has converged.

In general, the greater the degree of decorrelated mutational events involving pre-emptive non-assimilatory changes, the more the simulation model predicts that the co-evolutionary dynamic would bias the hypothesis space until only one grammatical system remained. If the mutation operator is prevented from creating principles or increasingly stronger defaults, as in the first series of experiments, then there is a limit to this effect, but removing this, as in the second series of experiments, simply strengthens this tendency.

14.6 Conclusions

In summary, extant models predict that genetic assimilation of grammatical information would have occurred given three crucial but plausible assumptions. First, communicative success via expressive languages with compositional syntax conferred a fitness benefit on their users. Secondly, the linguistic environment for adaptation of the language faculty consistently provided grammatical generalizations to be genetically assimilated. Thirdly, at least some of these generalizations were neurally and genetically encodable with sufficient correlation to enable genetic assimilation. The simulation experiments I describe show that these assumptions can be incorporated in a precise model which reliably shows genetic assimilation under conditions that support ongoing successful communication with an expressive language.

The simulation model predicts that if language confers no fitness benefit but the acquisition procedure is under genetic control, genetic drift would result in evolution of non-learners and thus non-linguistic populations. It also predicts that, for there to be no grammatical generalizations capable of being genetically assimilated, language change would need to be impossibly rapid, to the point where speech communities would break down. Finally, it predicts that if genotype and phenotype are decorrelated to the extent that assimilation is blocked, the resultant co-evolutionary dynamic would lead inexorably towards simpler but less expressive subset languages. Thus, the case for genetic assimilation as the primary mechanism of the evolution of the language faculty remains, in my opinion, strong.

Nevertheless, the co-evolutionary perspective on genetic assimilation of grammatical information raises two important caveats. First, as languages themselves are adapted to be learnable (as well as parsable and expressive) and as languages change on a historical timescale, some of the grammatical properties of human languages were probably shaped by the process of cultural transmission of (proto)language via more general-purpose learning (e.g. Kirby 1998; Brighton 2002) prior to the evolution of the fully formed language faculty. Secondly, whether the subsequent evolution of this faculty was assimilative, encoding generalizations manifest in the linguistic environment, or pre-emptive, with mutations creating side-effects causing linguistic selection for new variants, the fit between the learning bias of the language faculty and extant languages is predicted to be very close.

It is important to emphasize that modelling and simulation, however careful and sophisticated, are not enough to establish the truth of what remains a partly speculative inference about prehistoric events. The value of the simulations, and related mathematical modelling and analysis, lies in uncovering the precise set of assumptions required to predict that genetic assimilation of grammatical information will or will not occur. Some of these assumptions relate to cognitive abilities or biases which remain in place today—these are testable. Others, such as the relative weight of factors relating to learnability and expressiveness in the LAgt fitness function in my simulation model remain largely speculative, though not, in principle, untestable, since they should, for example, affect attested grammatical changes, including those under intensive study right now (e.g. Kegl et al. 1999). Other assumptions, such as the degree of correlation between genetic and neural encoding, are theoretically plausible but empirically untestable using extant techniques.

FURTHER READING

Jablonka and Lamb (1995) describe Waddington's work and the concept of genetic assimilation. Durham's (1991) theory of gene-culture interactions provides the basis for a co-evolutionary account of grammatical assimilation. Deacon (1997) argues in an accessible manner for the co-evolutionary perspective on language and its acquisition, adopted here. Bertolo (2001) is a good overview of recent work on parameter setting. Cosmides and Tooby (1996) make the case for integrating the Bayesian learning framework with evolutionary theory as a general model of human learning. Briscoe (2003) summarizes recent work on genetic assimilation of grammatical information.

15 Acquisition and evolution of quasi-regular languages: two puzzles for the price of one

MATTHEW ROBERTS, LUCA ONNIS, AND NICK CHATER

15.1 Introduction

Natural languages are most often characterized as a combination of rule-based generalization and lexical idiosyncrasy. The English past tense is a familiar case, in which the irregular form *went* replaces the expected +*ed* construction **goed*. Baker (1979) notes that this is a relatively benign example for learners, since irregular forms are frequently encountered in the course of their linguistic experience. The experience of the form *went* may block **goed*, if the learner assumes that verbs typically have a single past tense form—thus, an observed alternative form can serve as evidence that an absent regular form is not allowed in the language (see, for instance, the Competition model, MacWhinney 1989). Much more troubling are cases where an apparently legal construction is idiosyncratically absent, without any alternative. The dative shift in English is a well-documented example:

(1) John gave/donated a book to the library
(2) John gave/*donated the library a book

In such cases we can think of linguistic rules as being quasi-regular: they license the combination of *some* members of syntactic categories, but not others. The difficulty of learning such idiosyncratic absences from partial input and without negative evidence (as is the case with natural language) has become notorious in the language acquisition literature. In particular, given that only a finite set of sentences is ever heard, out of the infinite set of possible sentences in a natural language, it is clear that mere absence of a linguistic form cannot be directly used as evidence that the form is not allowed. However, such 'holes' are clearly specific to particular natural languages, and hence cannot be explained by an appeal to innate linguistic principles. This problem has been regarded as so severe that it has been labelled Baker's paradox, and viewed as raising logical problems for the theory of language acquisition (e.g. Baker and McCarthy 1981).[1]

The approach we adopt here is to apply a general principle of learning to explain how linguistic idiosyncrasies can be acquired. Note that the mechanism must be sufficiently flexible to capture the huge range of idiosyncrasies across a vast range of linguistic contexts. Moreover, the existence of such a mechanism is required, we contend, to explain the existence of idiosyncrasies in language: idiosyncrasies could not have emerged or survived in its absence, as they would have been winnowed out by learning failures by successive linguistic generations. In this respect, Baker's paradox raises a secondary paradox for language evolution. The puzzle of how language acquisition processes can capture what appear to be idiosyncratic 'holes' in the language also raises the puzzle of how difficult-to-acquire linguistic patterns emerge and are transmitted in the development of languages. Note that, on pain of circularity, whatever learning mechanisms are responsible for learning such idiosyncrasies must pre-date the emergence of such idiosyncrasies. That is, we cannot view the idiosyncratic nature of language as a stable environment to which the biological basis for language acquisition adapted, because without

---

[1] Many writers have argued that the general problem of language acquisition inevitably necessitates innate language-learning modules: 'no known "general learning" mechanism can acquire a natural language solely on the basis of positive or negative evidence, and the prospects of finding any such domain-independent device seem rather dim' (Hauser et al. 2002: 1577. See also Chomsky 1957; Pinker 1989). Gold (1967) has shown that language identification 'in the limit' is impossible for a broad class of formal languages. (Learning in the limit requires that the learner eventually identifies the language correctly, after it has received a sufficiently large corpus, and maintains that correct hypothesis however much further linguistic input is received. Identifying a language means that the learner can correctly decide which sentences do or do not belong to the language. Note that learning in the limit does not require that the learner can determine when learning has been successful.) By contrast, Horning (1969) has shown that grammatical inference is possible in a probabilistic sense, for languages generated by stochastic, context-free grammars. More recently, Chater and Vitányi (ms.) have shown that such inference is possible for any computable language, including, *a fortiori*, any grammars involving context sensitivity and/or transformations if the goal is (arbitrarily close) agreement between the learner's language with the target language. The method that underpins Chater and Vitányi's theoretical result is practically implemented in the simulations described here—the learner seeks the simplest description of the corpus it has received.

relevant prior learning mechanisms already established, language could not have developed with such idiosyncrasies in the first place.

In this chapter we consider two questions for language evolution raised by the existence of these idiosyncrasies. The first is a problem of transmission: what kind of learning mechanism could ensure the stability of idiosyncratic absences across generations and be sufficiently flexible and general to pre-date their emergence? The second is one of emergence: even assuming that such a mechanism exists, what conditions might give rise to these irregularities?

The remainder of the chapter falls into five main sections. In section 15.2 we discuss the ubiquity of quasi-regular constructions. In section 15.3 we outline why they constitute such an apparently difficult learning problem. We then discuss the relationship between acquisition and evolution, in particular the idea that any hard learning problem for culturally transmitted information entails evolutionary puzzles. In section 15.4 we present a model that is able to learn quasi-regular structures in a rudimentary language from positive evidence alone, using a very general learning principle: simplicity. The model learns by creating competing hypothetical grammars to fit the language to which it has been exposed, and choosing the simplest. As an explicit metric for simplicity we use Minimum Description Length (MDL), a mathematical idea grounded in Kolmogorov complexity theory (Li and Vitányi 1997). In acquiring quasi-regular language structures, our model addresses the transmission/acquisition problem. In section 15.5 we detail several simulations based on an Iterated Learning Model (ILM, e.g. Kirby 2001; Brighton, Kirby, and Smith, Chapter 13) in which a probabilistically generated artificial language is transmitted over 1,000 generations of simplicity-based learners. The results of these simulations chart not only the stability but also the emergence of quasi-productivities in the language. In particular we show that:

1. Exceptions are stable across successive generations of simplicity-driven learners.
2. Under certain conditions, statistical learning using simplicity can account for the emergence of quasi-productivity in a language.

In section 15.6 we discuss the results of the ILM simulations, in particular the conditions in which quasi-regular structures might emerge.

15.2 Baker's paradox and linguistic quasi-productivity

A mainstay of linguistic analysis is the concept that human languages are composed of a limited number of basic units (features, segments, syllables, morphemes, words, phrases, clauses, etc.) that can be combined by a small number of generative rules to create larger units. Postulating the existence of recursive rules allows for an infinite number of sentences to be created. This generativity goes well beyond theoretical linguistic description, as it is typically taken to be embodied in the psychological mechanisms responsible for acquiring and representing linguistic rules and units.

Although the capacity to generalize from a limited set of examples to novel instances is an uncontroversial aspect of human cognition, a puzzle that has attracted linguists is that natural languages, although productive, are never fully regular. There appear to be finely tuned lexical and syntactic selectional constraints that native speakers are aware of. Expected regular structures may either be replaced (e.g. *went* for **goed*) or they may be disallowed completely. These semi-productive structures may be seen as a special case of irregularity where the irregular form is absent; in other words, there seems to be an unfilled slot that constrains open-ended productivity. Consider, for instance, a transformational rule such as *to be* Deletion (after Baker 1979):

(3) $X - to\ be - Y \rightarrow X,\ \emptyset,\ Y$
(4) The baby seems/appears/happens to be sleepy
(5) The baby seems/appears/happens to be sleeping
(6) The baby seems/?appears/*happens sleepy
(7) The baby *seems/*appears/*happens sleeping

The transformational rule in (3) is misleading with regard to the perfectly plausible but ungrammatical predictions that it gives for *happen* (and perhaps *appear*) in (6) and for *seem, appear,* and *happen* in (7). Such 'unfilled slots' cannot be accounted for by the general rule. Similarly, consider the lexical constraints on the collocations between, for instance, adjectives and nouns below:

(8) strong/high/*stiff winds
(9) strong /*high/*stiff currents
(10) strong/*high/stiff breeze

Quasi-productivities are ubiquitous in the lexicon, and it has been proposed that they constitute a considerable portion of syntax as well (for a discussion of the vast range of syntactic idiosyncrasies, including *wh*-movement and subjacency, see Culicover 1999). In standard generative grammar these 'syntactic nuts' have traditionally been disregarded as the 'periphery' of the language system, where the 'core' is a set of general fully regular principles requiring a minimum of stipulation. Most syntactic constructions, however, are subject to varying degrees of lexical idiosyncrasy. Consider another familiar example, the constraints on the dative shift transformation:

(11) $NP_1 - V - NP_2 - to\ NP_3 \rightarrow NP_1, V, NP_3, NP_2$ (optional)
(12) We sent the book to George
(13) We sent George the book
(14) We reported the accident to the police
(15) *We reported the police the accident

Indeed, as has been argued by Culicover (1999), and others within the general movement of construction grammar (Goldberg 2003), such idiosyncrasies may be so ubiquitous that the 'periphery' of standard linguistic theory may encroach deep into the 'core' of standard linguistic theory—so much so, that explanatory principles and learning mechanisms required to deal with the periphery might even deal with the core as a limiting case.

To see why the presence of semi-productive regularities represents a particularly difficult learning problem, we now consider arguments concerning language learnability and the contribution of innate linguistic constraints.

15.3 The logical problem of language acquisition

At a general level, the so-called logical problem of language acquisition is that learning a quasi-regular language from experience alone is impossible, because linguistic experience is too incomplete and contradictory. In the first place, learners observe only a limited set of the infinite number of utterances in their language. From this, they must distinguish a certain set of 'grammatical' utterances among all the other utterances that they have never heard and may never produce. The problem is particularly acute when considering the case of quasi-productivities which yield Baker's paradox (also known as the projection problem). Baker (1979) noted that quasi-productive regularities such as those above pose a genuine puzzle for any account of language acquisition. This is principally because the unfilled slots they create in the language occur *within* the space of allowable sentences and nonetheless are somehow blocked by language learners. A crucial tenet of the logical problem is that indirect negative evidence in the form of absence is not sufficient to constrain the learner's hypotheses about the correct grammar, because there are many linguistic sentences that a learner has never heard but are nonetheless grammatical (Pinker 1984). There are therefore many hypothesis grammars that would be consistent with the positive data available. It is suggested that such a hard learning problem necessitates the existence of powerful innate linguistic tools. However, the paradox raised by Baker is that even postulating a universal grammar that restricts the search space for potential grammars does not solve this particular problem, since unfilled slots are highly idiosyncratic across languages. Language-specific omissions of the kind we have described must therefore be determined by the learner on the basis of experience; they cannot stem from universal principles.

Nor is it the case that this apparently intractable computational problem will disappear in the face of simple appeal to semantics. Bowerman (1996) noted that it can be misleading to predict syntactic behaviour from semantics: for instance, *donate* and *give* in the examples (1) and (2) have similar semantics but *donate* does not allow for dative shift. It is worth noting that younger speakers of English will often fail to judge the phrase *John donated the library a book* as ungrammatical. This may be an example of regularization, but this does not weaken the argument. Consider also the following data:[2]

(16) John waved Mary goodbye
(17) John waved goodbye to Mary
(18) *John said Mary hello
(19) John said hello to Mary

or, again from Baker:

(20) It is likely that John will come
(21) It is possible that John will come
(22) John is likely to come
(23) *John is possible to come

[2] Our thanks to an anonymous reviewer for providing this set of examples.

Hence, we argue that some degree of arbitrariness must be accounted for in quasi-regular constructions (see also Culicover 1999, on the case for at least partial independence of syntax from semantics in the case of unfilled slots). If idiosyncrasy is to be found at the core of grammar and can neither be accounted for by universal principles nor completely semantically determined, it must be learnable from experience. Before we consider how such learning might occur, we consider why the existence of this acquisition problem entails two equally puzzling evolution problems.

The logical problem of language acquisition can be seen as the starting argument for raising a paradox about the evolution of natural languages: first, if quasi-regular structures in languages are such hard cases for the learner, why are they so pervasive in contemporary natural languages? More specifically, why do not we see the emergence over time of simpler, more easily learnable languages? Secondly, the speculation that irregularities should tend to be replaced by regular forms over time leads immediately to a second puzzle: how did such language become quasi-regular in the first place?

15.4 A solution to the acquisition problem

In this section we first outline the simplicity principle and Minimum Description Length (MDL) as a metric for simplicity. We then describe how this forms the basis of a language learning mechanism, detail a rudimentary toy language for use in simulations, and give details of a single-learner simulation in which a learner agent learns idiosyncratic exceptions. Using this machinery, we show, for this rudimentary language, how it is possible to acquire quasi-regular patterns in a language, from positive evidence, by preferring the grammar that corresponds to the simplest representation of the corpus that has been encountered. Roughly, the simplicity principle allows learners to determine when absence of a particular construction from the corpus can be taken as evidence that it is genuinely blocked. This general type of approach to Baker's paradox has been discussed by a range of authors (Dowman 2000; Stolcke 1994).

15.4.1 *The simplicity principle and MDL*

From an abstract point of view, learning from experience can be thought of as finding patterns in a finite set of data. Any finite set of data is consistent with an infinite number of possible patterns; the problem is how to choose between them. The simplicity principle (e.g. Chater 1999) asserts that the cognitive system will always prefer simpler patterns over more complex ones. The mathematical theory of Kolmogorov complexity provides an elegant way to think about simplicity through two key insights (Li and Vitányi 1997). Firstly, the length of the shortest program in a universal programming language (for example, any conventional computer language, such as C++ or Java) that regenerates an object is a natural measure of the complexity of that object. Secondly, the length of that program is independent of the choice of the specific universal programming language, up to a constant. This length is known as the Kolmogorov complexity of an object. This approach has yielded a rich mathematical literature (Li and Vitányi 1997), and a number of theoretical results concerning language learnability from positive evidence (e.g. Chater and Vitányi ms.), but is problematic from a practical point of view, in that Kolmogorov complexity itself is incomputable. This provides the motivation for practical variants of this approach, where complexity is measured using restricted statistical coding schemes, rather than the full power of a universal programming language (Rissanen 1987, 1989; Wallace and Freeman 1987). It is not necessary to discover the *actual* binary encoding of an object: it is possible to deal only in code *lengths*, i.e. the number of bits necessary to describe an object or event. This figure can be specified if a probability can be associated with that object or event (Shannon 1948), using standard information theory. Highly probable or frequent objects or events are associated with short (simple) encodings.

15.4.2 *Simplicity-based language learning: the learner as gambler*

The simplicity principle, outlined above, demonstrates how the simplest model of experience can be thought of as that represented by the shortest binary code. In this instance the binary code must represent two things: firstly a hypothesis, or grammar, that describes the language to which the learner is exposed. Secondly, all the language that has been heard must be represented *under the hypothesis*. This may be expressed formally as (24):

(24) $C = C(H) + C(D|H)$

where C is the total length of code (in bits), C(H) is the number of bits necessary to specify the hypothesis (grammar) and C(D|H) is the number of bits necessary to specify the data (all the language heard) given the hypothesis. The length of code necessary to represent data will differ between hypotheses.

Our model of the learner does not acquire vocabulary or induce categories and rules from scratch. We take productive rules to be already learned. Thus, our model is already at the stage at which children make errors of overgeneralization. The task is to spot which of the constructions allowable under the rule are in fact blocked—to find the holes in the language. Learning proceeds by a series of 'gambles'. The learner bets that a particular construction is not allowed and that it will therefore never be encountered. In making this gamble it must specify the construction as part of a new hypothesis, H. Coding this specification requires some bits of information, so the complexity of the new hypothesis increases. However, the learner has reduced the number of allowable constructions that it can expect to encounter. It has therefore increased the probability of those remaining. The number of bits required to specify future data under the new hypothesis is therefore reduced. Thus, if it is true that the construction is not allowed, the learner will gradually win back the number of bits that it gambled in specifying the exception. As more language is heard, the new hypothesis will eventually come to be associated with a shorter code length than the original. If the gamble is inappropriate, however, the learner will encounter a construction that it has wrongly presumed to be disallowed. This construction is now associated with a very low probability, so the learner will incur a high bit-cost in encoding it under the erroneous hypothesis. Our model generates a new hypothesis every time it gambles on a particular construction, with all hypotheses running in parallel. The preferred hypothesis is always that associated with the shortest code length.

Onnis, Roberts, and Chater (2002) show that a batch learner (i.e. a learner that runs all calculations after the entire corpus has been encountered) employing this strategy is able to distinguish genuine constructions from blocked ones as a result of exposure to data from the CHILDES database of child-directed speech (MacWhinney 2000). Here, we implement an online version that was able to postulate exceptions and create new hypotheses during the course of exposure to a rudimentary toy language. Algorithmic details are given at the end of this chapter in Appendix 15.1; the following two sections describe the toy language and the learner's ability to discover exceptions in it.

15.4.3 *Learning a rudimentary language*

A toy language was used to simplify the simulation. It consisted of two syntactic categories, A and B, and two production rules, S_1 and S_2. The categories A and B each contained four words. The language also contained an exception element, specifying sentences that were producible under the rewrite rules but were disallowed. Each sentence contained only two words, AB or BA. The language may be expressed formally as in (25):

(25) $S_1 \rightarrow AB$,
$\quad S_2 \rightarrow BA$,
$\quad A \rightarrow \{a_1, a_2, a_3, a_4\}$,
$\quad B \rightarrow \{b_1, b_2, b_3, b_4\}$,
$\quad * \rightarrow \{(a_2 b_1), (a_2 b_2), (a_2 b_3), (a_2 b_4), (b_1 a_1), (b_2 a_1), (b_3 a_1), (b_4 a_1)\}$

where the examples generated by $*$ are blocked. This language can mimic the pattern of alternations, for example, in transitive and intransitive verb constructions. In English, verbs can nominally occur in either a transitive or an intransitive context, but some are blocked from occurring in one or the other. This is analogous to the patterns in our toy language, where items in either category may in principle occur in both first and second positions, but can be blocked from doing so by entries in the exceptions element. This is illustrated in Figure 15.1.

Samples of the language were produced by a parent agent and experienced by a learner agent. We assume that parents and learners share knowledge of word frequency. This allows both of them to associate each word with a probability of occurrence. Sentence probabilities are taken to be the product of two probabilities: that of the first word and that of the second word, given the first. Parent agents use these probabilities to produce samples of the language stochastically. Learners use them to calculate code lengths (in bits) for different hypotheses. We assume that word frequencies are distributed according to Zipf's law (Zipf 1949), a ubiquitous power law distribution in natural language (Bell, Cleary, and Witten 1990): if we rank words in terms of frequency, then frequency of

Transitive	Intransitive
cut (*I cut the cake*)	cut (**I cut*)
fall (**I fell the bicycle*)	fall (*I fell*)
break (*I broke the cup*)	break (*The window broke*)

AB	BA
$a_1 B$	$*Ba_1$
$*a_2 B$	Ba_2
$a_3 B, a_4 B$	Ba_3, Ba_4

FIG 15.1 The structure of the toy language mimics that of Baker's Paradox for alternations. a_1 and a_2 could be blocked from occurring in BA and AB constructions respectively by entries in the exceptions element such as $a_2 b_1$, $a_2 b_2$ or $b_1 a_1$, $b_2 a_1$ etc. For the first-generation agent in each simulation, however, all As occurred in both contexts (that is, they were 'alternating'). *Cut* and *fall* are non-alternating verbs; *break* is an alternating verb. Levin (1993) provides an extensive list of alternations in English.

any word is the inverse of its rank. Details are given in Appendix 15.1 below.

Learner agents begin with a single, completely regular hypothesis about the language, namely, all sentences are allowed. This is equivalent to (25) with the exceptions element empty. As they experience samples of the language, the learner agents compare the probability of each sentence with the total number of sentences they have heard. A new hypothesis is generated if the total exceeds a threshold (where the threshold is a function of sentence probability; thus, the threshold is different for each sentence). Each new hypothesis is simply a clone of the most recent hypothesis to be generated (or the original, if it is the first) with the addition of the sentence in question to the exceptions element. This addition entails an increment in the code length associated with the new hypothesis, and a rescaling of the probabilities for the remaining sentences.

Each sentence encountered entails an increment in the number of bits associated with each hypothesis, but since the creation of a new hypothesis involves rescaling sentence probabilities, this increment differs between hypotheses. All algorithmic details are given in Appendix 15.1. Figure 15.2 illustrates the code lengths associated with all the hypotheses entertained by a learner agent after exposure to fifty sentences of a language containing eleven exceptions.

Figure 15.2 illustrates that the learner agent creates many hypotheses, but that the shortest code length is associated with the one that matches the language to which it was exposed. It is important to note that the sentence comprising the two least frequent words was associated with a probability of approximately 1/100. It was therefore highly unlikely that it

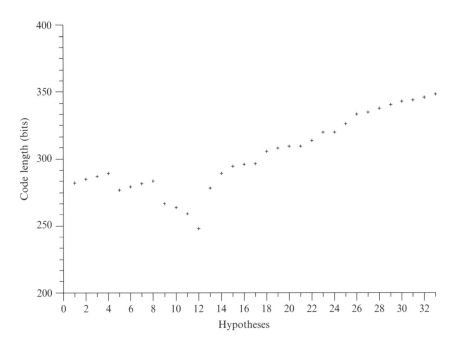

FIG. 15.2 The code length (number of bits) associated with each hypothesis grammar entertained by a learner after exposure to fifty sentences of a language containing eleven exceptions. The shortest code length is obtained by the twelfth hypothesis, i.e. the one containing eleven exceptions (the first contains none, being completely regular). Although it is not obvious from the figure, the twelfth hypothesis specifies exactly the eleven exceptions contained in the language.

would have occurred in a corpus of fifty sentences. In addition, the learner received no feedback on its learning, other than more samples of the language. These conditions mirror to a modest extent the 'poverty of the stimulus', according to which children never hear all the possible sentences of a language and do not typically receive explicit negative feedback. Note that our language contains, of course, no semantics and has no communicative function: we do not attempt to model the relationship between meanings-signals-referents nor try to give functional explanations of language change as in other models. In general, however, part of the fascination of the constructions investigated here is that their idiosyncrasy does not seem to be primarily semantically or functionally determined.

In spite of these restrictions, the learner agent was nonetheless able to distinguish between admissible and inadmissible sentences which it had

	a₁	a₂	a₃	a₄	b₁	b₂	b₃	b₄
a₁	*	*	*	*				
a₂	*	*	*	*	*	*	*	*
a₃	*	*	*	*				
a₄	*	*	*	*				
b₁	*				*	*	*	*
b₂	*				*	*	*	*
b₃	*				*	*	*	*
b₄	*				*	*	*	*

FIG. 15.3 Sentences allowable under (25). Rows are first words, columns are second words. The rewrite rules license half the sentences in this table; blocked sentences are denoted *. Our learner was able to discover exceptions to the rules such as a_2 appearing in first position or a_1 appearing in second position.

not heard. It is also worth noting that this mechanism need not be restricted to spotting the idiosyncratic absence of single sentences: the same process could equally well be used to recover from errors of overgeneralization made as a consequence of (for example) semantic contexts. To see why this is so, it is helpful to consider how the sentences allowable under a grammar such as (25) can be represented in a contingency table such as Figure 15.3, in which rows and columns may represent any set of objects and contexts.

We suggest that a simplicity-based learning mechanism such as that outlined above is sufficiently powerful and general to offer a solution to the first of the evolutionary questions we posed, namely the transmission problem—i.e. once quasi-regularity is established, a learner can, in principle at least, learn this quasi-regularity, avoiding overgeneralization by using the simplicity principle. We now place the single learner in the context of an Iterated Learning Model (ILM) to consider the second question: under what conditions do such idiosyncrasies emerge?

15.5 Language learning over generations

15.5.1 *ILM simulations*

Although developed independently, our model proposes an MDL learner embedded within an Iterated Learning Model (ILM), which has been used extensively by Kirby and colleagues, and others (e.g. Kirby 2001; Brighton 2002; Teal and Taylor 2000; Zuidema 2003; Brighton, Kirby, and Smith, Chapter 13). In the ILM, parent agents generate language for children agents, who in turn, become parents for the next generation of learners.

A simplifying assumption is that there is one agent per generation, so issues of population dynamics are neglected. All agents were 'genetically' homogeneous: all were equipped with identical learning facility and started from the same point in their development. The first generation agent was exposed to probabilistically generated samples of the completely regular toy language used in the single-learner simulation. Subsequent agents were exposed to probabilistically generated samples of the language as learned by the preceding generation. Although complete regularity at the outset is probably unrealistic, our intent is not so much to replicate a historic development of languages as to test the conditions for the emergence and stability of irregularities. We test this in the least favourable condition for their emergence, i.e. an ideal, fully regular language.

The mean number of sentences heard by each agent was the same within each simulation, but varied between simulations. In different simulations, successive generations of learners heard between twenty-five and sixty-five sentences. Again, it was unlikely that any agent was exposed to all the sentences in the language, and agents received no negative feedback on their learning. When an agent had been exposed to the required number of sentences, one hypothesis entertained by that agent was selected. This hypothesis was then used as the basis for generating the sentences that would be heard by the succeeding generation. The hypothesis chosen was always that associated with the simplest interpretation, namely that with the shortest code length.

15.5.2 *Results*

Figure 15.4 charts the emergence and stability of exceptions in four simulations. The number of sentences heard by each generation was critical to both. Where each generation heard a short corpus (mean number of sentences, n, of 30, Figure 15.4(a)), exceptions frequently emerged but were highly unstable: they rarely remained in the language for more than a few generations. With a long corpus (mean n = 60, Figure 15.4(d)) exceptions were less likely to emerge; in contrast to Figures 15.4(a) – (c), no exceptions emerged for almost 400 generations. However, once they had emerged they were much less likely to be lost from the language than with shorter corpora.

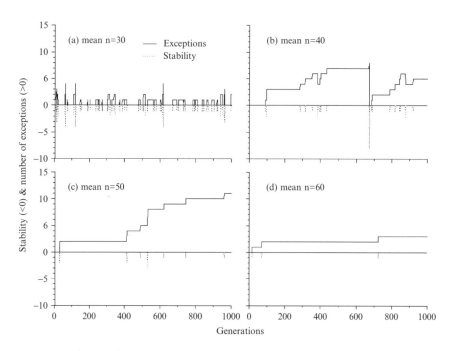

Fig. 15.4 The number of exceptions contained in the language transmitted by each learner to the subsequent generation in four simulations with differing corpus sizes. Where the number of exceptions was stable across several generations—for example seven exceptions in (b) or the final 250 generations of (d)—the sentences specified as exceptions were the same for each generation.

Figure 15.4 suggests that exceptions are posited during the early stages of language acquisition. With a relatively small amount of data, learners may postulate that the language contains many exceptions that do not in fact exist. As more data becomes available, such early hypotheses are either confirmed or exposed as spurious. These simulations suggest a trade-off between emergence and stability of exceptions. The crucial factor mediating this trade-off is the amount of language heard by each generation. If each generation hears a great deal of data relative to the size of the language, exceptions are unlikely to emerge: any that are posited will later be shown to be false. However, if exceptions are to be stable, each generation must hear enough language to learn the exceptions that existed in the previous generation.

15.6 Discussion and conclusion

We started by noting that most phenomena in natural languages seem to be of a quasi-regular nature, which traditionally poses a learnability problem. Baker's paradox arises whenever the child has to recover from perfectly plausible and attested overgeneralizations such as (26) (Bowerman 1982), which is ungrammatical in standard English, without the aid of direct negative evidence.

(26) *I gave my mummy it

Because a putative universal grammar can only capture general syntactic behaviours, many syntactic constructions have to be learned from experience. We contended that if the acquisition of such idiosyncrasies is hard, then their transmission over generations of speakers should be 'filtered out' over time to improve learnability and communication. We subsequently presented a computational simulation where such hard cases are in fact successfully learned and transmitted from positive evidence. Our solution to the learning problem is that a learning bias toward simplicity of representation makes language learnable from experience. This bias need not be specific to language—indeed, simplicity principles have been used in linguistic contexts (Brent and Cartwright 1996; Goldsmith 2001; Wolff 1982) and non-linguistic contexts (e.g. perception, Hochberg and McAlister 1953; van der Helm and Leeuwenberg 1996; categorization, Pothos and Chater 2002), and have even been viewed as general frameworks for cognition (e.g. Chater 1999; Wolff 1991). In our model there is no *a priori* 'correct' grammar, i.e. a grammar that is valid prior to linguistic experience. The development of the final-state grammar corresponding to adult linguistic competence is a matter of choosing the simplest competing grammar.

The quest for simplicity is hardly a new idea, and appears, for instance, in the early works of Chomsky (1955/1975, 1965: 25): under the notion of markedness, the grammar being constructed directly reflects the linguistic input. If the input contains information that points to a certain complex grammatical relation, the learner will acquire it, but if the input lacks such information, the principles that govern generalization will prevent the learner from constructing the more complex grammar. The markedness approach was abandoned in generative linguistics, in part because of the lack of a metric for establishing the simplicity of grammars, and partially owing to the rise of the 'poverty of the stimulus argument', whereby linguistic experience seems hopelessly unreliable. Such caveats are dealt with in this chapter: firstly, the MDL approach provides a quantitative metric for simplicity; secondly, the poverty of the stimulus instantiated in the transmission bottleneck seems a necessary precondition for the emergence of exceptions, rather than a hindrance to language evolution. There is a critical size for the bottleneck: too little or too much exposure to the language fails to yield stable patterns of quasi-productivity.[3]

Another defining feature of the simulations described in this chapter is that they rely on word frequencies to assign probabilities to sentences. We have also assumed that the distribution of word frequencies follows Zipf's law (Zipf 1949). These assumptions merit some discussion. There are two important reasons for applying a power law distribution to word frequency: firstly, it has been shown in the past to have important implications for the emergence of irregularities in ILM simulations of language evolution (e.g. Kirby 2001), and secondly, such frequency distributions are ubiquitous in natural language.

Kirby (2001) has shown that benign irregularities will spontaneously emerge in compositional language structure if frequency distributions follow Zipf's law.[4] When this is the case, the very frequent phrases at the 'head' of the distribution are shortened to irregular forms, resulting in selection under a similar MDL metric to that described here. This phenomenon does not appear to occur when frequencies do not follow a power law. We can see the impact of Zipf's law on our simulations by considering the likely results if word frequencies had been evenly distributed (i.e. if all sentences had been assigned equal probability). In such a

---

[3] Brighton (2002) and Kirby (2001) found that both compositionality and irregularity emerge thanks to the bottleneck. Interestingly, we seem to have modelled the reverse timecourse to Brighton's simulations, which start with a non-compositional language to attain compositionality. The converging end-point is, however, a stable state of quasi-regularity modulated by the bottleneck.

[4] We investigate the case of accidentally unfilled slots in syntactic paradigms. In contrast, Kirby models the case of slots filled by irregular forms, for instance the emergence and replacement of *went* for **goed*. Baker called these 'benign' exceptions vis-à-vis the learnability paradox: recovery from overgeneralization of **goed* can be safely arrived at by positive evidence, as the correct alternative *went* is present in the input. In addition, Kirby models meaning, and the pressure to invent random forms for meanings for which no rule exists is what gives rise to the irregularities in the first place. Because we purposely modelled the emergence of quasi-productivities without a meaning space, comparisons with Kirby's work can only be indirect.

case, the threshold number of sentences for learning a particular exception would have been the same for every sentence. Thus, the learner would either encounter enough sentences to learn all the exceptions at once, or would not learn any exceptions at all. Any sentences not encountered before the threshold was reached would be posited as exceptions. It is not impossible that exceptions would emerge and survive under such conditions, but it seems unlikely that we would see the patterns of emergence and stability outlined above.

In following Zipf's law, the frequency distribution of words in our toy language mirrors that found in natural languages: word frequencies in natural language text and corpora follow such distributions quite precisely, as do a number of other natural-language statistics (Bell et al. 1990). The assumption that the probability of a given sentence is perceived as a function of word frequencies is more controversial. It seems highly unlikely that this would be exclusively the case in natural language; we would be surprised if factors such as semantics and phonology did not play a role. However, no factors other than the frequency and collation statistics were available in our language. We contend that it is a plausible assumption that these factors also play a role in determining our perceptions of the probability of a particular sentence occurring. We speculate that in the absence of other factors they must determine them exclusively.

Anecdotally, it seems that young speakers are losing the Germanic/Latinate distinction that allows dative shift for *give* but not for *donate*. Hence **John donated the library a book* is more likely to be accepted as grammatical in contemporary usage. However, **John said Mary hello* is more resistant to regularization, perhaps because *donate* is a low-frequency verb whereas *say* has a high frequency. We have ourselves found that our intuitions concerning 'holes' in the language are surprisingly volatile—we find it hard to reject some of the ungrammatical examples when we have used them several times as examples in our discussions. The same 'lifelong learning' phenomenon also affects linguists who feel that subjacency violations become weaker the more often they produce them (Culicover 1996). This is consistent with our model. In addition, syntactic constructions such as dative shift may undergo local regularization while still preserving idiosyncratic behaviour in some other area (*wave/say hello*, or *send/report*). More interestingly, our simulation results defy intuition in that a reverse trend from local regularity to idiosyncratic behaviour can also occur.

Although relatively stable, a given idiosyncrasy may die out quickly, being replaced by new idiosyncrasies or by a regularized form. Local structural reorganizations of syntactic paradigms (such as dative shift for *donate*) can take place within a *single* generation. An implication of our model, not tested directly, is that linguistic diversity will emerge spontaneously in different spatially distributed linguistic communities, even in those that share a similar culture, as attested in different varieties of English in the English-speaking world. These considerations remain speculative as we have not attempted to model language change driven by social factors, language contact, multilingualism, or other factors; see Chapter 16 in this volume, by Solan et al.

In this chapter we have shown that a potentially hard problem of language acquisition, that of quasi-regularity, gives rise to a paradox of language evolution. We have shown that the acquisition problem may be solved by incorporating a learning bias towards simplicity. This solution goes some way towards resolving a related paradox in language evolution: given sufficient exposure to samples of language, quasi-regular structures are learnable, and hence stable over generations. In addition to this we have shown that under some conditions, quasi-regular structures may emerge in a language even if it were initially completely productive. However, we make no assumptions as to the origins of language in the human species. The starting point of a fully regular language should not be taken as a hypothesis about historical languages. Rather, it served the purpose of demonstrating that quasi-regular structures may emerge spontaneously, and hence constitute a natural, stable equilibrium for languages across time.

It is worth mentioning the striking analogy between natural languages and many complex systems in the natural world (see also Oudeyer, Chapter 4). The sciences of complexity have recently started to note that most natural phenomena are truly complex, i.e. they occur at a transition point between two extremes, perfect regularity on the one side and pure randomness on the other (Flake 1998). Perfect regularity is orderly and allows for high compressibility, whereas randomness is by its nature unpredictable and therefore defies compression (Gell-Mann 1995). If syntactic constructions were completely idiosyncratic (irregular) they could only be learned by heart and no generalization to novel instances would be possible. On the other side, the sort of innate constraints for acquisition postulated by a universal grammar and characterized in terms of maximally general and universal syntactic principles would lead all languages to develop perfectly compressible grammars, which is not the case for natural languages in the world. For example, a truly general transformational rule like dative shift raises the projection problem noted by Baker, as it predicts that *We reported the police the accident* is grammatical. Hence, the very existence of irregular, idiosyncratic, and quasi-regular forms, so widespread and stable in natural languages, suggests that they are arbitrary and unconstrained except by the requirement that they be computable, i.e. learnable (see also Culicover 1999). A language-learning mechanism must be capable of accommodating the irregular, the exceptional, and the idiosyncratic. We have proposed that a general-purpose learning mechanism driven by simplicity has the computational power to do so.

ACKNOWLEDGEMENTS

This work was supported by European Union Project HPRN-CT-1999-00065 and ESRC grant R42200134569. Luca Onnis is now at the Department of Psychology, Cornell University.

FURTHER READING

To find out more about simplicity as a general principle of cognition, Chater (1996) and Chater (1999) are exhaustive readings. A more technical reading on simplicity applied to language learning from positive evidence is Chater and Vitányi (ms.). From a linguist's perspective, Culicover (1999) is a very useful book, with in-depth linguistic analyses uncovering many puzzling irregularities in English and other languages. Culicover argues that such 'syntactic nuts' should be centre stage in a theory of language acquisition, rather than being relegated to the periphery of linguistic enquiry.

Appendix 15.1

Probabilistic generation of language samples

For the language to be probabilistically generated and understood, it was necessary to assign several sets of probabilities. We made the initial idealization that the probability of any given sentence equalled the product of the probabilities of its components. Thus, constructions comprising high-frequency words were taken to be much more probable than those comprising low-frequency words. We assigned relative frequencies to individual words by applying Zipf's law (Zipf

1948), which states that the relative frequency of any word is given as the inverse of its rank. This distribution is frequently encountered in natural languages (see, for example, Bell et al. 1990).

Our simulations began by arbitrarily ranking both classes of words, As and Bs. The probability of a word occurring in a particular distributional context is then given as:

$$p(w_i) = \frac{f(w_i)}{\sum_j f(w_j)} \tag{1}$$

where $p(w_i)$ is the probability of the word i, $f(w_i)$ is the frequency of that word, and $\sum_j f(w_j)$ is the sum of the frequencies of all the words that might occur in the given context. Any sentence involves two such probabilities, $p(w1)$, the probability of the first word and $p(w2 \mid w1)$, the probability of the second word in the context of the first. $p(w1)$ is given by equation (1) with $\sum_j f(w_j)$ operating over all eight words. For $p(w2 \mid w1)$, $\sum_j f(w_j)$ operates over the distribution of second words associated with $w1$. If no exceptions are specified (as at the beginning of the simulation, and for each learner's initial hypothesis), there were always four possible second words. In hypotheses where exceptions were specified, however, the number of possible second words varied between first words. The first agent heard language generated from a completely regular hypothesis. Subsequent agents heard language generated from the favoured hypothesis of their parent agent. Sentences were generated by stochastically selecting a first word and then a second, given the first, and using the probabilities stipulated by the hypothesis in question.

Hypothesis selection using Minimum Description Length

Agents chose between competing hypotheses by selecting the one specified with the shortest binary code. The code for each hypothesis specified both the hypothesis itself and all the encountered data as a function of that hypothesis. It was possible to specify both the hypothesis and the data in exactly the same way. All learners entertained one initial hypothesis, which was completely regular. Each sentence consisted of a pair of A and B words in either order. The only difference between this and later hypotheses was the number of exceptions specified. The code length necessary to specify the syntactic categories A and B and the production rules were identical for every hypothesis and therefore need not be considered. The only variable element that needed to be specified was the set of exceptions. This element, when it was not empty, consisted of a set of sentences of exactly the same form as those generated as samples of the language. The code length to specify an exception was therefore exactly the same as the code length necessary to specify that sentence, were it to be encountered as data. This is given by the general formula for encoding an object or event with a binary code of length $c(x)$, when it is associated with a probability p (Shannon 1948):

$$c(x) = \log_2 \frac{1}{p(x)} \qquad (2)$$

Following equation (2), the code length necessary to specify a sentence $w1,w2$ is given as:

$$c(w1,w2) = \log_2 \frac{1}{p(w1) \times p(w2|w1)} \qquad (3)$$

where $c(w1, w2)$ is the number of bits necessary to specify $w1,w2$; $p(w1)$ is the probability of the first word; and $p(w2|w1)$ the probability of the second word given the first. These values are found using equation (1). In the event that the sentence $w1w2$ was specified as an exception under the hypothesis in question, the code length necessary to specify it was:

$$c(w1,w2) = \log_2 \frac{1}{p(w1) \times p(w2)} \qquad (4)$$

where $p(w2)$ is the probability of $w2$ independent of $w1$. The second word is therefore coded as if it were one of eight possibilities, rather than one of four. This reduces the perceived probability of the sentence and increases the code length associated with it. In this way, hypotheses that posited spurious exceptions were punished with longer data code lengths when those exceptions were encountered. As mentioned above, each learner agent began by entertaining a single completely regular hypothesis without any exceptions. Initially, therefore, all data was coded under one hypothesis only. As more hypotheses emerged, they ran in parallel with previous ones so that data was coded under all hypotheses simultaneously. Each new hypothesis was a clone of its immediate predecessor, with the addition of one exception. Thus, the initial hypothesis contained no exceptions, the second contained one, the third, two, and so on. A new exception was postulated when a particular construction or sentence, x, had never been heard and an MDL-derived parameter, equation (5), was satisfied:

$$Np(x) > \log_2 \frac{1}{p(x)} \qquad (5)$$

where N is the total number of sentences heard so far. This parameter merits some discussion. A learner's decision to posit a particular sentence as an exception is dependent on two pieces of data: the total number of sentences heard and the number of times that the sentence in question has been heard. How these are combined to determine the precise point at which an exception is posited is to some extent arbitrary. For simplicity, we will only consider the case in which no sentence is ever posited as an exception if it has been encountered in the data. The critical value that determines when a particular sentence is posited as an exception is therefore the number of sentences that have been heard. Two normative criteria for this threshold exist: on the one hand it should not be so low that the learner concludes there is an exception when in fact none exists; on the other hand, the learner should not fail to spot genuine exceptions after exposure to a reasonable amount of data. The consequences of failure to meet either of these criteria can be seen in both cognitive and linguistic terms. Both will result in longer code lengths than necessary: the former will incur long data codes when it encounters the sentences that it has specified as exceptions; the latter will incur long data codes that it could reasonably have avoided by specifying exceptions earlier. Linguistically, in the former case the learner will have legitimate sentences pruned from its productive repertoire; in the latter it will continue to produce illegitimate sentences for longer than necessary.

In these simulations, not all sentences were equally probable. Less probable (and absent) sentences should require more language to be encountered before they could be considered exceptions. This was taken into account by making use of a general derivation (not specific to these simulations) based on the premise that an exception should be postulated at the point at which the investment of bits necessary to specify it would have been recouped had it been postulated before any language was heard.

Suppose that a learner wants to know whether to consider x as an exception, where $p(x)$ is the probability of x. If it is postulated as an exception, we can increase the probability of the other sentences that have not been ruled out. These probabilities used to sum to $1-p(x)$ but with x as an exception they now sum to 1. The most neutral way to rescale these probabilities is to multiply them all by the same factor $\frac{1}{1-p(x)}$. This increase means that the code for each item reduces by $\log_2 \frac{1}{1-p(x)}$ (see equation (2)). Thus if the learner hears a corpus of N sentences, never encountering x and having postulated x as an exception, it will make a saving of $N\log_2 \frac{1}{1-p(x)}$ over the whole corpus. Thus x may be postulated as an exception when this saving exceeds the cost of specifying x as an exception:

$$N \log_2 \frac{1}{1 - p(x)} > \log_2 \frac{1}{p(x)} \tag{6}$$

If we assume that $p(x)$, the probability of a particular sentence is small (i.e. near 0), a Taylor expansion gives that $\log_2 \frac{1}{1-p(x)}$ approximately equals $p(x)$. From this we can conclude that a learner can recoup the 'cost' of specifying an exception, x, if equation (5) holds.

16 Evolution of language diversity: why fitness counts

ZACH SOLAN, EYTAN RUPPIN, DAVID HORN, AND SHIMON EDELMAN

16.1 Introduction

Many recent studies exploring the evolution of language in a population of communicating agents assume that the possession of a common language increases the fitness of its users (e.g. Cangelosi 2001; Reggia et al. 2001; Nowak et al. 1999; K. Smith 2001). Language-conferred fitness is defined as the increase in individual survival probability that stems from successful communication: a group whose members communicate well is supposed to leave, on average, more offspring. Although the assumption that language increases human evolutionary fitness is intuitively appealing, its validity needs to be examined in the light of indications that a coherent language can emerge in the absence of language-related fitness (Kirby 2000; Oliphant 1999; Oliphant and Batali 1997; Briscoe, Chapter 14)—for example, through a combination of genetic drift and random population diffusion.

The present chapter examines and compares the effects of fitness and of neutral drift on the emergence of coherent languages. Our approach is motivated both by communication models employed in studies of language evolution (Nowak et al. 2000; Nowak et al. 1999; Nowak and Krakauer 1999; Komarova and Nowak 2001; Kirby 2000; Kirby 2002a; Batali 1998), and by migration models that are widely used in population genetics, such as the island model (Wright 1931) and migration matrix (Bodmer and Cavalli-Sforza 1968). Specifically, we integrate communication and migration effects by constructing a system of several distinct populations that exchange migrants at a controlled rate; within each population, evolutionary dynamics of language are governed by the communication model.

The spread of languages within and between populations in this model can be compared to empirical data on linguistic diversity, a field of study that has been drawing increasing attention over recent years (Nichols 1992; Nettle 1999). Although there are as many as 6500 known languages, about 95 per cent of the world population speaks only 100 languages. The distribution of languages around the world is far from uniform (Grimes 2001). Hundreds of languages have evolved in Africa and Oceania, while very few appear to have evolved in North America and Europe (unless most of those that did died off in prehistoric times). Examining the distribution of languages, most of which are nearly extinct, can shed light on the evolutionary forces that were involved in their emergence.

The markedly uneven geographic distribution both of the emergence of languages and of their disappearance suggests that powerful dynamic mechanisms are at work. The evolutionary dynamics behind linguistic diversity can be explored using computational simulations, as in Nettle (1999) and Livingstone (2000). Nettle's work concerned vowel learning in the presence of migration, in a population distributed over a 7×7 spatial grid, with twenty individuals at each position. Each new offspring learned two continuous parameters (the first two formants), by sampling their values among all the adults in its group. Individuals thus learned the approximate average values of the parameters in their group. Each simulation typically lasted for several hundreds of generations. To simplify the calculations and to keep the group sizes constant, migration always involved an exchange of individuals between two groups.

Nettle examined the dynamics of this system under three modes of fitness influence. The first of these was the neutral mode, corresponding to an absence of selection pressure. In that mode the individuals simply learned by averaging the values of the two continuous parameters among the adults in their social group. The second mode was functional selection, based on the notion that some variables may confer fitness because they make language easier to learn or use. In Nettle's version of the functional selection mode, if the distance between any two phonemes is less than a critical value, then one of the phonemes is moved randomly in the formant space until the critical distance is re-established (note that this process amplifies within-group differences). The third mode of fitness influence corresponded to raising the social status of some individuals in each group, and having the new offspring learn selectively from the high-ranking adults in their group. Nettle found that in the absence of social selection even a very low level of migration destroys local diversity. Social selection was found to contribute very strongly both to diversity and to its stability in the face of higher migration rates. Finally, functional selection was seen to amplify and reinforce diversity, but could not bring this about on its own.

Livingstone's work (Livingstone 2000; Livingstone and Fyfe 2000) suggests that no functional benefits are required to create linguistic diversity and that language diversity may be a natural consequence of the adaptively neutral cultural evolution of language. Livingstone studied a computational model based on the evolutionary dynamics of a population of communicating individuals. These were simulated by simple artificial neural networks that mapped signals to meanings (once an agent is presented with a meaning, a signal is produced, and vice versa). In contrast to Nettle's work, Livingstone's study did not address the issue of migration forces and was based solely on the transmission of signal–meaning maps between generations.

16.2 The model

In the present work, we extend Nettle's migration matrix model, controlling the population exchange between spatially separated 'islands' by introducing a measure of individual fitness based on communication success (Hurford 1989; Nowak et al. 1999). Thus, in our model both the individual and the social fitness are determined by the communication performance, rather than by external parameters. In addition, we allow true matrix-controlled migration (compared to symmetric swapping of individuals used by Nettle).

The population we study consists of n individuals $(I_1 \ldots I_n)$ that can exchange m possible signals $(S_1 \ldots S_m)$. For each individual, the signal exchange is described by two matrices, P and Q, the first one defining production and the second comprehension. The elements P_{ij} of the production matrix P are the probabilities that a certain individual will refer to object i with signal j. Thus, the production matrix can be seen as a look-up table for generating signals associated with a specific object. The elements q_{ji} of the comprehension matrix Q are the probabilities that an individual will associate signal j with object i. As in Nowak's work, the ability of two individuals to communicate depends on their comprehension and production matrices. To measure this communication ability, a payoff function is introduced. The payoff $F(I_i, I_j)$ corresponds to the mutual understanding between the individuals I_i and I_j and is calculated from the four matrices Q and P of the two individuals (a more detailed description of the model can be found in Appendix 16.1 at the end of this chapter).

The evolution of language in this model is based on lexicon transmission from one generation to the next. In each iteration, the newly generated population are treated as students (listeners), while the old generation are treated as the teachers (speakers). The students select their role models according to the learning mode chosen for the given simulation (the learning modes are described below). Each teacher uses its look-up table of objects (matrix P) to produce k signals. Note that in principle an object can be associated with several signals. Each student receives the signals and keeps a record (represented by the association matrix A) of the number of times a specific object is associated with a specific signal. This record is used at the end of the learning stage to build the comprehension and the production matrices of the new individual.

The maximum payoff for a P, Q pair is obtained for matrices P that have at least one *1* in every column, which means that each object is associated with only one signal. A more detailed analysis reveals that (a) this optimal state is an absorbing state of the system, and (b) an optimal learning mechanism will ultimately reach this state as there is an apparent bias in favour of one-to-one mappings between objects and words (K. Smith 2002). When learning is complete and all the individuals have acquired their association matrices, the old generation is removed from the simulation (i.e. there is no overlap between generations), and the simulation calculates the Q and P matrices for the remaining individuals. The Q and P matrices of each individual are calculated using its association matrix A.

Three learning modes were implemented and compared:

1. **Parental learning with fitness** (LINEAR SELECTION). In this mode, the offspring learn from their parents, with individuals that communicate well producing more offspring. Of the many possible fitness functions linking the number of offspring with the communication payoff, we chose linear fitness.

2. **Parental learning with no fitness** (DRIFT). In this mode, there is no advantage to individuals who communicate well.

3. **Role model** (SOCIAL SELECTION). In this mode, the members of a group acquire their language from a few selected 'role model' individuals, singled out by their ability to communicate with their group members.

The migration component of our model is very similar to the original n-island approach of Wright (1931), and to the migration matrix approach of Bodmer and Cavalli-Sforza (1968). The island model assumes that individuals migrate from one subpopulation to another. In the initial state each subpopulation consists of N individuals in M subpopulations. In each cycle, the migration rate M_{ij} determines the number of individuals relocating from population i to population j.

The migration rates, which are preset at the beginning of the simulation, may be the same for all subpopulations, or may vary according to some external factors (i.e. geographical distance). In the next section we address first the simple case in which the migration rates are fixed for all subpopulations; the more realistic case in which migration rates depend on geographical distances is treated later.

16.3 Results

We first analysed the diversity of languages that evolved under each of the three fitness modes, by considering two kinds of indicators: (i) the *internal payoff*, which is the average payoff within a subpopulation, and (ii) the *external payoff*, which is the average payoff between individuals across the whole population. The migration matrix entries were constant and equal for all groups (in the more realistic case the migration matrix is merely symmetric). Figure 16.1(a) illustrates the time course of the internal and external payoffs across generations in the DRIFT mode. Notice that after the first 500 generations, the internal payoff is higher than the external payoff. After 2000 generations, only one dominant language is left, at which point the internal payoff is equal to the external payoff. The same phenomenon was observed in the SOCIAL SELECTION mode, where, however, it took much longer for one dominant language to emerge. In comparison, in the LINEAR SELECTION mode (linear fitness), a diversity of languages is obtained under high internal and low external payoff.

To visualize the process of language development, one may consider the distance matrix whose elements d_{ij} correspond to the quality of understanding between any two individuals within the entire population:

$$(1) \quad d(ij) = 1 - F(I_i, I_j)/n$$

where $F(I_i, I_j)$ is the communication payoff between individuals I_i and I_j. Note that $d = 0$ means maximal understanding between two individuals, and $d = 1$ means no understanding. A simulation with ten subpopulations of fifty individuals each yields a 500×500 distance matrix. The diagonal values are all equal to zero, because each individual understands itself perfectly. Such a distance matrix captures the mutual understanding between individuals, regardless of their subpopulation relation. To visualize the interaction between the individuals, one can represent each of them as a point in a multidimensional 'understanding space' in which the Euclidean distance between two points corresponds to the mutual understanding between the corresponding individuals. In such a representation, a subpopulation that shares the same language will appear as a cluster whose size is determined by its level of understanding (internal payoff value): a subpopulation whose members have a high degree of mutual understanding will appear as a tight cluster. For visualization purposes, we embed the understanding space into two dimensions, using a well-known technique (multidimensional scaling, or MDS; Shepard 1980). The resulting maps afford a certain insight into the pattern of subpopulations in each cycle. Figure 16.2 presents a sequence of snapshots of the understanding space, taken every 200 generations in the DRIFT, SOCIAL SELECTION, and LINEAR SELECTION modes.[1]

In the DRIFT mode, the first several snapshots contain several clusters of languages; eventually, the clusters become unstable, that is, most of the languages become extinct and one language prevails. In comparison, in the SOCIAL SELECTION mode the system passes through a stage with several discrete clusters; after 2000 generations one dominant language remains. Likewise, in the LINEAR SELECTION mode, ten subpopulations

---

[1] The circular cluster arrangement is an artifact that arises when MDS is applied to data that contain many equidistant pairs of points (Kruskal 1977).

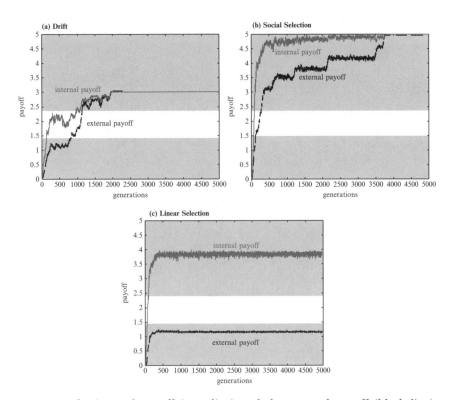

FIG. 16.1 The internal payoff (grey line) and the external payoff (black line) in successive generations (the maximum possible payoff according to equation (2) in Appendix 16.1 is equal to the number of distinct signals m = 5). The upper band of the graph corresponds to a situation with one dominant language (all individuals understand each other regardless of their location). When the grey curve is in the upper band and the black one in the lower band, individuals within the subpopulations understand each other but not the members of other subpopulations (in other words, several languages coexist). In this run we simulated ten subpopulations of fifty individuals each. The migration rate between the islands was constant and equal to 0.01 (1 per cent of migration per generation).

stabilize after 200 generations; after 800 generations only six of these are left. In Figure 16.2, there is a large cluster in the DRIFT mode; in the SOCIAL SELECTION mode each of the much smaller clusters eventually converges to a single dot. These singleton clusters represent subpopulations with the most efficient language (recall that the size of a cluster is determined by its internal payoff value). In this sequence, all the clusters become singletons with the maximal internal payoff, which means that this fitness mode finds an optimally efficient language, but cannot converge on a stable multiple-language situation.

Figure 16.3 presents a sensitivity analysis of the three fitness modes for different migration rates. The only mechanism that remained stable against a higher rate of migration was the LINEAR SELECTION mode with linear fitness. Even in that mode, however, the system converged to a single language when the migration rate exceeded a critical value (about 4 per cent).

Figure 16.4 illustrates a more realistic scenario, in which the subpopulations are randomly located on a 50×50-cell, and the migration rate between the groups is not fixed but is determined geographically, as a Gaussian function of their distance. The MDS snapshots of the simulation were taken over three different iterations. As before, in this simulation too only the linear fitness mode can preserve the coexistence of several distinct languages. Furthermore, because of the geographical distance effect, subpopulations that are located close to each other are those whose languages are the first to merge.

16.4 Discussion

In the language evolution literature, one frequently encounters arguments based on the intuitive assumption that successful communication leads eventually to an increased chance of individual survival. This assumption occupies a prominent place in many models of language evolution, despite the scarcity of evidence supporting it. In this work, we addressed this issue by studying the evolutionary dynamics of language diversity with and without language-conferred fitness.

Our model, which combines the shared lexicon approach (Hurford 1989; Nowak et al. 1999) with island migration methods (Nettle 1999), allowed us to compare the relative contributions of language fitness and of population migration to language diversity. As in previous models (Nettle 1999; Livingstone 2000), the underlying assumption is that the source of the diversity in the model is the initial randomness of the populations. Although it is not intended to produce precise quantitative predictions,

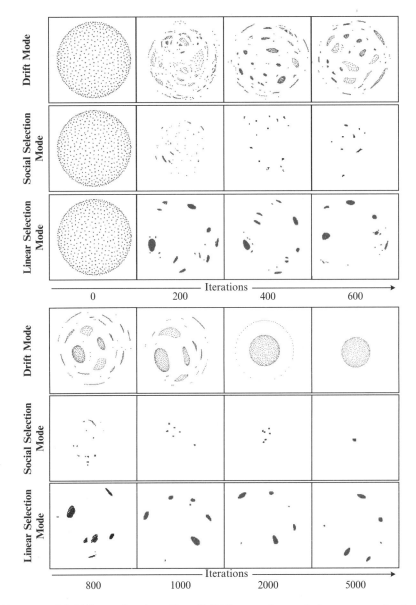

Fig. 16.2 Multidimensional scaling (MDS) snapshots of the communication distance matrix under each of the three fitness modes. The circular arrangement of the clusters is a well-known artifact introduced by MDS (Kruskal 1977), which is of no import in the present case (we are interested in the number of clusters and their shapes and not in their mutual arrangement).

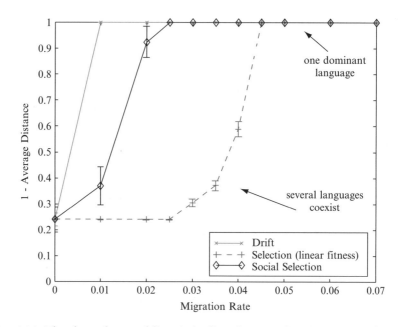

Fɪɢ. 16.3 The dependence of linguistic diversity on migration rate under the three fitness modes (DRIFT, grey line; SOCIAL SELECTION, solid line; and LINEAR SELECTION, dashed line). The abscissa shows the migration rate and the ordinate shows the internal–external payoff ratio, computed after 5000 generations by averaging the distance defined by equation (1). A ratio of 1 corresponds to a single dominant language; low ratios indicate high linguistic diversity.

this approach makes it possible to study the general dynamics of the evolution of language diversity. In particular, the behaviour of the model in time and space offers some insights into the patterns of present-day linguistic diversity.

Our computational results differ from those of Nettle (1999) and Livingstone (e.g. Livingstone 2000), most likely due to differences in the manner in which linear selection pressure and social effects have been implemented. In Nettle's model, these factors were not influenced by the ability of the individuals to communicate; in comparison, in the present study mutual understanding between individuals was the key factor shaping the evolutionary dynamics. Livingstone's study, on the other hand, explored the effects of signal transmission but left out migration.

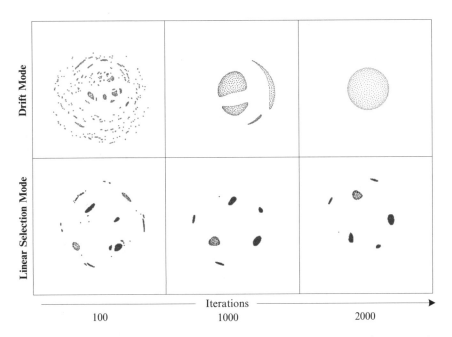

Fig. 16.4 A spatial migration model. The migration rate between the groups is determined by a Gaussian function of their distance on a 50 × 50 grid. The figure shows the MDS snapshots of the state of the simulation, taken over three different iterations.

The results of our simulations suggest that the contribution of language to the fitness of individuals and the migration of individuals between subpopulations can indeed account for the evolution of language diversity. While fitness contributes positively to diversity, the contribution of migration is negative. We found that in the DRIFT and SOCIAL SELECTION conditions it takes much longer for the system to reach a steady state, and that even a very small migration rate suffices for one language to become dominant. In the LINEAR SELECTION case, when the fitness of individuals is assumed to be proportional to the success of their shared communication, the subpopulations stabilize quite rapidly to form several distinct languages. In this case, only relatively high migration rates will force the system into a regime of one dominant language. Thus, given the continued presence of linguistic diversity and migration forces in the world, our results strongly suggest that fitness-based (linear) selection is at work in governing the evolutionary dynamics of language.

For each one of the cases (DRIFT, SOCIAL SELECTION, and LINEAR SELECTION), a critical value of the migration rate can be identified, beyond which only one language can exist in the long run. This phenomenon offers a simple explanation for the transformation of social networks into linguistically bounded groups. One of the best known phenomena in linguistic diversity is the existence of small societies in which distinct languages rather than continua of dialects are found. According to our findings, such sharp linguistic boundaries can arise when migration rates depend on geographical and sociological factors. Thus, in those locations where the migration rate is above the critical value, the languages will be fused into one; in locations that share a lower rate of migration, languages will remain divided. This situation was obtained in simulation 2 (see Figure 16.4), where in the linear selection mode, seven out of the initial ten groups survived, as their migration rate was below the critical value. However, this phenomenon was not observed in the absence of linear selection (i.e. in the DRIFT and SOCIAL SELECTION modes), as the migration rate among the groups exceeded the critical value, which in these modes is much lower. The effect of migration thus drives languages in these modes into extinction very quickly. We remark that the consistent and stable emergence either of one dominant language or of linguistic diversity for different values of a control parameter—the migration rate—has an intriguing analogy in solid-state physics: when certain materials are cooled rapidly, they crystallize heterogeneously (several crystals develop), while a slow gradual annealing of the same material leads to a homogeneous crystallization.

Our analysis predicts that in places where the migration rate is beneath the critical value, the diversity will be relatively high, while in places where it exceeds the critical value the level of diversity will be much lower. To examine this prediction, one may consider processes known to affect both migration rates and the level of language diversity. One such factor is *ecological risk*, suggested by Nettle (1999), which is defined as the probability of a household facing a temporary shortfall in food production. People tend to migrate more in regions with higher ecological risk; Nettle showed that in places where the risk factor (and therefore the migration rate) is low, the level of diversity is high, and vice versa. Another relevant factor is social networks: where such networks exist, the level of diversity is low (e.g. Niger), while in places where the social networks are less developed (e.g. Papua New Guinea) the level of linguistic diversity is much higher. Bringing additional factors, such as means of transportation, mobility, and average distance among subpopulations into the picture should lead to a better understanding of the relation between migration rates and language diversity.

Another prediction of our model concerns the development of language diversity over time. Specifically, our model predicts a non-constant rate of language evolution, where the appearance of new languages is very rapid (the first stage of language evolution takes very few iterations), and the extinction of languages is slow (see Figure 16.2). Dixon (1997) has proposed a controversial model (cf. Joseph 2001) of the development of language over time, building on ideas from biological evolution (Eldredge and Gould 1972). In his 'punctuated equilibrium' model, language evolution undergoes periods of rapid expansion, during which many languages evolve, interspersed with long periods of near-equilibrium, during which languages diffuse and converge, as societies interact, intermarry, fission, and fuse. In comparison to Dixon's, our approach needs not postulate *ad hoc* discrete evolutionary stages: the variable rate of language evolution, spread, and disappearance emerges from the dynamics of the underlying processes of differentiation and drift.

FURTHER READING

For Dixon's model of punctuated equilibrium in language evolution, see Dixon (1997). On linguistic diversity, see Nettle (1999) and Nichols (1992). On communication models employed in studies of language evolution, see Nowak, Plotkin, and Krakauer (1999).

Appendix 16.1

The population we study consists of n individuals ($I_1 \ldots I_n$) that can exchange m possible signals ($S_1 \ldots S_m$). For each individual, the signal exchange is described by two matrices, P and Q, the first one defining production and the second comprehension. The elements p_{ij} of the production matrix P are the probabilities that a certain individual will refer to object i with signal j; each row in the matrix P sums to 1. The elements q_{ji} of the comprehension matrix Q are the probabilities that an individual will associate signal j with object i; here too each row sums to 1. The payoff value corresponds to the mutual understanding between the two individuals; an individual's average payoff is calculated by summing its payoff with respect to each of its group members, divided by the group size (see equation (2)).

$$F(I_k, I_l) = \frac{1}{2} \sum_{i=1}^{n} \sum_{j=1}^{m} (p_{ij}^{(k)} q_{ji}^{(l)} + p_{ij}^{(l)} q_{ji}^{(k)})$$

$$F(I_u) = \frac{1}{n-1} \sum_{v \neq u} F(I_u, I_v)$$

(2)

The evolution of language in this model is based on lexicon transmission from one generation to the next. Individual I_k learns from I_l by sampling the responses of I_l to every object. This is incorporated in the model by sequentially scanning the rows of I_l's production matrix (each row corresponds to a different object). For each row, the agent produces k random signals according to the probabilities listed. The listener I_k undergoes a 'learning phase' in which it updates its association matrix A; this is an n × m matrix whose entries a_{ij} specify how often the individual has observed the object i being referred to by the signal j. The Q and P matrices are both derived from A according to equation (3).

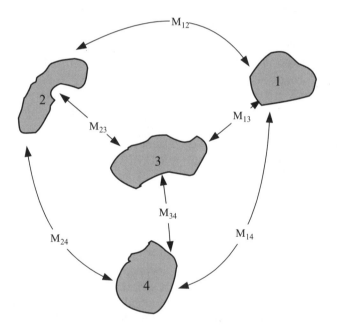

FIG. 16.5 The island migration model (general case). The island model assumes that individuals migrate from one subpopulation to another with different migration rate values. Initially, there are N individuals in each of the M subpopulations. In every cycle, the migration rate M_{ij} determines the number of individuals relocating from population i to population j. The migration rates M_{ij} can be arranged in a migration matrix.

The three learning modes we considered are: Parental learning with fitness (LINEAR SELECTION), Parental learning with no fitness (DRIFT), and Role model (SOCIAL SELECTION).

$$q_{ji} = \frac{a_{ij}}{\sum_{l=1}^{n} a_{lj}} \quad p_{ij} = \frac{a_{ij}}{\sum_{l=1}^{m} a_{il}} \tag{3}$$

The migration component of our model is very similar to the original n-island approach of Wright (1931), and to the migration matrix approach of Bodmer and Cavalli-Sforza (1968). The former assumes that individuals migrate from one subpopulation to another with the same rate, which means that the distances between subpopulations are not taken into account (cf. matrix M_1 in equation (4) and Figure 16.5). In the latter approach, the migration rates between subpopulations can be different, for example depending on distance (cf. matrix M_2 in equation (4) and Figure 16.5). In our implementation, each subpopulation consisted of N individuals. In each cycle, the migration rate determined the number of individuals relocating from one island to another; a migration matrix controlled the migration rate between the subpopulations.

$$M_1 = \begin{pmatrix} 0 & m & m & m \\ m & 0 & m & m \\ m & m & 0 & m \\ m & m & m & 0 \end{pmatrix} \quad M_2 = \begin{pmatrix} 0 & m & \frac{m}{2} & \frac{m}{4} \\ m & 0 & m & \frac{m}{2} \\ \frac{m}{2} & m & 0 & m \\ \frac{m}{4} & \frac{m}{2} & m & 0 \end{pmatrix} \tag{4}$$

17 Mutual exclusivity: communicative success despite conceptual divergence

ANDREW D. M. SMITH

17.1 Introduction

Traditional explanatory accounts of the evolution of language frequently appeal to a 'conventional neo-Darwinian process' (Pinker and Bloom 1990: 707), assuming that humans have evolved an innate, genetically encoded language acquisition device, which specifies a formal coding of universal grammar (Chomsky 1965), and which evolved incrementally through a series of steps via natural selection (Jackendoff 2002). An alternative approach focuses instead on the evolution of linguistic structures themselves, as utterances used and understood by speakers and hearers (Christiansen 1994; Croft 2000). Under the latter approach, the continual cycle of expressing and reinterpreting these utterances (Hurford 2002b) drives the cultural evolution of language. Other things being equal, languages which can be readily interpreted and expressed through this cycle are more likely to persist than those which cannot. An explanation of the evolution of syntactic structure is considered to be the Holy Grail of evolutionary linguistics by researchers in both these traditions, because syntax has been seen as the defining characteristic which separates human language from animal communication systems, and in recent years, computational simulations have been used extensively to shed light on this issue. Kirby (2002a), for example, shows that structured signals can develop from unstructured signals through the analysis of signal–meaning pairs and the subsequent generalization of rules based on the analysis; similar accounts are presented by Batali (2002), whose agents combine and modify phrases based on exemplars of signal–meaning mappings which they receive, and by Brighton (2002), who shows how the poverty of the stimulus is an important factor in the emergence of compositional syntax.

Despite these exciting findings, however, there are some problematic assumptions in models such as these. In particular, the emergence of syntactic structure in the signal space is a direct result of the signals' explicit association with predefined meanings (Nehaniv 2000), and of the explicit transfer of meaning in communication (A. Smith 2001). Furthermore, the models often rely on reinforcement learning to guide the learners, although error signals are widely rejected in language acquisition (Bloom 2000). I have, however, developed a model of meaning creation and communication which addresses these problems and have shown that communication can succeed through the inference of meaning (A. Smith 2001, 2003a, 2003b). Crucially, inferential communication allows the development of communication between individuals who do not necessarily share exactly the same internal representations of meaning. This flexibility then opens the possibility of a realistic evolutionary scenario, by allowing both for the necessary variation among individuals, and also for mutations which might enhance the inferential capabilities of one individual, while still allowing them to be communicatively consistent with the rest of the population.

In this chapter, I extend my inferential model to explore the usefulness of one of the main psycholinguistic acquisition biases which has been proposed to explain how children learn the meaning of words without explicit meaning transfer, namely Markman's (1989) *mutual exclusivity assumption*. The remainder of the chapter is divided into four parts: in section 17.2, I describe the signal redundancy paradox which is contained in other models; this predetermines the outcomes which are achieved, and, to a large extent, undermines the strength of their conclusions. In section 17.3, I focus further on Quine's (1960) famous problem of the indeterminacy of meaning, and on proposals made by psychologists and psycholinguists to explain how children manage to solve this problem when they acquire language, including, of course, the mutual exclusivity assumption. In section 17.4, I briefly describe my model of individual, independent meaning creation and negotiated communication which avoids these pitfalls and yet still allows successful communication. I show, crucially, that there is a strong relationship between levels of meaning coordination and communicative success. Finally, in section 17.5, mutual exclusivity is added to the model, and I show that, in contrast to expectations based on my earlier models, this can lead to high levels of communicative success despite agents having divergent conceptual structures.

17.2 The signal redundancy paradox

Kirby (2002a) and Batali (2002), among others, have shown how the simple ability to generalize can result in the emergence of a compositional, 'syntactic' communication system. In their simulations, agents initially create idiosyncratic rules to represent each different meaning they need to express, and each of these rules generates just one signal. Over time, coincidental matches occur between parts of signals and parts of meaning, and the agents create more general rules based on these matches; these rules use symbolic variables and can therefore generate more than one signal. Brighton (2002) shows that if there are pressures on agents which limit their exposure to the language, such as the poverty of the stimulus, then the agents are more likely to encounter general rules than idiosyncratic ones, and so these general rules are preferentially replicated over generations, leading to the eventual evolution of a fully compositional communication system, where the meaning of a signal is made up of a combination of the meanings of its parts and an algorithm for joining these together. The successful emergence of syntax in such models, however, is completely dependent on the signals being explicitly coupled to meanings which have a predefined and complex structure. It is not coincidental that the emergent syntactic structure parallels this semantic structure exactly, as the semantic structure is effectively used as a template against which the syntactic structure is constructed.

17.2.1 *Explicit meaning transfer*

Figure 17.1 shows a schematic diagram of the linguistic transfer in such a communicative model, where the utterances are made up of pairs of signals and meanings. We can see that the speaker (on the left of Figure 17.1) utters a signal *zknvrt*, which is received by the hearer. Simultaneously, the meaning in the speaker's brain, represented in Figure 17.1 by three symbols meant to resemble apples, is transferred directly to the hearer's brain. This explicit linkage of signal and meaning in the communication process means that it is a trivial task for the hearer to learn the association between them.

Models which make this idealization, therefore, ignore one of the most important and difficult problems facing researchers into the acquisition of

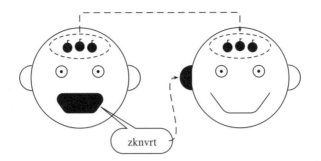

Fɪɢ. 17.1 A communicative episode which consists of the explicit transfer of both a signal, *zknvrt*, and a meaning, 'three apples', from speaker to hearer.

language, namely Quine's famous problem of the indeterminacy of meaning. Quine (1960) presented an imaginary anthropologist, who observes a speaker of an unfamiliar language uttering the word *gavagai* while pointing to a rabbit, and then shows that, logically, *gavagai* has an infinite number of possible meanings and, moreover, that the collection of further relevant information by the anthropologist will never reduce the number of possible hypotheses which will be consistent with the data; no matter how much evidence is collated, the meaning of *gavagai* can never be determined.

The consequences of the idealization of the learning process as shown in Figure 17.1 are considerable, not least because if meanings are explicitly and accurately transferable by telepathy, then the signals are not actually being used to convey meaning, and their very role in the model must be called into question; if the agents can transfer meanings between each other, there can be no justification for them to waste time and energy worrying about learning a redundant additional system of signalling. This paradox, which I call the *signal redundancy paradox*, arises whenever meanings are explicitly transferred in communication:

- If the meanings are transferable, then the signals are redundant;
- But if the signals are removed, then to what extent does the model represent communication?

The most obvious way out of this paradox is to conclude that meanings *cannot* be explicitly transferred, but must be inferred from elsewhere.

17.2.2 *Accessibility and privacy*

If there is no explicit meaning transfer, however, how does a hearer know which meaning to associate with a particular signal? The hearer must be able to infer a meaning from somewhere; the most obvious and general source for this is surely the environment in which the agent is placed. This in turn suggests that at least some of the meanings that agents talk about are used to *refer* to objects and events which actually happen in the environment. In this way, the agents' meanings are grounded (Harnad 1990); without the possibility of inferring the reference of the signals, real communication cannot emerge. Indeed, the existence of an external world from which meaning can be inferred is crucial to a realistic model of meaning, for without it, any 'meanings' are necessarily abstract and pre-defined. If the meanings do not identify anything in the world, or do not have reference, they can only be communicated through explicit transfer, which of course entails the signal redundancy paradox.

In order to avoid the signal redundancy paradox, therefore, there must be at least three levels of representation in the model, as shown in Figure 17.2:

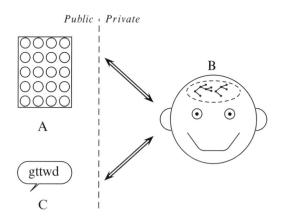

FIG. 17.2 A model of communication which avoids the signal redundancy paradox must have three levels of representation for the agents: an external environment (A); an internal, private semantic representation, represented by the trees in the agent's brain (B); and public signals (C). The mappings between A and B, and between B and C, represented by the arrows, must also be private and inaccessible to other agents.

A: an external environment, which is public and accessible to all, which provides the motivation and source for meaning creation;
B: a private, agent-specific internal representation of meaning, which is not perceptible to others;
C: a set of signals, which can be transmitted between agents and is in principle public.

The mere existence of an external world, as for instance in Hutchins and Hazlehurst's (1995) model of the emergence of a shared vocabulary, is not sufficient to avoid the paradox; if the agents' meanings are publicly accessible, either directly as in Hutchins and Hazlehurst's model where the external scenes *are* the meanings, or indirectly through an accessible mapping between the environment and the meanings, then the signals are again rendered unnecessary. For this reason, note in Figure 17.2 that the mappings between A and B and between B and C fall to the right-hand side of the demarcation line between the public and private domains.

17.2.3 *Inferential communication*

There are at least two possible explanations for how the agents come to have meanings which refer to things in their environment: either the meanings are innate, and have evolved through biological evolution, or they are created by the agents, as a result of their interactions with the environment. Innate meanings are not inherently implausible, but they seem to require either that the number of meanings useful to the agents is small and fixed, or that the world in which the agents exist is very stable and unchanging, so that the evolved meanings which were useful to their ancestors are still of use to the current generation. In practice, then, it is more reasonable to assume that the agents have an innate quality space, as suggested by Quine (1960), within which they create meanings anew in each generation, based on empirical testing of their environment, which allows them to discover which distinctions are communicatively relevant.

Thinking of the communicative function of language as a simple coding system between signals and meanings, however, is problematic not just in terms of the communication model itself, but also in terms of the evolution of such a system. From this perspective, it is important to remember that language is necessarily both reciprocal and cultural. There is no advantage, therefore, in a mutant obtaining a language acquisition device if others do not have one. In addition, however, there is no advantage in *many* mutants having a language acquisition device, if there is no language existing in the community for them to acquire. As Origgi and Sperber (2000) point out, a mutation which allows individuals to infer the meanings of signals can not only provide an explanation for how language got started, through the accidental discovery of what another is referring to, but can also provide a plausible account of the progressive complexification of language. For instance, a mutation which promotes the construction of a more complex semantic representation does not, in an inferential model, cause catastrophic effects on communication due to the ensuing mismatch between the speaker's meaning and the hearer's meaning; instead, because communication is based on reference, individuals can have very different internal representations of meanings, and yet still communicate successfully, as I have shown through simulation experiments (A. Smith 2003b). Those without the enhanced semantic representation can still communicate with everyone in blissful ignorance, while the mutants might receive an advantage in more accurate or detailed inference of the meaning, and might, in time, develop new symbols to represent the patterns they find in this structure. Indeed, this process of structural development is most obviously attested in historical processes of language change, particularly in the case of grammaticalization (Hopper and Traugott 1993), where (more complex) grammatical markers such as case markers and complementizers are created from (less complex) lexical items over generations of inference, a process which has been explicitly described as 'context-induced reinterpretation' (Heine and Kuteva 2002a: 3).

The model I describe, then, departs from previous accounts which assume that language learning is merely equivalent to learning a mapping between signals and predefined meanings. Instead, I argue that it must include at least the construction of empirical meanings, learning which of these meanings are relevant, and learning a mapping between meanings and signals through the inference of meaning in context.

17.3 Overcoming indeterminacy

Learning the meanings of words, of course, is utterly unremarkable to children, who effortlessly overcome Quine's problem of indeterminacy; a common suggestion for how this happens is that they are explicitly taught by parents and teachers, by being given feedback on their use of words. Despite the intuitive appeal of this idea, it is actually very rarely observed in practice, and is by no means culturally universal. Lieven (1994), for instance, describes cultures in which parents do not even speak to their children in the initial stages of acquisition, much less provide them with either encouragement or discouragement about their use of words. Bloom (2000), furthermore, describes a study on mute children who clearly could not receive feedback on their own speech, and yet still developed language normally. In view of this, researchers have explored the existence of other representational constraints within the learners themselves which predispose them to disregard some of the theoretically possible meanings, thus reducing the size of the set of semantic hypotheses, thereby making the set finite and making Quine's problem soluble.

Macnamara (1972), for instance, argues that children naturally represent their environment in terms of the objects within it, and that, when learning words, they have a similar *object bias*, under which they automatically assume that a new word refers to a whole object, rather than particular parts or properties thereof. The object bias is indeed a very useful tool in explaining how children might bootstrap language acquisition, but it is not a sufficient explanatory tool for the larger problem, and many additional biases or restrictions have also been proposed in order to account for more complex facets of word learning. Landau, Smith, and Jones (1988), for instance, discovered experimentally that children are more likely to categorize new objects in terms of their shape, rather than other perceptual features. Markman and Hutchinson (1984) have shown that children categorize objects taxonomically (grouping on the basis of type) rather than thematically (grouping on the basis of relationships between them) when they are learning words, but not otherwise. For instance, when word learning is not involved, a car and a car tyre can be grouped together thematically, but when the car is given a name, and the children asked to find another object which can be called by the same name, they are much more likely to find the taxonomically related bicycle.

Interpretation biases, too, have often been proposed; in particular, many of these suggestions, by for instance Barrett (1986), Clark (1987), and Markman (1989), can be summarized by the proposal that 'children should construct mutually exclusive extensions of the terms they acquire' (Merriman and Bowman 1989: 1). Although there are slight differences between these suggestions in terms of their theoretical and explanatory emphasis, in this chapter I will consider them as related versions of an overarching *mutual exclusivity assumption.* Merriman and Bowman (1989) analyse the implications behind mutual exclusivity, and propose three crucial ways in which the bias could affect the learning of new words; the most important of these, and the only one which does not rely on the explicit naming of objects, is through the *disambiguation of reference.* This phenomenon has been shown experimentally a number of times, particularly by Markman and Wachtel (1988), who describe experiments in which young children were presented with random pairs of objects, one of which is familiar to them, such as a banana or a spoon, and one of which is unfamiliar, such as a lemon-wedge presser or a pair of tongs. The children, on being presented with both objects, were asked by the experimenters to 'show me the *x*', where *x* was a randomly chosen nonsense syllable. Markman and Wachtel found that the children are much more likely to interpret *x* as referring to the tongs, rather than the banana; they hypothesize that this is because the children already understand a word which means BANANA, and they assume, under the mutual exclusivity bias, that '[w]hen children hear a novel term in the presence of a familiar and unfamiliar object, children are able to use mutual exclusivity to determine the referent of the novel term' (Markman and Wachtel 1988: 128). In section 17.5, I explore how mutual exclusivity can improve the levels of communicative success relative to the shared conceptual structure of agents in my model.

17.4 Details of the model

17.4.1 *Independent meaning creation*

Before investigating the effects of mutual exclusivity, however, it is useful to give a brief description of my basic model of meaning creation and communication, which takes as its starting point the model initially described by Steels (1996). A simple model world is simulated, containing a number of objects, each of which can be described in terms of the values of their observable features. Feature values in the model are real numbers, pseudo-randomly generated in the range [0.0 . . . 1.0]; the features themselves, however, are deliberately abstract, with neither specific nor predefined meanings, although for ease of understanding, they can of course be considered analogous to features in human language such as 'height', 'smell', or 'colour'. Simulated agents interact with the objects in the world using *sensory channels*; they have the same number of sensory channels as the objects have features, and there is a one-to-one mapping between them. Sensory channels are sensitive to the feature values of the objects; specifically, they can detect whether a particular feature value falls between two bounds on a sensory channel. The process of meaning creation takes place through *refinement*, or the splitting of a channel's sensitivity range into two discrete segments of equal size. This results in the formation of two new categories, each sensitive to half the original range. Each category is itself a candidate for further refinement, so producing, over time, a hierarchical, dendritic structure, with the nodes on the tree representing categories, or *meanings* (Steels 1999). Such structures are shown schematically in the agent's private semantic representation in Figure 17.2.

Interaction with the environment occurs through Steelsian discrimination games, which are made up of the following four constituent parts:

scene-setting: the agent is presented with a specific set of objects, called the *context*, one of which is chosen to be the *target* of discrimination.

categorization: the agent goes through all the objects in the context, returning for each an association with one or more of its existing semantic representations.

discrimination: the agent tries to find a distinctive category for the target. A category is distinctive if it is a valid representation of the target, and is not a valid representation of any other object in the context.

adaptation: the agent modifies its internal conceptual structure, by refining one of the sensory channels.

Adaptation of an agent's conceptual structure is triggered by failure in a discrimination game. Each agent has a *tree-growth strategy* for choosing a channel for refinement, which is based on its cognitive biases and/or the details of the particular discrimination game which failed, as described in A. Smith (2003b). In a stable world, the agents will eventually always develop a conceptual structure which can succeed in describing every object in the world. Different agents, however, will create different conceptual structures which will each be able to distinguish objects in the world, and so it is useful to be able to measure the level of meaning similarity between the conceptual structures of the two agents (A. Smith 2003a).

17.4.2 *Introspective obverter*

Having established that agents can create meanings which are helpful in describing the world around them, I simulate communication without explicit meaning transfer and without feedback by providing the agents with the ability to create simple signals and transmit them without error, and also providing them with a mechanism for associating signals and meanings, an individual dynamic lexicon (A. Smith 2003a). In a communication episode, one agent (the speaker) is trying to convey a meaning to another agent (the hearer) by the use of a signal.

Preparatory to communication, a successful discrimination game provides the speaker with a distinctive meaning which has identified the target object from others in the context, and it is this meaning which the speaker tries to convey; it utters a signal to represent the meaning, either taking one from its lexicon, or, if none suitable exists, creating a new one at random. The hearer then tries to infer the meaning of the signal from the context in which it is heard, attempting to deduce which of the objects in the context was identified by the speaker. Successful communication is defined by *referent identity*, which occurs when the object identified by the speaker is the same object as that identified by the hearer. Note that it is not necessary that the agents use the same agent-internal meaning, only that both agents pick out the same object in the world. Importantly, neither speaker nor hearer is given any feedback on whether the communication episode is successful.

This communication model, therefore, relies neither on explicit meaning transfer, nor on feedback guiding learning. The algorithms which determine the agents' behaviour, however, are crucial to its success, and are based on Oliphant and Batali's (1997) strategy for achieving an accurate communication system in a population of agents, which they dub *obverter*. Essentially, the obverter strategy boils down to the speaker choosing signals which it knows the hearer will understand correctly, rather than choosing signals that it might prefer to say. Unfortunately, true obverter learning in the theoretical situation defined by Oliphant and Batali assumes that the speaker has access to the lexicons of the other members of the population, so that it can choose the optimal signal for each meaning. Such mind reading is of course unrealistic, and returns us, more damagingly, to a telepathic world and the signal redundancy paradox. In order to maintain the benefits of obverter, whilst also avoiding any reliance on telepathy, I implement a modification to the obverter algorithm, in which I allow the agent to read only its own mind. The agent therefore uses introspection as a basis for decision making, choosing a signal which *it itself* would be most likely to understand if it heard the signal in this context.

Choosing a signal is relatively straightforward, but interpreting that signal is much more difficult; the hearer, to whom this task falls, knows neither the object to which the speaker is referring, nor the meaning which the speaker has in mind for the signal. The hearer creates a list of *possible meanings* or semantic hypotheses, containing every meaning in its conceptual structure which identifies *any one* of the objects in the context and distinguishes it from all the other objects in the context. The hearer has no reason to prefer any one of these possible meanings over another yet, so each of them is paired with the signal in the hearer's lexicon. Having done this for all the possible meanings, the hearer searches through its list of semantic hypotheses, and chooses the meaning m in which it has the highest confidence, which is, as Vogt and Coumans (2003) explain, the highest conditional probability that, given the current signal, the meaning m is expected. The object which the chosen meaning identifies is then compared to the original target object of the speaker's discrimination game to determine the success of the communicative episode.

17.4.3 *Communicative success*

I have shown previously (A. Smith 2003b) that in such a model, where the agents infer the meanings of words from the contexts in which they hear them, the percentage of successful communicative episodes, or the communicative success rate κ, is highly dependent on the level of conceptual similarity σ between the agents. I experiment with various cognitive biases, environmental factors, and meaning-creation strategies, to discover the circumstances under which high levels of conceptual similarity are most likely to occur, and show moreover that in a randomly generated world, the agents cannot improve on creating meanings based on their cognitive biases, using a *probabilistic* tree-growth strategy; high levels of conceptual similarity will always arise if the agents share similar values of these biases. In a structured or clumpy world, on the other hand, then it is much better for the agents to use a more *intelligent*, ecologically rational

(Gigerenzer and Todd 1999) tree-growth strategy, which can exploit the information in the environmental structure to a much greater degree.

17.5 Mutual exclusivity

17.5.1 *Implementation*

Successful communication, therefore, can emerge without the need for innate meanings and without meanings being explicitly transferred between agents, if the agents use introspective obverter to choose signals. On the other hand, communicative success rates are highly correlated with levels of meaning similarity; the exact relationship varies according to the experimental conditions, but it is always a logarithmic curve with communicative success in general slightly higher than meaning similarity. In this section, I implement the mutual exclusivity bias in the model, to see what effects its inclusion has on the development both of coordinated meanings and successful communication. Two factors, in particular, are crucial in triggering the use of mutual exclusivity, and must be taken into account in developing the model, namely:

signal novelty: the utterance in question is novel, and unfamiliar to the learner;

disambiguation of reference through prior knowledge: the learner reduces the set of meanings under consideration by excluding all objects for which it already understands a word.

Under normal circumstances within my model, the hearer would, on hearing an unfamiliar word in context, build a set of all possible semantic hypotheses and use these to decipher the utterance, as described in section 17.4. Disambiguating the reference of the utterance through prior knowledge, therefore, will allow this set of semantic hypotheses to be reduced; the agent works through the objects in the context, and excludes from consideration all those objects for which it already knows an appropriate word, namely a word which the agent would use, in this context, to describe the object, and which therefore represents a distinctive meaning which would distinguish this object from all the other objects in the current context. The agent is then left with a set of *unfamiliar* objects, and it assumes that the speaker must be referring to one of these. Its list of semantic hypotheses is therefore based only on these unfamiliar objects, from which the agent interprets the word as before, choosing the meaning in which it has the highest confidence probability.

In addition to this, however, Markman and Wachtel also hypothesize that mutual exclusivity can help the child to develop new meanings, when it cannot interpret an unfamiliar word, because 'children would be left with a word for which they have not yet figured out a meaning. This should then motivate children to find a potential meaning for the novel term' (Markman and Wachtel 1988: 153). If no interpretation at all is possible, therefore, i.e. there are no appropriate meanings which distinguish any of the unfamiliar objects from all the others in the context, then the agent searches through the unfamiliar objects in turn, trying to create a new, appropriate meaning which will be suitable to describe it in this context. It tests potential refinements on its sensory channels, until it finds a node which, once refined, will distinguish this object from all the other objects in the context, and then creates this new meaning, associating it with the unfamiliar signal.

The hearer's meaning-creation process is now very different from the speaker's, both in the mechanism by which it is triggered and in the algorithm through which it is implemented; meaning creation in the hearer now occurs as a result of encountering an unfamiliar word and is a direct attempt to find a relevant interpretation of this word, but in the speaker occurs as a result of failure to discriminate a target object. This implementation of the mutual exclusivity bias differs from my earlier implementation of the principle of contrast (A. Smith 2003b); although both sets of simulations use the same framework of meaning creation and communication, in the earlier simulations, the agent did not divide the context into two sets of familiar and unfamiliar words before interpretation, so the list of semantic hypotheses was not reduced, and the meaning-creation process was triggered very infrequently.

17.5.2 *Experimental results*

In the results reported here, the agents in the model each had five sensory channels with cognitive biases distributed uniformly, and the objects in the world were generated randomly. Each simulation consists of 5000 discrimination and communication episodes, and was run fifty separate times, after which the levels of meaning similarity σ and communicative success κ were then averaged, and expressed together with 95 per cent confidence intervals (CI).

Table 17.1 shows that in this randomly generated world, for both the probabilistic and intelligent tree-growth strategies, the levels of communicative success are indeed slightly higher than those of meaning similarity, as we would expect. On the other hand, we can also see that, in contrast to the experiments in A. Smith (2003b), there is no significant difference between the tree-growth strategies, as their confidence intervals overlap; the large differences I found previously in levels of meaning similarity between these tree-growth strategies are almost completely neutralized if the hearer uses mutual exclusivity to guide its interpretation and meaning creation.

Table 17.2, on the other hand, shows similar experiments in a simulated clumpy world, where the objects are grouped together and given identical values on some features, so that they are *a priori* indistinguishable on that sensory channel.

I have shown previously (A. Smith 2003b) that the intelligent strategy will produce much higher levels of meaning similarity σ under these circumstances, as it is much more able to exploit the underlying informa-

TABLE 17.1 *Meaning similarity σ, communicative success κ, in a randomly generated world.*

Tree-growth strategy	Meaning similarity		Communicative success	
	Mean ($\bar{\sigma}$)	CI	Mean ($\bar{\kappa}$)	CI
Probabilistic	0.53	(0.50–0.56)	0.70	(0.67–0.72)
Intelligent	0.59	(0.56–0.63)	0.73	(0.70–0.76)

TABLE 17.2 *Meaning similarity σ, communicative success κ, in a clumpy, structured world.*

Tree-growth strategy	Meaning similarity		Communicative success	
	Mean ($\bar{\sigma}$)	CI	Mean ($\bar{\kappa}$)	CI
Probabilistic	0.35	(0.33–0.37)	0.81	(0.79–0.83)
Intelligent	0.92	(0.88–0.95)	0.90	(0.88–0.92)

tion structure in the environment. We can indeed see in Table 17.2 that meaning similarity is much improved under the intelligent tree-growth strategy, as this would predict. Much more interestingly, however, the levels of communicative success in these experiments no longer bear any close relationship with the levels of meaning similarity. We can see that the communicative success levels are very high under both strategies; in particular, even when agents have very dissimilar conceptual structures ($\sigma = 0.35$) under the probabilistic strategy, the use of mutual exclusivity means that the hearer can learn to associate the relevant meanings with the signals and communicate much more successfully than results without mutual exclusivity would suggest.

Agents have different meaning-creation processes, which promote very different patterns of conceptual growth. Specifically, the speaker, who creates meaning in response to discrimination game failure, has much more conceptual structure than the hearer, who creates meaning in response to the need to understand unfamiliar words. Moreover, in accordance with Grice's (1975) conversational principles, the agents use meanings in communication which provide sufficient information to identify the target object, but which are not unnecessarily specific. The meanings which the hearer creates under these circumstances are therefore necessarily communicatively relevant, because they can be used to discriminate at least one unfamiliar object from a group of others and therefore describe that object within a communicative episode.

Although the hearer has far fewer meanings, this leads to a situation where those meanings it does have are more relevant and useful for communication, and so the level of communicative success is much higher than might be expected.

17.6 Summary

I have presented in this chapter a model of independent meaning creation and communication which avoids the signal redundancy paradox and can yet produce successful communication through the inference of meaning from context. The inference of meaning is a crucial factor in the evolution of language, because it can explain both the genesis and the incremental development and complexification of negotiated communication systems. Individuals with non-identical semantic representations are able to communicate successfully, while *variation*, necessary to drive language change, and *flexibility*, necessary to allow mutation in semantic representation without catastrophic communication breakdown, both occur naturally as by-products of the meaning-inference process itself.

The level of meaning similarity between agents has previously been shown to be very important in predicting the likely level of communicative success, in earlier simulations. In the experiments presented here, however, I have introduced an assumption of mutual exclusivity into the hearer's interpretation process, and the creation of meaning in order to disambiguate the reference of unfamiliar words. These modifications lead to the development of fewer, but more relevant meanings in the hearer's conceptual structure, and lower levels of meaning similarity between agents; despite this conceptual divergence, using the mutual exclusivity bias produces relatively high levels of communicative success. Biases such as mutual exclusivity, therefore, might have evolved because they allow communicative systems based on the inference of meaning to be shared between individuals with different conceptual structures.

FURTHER READING

Bloom (2000) provides an ideal starting point for investigating the many aspects of children's word learning. A more detailed discussion of the mutual exclusivity bias in particular, including its theoretical implications and experimental evidence for its development, can be found in Merriman and Bowman (1989). Briscoe (2002) is an important collection of papers for those interested in computational simulations of language evolution, while the particular model of communication and meaning creation described here was inspired by that described in Steels (1999).

ACKNOWLEDGEMENTS

Andrew Smith was supported by ESRC Research Grant RES-000-22-0266.

References

Abler, W. L. (1989). On the particulate principle of self-diversifying systems. *Journal of Social and Biological Structures* 12: 1–13.

Aboitiz, F. and García, R. (1997). The evolutionary origin of the language areas in the human brain. A neuroanatomical perspective. *Brain Research Reviews* 25: 381–96.

Aitchison, J. (1995). *Language change: progress or decay?* Cambridge: Cambridge University Press.

Anderson, M. (1994). *Sexual selection.* Princeton, NJ: Princeton University Press.

Anderson, S. R. (1992). *A-morphous morphology.* Cambridge: Cambridge University Press.

—— (1993). Wackernagel's revenge: clitics, morphology, and the syntax of second position. *Language* 69: 68–98.

—— (2000). Towards an optimal account of second-position phenomena. In J. Dekkers, F. van der Leeuw, and J. van de Weijer (eds.), *Optimality theory: phonology, syntax and acquisition.* Cambridge: Cambridge University Press, 302–33.

Arbib, M. A. (1981). Perceptual structures and distributed motor control. In V. B. Brooks (ed.), *Handbook of physiology—the nervous system. II: Motor control.* Bethesda, MD: American Physiological Society, 1449–80.

—— (2002). The mirror system, imitation, and the evolution of language. In K. Dautenhahn and C. Nehaniv (eds.), *Imitation in animals and artifacts.* Cambridge, MA: MIT Press, 229–79.

—— (2003). Schema theory. In M. A. Arbib (ed.), *The handbook of brain theory and neural networks* (2nd edn.). Cambridge, MA: MIT Press, 993–8.

—— (2004). Interweaving protosign and protospeech: further developments beyond the mirror. *Interaction Studies: Social Behaviour and Communication in Biological and Artificial Systems* (forthcoming).

—— (2005). From monkey-like action recognition to human language: an evolutionary framework for neurolinguistics. *Behavioral and Brain Sciences* (forthcoming).

—— and Bota, M. (2003). Language evolution: neural homologies and neuroinformatics. *Neural Networks* 16: 1237–60.

—— Oztop, E., and Zukow-Goldring, P. (2004). Language and the Mirror System: a perception/action based approach to communicative development.

Cognition, Brain, Behavior. Special issue on developmental cognitive neuroscience (forthcoming).

Arnauld, A. and Lancelot, C. (1660/1997). *Grammaire générale et raisonnée.* Paris: Editions Allia.

Aronoff, M. (1994). *Morphology by itself: stems and inflectional classes.* Cambridge, MA: MIT Press.

Avikainen, S., Kulomaeki, T., and Hari, R. (1999). Normal movement reading in Asperger subjects. *Neuroreport: For Rapid Communication of Neuroscience Research* 10: 3467–70.

Azeb, A. (2001). *The Maale language.* Leiden: CNWS.

Baker, C. L. (1979). Syntactic theory and the projection problem. *Linguistic Inquiry* 10: 522–81.

Baker, C. L. and McCarthy, J. J. (eds.) (1981). *The logical problem of language acquisition.* Cambridge, MA: MIT Press.

Baker, M. C. (2001). *The atoms of language: the mind's hidden rules of grammar.* New York: Basic Books.

Baldwin, J. M. (1896). A new factor in evolution. *American Naturalist* 30: 441–51.

Ball, P. (2001). *The self-made tapestry: pattern formation in nature.* Oxford: Oxford University Press.

Barrett, M. D. (1986). Early semantic representations and early word usage. In S. A. Kuczaj and M. D. Barrett (eds.), *The acquisition of word meaning.* New York: Springer, 39–67.

Batali, J. (1998). *Computational simulations of the emergence of gramma*r. In Hurford et al. (eds.), 405–26.

—— (2002). The negotiation and acquisition of recursive grammars as a result of competition among exemplars. In Briscoe (ed.), 111–72.

Beavon, K. (1985). Two relativization strategies in Kɔɔzime discourse. *Journal of West African Languages XV.* 1: 31–56.

Beck, B. B. (1982). Chimpocentrism: bias in cognitive ethology. *Journal of Human Evolution* 11: 3–17.

Bednarz, J. C. (1988). Cooperative hunting in Harris' hawks (*Parabuteo unicinctus*). *Science* 239: 1525–7.

Bekoff, M., Allen, C., and Burghardt, G. M. (eds.) (2002). *The cognitive animal.* Cambridge MA: MIT Press.

Bell, T. C., Cleary, J. G., and Witten, I. H. (1990). *Text compression.* Upper Saddle River, NJ: Prentice-Hall.

Bergman, T. J., Beehner, J. C., Cheney, D. L., and Seyfarth, R. M. (2003). Hierarchical classification by rank and kinship in baboons. *Science* 302: 1234–6.

Bertolo, S. (2001). A brief overview of learnability. In S. Bertolo (ed.), *Language acquisition and learnability.* Cambridge: Cambridge University Press, 1–14.

Berwick, R. C. (1998). Language evolution and the Minimalist Program: the origins of syntax. In Hurford et al. (eds.), 320–40.

Bickerton, D. (1990). *Language and species.* Chicago, IL: University of Chicago Press.

—— (1995). *Language and human behavior.* Seattle, WA: University of Washington Press.

—— (1998). Catastrophic evolution: the case for a single step from protolanguage to full human language. In Hurford et al. (eds.), 341–58.

—— (2000). How protolanguage became language. In Knight et al. (eds.), 264–84.

Bilmes, J. A. (1998). *A gentle tutorial on the EM algorithm and its application to parameter estimation for Gaussian mixture and hidden Markov models.* University of California, Berkeley, technical report TR-97–021.

Blackmore, S. (1999). *The meme machine.* Oxford: Oxford University Press.

Bloom, P. (2000). *How children learn the meanings of words.* Cambridge, MA: MIT Press.

Bodmer, W. F. and Cavalli-Sforza, L. L. (1968). A migration matrix model for the study of random genetic drift. *Genetics* 59: 565–92.

Boesch, C. and Boesch, H. (1989). Hunting behavior of wild chimpanzees in the Taï National Park. *American Journal of Physical Anthropology* 78: 547–73.

Borsley, R. D. and Roberts, I. G. (eds.) (1996). *The syntax of the Celtic languages: a comparative perspective.* Cambridge: Cambridge University Press.

Botha, R. P. (2002). Did language evolve like the vertebrate eye? *Language and Communication* 22: 131–58.

Bowerman, M. (1982). Evaluating competing linguistic models with language acquisition data: implications of developmental errors with causative verbs. *Quaderni di semantica* 3: 5–66.

—— (1996). Argument structure and learnability: is a solution in sight? *Proceedings of the Berkeley Linguistics Society* 22: 454–68.

Brakke, K. and Savage-Rumbaugh, E. S. (1995). The development of language skills in bonobo and chimpanzee. I: comprehension. *Language and Communication* 15: 121–48.

—— —— (1996). The development of language skills in Pan: II: production. *Language and Communication* 16: 361–80.

Brauth, S., Liang, W., Roberts, T. F., Scott, L. L., and Quinlan, E. M. (2002). Contact call-driven zenk protein induction and habituation in telencephalic auditory pathways in the budgerigar (*Melopsittacus undulatus*): implications for understanding vocal learning processes. *Learning and Memory* 9: 76–88.

Brent, M. R. and Cartwright, T. A. (1996). Distributional regularity and phonotactic constraints are useful for segmentation. *Cognition* 61: 93–125.

Brighton, H. (2002). Compositional syntax from cultural transmission. *Artificial Life* 8: 25–54.

Briscoe, E. (1999). The acquisition of grammar in an evolving population of language agents. *Electronic Transactions of Artificial Intelligence.* Special Issue,

16: Machine Intelligence, S. Muggleton, (ed.), Vol. 3(B), <http://www.etaij.org>, 44–77.

—— (2000a). Grammatical acquisition: inductive bias and coevolution of language and the language acquisition device. *Language* 76: 245–96.

—— (2000b). Evolutionary perspectives on diachronic syntax. In S. Pintzuk, G. Tsoulas, and A. Warner (eds.), *Diachronic syntax: models and mechanisms.* Oxford: Oxford University Press, 75–108.

—— (2002). Grammatical acquisition and linguistic selection. In Briscoe (ed.), 255–300.

—— (ed.) (2002). *Linguistic evolution through language acquisition: formal and computational models.* Cambridge: Cambridge University Press.

—— (2003). Grammatical assimilation. In Christiansen and Kirby (eds.), 295–316.

Brooks, R. A. (1999). *Cambrian intelligence.* Cambridge, MA: MIT Press.

Browman, C. P. and Goldstein, L. F. (1986). Towards an articulatory phonology. *Phonology Yearbook* 3: 219–52.

Browman, C. P. and Goldstein, L. F. (1991). Tiers in articulatory phonology, with some implications for casual speech. In J. Kingston and M. E. Beckman (eds.), *Papers in laboratory phonology. Volume I: Between the grammar and the physics of speech.* Cambridge: Cambridge University Press, 341–76.

—— —— (1992). Articulatory phonology: an overview. *Phonetica* 49: 155–80.

—— —— (1995). Dynamics and articulatory phonology. In T. van Gelder and R. F. Port (eds.), *Mind as motion.* Cambridge, MA: MIT Press, 175–93.

—— —— (2000). Competing constraints on intergestural coordination and self-organization of phonological structures. *Les Cahiers de l'ICP, Bulletin de la Communication Parlée* 5: 25–34.

Bullock, S. and Todd, P. M. (1999). Made to measure: ecological rationality in structured environments. *Minds and Machines* 9: 497–541.

Burgess, N., Jeffery, K. F., and O'Keefe, J. (eds.) (1999). *The hippocampal and parietal foundations of spatial cognition.* Oxford: Oxford University Press.

Bybee, J. (1985). *Morphology: a study of the relation between meaning and form.* Amsterdam: John Benjamins.

Byers B. E. and Kroodsma, D. E. (1992). Development of two song categories by chestnut-sided warblers. *Animal Behaviour* 44: 799–810.

Byrne, R. W. (2003). Imitation as behavior parsing. *Philosophical Transactions of the Royal Society of London, B Series* 358: 529–36.

Calvin, W. H. and Bickerton, D. (2000). *Lingua ex machina: reconciling Darwin and Chomsky with the human brain.* Cambridge, MA & London: MIT Press.

Cameron-Faulkner, T. and Carstairs-McCarthy, A. (2000). Stem alternants as morphological signata: evidence from blur avoidance in Polish nouns. *Natural Language and Linguistic Theory* 18: 813–35.

Cangelosi, A. (2001). Evolution of communication and language using signals, symbols, and words. *IEEE Transactions on Evolutionary Computation* 5: 93–101.

—— and Parisi, D. (eds.) (2002). *Simulating the evolution of language*. London: Springer.

Cantalupo, C. and Hopkins, W. D. (2001). Asymmetric Broca's area in great apes—a region of the ape brain is uncannily similar to one linked with speech in humans. *Nature* 414: 505.

Carnie, A. and Guilfoyle, E. (eds.) (2000). *The syntax of verb initial languages*. Oxford: Oxford University Press.

Carr, P. (2000). Scientific realism, sociophonetic variation, and innate endowments in phonology. In N. Burton-Roberts, P. Carr, and G. Docherty (eds.), *Phonological knowledge: conceptual and empirical issues*. Oxford: Oxford University Press, 67–104.

—— (forthcoming). Universal Grammar and syntax/phonology parallelisms. In Honeybone and Bermúdez-Otero (eds.).

Carré, R. and Mrayati, M. (1990). Articulatory-acoustic-phonetic relations and modelling, regions and modes. In A. Marchal and W. J. Hardcastle (eds.), *Speech production and speech modelling*. Dordrecht: Kluwer Academic Publishers, 211–40.

Carstairs-McCarthy, A. (1994). Inflection classes, gender and the Principle of Contrast. *Language* 70: 737–88.

—— (1998). Synonymy avoidance, phonology and the origin of syntax. In Hurford et al. (eds.), 279–96.

—— (1999). *The origins of complex language: an inquiry into the evolutionary beginnings of sentences, syllables, and truth*. Oxford: Oxford University Press.

—— (2000). The distinction between sentences and noun phrases: an impediment to language evolution? In Knight et al. (eds.), 248–63.

—— (2002). *An introduction to English morphology: words and their structure*. Edinburgh: Edinburgh University Press.

Chaminade, T., Meary, D., Orliaguet, J.-P., and Decety, J. (2001). Is perceptual anticipation a motor simulation? A PET study. *Brain Imaging* 12: 3669–74.

—— Meltzoff, A. N., and Decety, J. (2002). Does the end justify the means? A PET exploration of the mechanisms involved in human imitation. *NeuroImage* 15: 318–28.

Changeux, J.-P. (1983). *L'homme neuronal*. Paris: Fayard.

—— (1985). *Neuronal man*. New York: Pantheon. (Current edition 1997, Princeton: Princeton University Press).

Chater, N. (1996). Reconciling simplicity and likelihood principles in perceptual organization. *Psychological Review* 103: 566–81.

—— (1999). The search for simplicity: a fundamental cognitive principle? *Quarterly Journal of Experimental Psychology* 52A: 273–302.

Chater, N. and Vitányi, P. (ms.). A simplicity principle for language learning: re-evaluating what can be learned from positive evidence.

Cheney, D. L. and Seyfarth, R. M. (1998). Why animals don't have language. In G. B. Peterson (ed.), *The Tanner lectures on human values, volume 19*. Salt Lake City, UT: University of Utah Press, 173–210.

Chomsky, N. (1955/1975). *The logical structure of linguistic theory*. Manuscript, Harvard University. Published by Plenum Press: New York and London.

—— (1957). *Syntactic structures*. Mouton: The Hague.

—— (1965). *Aspects of the theory of syntax*. Cambridge, MA: MIT Press.

—— (1966). *Cartesian linguistics*. New York: Harper and Row.

—— (1967). Recent contributions to the theory of innate ideas. *Synthese* 17: 2–11.

—— (1968). *Language and mind*. New York: Harcourt, Brace & World.

—— (1975). *Reflections on language*. New York: Pantheon.

—— (1980). *Rules and representations*. London: Basil Blackwell.

—— (1981). *Lectures on government and binding*. Dordrecht: Foris.

—— (1982). *The generative enterprise. A discussion with Riny Huybregts and Henk van Riemsdijk*. Dordrecht: Foris Publications.

—— (1986). *Knowledge of language: its nature, origin and use*. New York: Praeger.

—— (1988). *Language and problems of knowledge: the Managua lectures*. Cambridge, MA: MIT Press.

—— (1993a). A minimalist program for linguistic theory. In Hale and Keyser (eds.), 1–52.

—— (1993b). *Language and thought*. Wakefield, RI: Moyer Bell.

—— (1995). *The Minimalist program*. Cambridge, MA: MIT Press.

—— (2000). *New horizons in the study of language and mind*. Cambridge: Cambridge University Press.

—— (2002). Roundtable Discussion, Fourth International Conference on the Evolution of Language, Harvard University, March 27–30.

—— and Halle, M. (1968). *The sound pattern of English*. New York: Harper and Row.

Christiansen, M. (1994). Infinite languages, finite minds: connectionism, learning and linguistic structure. PhD thesis, University of Edinburgh.

—— and Kirby, S. (eds.) (2003). *Language evolution*. Oxford: Oxford University Press.

Chumbow, B. (1977). Relatives as determiners: a case from Ngemba. In P. F. A. Kotey and H. Der-Houssikian (eds.), *Language and linguistic problems in Africa. Proceedings of the VII conference on African linguistics*. Columbia, SC: Hornbeam Press, 283–302.

Clancey, W. J. (1997). *Situated cognition*. Cambridge: Cambridge University Press.

Clark, R. and Roberts, I. G. (1993). A computational model of language learnability and language change. *Linguistic Inquiry* 24: 299–345.

Clark, E. V. (1987). The principle of contrast: a constraint on language acquisition. In B. MacWhinney (ed.), *Mechanisms of language acquisition*. London: Lawrence Erlbaum, 1–33.

Cobas, A. and Arbib, M. A. (1992). Prey-catching and predator-avoidance in frog and toad: defining the schemas. *Journal of Theoretical Biology* 157: 271–304.

Comrie, B. (1989). *Language universals and linguistic typology. Syntax and morphology* (2nd edn). Oxford: Blackwell/Chicago, IL: University of Chicago Press.

—— (1992). Before complexity. In Hawkins and Gell-Mann (eds.), 193–211.

—— (1998). Rethinking the typology of relative clauses. *Language Design* 1: 59–86.

—— and Kuteva, T. (2004). The evolution of language and elaborateness of grammar. Paper presented at the Fifth International Conference on the Evolution of Language, Leipzig, March 31–April 3.

—— —— (forthcoming). Relativization strategies in the languages of the world. In M. Haspelmath, M. Dryer, D. Gil, and B. Comrie (eds.), *World atlas of language structures*. Oxford: Oxford University Press.

Cooper, F. S., Gaitenby, J., and Nye, P. W. (1984). Evolution of reading machines for the blind: Haskins Laboratories research as a case history. *Journal of Rehabilitation Research and Development* 21: 51–87.

Corballis, M. C. (2002). *From hand to mouth: the origins of language*. Princeton, NJ: Princeton University Press.

Cosmides, L. and Tooby, J. (1996). Are humans good intuitive statisticians after all? Rethinking some conclusions from the literature on judgement under uncertainty. *Cognition* 58: 1–73.

Costello, F. J. and Keane, M. T. (2000). Efficient creativity: constraint guided conceptual combination. *Cognitive Science* 24: 299–349.

Crockford, C. and Boesch, C. (2003). Context-specific calls in wild chimpanzees, *Pan troglodytes verus*: analysis of barks. *Animal Behaviour* 66: 115–25.

Croft, W. (1990). *Typology and universals*. Cambridge: Cambridge University Press.

—— (2000). *Explaining language change: an evolutionary approach*. Harlow: Pearson.

Crothers, J. (1978). Typology and universals of vowels systems. In J. H. Greenberg, C. A. Ferguson, and E. A. Moravcsik (eds.), *Universals in human language. Volume 2: Phonology*. Stanford, CA: Stanford University Press, 93–152.

Culicover, P. W. (1996). Adaptive learning and concrete minimalism. In C. Koster and F. Wijnen (eds.), *Proceedings of the Groningen Assembly on Language Acquisition (GALA 1995)*. Groningen: Center for Language and Cognition, 165–74.

—— (1999). *Syntactic nuts*. Oxford: Oxford University Press.

Damper, R. and Harnad, S. (2000). Neural network modeling of categorical perception. *Perception and Psychophysics* 62: 843–67.

Danchev, A. and Kytö, M. (1994). The construction *be going to* + *infinitive* in Early Modern English. In D. Kastovsky (ed.), *Studies in Early Modern English*. Berlin/New York: Mouton de Gruyter, 59–77.

Dapretto, M. and Bjork, E. L. (2000). The development of word retrieval abilities in the second year and its relation to early vocabulary growth. *Child Development* 71: 635–48.

Darwin, C. (1871/1971). *The descent of man and selection in relation to sex*. London: Prometheus Books.

—— (1872/1998). *The expression of the emotions in man and animals*. Oxford: Oxford University Press.

Dawkins, R. (1976). Hierarchical organization: a candidate principle for ethology. In P. P. G. Bateson and R. A. Hinde (eds.), *Growing points in ethology*. Cambridge: Cambridge University Press, 7–54.

—— (1986). *The blind watchmaker*. London: Penguin Books.

Deacon, T. W. (1992). Brain-language coevolution. In Hawkins and Gel-Mann (eds.), 49–83.

—— (1997). *The symbolic species: the co-evolution of language and the brain*. New York: W. W. Norton. (Also published 1998 as *The symbolic species: the co-evolution of language and the human brain*, London: Penguin Books.)

de Boer, B. (2000). Self-organization in vowel systems. *Journal of Phonetics* 28: 441–65.

—— (2001a). *The origins of vowel systems*. Oxford: Oxford University Press.

—— (2001b). Infant-directed vowels are easier to learn for a computer model. *Journal of the Acoustical Society of America* 110: 2703.

—— and Kuhl, P. K. (2003). Investigating the role of infant-directed speech with a computer model. *Acoustics Research Letters Online* 4: 129–34.

Delius, J. D. and Siemann, M. (1998). Transitive responding in animals and humans: exaptation rather than adaptation? *Behavioural Processes* 42: 107–37.

Dempster, A., Laird, N., and Rubin, D. (1977). Maximum likelihood from incomplete data via the EM algorithm. *Journal of the Royal Statistical Society, series B* 39: 1–38.

Dessalles, J.-L. (2000). *Aux origines du langage*. Paris: Hermes Science Publications.

Diessel, H. and Tomasello, M. (2000). The development of relative clauses in spontaneous child speech. *Cognitive Linguistics* 11: 131–51.

Di Sciullo, A.-M. and Williams, E. (1987). *On the definition of word*. Cambridge, MA: MIT Press.

Dixon, R. (1997). *The rise and fall of languages*. Cambridge: Cambridge University Press.

Donald, M. (1991). *The origins of the modern mind*. Cambridge, MA: Harvard University Press.

Dowman, M. (2000). Addressing the learnability of verb subcategorizations with Bayesian inference. In L. R. Gleitman and A. K. Joshi (eds.), *Proceedings of the Twenty-Second Annual Conference of the Cognitive Science Society*. Mahwah, NJ: Lawrence Erlbaum Associates, 107–12.

Dressler, W. U. (1985a). *Morphonology: the dynamics of derivation*. Ann Arbor, MI: Karoma.

—— (1985b). Typological aspects of Natural Morphology. *Acta Linguistica Hungarica* 35: 51–70.

—— Mayerthaler, W., Panagl, O., and Wurzel, W. U. (eds.) (1987). *Leitmotifs in natural morphology*. Amsterdam: John Benjamins.

Dreyfus, H. L. (1972). *What computers still can't do* (2nd edn.). Cambridge, MA: MIT Press.

Dunbar, R. (1996). *Grooming, gossip and the evolution of language*. London: Faber and Faber.

—— (1998). Theory of mind and the evolution of language. In Hurford et al. (eds.), 92–110.

—— (2004). Knowing primates: can you guess what I'm thinking? *New Scientist* 2451: 44–5.

Durham, W. (1991). *Coevolution, genes, culture and human diversity*. Pala Alto, CA: Stanford University Press.

Eckardt, W. and Zuberbühler, K. (2004). Cooperation and competition in two forest monkeys. *Behavioral Ecology* 15: 400–11.

Eimas, P. D., Siqueland, P., Jusczyk, P., and Vigorito, J. (1971). Speech perception in infants. *Science* 212: 303–6.

Eldredge, N. and Gould, S. J. (1972). Punctuated equilibria: an alternative to phyletic gradualism. In T. Schopf (ed.), *Models in paleobiology*. San Francisco, CA: Freeman, Cooper, 82–115.

Elman, J. L., Bates, E. A., Johnson, M. H., Karmiloff-Smith, A., Parisi, D., and Plunkett, K. (1996). *Rethinking innateness: a connectionist perspective on development*. Cambridge, MA: MIT Press.

Emonds, J. E. (2002). A common basis for syntax and morphology: tri-level lexical insertion. In P. Boucher (ed.), *Many morphologies*. Somerville, MA: Cascadilla Press, 235–62.

Enard, W., Przeworski, M., Fisher, S. E., Lai, C. S. L., Wiebe, V., Kitano, T., Monaco, A. P., and Pääbo, S. (2002). Molecular evolution of FOXP2, a gene involved in speech and language. *Nature* 418: 869–72.

Evans, C. S., Macedonia, J. M., and Marler, P. (1993). Effects of apparent size and speed on the response of chickens, *Gallus gallus*, to computer-generated simulations of aerial predators. *Animal Behaviour* 46: 1–11.

Evans, D. L. (1987). Dolphins as beaters for gulls? *Bird Behaviour* 7: 47–8.

Fadiga, L., Craighero, L., Buccino, G., and Rizzolatti, G. (2002). Speech listening specifically modulates the excitability of tongue muscles: a TMS study. *European Journal of Neuroscience* 15: 399–402.

Fadiga, L., Fogassi, L., Pavesi, G., and Rizzolatti, G. (1995). Motor facilitation during action observation: a magnetic stimulation study. *Journal of Neurophysiology* 73: 2608–11.

Fagg, A. H. and Arbib, M. A. (1998). Modelling parietal-premotor interactions in primate control of grasping. *Neural Networks* 11: 1277–303.

Fentress, J. C. (1983). Hierarchical motor control. In M. Studdert-Kennedy (ed.), *Psychobiology of language*. Cambridge, MA: MIT Press, 40–61.

Ferguson, C. A. (1964). Baby talk in six languages. *American Anthropologist* 66: 103–14.

Fernald, A. (1985). Four-month-old infants prefer to listen to motherese. *Infant Behavior and Development* 8: 181–95.

—— and Kuhl, P. (1987). Acoustic determinants of infant preference for motherese speech. *Infant Behavior and Development* 10: 279–93.

—— Taeschner, T., Dunn, J., Papousek, M., de Boysson-Bardies, B., and Fukui, I. (1989). A cross-language study of prosodic modifications in mothers' and fathers' speech to preverbal infants. *Journal of Child Language* 16: 477–501.

Fernandez, J. (1982). *Bwiti: an ethnography of the religious imagination in Africa*. Princeton, NJ: Princeton University Press.

Ferrari, P. F., Gallese, V., Rizzolatti, G., and Fogassi, L. (2003). Mirror neurons responding to the observation of ingestive and communicative month actions. *European Journal of Neuroscience* 17: 1703–14.

Fisher, R. A. (1930). *The genetical theory of natural selection*. Oxford: Clarendon Press.

Fisher, S. E., Vargha-Khadem, F., Watkins, K. E., and Monaco, A. P. (1998). Localisation of a gene implicated in a severe speech and language disorder. *Nature Genetics* 18: 168–70.

Fitch, W. T. (2000). The evolution of speech: a comparative review. *Trends in Cognitive Science* 4: 258–67.

—— and Hauser, M. D. (2004). Computational constraints on syntactic processing in a nonhuman primate. *Science* 303: 377–80.

Fitzpatrick, J. M. (2002). On minimalist approaches to the locality of movement. *Linguistic Inquiry* 33: 443–64.

Flake, G. W. (1998). *The computational beauty of nature*. Cambridge, MA: MIT Press.

Fogassi, L. (2000). Mirror neurons and language origin. Paper presented at the International Conference on the Development of Mind, Tokyo, Japan, August 2000.

—— and Ferrari, P. F. (2005). Mirror neurons, gestures and language evolution. In C. Abry, A. Vilain, and J.-L. Schwartz (eds.), *Vocalize to localize*. Special issue of *Interaction Studies: Social Behaviour and Communication in Biological and Artificial Systems* (forthcoming).

—— Gallese, V., Fadiga, L., and Rizzolatti, G. (1998). Neurons responding to the sight of goal directed hand/arm actions in the parietal area PF (7b) of the macaque monkey. *Society for Neuroscience Abstracts* 24: 257.

Forestell, P. H. and Herman, L. M. (1988). Delayed matching of visual materials by a bottlenosed dolphin aided by auditory symbols. *Animal Learning and Behavior* 16: 137–46.

Fowler, C. A. (1996). Speaking. In H. Heuer and S. Keele (eds.), *Handbook of perception and action. Volume 2: Motor skills.* London: Academic Press, 503–60.

Fox, B. and Thompson, S. (1990). A discourse explanation of 'The Grammar' of relative clauses in English conversation. *Language* 66: 297–316.

Frajzyngier, Z. (1996). *Grammaticalization of the complex sentence. A case study in Chadic.* Amsterdam/Philadelphia: John Benjamins.

Franks, B. (1995). Sense generation: a 'quasi-classical' approach to concepts and concept combination. *Cognitive Science* 19: 441–506.

von Frisch, K. (1973). Decoding the language of the bee. Paper presented at the Nobel Lecture, 12 December 1973.

——— (1974). *Animal architecture.* London: Hutchinson.

——— (1993). *The dance language and orientation of bees.* Cambridge, MA: Harvard University Press.

Fukunaga, K. (1990). *Introduction to statistical pattern recognition.* Boston, MA: Academic Press.

Gagné, C. L. (2000). Relation-based combinations versus property-based combinations: a test of the CARIN theory and dual-process theory of conceptual-combination. *Journal of Memory and Language* 42: 365–89.

—— (2001). Relation and lexical priming during the interpretation of noun–noun combinations. *Journal of Experimental Psychology: Learning, Memory and Cognition* 27: 236–54.

Galileo, G. (1632/1953). *Dialogue on the great world systems, in the Salusbury translation* (ed. Giorgio de Santillana). Chicago, IL: University of Chicago Press.

Gardner, H. (1985). *The mind's new science.* New York: Basic Books.

Gell-Mann, M. (1995). *The quark and the jaguar: adventures in the simple and the complex.* New York: W. H. Freeman.

Georgopoulos, A., Kettner, R., and Schwartz, A. (1988). Primate motor cortex and free arm movement to visual targets in three-dimensional space. II: Coding of the direction of movement by a neuronal population. *Journal of Neurosciences* 8: 2928–37.

Gergely, G., Bekkering, H., and Kiraly, I. (2002). Developmental psychology: rational imitation in preverbal infants. *Nature* 415: 755.

Gerken, L. A. and McIntosh, B. (1993). The interplay of function morphemes and prosody in early language. *Developmental Psychology* 29: 448–57.

Ghazanfar, A. A. (ed.) (2003). *Primate audition: ethology and neurobiology.* Boca Raton, FL: CRC Press.

Gibson, J. J. (1979). *The ecological approach to visual perception.* Boston, MA: Houghton Mifflin.

Gigerenzer, G. and Todd, P. M. (1999). Fast and frugal heuristics: the adaptive toolbox. In G. Gigerenzer, P. M. Todd, and the ABC Research Group (eds.), *Simple heuristics that make us smart*. Oxford: Oxford University Press, 3–34.

Givón, T. (1971). Historical syntax and synchronic morphology: an archaeologist's field trip. *Chicago Linguistic Society* 7: 394–415.

—— (1995). *Functionalism and grammar*. Amsterdam: John Benjamins.

Gold, E. M. (1967). Language identification in the limit. *Information and Control* 10: 447–74.

Goldberg, A. (2003). Constructions: a new theoretical approach to language. *Trends in Cognitive Sciences* 7: 219–24.

Goldsmith, J. (2001). Unsupervised learning of the morphology of a natural language. *Computational Linguistics* 27: 153–98.

Goldstein, L. F. (2003). Emergence of discrete gestures. Paper presented at the Fifteenth International Congress of Phonetic Sciences, Barcelona.

—— Pouplier, M., Chen, L., Saltzman, E., and Byrd, D. (forthcoming). Dynamic action units slip in speech production errors. *Journal of Phonetics*.

Goodall, J. (1986). *The chimpanzees of Gombe: patterns of behavior*. Cambridge, MA: Harvard University Press.

Gould, S. J. (1979). Panselectionist pitfalls in Parker & Gibson's model of the evolution of intelligence. *Behavioral and Brain Sciences* 2: 385–6.

—— (1993). *Eight little piggies: reflections in natural history*. New York: W. W. Norton.

—— and Vrba, E. S. (1982). Exaptation—a missing term in the science of form. *Paleobiology* 8: 4–15.

Gouzoules, S., Gouzoules, H., and Marler, P. (1984). Rhesus monkey (*Macaca mulatta*) screams: representational signalling in the recruitment of agonistic aid. *Animal Behaviour* 32: 182–93.

Greenfield, P. M. (1972). Studies in mother–infant interactions: toward a structural-functional approach. *Human Development* 15: 131–8.

—— (1991). Language, tools and brain: the ontogeny and phylogeny of hierarchically organized sequential behavior. *Behavioral and Brain Sciences* 14: 531–95.

—— Brazelton, T. B., and Childs, C. (1989). From birth to maturity in Zinacantán: ontogenesis in cultural context. In V. Bricker and G. Gossen (eds.), *Ethnographic encounters in Southern Mesoamerica: celebratory essays in honor of Evon Z. Vogt*. Albany, NY: Institute of Mesoamerican Studies, SUNY Press, 177–216.

—— Nelson, K., and Salzman, E. (1972). The development of rulebound strategies for manipulating seriated nesting cups: a parallel between action and grammar. *Cognitive Psychology* 3: 291–310.

—— and Savage-Rumbaugh, E. S. (1990). Grammatical combination in *Pan paniscus*: processes of learning and invention in the evolution and development of language. In S. T. Parker and K. R. Gibson (eds.), *'Language' and intelligence in monkeys and apes: comparative developmental perspectives.* Cambridge: Cambridge University Press, 540–78.

—— —— (1991). Imitation, grammatical development, and the invention of protogrammar by an ape. In N. A. Krasnegor, D. M. Rumbaugh, R. L. Schiefelbusch, and M. Studdert-Kennedy (eds.), *Biological and behavioral determinants of language development.* Hillsdale, NJ: Lawrence Erlbaum, 235–58.

Grice, H. P. (1975). Logic and conversation. In P. Cole and J. L. Morgan (eds.), *Syntax and semantics 3: speech acts.* New York: Academic Press, 41–58.

Grieser, D. L. and Kuhl, P. K. (1988). Maternal speech to infants in a tonal language: support for universal prosodic features in motherese. *Developmental Psychology* 24: 14–20.

Grimes, P. (2001). *Ethnologue: languages of the world* (14th edn.). Dallas, TX: SIL International.

Guenther, F. and Gjaja, M. (1996). Magnet effect and neural maps. *Journal of the Acoustical Society of America* 100: 1111–21.

Gustafson, K. T. (1993). The effect of motherese versus adult-directed speech on goodness ratings of the vowel /i/. MSc. thesis, University of Washington.

Gyger, M., Marler, P., and Pickert, R. (1987). Semantics of an avian alarm call system: the male domestic fowl, *G. domesticus*. *Behaviour* 102: 15–40.

Hailman, J. P. and Ficken, M. S. (1987). Combinatorial animal communication with computable syntax: chick-a-dee calling qualifies as 'language' by structural linguistics. *Animal Behaviour* 34: 1899–1901.

Hale, K. and Keyser, S. J. (eds.) (1993). *The view from Building 20: essays in linguistics in honor of Sylvain Bromberger.* Cambridge MA: MIT Press.

Halle, M. and Marantz, A. (1993). Distributed Morphology and the pieces of inflection. In Hale and Keyser (eds.), 111–76.

Hare, M. and Elman, J. L. (1995). Learning and morphological change. *Cognition* 56: 61–98.

Harnad, S. (1990). The symbol grounding problem. *Physica* D 42: 335–46.

Harris, J. (1994). *English sound structure.* Oxford: Blackwell.

Haspelmath, M. (2002). *Understanding morphology.* London: Arnold.

Hauser, M. D. (1996). *The evolution of communication.* Cambridge, MA: MIT Press.

—— (1998). Functional referents and acoustic similarity: field playback experiments with rhesus monkeys. *Animal Behaviour* 55: 1647–58.

—— Chomsky, N., and Fitch, W. T. (2002). The faculty of language: what is it, who has it, and how did it evolve? *Science* 298: 1569–79.

—— Evans, C. S. and Marler, P. (1993). The role of articulation in the production of rhesus monkey (*Macaca mulatta*) vocalizations. *Animal Behaviour* 45: 423–33.

Hauser, M. D., Newport, E. L., and Aslin, R. N. (2001). Segmentation of the speech stream in a non-human primate: statistical learning in cotton-top tamarins. *Cognition* 78 B: 53–64.

Hawkins, J. A. and Gell-Mann, M. (eds.) (1992). *The evolution of human language.* Santa Fe, NM: Addison-Wesley.

Heavey, L., Phillips, W., Baron-Cohen, S., and Rutter M. (2000). The awkward moments test: a naturalistic measure of social understanding in autism. *Journal of Autism and Developmental Disorders* 30: 225–36.

Heine, B. (1993). *Auxiliaries. Cognitive forces and grammaticalization.* New York and Oxford: Oxford University Press.

—— Claudi, U., and Hünnemeyer, F. (1991). *Grammaticalization: a conceptual framework.* Chicago, IL: Chicago University Press.

—— and Kuteva, T. (2002a). *World lexicon of grammaticalization.* Cambridge: Cambridge University Press.

—— —— (2002b). On the evolution of grammatical forms. In Wray (ed.), 376–97.

—— —— (forthcoming). On contact-induced grammaticalization. *Studies in Language.*

Hendrick, R. (1990). Breton pronominals, binding and barriers. In Hendrick (ed.), 121–65.

—— (ed.) (1990). *Syntax and Semantics 23: The syntax of the modern Celtic languages.* San Diego, CA: Academic Press.

Hewes, G. (1973). Primate communication and the gestural origin of language. *Current Anthropology* 14: 5–24.

Hewson, J. and Bubenik, V. (1997). *Tense and aspect in Indo-European languages. Theory, typology, diachrony.* Amsterdam/Philadelphia: John Benjamins.

Hochberg J. and McAlister, E. (1953). A quantitative approach to figural goodness. *Journal of Experimental Psychology* 46: 361–4.

Hockett, C. F. (1958). *A course in modern linguistics.* New York: MacMillan.

—— (1960). The origin of speech. *Scientific American* 203: 88–111.

Honeybone, P. and Bermúdez-Otero, R. (eds.) (forthcoming). *Linguistic knowledge: perspectives from phonology and from syntax* (Special issue of *Lingua*).

Hopkins, W. D., Marino, L., Rilling, J. K., and MacGregor, L. A. (1998). Planum temporale asymmetries in great apes as revealed by magnetic resonance imaging (MRI). *Neuroreport* 9: 2913–18.

Hopper, P. J. and Traugott, E. C. (1993). *Grammaticalization.* Cambridge: Cambridge University Press.

Horning, J. J. (1969). A study of grammatical inference. PhD thesis, Stanford University.

Huber, L., Voelkl, B., and Rechberger, S. (1997). New methods of analysing the copying fidelity of socially learning animals. Paper presented at the Twenty-fifth International Ethological Congress, Vienna, August 1997.

Hulse, S. H., Humpal, J., and Cynx, J. A. (1984). Processing of rhythmic sound structures by birds. *Annals of the New York Academy of Sciences* 423: 407–19.

von Humboldt, W. (1836). *Über die Verschiedenheit des menschlichen Sprachbaues*. Berlin: Druckerei der Königlichen Akademie der Wissenschaften.

Hurford, J. R. (1989). Biological evolution of the Saussurean sign as a component of the language acquisition device. *Lingua* 77: 187–222.

—— (1998). Introduction: the emergence of syntax. In Hurford et al. (eds.), 299–304.

—— (2002a). The roles of expression and representation in language evolution. In Wray (ed.), 311–34.

—— (2002b). Expression/induction models of language evolution: dimensions and issues. In Briscoe (ed.), 301–44.

—— (2004). Language beyond our grasp: what mirror neurons can, and cannot, do for language evolution. In D. Kimbrough Oller and U. Griebel (eds.), *Evolution of communication systems: a comparative approach*. Cambridge, MA: MIT Press, 297–314.

Hurford, J., Studdert-Kennedy, M., and Knight, C. (eds.) (1998). *Approaches to the evolution of language: social and cognitive bases*. Cambridge: Cambridge University Press.

Hutchins, E. and Hazlehurst, B. (1995). How to invent a lexicon: the development of shared symbols in interaction. In N. Gilbert and R. Conte (eds.), *Artificial societies: the computer simulation of social life*. London: UCL Press, 157–89.

Iskarous, K. R. (forthcoming). Patterns of tongue movement. *Journal of Phonetics*.

Jablonka, E. and Lamb, M. (1995). *Epigenetic inheritance and evolution*. Oxford: Oxford University Press.

Jackendoff, R. (1999). Possible stages in the evolution of the language capacity. *Trends in Cognitive Sciences* 3: 272–9.

—— (2002). *Foundations of language: brain, meaning, grammar, evolution*. Oxford: Oxford University Press.

Jacob, F. (1977). The linguistic model in biology. In D. Armstrong and C. H. van Schoonefeld (eds.), *Roman Jakobson: echoes of his scholarship*. Lisse: de Ridder, 185–92.

Jakobson, R. (1970). Linguistics. *Main Trends of Research in the Social and Human Sciences, Part 1*. Paris/The Hague: UNESCO/Mouton, 419–63.

Jarvis, E. D. (2004). Learned birdsong and the neurobiology of human language. *Annals of the New York Academy of Sciences* 1016: 749–77.

—— and Mello, C. V. (2000). Molecular mapping of brain areas involved in parrot vocal communication. *Journal of Comparative Neurology* 419: 1–31.

Jespersen, O. (1933). *Language. Its nature, development and origin*. London: George Allen & Unwin.

Johnson-Pynn, J., Fragaszy, D. M., Hirsh, E. M., Brakke, K.E., and Greenfield, P. M. (1999). Strategies used to combine seriated cups by chimpanzees (*Pan troglodytes*), bonobos (*Pan paniscus*), and capuchins (*Cebus apella*). *Journal of Comparative Psychology* 113: 137–48.

Jones, S., Martin, R., and Pilbeam, D. (eds.) (1992). *The Cambridge encyclopedia of human evolution*. Cambridge: Cambridge University Press.

Joos, M. (1948). *Acoustic phonetics* (Language Monograph No. 23). Baltimore, MD: Linguistic Society of America.

Joseph, B. (2001). Review of R. M. W. Dixon, *The rise and fall of languages. Journal of Linguistics* 37: 180–6.

Jusczyk, P. W. (1997). *The discovery of spoken language*. Cambridge, MA: MIT Press.

Kager, R. (1999). *Optimality theory*. Cambridge: Cambridge University Press.

Kaminski, J., Call, J., and Fischer, J. (2004). Word learning in a domestic dog: evidence for 'fast mapping'. *Science* 304: 1682–3.

Kandel, E. R., Schwartz, J. H., and Jessell, T. M. (2001). *Principles of neural science* (4th edn.). New York: McGraw-Hill.

Kauffman, S. (1993). *The origins of order: self-organization and selection in evolution*. New York: Oxford University Press.

—— (1995). *At home in the universe: the search for laws of self-organization and complexity*. Oxford: Oxford University Press.

Keenan, E. (1976). Towards a universal definition of 'subject'. In C. Li (ed.), *Subject and topic*. New York: Academic Press, 303–33.

—— and Comrie, B. (1977). Noun phrase accessibility and universal grammar. *Linguistic Inquiry* 8: 77–100.

Kegl, J., Senghas, A., and Coppola, M. (1999). Creation through contact: sign language emergence and sign language change in Nicaragua. In M. DeGraff (ed.), *Language creation and language change: creolization, diachrony, and development*. Cambridge, MA: MIT Press, 179–238.

Kelemen, J. and Sosík, P. (eds.) (2001). *Advances in artificial life: Proceedings of the Sixth European Conference on Artificial Life*. Berlin and Heidelberg: Springer.

Kilani-Schoch, M. (1988). *Introduction à la morphologie naturelle*. Berne: Lang.

Kiparsky, P. (1982). From cyclic phonology to Lexical Phonology. In H. van der Hulst and N. Smith (eds.), *The structure of phonological relations (Part I)*. Dordrecht: Foris, 131–75.

Kirby, S. (1998). Fitness and the selective adaptation of language. In Hurford et al. (eds.), 359–83.

—— (1999). *Function, selection, and innateness: the emergence of language universals*. Oxford: Oxford University Press.

—— (2000). Syntax without natural selection: how compositionality emerges from vocabulary in a population of learners. In Knight et al. (eds.), 303–23.

—— (2001). Spontaneous evolution of linguistic structure: an iterated learning model of the emergence of regularity and irregularity. *IEEE Transactions on Evolutionary Computation* 5: 102–10.

—— (2002a). Learning, bottlenecks and the evolution of recursive syntax. In Briscoe (ed.), 173–203.

—— (2002b). Natural language from artificial life. *Artificial Life* 8: 185–215.

—— and Hurford, J. (1997). Learning, culture and evolution in the origin of linguistic constraints. In P. Husbands and I. Harvey (eds.), *Fourth European Conference on Artificial Life*. Cambridge, MA: MIT Press, 493–502.

É. Kiss, K. (2002). *The syntax of Hungarian*. Cambridge: Cambridge University Press.

Kitahara, H. (1997). *Elementary operations and optimal derivations*. Cambridge, MA: MIT Press.

Klavans, J. L. (1985). The independence of syntax and phonology in cliticization. *Language* 62: 95–120.

Klein, W. and Perdue, C. (1997). The Basic Variety, or: Couldn't language be much simpler? *Second Language Research* 13: 301–47.

Klima, E. S. and Bellugi, U. (1979). *The signs of language*. Cambridge, MA: Harvard University Press.

Kluender, K. R. (1991). Effects of first formant frequency on VOT judgments result from processes not specific to humans. *Journal of the Acoustical Society of America* 67: 971–95.

—— Diehl, R., and Killeen, P. R. (1987). Japanese quail can learn phonetic categories. *Science* 237: 1195–7.

—— and Lotto, A. J. (1994). Effects of first formant onset frequency on [−voice] judgments result from general auditory processes not specific to humans. *Journal of the Acoustical Society of America* 95: 1044–52.

Knight, C., Studdert-Kennedy, M., and Hurford, J. (eds.) (2000). *The evolutionary emergence of language: social function and the origins of linguistic form*. Cambridge: Cambridge University Press.

Kobayashi, T. and Kuroda, T. (1987). *Morphology of crystals* (Part B, ed. I. Sunagawa). Tokyo: Terra Scientific.

Kodric-Brown, A. and Brown, J. H. (1984). Truth in advertising: the kind of traits favoured by sexual selection. *American Naturalist* 124: 309–23.

Kohler, E., Keyser, C., Umiltá, M. A., Fogassi, L., Gallese, V., and Rizzolatti, G. (2002). Hearing sounds, understanding actions: action representation in mirror neurons. *Science* 297: 846–8.

Kohler, K. J. (1998). The development of sound systems in human language. In Hurford et al. (eds.), 265–78.

Komarova, N. L. and Nowak, M. A. (2001). The evolutionary dynamics of the lexical matrix. *Bulletin of Mathematical Biology* 63: 451–85.

Kroodsma, D. E. (1979). Vocal dueling among male marsh wrens: evidence for ritualized expressions of dominance/subordinance. *Auk* 96: 506–15.

Kruskal, J. B. (1977). The relationship between multidimensional scaling and clustering. In J. V. Ryzin (ed.). *Classification and clustering*. New York: Academic Press, 17–44.

Kuczaj, S. A. (1998). Is an evolutionary theory of language play possible? *Cahiers de Psychologie Cognitive* 17: 135–54.

Kuhl, P. K., Andruski, J. E., Chistovich, I. A., Chistovich, L. A., Kozhevikova, E., Rysinka, V. L., Stolyarova, E. I., Sundberg, U., and Lacerda, F. (1997). Cross-language analysis of phonetic units in language addressed to infants. *Science* 277: 684–6.

Kuteva, T. (2001). *Auxiliation: an inquiry into the nature of grammaticalization*. Oxford: Oxford University Press.

—— and Comrie, B. (forthcoming). The typology of relative clause formation in African languages. In E. Voeltz (ed.), *African Studies*. Amsterdam: John Benjamins.

Ladefoged, P. (1982). *A course in phonetics*. San Diego, CA: Harcourt Brace Jovanovitch.

—— and Maddieson, I. (1996). *The sounds of the world's languages*. Oxford: Blackwell.

Lakoff, G. (1972). Hedges: a study in meaning criteria and the logic of fuzzy concepts. In P. Peranteau, J. Levi, and G. Phares (eds.), *Papers from the Eighth Regional Meeting of the Chicago Linguistic Society*, 183–228.

Landau, B., Smith, L. B., and Jones, S. S. (1988). The importance of shape in early lexical learning. *Cognitive Development* 3: 299–321.

Langer, J. (1986). *The origins of logic*. New York: Academic Press.

Lashley, K. S. (1951). The problem of serial order in behaviour. In L. Jeffress (ed.), *Cerebral mechanisms in behaviour: the Hixon Symposium*. New York: Wiley, 112–36.

Lass, R. (1990). How to do things with 'junk': exaptation in language evolution. *Journal of Linguistics* 26: 79–102.

Leonard, M. L. and Picman, J. (1987). The adaptive significance of multiple nest building by male marsh wrens. *Animal Behaviour* 35: 271–7.

Levelt, W. J. M. (1989). *Speaking: from intention to articulation*. Cambridge, MA: MIT Press.

Levi, J. (1978). *The syntax and semantics of complex nominals*. New York: Academic Press.

Levin, B. (1993). *English verb classes and alternations: a preliminary investigation*. Chicago, IL and London: University of Chicago Press.

Levy, L. S. and Joshi, A. K. (1979). Skeletal structural descriptions. *Information and Control* 39: 192–211.

Li, M. and Vitányi, P. (1997). *An introduction to Kolmogorov complexity theory and its applications* (2nd edn.). Berlin: Springer.

Liberman, A. M., Cooper, F. S., Shankweiler, D. P. and Studdert-Kennedy, M. (1967). Perception of the speech code. *Psychological Review* 74: 431–61.

Lieber, R. (1992). *Deconstructing morphology: word formation in syntactic theory*. Chicago, IL: University of Chicago Press.

Lieberman, P. (1984). *The biology and evolution of language.* Cambridge, MA: Harvard University Press.

—— (2000). *Human language and our reptilian brain. The subcortical bases of speech, syntax, and thought.* Cambridge, MA: Harvard University Press.

Lieven, E. V. M. (1994). Crosslinguistic and crosscultural aspects of language addressed to children. In C. Gallaway and B. J. Richards (eds.), *Input and interaction in language acquisition.* Cambridge: Cambridge University Press, 56–73.

Lightfoot, D. (1991). Subjacency and sex. *Language and Communication* 11: 67–9.

—— (1999). *The development of language: acquisition, change, and evolution.* Oxford: Blackwell.

—— (2000). The spandrels of the linguistic genotype. In Knight et al. (eds.), 231–47.

Liljencrants, J. and Lindblom, B. (1972). Numerical simulation of vowel quality systems: the role of perceptual contrast. *Language* 48: 839–62.

Lindblom, B. (1986). Phonetic universals in vowel systems. In J. Ohala and J. Jaeger (eds.), *Experimental phonology.* Orlando, FL: Academic Press, 13–44.

—— (1992). Phonological units as adaptive emergents of lexical development. In C. A. Ferguson, L. Menn, and C. Stoel-Gammon (eds.), *Phonological development: models, research, implications.* Timonium, MD: York Press, 131–63.

—— (1998). Systemic constraints and adaptive change in the formation of sound structure. In Hurford et al. (eds.), 242–64.

—— (2000). Developmental origins of adult phonology: the interplay between phonetic emergents and the evolutionary adaptations of sound patterns. *Phonetica* 57: 297–314.

—— and Maddieson, I. (1988). Phonetic universals in consonant systems. In L. M. Hyman and C. N. Li (eds.), *Language, speech and mind.* London and New York: Routledge, 62–78.

Liner, E. (1977). Restrictive and non-restrictive relative clauses in Swahili. In P. F. A. Kotey and H. Der-Houssikian (eds.), *Language and linguistic problems in Africa. Proceedings of the Seventh Conference on African Linguistics.* Columbia, SC: Hornbeam Press, 269–82.

Liu, H.-M., Tsao, F.-M. and Kuhl, P. K. (2000). Support for an expanded vowel triangle in Mandarin motherese. *International Journal of Psychology* 35: 337.

Livingstone, D. (2000). *Neutral evolution and linguistic diversity.* Technical Report 9, University of Paisley, Computing and Information Systems.

—— and Fyfe, C. (2000). Modelling language-physiology coevolution. In Knight et al. (eds.), 199–215.

Locke, J. L. (1993). *The child's path to spoken language.* Cambridge, MA: Harvard University Press.

McCloskey, J. (1990). Resumptive pronouns, Ā-binding and levels of representation in Irish. In Hendrick (ed.), 199–248.

Macedonia, J. M. (1990). What is communicated in the antipredator calls of lemurs: evidence from playback experiments with ring-tailed and ruffed lemurs. *Ethology* 86: 177–90.

—— and Evans, C. S. (1993). Variation among mammalian alarm call systems and the problem of meaning in animal signals. *Ethology* 93: 177–97.

McFarland, W. L. and Morgane, P. J. (1966). Neurological, cardiovascular, and respiratory adaptations in the dolphin, *Tursiops truncatus*. *Proceedings of the Annual Convention of the American Psychological Association*, 167–8.

MacLarnon, A. (1993). The vertebral canal. In A. Walker and R. Leakey (eds.), *The Nariokotome Homo erectus skeleton*. Cambridge, MA: Harvard University Press, 359–90.

Macnamara, J. (1972). The cognitive basis of language learning in infants. *Psychological Review* 79: 1–13.

MacNeilage, P. F. (1998). The Frame/Content theory of evolution of speech production. *Behavioral and Brain Sciences* 21: 499–511.

—— and Davis, B. (2004). The Frame/Content theory of evolution of speech: a comparison with a gestural origins alternative. *Interaction Studies: Social Behaviour and Communication in Biological and Artificial Systems* (forthcoming).

MacWhinney, B. (1989). Competition and lexical categorization. In R. Corrigan, F. Eckman, and M. Noonan (eds.), *Linguistic categorization*. New York: John Benjamins, 195–242.

—— (2000). *The CHILDES project: tools for analyzing talk* (3rd edn.). Mahwah, NJ: Lawrence Erlbaum.

McWhorter, J. H. (2001a). The world's simplest grammars are creole grammars. *Linguistic Typology* 5: 125–66.

—— (2001b). *The power of Babel: a natural history of language*. London: Heinemann.

Maddieson, I. (1984). *Patterns of sound*. Cambridge: Cambridge University Press.

Marchese, L. (1986). *Tense/aspect and the development of auxiliaries in Kru languages*. Arlington, TX: Summer Institute of Linguistics and University of Texas, Arlington.

Markman, E. M. (1989). *Categorization and naming in children: problems of induction*. Cambridge, MA: MIT Press.

—— and Hutchinson, J. E. (1984). Children's sensitivity to constraints on word meaning: taxonomic vs. thematic relations. *Cognitive Psychology* 16: 1–27.

—— and Wachtel, G. F. (1988). Children's use of mutual exclusivity to constrain the meaning of words. *Cognitive Psychology* 20: 121–57.

Marler, P. (1970). A comparative approach to vocal learning: song development in white-crowned sparrows. *Journal of Comparative and Physiological Psychology* 71: 1–25.

—— (1973). Speech development and bird song: are there any parallels? In G. A. Miller (ed.), *Communication, language, and meaning.* New York: Basic Books, 73–83.

Marr, D. (1977). Artificial intelligence: a personal view. *Artificial Intelligence* 9: 37–48.

—— (1982). *Vision.* New York: W. H. Freeman and Company.

Marshall, A., Wrangham, R., and Clark Arcadi, A. (1999). Does learning affect the structure of vocalizations in chimpanzees? *Animal Behaviour* 58: 825–30.

Martin, C. (1991). *The rainforests of West Africa: ecology, threats, conservation.* Basel: Birkhäuser.

Matthews, P. H. (1997). *The concise Oxford dictionary of linguistics.* Oxford: Oxford University Press.

May, D. L. (1996). The behaviour of African Grey parrots in the rainforest of the Central African Republic. *Psittascene* 8: 8–9.

Mayerthaler, W. (1981). *Morphologische Natürlichkeit.* Wiesbaden: Athenaion.

Mayley, G. (1996). Landscapes, learning costs and genetic assimilation. In P. Turney, D. Whitley, and R. Anderson, (eds.), *Evolution, learning and instinct: 100 years of the Baldwin effect.* (Special issue of *Evolutionary Computation,* 4). Cambridge, MA: MIT Press, 213–34.

Maynard Smith, J. (1965). The evolution of alarm calls. *American Naturalist* 99: 59–63.

Mayr, E. (1982). *The growth of biological thought.* Cambridge, MA: Harvard University Press.

Mealey, L., Daood, C., and Krage, M. (1996). Enhanced memory for faces associated with potential threat. *Ethology and Sociobiology* 17: 119–28.

Medina, L. and Reiner, A. (2000). Do birds possess homologues of mammalian primary visual, somatosensory, and motor cortices? *Trends in Neurosciences* 23: 1–12.

Meltzoff, A. N. and Moore, M. K. (1997). Explaining facial imitation: a theoretical model. *Early Development and Parenting* 6: 179–92.

Merriman, W. E. and Bowman, L. L. (1989). The mutual exclusivity bias in children's word learning. *Monographs of the Society for Research in Child Development* 54.

Miller, G. E. (2000). *The mating mind. How sexual choice shaped the evolution of human nature.* London: Heinemann.

Mitani, J. C. and Marler, P. (1989). A phonological analysis of male gibbon singing behavior. *Behaviour* 109: 20–45.

Molencki, R. (2000). Parallelism vs. asymmetry. In O. Fischer, A. Rosenbach, and D. Stein (eds.), *Pathways of change: grammaticalization in English.* Amsterdam/Philadelphia: John Benjamins, 311–28.

Morgan, J. L. and Demuth, K. (eds.) (1996). *Signal to syntax: bootstrapping from speech to grammar in early acquisition.* Mahwah, NJ: Lawrence Erlbaum.

Morgane, P. J., Jacobs, M. S., and Galaburda, A. (1986). Evolutionary morphology of the dolphin brain. In R. J. Schusterman, J. A. Thomas, and F. G. Woods (eds.), *Dolphin cognition and behavior: a comparative approach.* Hillsdale, NJ: Lawrence Erlbaum, 5–29.

Neal, K. B. (1996). Development of a vocalization in a Grey parrot. Senior thesis, University of Arizona, Tucson.

Nehaniv, C. L. (2000). The making of meaning in societies: semiotic and information-theoretic background to the evolution of communication. In B. Edmonds and K. Dautenhahn (eds.), *Proceedings of the AISB symposium: Starting from society—the application of social analogies to computational systems.* (Special issue of *Journal of Artificial Societies and Social Simulation*, 4), 73–84.

Nemeth, E. and Bibok, K. (eds.) (2001). *Pragmatics and the flexibility of word meaning.* London: Elsevier.

Nettle, D. (1999). *Linguistic diversity.* Oxford: Oxford University Press.

—— (2001). *Strong imagination: madness, creativity and human nature.* Oxford: Oxford University Press.

Newmeyer, F. J. (1998a). *Language form and language function.* Cambridge, MA: MIT Press.

—— (1998b). On the supposed 'counterfunctionality' of universal grammar: some evolutionary implications. In Hurford et al. (eds.), 305–19.

—— (2000). On the reconstruction of 'Proto-World' word order. In Knight et al. (eds.), 372–88.

—— (2002). Uniformitarian assumptions and language evolution research. In Wray (ed.), 359–75.

Newport, E. L., Gleitman, H., and Gleitman, L. R. (1977). Mother, I'd rather do it myself: some effects and non-effects of maternal speech style. In C. E. Snow and C. A. Ferguson (eds.), *Talking to children.* Cambridge: Cambridge University Press, 109–49.

Nguyen, D.-H. (1987). Vietnamese. In B. Comrie (ed.), *The world's major languages.* London: Croom Helm, 777–96.

Nichols, J. (1992). *Linguistic diversity in space and time.* Chicago, IL and London: University of Chicago Press.

Nittrouer, S. (1993). The emergence of mature gestural patterns is not uniform: evidence from an acoustic study. *Journal of Speech and Hearing Research* 36: 959–72.

Niyogi, P. and Berwick, R. (1997). Evolutionary consequences of language learning. *Linguistics and Philosophy* 20: 697–719.

Nottebohm, F. (1970). Ontogeny of bird song. *Science* 167: 950–6.

—— (1980). Brian pathways for vocal learning in birds: a review of the first ten years. *Progress in Psychobiology and Physiological Psychology* 9: 85–124.

—— (1991). Reassessing the mechanisms and origins of vocal learning in birds. *Trends in Neurosciences* 14: 206–11.

Nowak, M. A. and Komarova, N. L. (2001). Towards an evolutionary theory of language. *Trends in Cognitive Sciences* 5: 288–95.

—— —— and Niyogi, P. (2001). Evolution of universal grammar. *Science* 291: 114–18.

—— and Krakauer, D. C. (1999). The evolution of language. *Proceedings of the National Academy of Sciences of the United States of America* 96: 8028–33.

—— Plotkin, J. B., and Jansen, V. A. A. (2000). The evolution of syntactic communication. *Nature* 404: 495–8.

—— —— and Krakauer, D. C. (1999). The evolutionary language game. *Journal of Theoretical Biology* 200: 147–62.

Nunes, J. (1995). The copy theory of movement and linearization of chains in the Minimalist Program. PhD thesis, University of Maryland, MD.

O'Grady, W., Dobrovolsky, M., and Katamba, F. (1997). *Contemporary linguistics* (3rd edn.). London: Longman.

Okanoya, K. (2002). Sexual display as a syntactical vehicle: the evolution of syntax in birdsong and human language through sexual selection. In Wray (ed.), 46–63.

Oliphant, M. (1999). The learning barrier: moving from innate to learned systems of communication. *Adaptive Behavior* 7: 371–84.

—— and Batali, J. (1997). Learning and the emergence of coordinated communication. *Center for Research on Language Newsletter* 11.

Onnis, L., Roberts, M., and Chater, N. (2002). Simplicity: a cure for overgeneralizations in language acquisition? In W. D. Gray and C. D. Shunn (eds.), *Proceedings of the Twenty-fourth Annual Conference of the Cognitive Science Society*, Mahwah, NJ and London: Lawrence Erlbaum, 720–5.

Origgi, G. and Sperber, D. (2000). Evolution, communication and the proper function of language. In P. Carruthers and A. Chamberlain (eds.), *Evolution and the human mind: modularity, language and meta-cognition*. Cambridge: Cambridge University Press, 140–69.

Oudeyer, P.-Y. (2001a). Coupled neural maps for the origins of vowel systems. In G. Dorffner, H. Bischof, and K. Hornik (eds.), *Proceedings of the International Conference on Artificial Neural Networks*. Berlin: Springer, 1171–6.

—— (2001b). Origins and learnability of syllable systems, a cultural evolutionary model. In P. Collet, C. Fonlupt, J. K. Hao, E. Lutton, and M. Schonenauer (eds.), *Artificial evolution*. Berlin: Springer, 143–55.

—— (2003). L'auto-organisation de la parole. PhD thesis, University Paris VI, <http://www.csl.sony.fr/~py/theseEnglish.html>.

Owings, D. H. and Hennessy, D. F. (1984). The importance of variation in sciurid visual and vocal communication. In J. O. Murie and G. R. Michener (eds.), *The biology of ground-dwelling squirrels*. Lincoln, NE: University of Nebraska Press, 167–200.

Oztop, E. and Arbib, M. A. (2002). Schema design and implementation of the grasp-related mirror neuron system. *Biological Cybernetics* 87: 116–40.

Oztop, E., Bradley, N., and Arbib, M. A. (2004). Infant grasp learning: a computational model. *Experimental Brain Research* 158: 480–503.

Parker, S. T. and Gibson K. R. (1977). Object manipulation, tool use, and sensorimotor intelligence as feeding adaptations in *Cebus* monkeys and great apes. *Journal of Human Evolution* 6: 623–41.

Parsons, L. M., Fox, P. T., Downs, J. H., Glass, T., Hirsch, T. B., Martin, C. C., Jerabek, P. A. and Lancaster, J. L. (1995).Use of implicit motor imagery for visual shape discrimination as revealed by PET. *Nature* 375: 54–8.

Passingham, R. (1993). *The frontal lobes and voluntary action.* Oxford: Oxford University Press.

Patterson, D. K. and Pepperberg, I. M. (1994). A comparative study of human and parrot phonation: acoustic and articulatory correlates of vowels. *Journal of the Acoustical Society of America* 96: 634–48.

—— —— (1998). Acoustic and articulatory correlates of stop consonants in a parrot and a human subject. *Journal of the Acoustical Society of America* 106: 491–505.

Pepperberg, I. M. (1983). Cognition in the African Grey parrot: preliminary evidence for auditory/vocal comprehension of the class concept. *Animal Learning and Behavior* 11: 179–85.

—— (1987a). Interspecies communication: a tool for assessing conceptual abilities in the Grey parrot (*Psittacus erithacus*). In G. Greenberg and E. Tobach (eds.), *Language, cognition, and consciousness: integrative levels.* Hillsdale, NJ: Lawrence Erlbaum, 31–56.

—— (1987b). Evidence for conceptual quantitative abilities in the African Grey parrot: labeling of cardinal sets. *Ethology* 75: 37–61.

—— (1987c). Acquisition of the same/different concept by an African Grey parrot (*Psittacus erithacus*): learning with respect to categories of color, shape, and material. *Animal Learning and Behavior* 15: 423–32.

—— (1988a). An interactive modeling technique for acquisition of communication skills: separation of 'labeling' and 'requesting' in a psittacine subject. *Applied Psycholinguistics* 9: 59–76.

—— (1988b). Acquisition of the concept of absence by an African Grey parrot: learning with respect to questions of same/different. *Journal of the Experimental Analysis of Behavior* 50: 553–64.

—— (1990). Cognition in an African Grey parrot (*Psittacus erithacus*): further evidence for comprehension of categories and labels. *Journal of Comparative Psychology* 104: 41–52.

—— (1992). Proficient performance of a conjunctive, recursive task by an African Grey parrot (*Psittacus erithacus*). *Journal of Comparative Psychology* 106: 295–305.

—— (1994). Evidence for numerical competence in an African Grey parrot (*Psittacus erithacus*). *Journal of Comparative Psychology* 108: 36–44.

—— (1999). *The Alex studies.* Cambridge, MA: Harvard University Press.

—— (2001). Avian cognitive abilities. *Bird Behavior* 14: 51–70.

—— (forthcoming a). Human speech: its learning and use by Grey parrots. In P. Marler and H. Slabbekoorn (eds.), *Nature's music.* New York: Academic Press.

—— (forthcoming b). Insights into vocal imitation in Grey Parrots (*Psittacus erithacus*). In S. Hurley and N. Chater (eds.), *Perspectives on imitation: from cognitive neuroscience to social science.* Cambridge, MA: MIT Press.

—— Brese, K. J., and Harris, B. J. (1991). Solitary sound play during acquisition of English vocalizations by an African Grey parrot (Psittacus erithacus): possible parallels with children's monologue speech. *Applied Psycholinguistics* 12: 151–78.

—— and Brezinsky, M. V. (1991). Relational learning by an African Grey parrot (*Psittacus erithacus*): discriminations based on relative size. *Journal of Comparative Psychology* 105: 286–94.

—— and Kozak, F. A. (1986). Object permanence in the African Grey parrot (*Psittacus erithacus*). *Animal Learning and Behavior* 14: 322–30.

—— Sandefer, R. M., Noel, D., and Ellsworth, C. P. (2000). Vocal learning in the Grey parrot: effect of species identity and number of trainers. *Journal of Comparative Psychology* 114: 371–80.

—— and Shive, H. (2001). Simultaneous development of vocal and physical object combinations by a Grey parrot (*Psittacus erithacus*): bottle caps, lids, and labels. *Journal of Comparative Psychology* 115: 376–84.

—— and Wilcox, S. E. (2000). Evidence for a form of mutual exclusivity during label acquisition by Grey parrots (*Psittacus erithacus*)? *Journal of Comparative Psychology* 114: 219–31.

—— Willner, M. R., and Gravitz, L. B. (1997). Development of Piagetian object permanence in a Grey parrot (*Psittacus erithacus*). *Journal of Comparative Psychology* 111: 63–75.

Perrins, C. (1968). The purpose of the high-intensity alarm call in small passerines. *Ibis* 110: 200–1.

Pfeifer, R. and Scheier, C. (1999). *Understanding intelligence.* Cambridge, MA: MIT Press.

Pinker, S. (1984). *Language learnability and language development.* Cambridge, MA: Harvard University Press.

—— (1989). *Learnability and cognition: the acquisition of argument structure.* Cambridge, MA: MIT Press.

—— (1994). *The language instinct.* New York: W. Morrow and Co.

—— and Bloom, P. (1990). Natural language and natural selection. *Behavioral and Brain Sciences* 13: 707–84.

Plumer, T. K. and Striedter, G. F. (2000). Auditory responses in the vocal motor system of budgerigars. *Journal of Neurobiology* 42: 79–94.

Pothos, E. and Chater, N. (2002). A simplicity principle in unsupervised human categorization. *Cognitive Science* 26: 303–43.

Poulos, G. (1994). *A linguistic analysis of Northern Sotho*. Pretoria: Via Africa Limited.

Povinelli, D. and Eddy, T. (2000). *What young chimpanzees know about seeing*. Oxford: Blackwell.

Pullum, G. K. (1996). Learnability, hyperlearning, and the poverty of the stimulus. In J. Johnson, M. L. Juge, and J. L. Moxley (eds.), *Proceedings of the Twenty-Second Annual Meeting of the Berkeley Linguistics Society. General session and parasession on the role of learnability in grammatical theory*. Berkeley, CA: Berkeley Linguistics Society, 498–513.

—— and Scholz, B. C. (2002). Empirical assessment of stimulus poverty arguments. *The Linguistic Review* 19: 9–50.

Quine, W. V. O. (1960). *Word and object*. Cambridge, MA: MIT Press.

Rackowski, A. and Travis, L. (2000). V-initial languages: X or XP movement and adverbial placement. In Carnie and Guilfoyle (eds.), 117–41.

Rainey, H. J., Zuberbühler, K., and Slater, P. J. B. (2004a). Hornbills can distinguish between primate alarm calls. *Proceedings of the Royal Society of London B series: Biological Sciences* 271: 755–759.

—— —— —— (2004b). The responses of black-casqued hornbills to predator vocalizations and primate alarm calls. *Behaviour* 141: 1263–77.

Ramsay, G. and Demolin, D. (2002). A comparative study of the sensory innervation of the vocal tract in humans and primates: possible implications for the development of speech motor control. Part I: the palate. Paper presented at the Fourth International Conference on the Evolution of Language, Harvard University, March 27–30.

Reggia, J. A., Schulz, R., Wilkinson, G., and Uriagereka, J. (2001). Conditions enabling the evolution of inter-agent signaling in an artificial world. *Artificial Life* 7: 3–32.

Ridley, M. (ed.) (1997). *Evolution*. Oxford: Oxford University Press.

Riede, T. and Zuberbühler, K. (2003a). Pulse register phonation in Diana monkey alarm calls. *Journal of the Acoustical Society of America* 113: 2919–26.

—— —— (2003b). The relationship between acoustic structure and semantic information in Diana monkey alarm calls. *Journal of the Acoustical Society of America* 114: 1132–42.

Rigby, K. (2002). The evolution of sex differences in cognition: mate choice, creativity and concept combination. PhD thesis, University of London.

—— and Franks, B. (2001). A mating of minds. Review of G. E. Miller, *The mating mind. How sexual choice shaped the evolution of human nature. Psycholoquy* 12/33. <http://psycprints.ecs.soton.ac. uk/archive/00000162/>.

Rissanen, J. (1987). Stochastic complexity. *Journal of the Royal Statistical Society, Series B*, 49: 223–39.

—— (1989). *Stochastic complexity and statistical inquiry*. Singapore: World Scientific.

Rizzolatti, G. and Arbib, M. A. (1998). Language within our grasp. *Trends in Neuroscience* 21: 188–94.

—— Craighero, L., and Fadiga, L. (2002). The mirror system in humans. In Stamenov and Gallese (eds.), 37–59.

—— Fadiga, L., Gallese, V., and Fogassi, L. (1996). Premotor cortex and the recognition of motor actions. *Cognitive Brain Research* 3: 131–41.

—— Fogassi, L., and Gallese, V. (2001). Neurophysiological mechanisms underlying the understanding and imitation of actions. *Nature Review Neurology* 2: 661–70.

Robinson, J. G. (1984). Syntactic structure in the vocalizations of wedge-capped capuchin monkeys (*Cebus olivaceus*). *Behaviour* 90: 46–79.

Rose, M. R. and Lauder, G. V. (eds.) (1996). *Adaptation*. London: Academic Press.

Roy, D. (2000). Learning visually grounded words and syntax of natural spoken language. *Evolution of Communication* 4: 33–56.

Ryan, M. J. (1990). Sexual selection, sensory systems, and sensory exploitation. In D. Futuyma and J. Antonovics (eds.), *Oxford surveys of evolutionary biology: volume 7*, 156–95.

Sanders, I. (2002). Human tongue, pharynx and vocal fold muscles contain slow tonic muscle, a distinct class of muscle that may have evolved for speech. Paper presented at the Fourth International Conference on the Evolution of Language, Harvard University, March 27–30.

—— (2004). The human tongue slows down to speak. Paper presented at the Fifth International Conference on the Evolution of Language, Max Planck Institute for Evolutionary Anthropology, Leipzig, Germany, March 31–April 3.

Saussure, F. de. (1916/1973). *Cours de linguistique générale* (ed. C. Bally, A. Sechehaye, and A. Riedlinger; critical edn. by T. de Mauro). Paris: Payot.

Savage-Rumbaugh, E. S., Shanker, S. G., and Taylor, T. J. (1998). *Apes, language and the human mind*. New York: Oxford University Press.

Schieffelin, B. B. (1985). The acquisition of Kaluli. In D. I. Slobin (ed.), *The crosslinguistic study of language acquisition. Volume 1: The data*. Hillsdale, NJ: Lawrence Erlbaum, 525–93.

—— and Ochs, E. (1983). A cultural perspective on the transition from prelinguistic to linguistic communication. In R. M. Golinkoff (ed.), *The transition from prelinguistic to linguistic communication*. Hillsdale, NJ: Lawrence Erlbaum, 115–31.

Schwartz J.-L., Boé, L.-J., Vallée, N., and Abry, C. (1997a). Major trends in vowel systems inventories. *Journal of Phonetics* 25: 233–53.

—— —— —— —— (1997b). The dispersion-focalization theory of vowel systems. *Journal of Phonetics* 25: 255–86.

Selkirk, E. O. (1982). *The syntax of words*. Cambridge, MA: MIT Press.

Senft, G. (1986). *Kilivila. The language of the Trobriand Islanders*. Berlin: Mouton de Gruyter.

Seyfarth, R. M., Cheney, D. L., and Marler, P. (1980). Vervet monkey alarm calls: semantic communication in a free-ranging primate. *Animal Behaviour* 28: 1070–94.

Shady, M. E. (1996). Infants' sensitivity to function morphemes. PhD thesis, State University of New York at Buffalo.

Shannon, C. E. (1948). A mathematical theory of communication. *Bell System Technical Journal* 27: 379–423 and 623–56.

Shaofu, C., Swartz, K. B., and Terrace, H. S. (1997). Knowledge of the ordinal position of list items in rhesus monkeys. *Psychological Science* 8: 80–6.

Shepard, R. N. (1980). Multidimensional scaling, tree-fitting, and clustering. *Science* 210: 390–7.

Shultz, S. (2001). Notes on interactions between monkeys and African crowned eagles in Tai National Park, Ivory Coast. *Folia primatologica* 72: 248–50.

Slocombe, K., and Zuberbühler, K. (2005). Agonistic screams in wild chimpanzees vary as a function of social role. *Journal of Comparative Psychology* 119(1) (forthcoming).

Smith, A. D. M. (2001). Establishing communication systems without explicit meaning transmission. In Kelemen and Sosík (eds.), 381–90.

—— (2003a). Evolving communication through the inference of meaning. PhD thesis, University of Edinburgh.

—— (2003b). Intelligent meaning creation in a clumpy world helps communication. *Artificial Life* 9: 175–90.

Smith, K. (2001). The importance of rapid cultural convergence in the evolution of learned symbolic communication. In J. Kelemen and P. Sosík (eds.), 637–40.

—— (2002). The cultural evolution of communication in a population of neural networks. *Connection Science* 14: 65–84.

—— Brighton, H., and Kirby, S. (2003). Complex systems in language evolution: the cultural emergence of compositional structure. *Advances in Complex Systems* 6: 537–58.

Sperber, D. (1994). Understanding verbal understanding. In J. Khalfa (ed.), *What is intelligence?* Cambridge: Cambridge University Press, 179–98.

—— (2000). Metarepresentations in an evolutionary perspective. In D. Sperber (ed.), *Metarepresentations.* Oxford: Oxford University Press, 117–37.

—— and Wilson, D. (1986). *Relevance.* Oxford: Blackwell.

Stamenov, M. and Gallese, V. (eds.) (2002). *Mirror neurons and the evolution of the brain and language.* Amsterdam/Philadelphia: John Benjamins.

Steels, L. (1996). Perceptually grounded meaning creation. In M. Tokoro (ed.), *Proceedings of the International Conference on Multi-agent Systems.* Cambridge, MA: MIT Press, 338–44.

—— (1997). Constructing and sharing perceptual distinctions. In M. van Someren and G. Widmer (eds.), *Proceedings of the European Conference on Machine Learning.* Berlin: Springer, 4–13.

—— (1998a). Synthesising the origins of language and meaning using co-evolution, self-organization and level formation. In Hurford et al. (eds.), 384–404.

—— (1998b). The origins of syntax in visually grounded robotic agents. *Artificial Intelligence* 103: 133–56.

—— (1999). *The Talking Heads experiment. Volume I: Words and meanings.* Antwerp: Laboratorium.

—— (2001). The methodology of the artificial. *Behavioral and Brain Sciences* 24: 1077–8.

—— and Kaplan, F. (2000). AIBO's first words: the social learning of language and meaning. *Evolution of Communication* 4: 3–32.

Sternberg, R. (1999). *Handbook of creativity.* Cambridge: Cambridge University Press.

Stevens, K. N. (1972). The quantal nature of speech: evidence from articulatory-acoustic data. In E. E. David and P. B. Denes (eds.), *Human communication: a unified view.* New York: McGraw-Hill, 51–66.

—— (1989). On the quantal nature of speech. *Journal of Phonetics* 1: 3–45.

Stoddard, P. K., Beecher, M. D., Horning, C. L. and Campbell, S. E. (1991). Recognition of individual neighbors by song in the song sparrow, a species with song repertoires. *Behavioral Ecology and Sociobiology* 29: 211–15.

Stokoe, W. C. (2001). *Language in hand: why sign came before speech.* Washington, DC: Gallaudet University Press.

Stolcke, A. (1994). Bayesian learning of probabilistic language models. PhD thesis, University of California, Berkeley.

Striedter, G. (1994). The vocal control pathways in budgerigars differ from those in songbirds. *Journal of Comparative Neurology* 343: 35–56.

Struhsaker, T. T. (1967). Auditory communication among vervet monkeys (*Cercopithecus aethiops*). In S. A. Altmann (ed.), *Social communication among primates.* Chicago, IL: University of Chicago Press, 281–324.

Studdert-Kennedy, M. (1987). The phoneme as a perceptuomotor structure. In A. Allport, D. G. MacKay, W. Prinz, and E. Scheerer (eds.), *Language perception and production.* London: Academic Press, 67–84.

—— (1998). The particulate origins of language generativity: from syllable to gesture. In Hurford et al. (eds.), 202–21.

—— (2000). Evolutionary implications of the particulate principle: imitation and the dissociation of phonetic form from semantic function. In Knight et al. (eds.), 161–76.

—— (2002). Mirror neurons, vocal imitation and the evolution of particulate speech. In Stamenov and Gallese (eds.), 207–27.

—— and Goldstein, L. F. (2003). Launching language: the gestural origin of discrete infinity. In Christiansen and Kirby (eds.), 235–54.

Studdert-Kennedy, M. and Goodell, E. W. (1995). Gestures, features and segments in early child speech. In B. de Gelder and J. Morais (eds.), *Speech and reading: a comparative approach*. Hove: Lawrence Erlbaum/Taylor and Francis, 65–88.

Stump, G. T. (2001). *Inflectional morphology: a theory of paradigm structure*. Cambridge: Cambridge University Press.

Sundara, M., Kumar Namasivayam, A., and Chen, R. (2001). Observation-execution matching system for speech: a magnetic stimulation study. *Neuroreport: For Rapid Communication of Neuroscience Research* 12: 1341–4.

Supalla, T. and Newport, E. (1978). How many seats in a chair? The derivation of nouns and verbs in American Sign Language. In P. Siple (ed.), *Understanding language through sign language research*. New York: Academic Press, 91–159.

Symons, D. (1992). On the use and misuse of Darwinism. In J. H. Barkow, L. Cosmides, and J. Tooby (eds.), *The adapted mind: evolutionary psychology and the generation of culture*. Oxford: Oxford University Press, 137–62.

Taglialatela, J. P., Savage-Rumbaugh, S., and Baker, L. A. (2003). Vocal production by a language-competent *Pan paniscus*. *International Journal of Primatology* 24: 1–17.

Taira, M., Mine, S., Georgopoulos, A. P, Murata, A., and Sakata, H. (1990). Parietal cortex neurons of the monkey related to the visual guidance of hand movement. *Experimental Brain Research* 83: 29–36.

Tallerman, M. (forthcoming). Challenging the syllabic model of 'syntax-as-it-is'. In Honeybone and Bermúdez-Otero (eds.).

Teal, T. K. and Taylor, C. E. (2000). Effects of compression on language evolution. *Artificial Life* 6: 129–43.

Terrace, H. S. (1979). *Nim*. New York: Knopf.

—— (1985). In the beginning was the 'name'. *American Psychologist* 40: 1011–28.

—— (2002). Serial expertise and the evolution of language. In Wray (ed.), 64–90.

—— (2005). Metacognition and the evolution of language. In H. S. Terrace and J. Metcalfe (eds.) *Metacognition: the missing link*. Oxford: Oxford University Press, 84–115.

Thompson, D. W. (1932). *On growth and form*. Cambridge: Cambridge University Press.

Todt, D. (1975). Social learning of vocal patterns and modes of their applications in Grey parrots. *Zeitschrift für Tierpsychologie* 39: 178–88.

Tomasello, M. (2003). Some surprises for psychologists. In M. Tomasello (ed.), *The new psychology of language. Volume 2: Cognitive and functional approaches to language structure*. Mahwah, NJ and London: Lawrence Erlbaum, 1–14.

—— and Call, J. (1997). *Primate cognition*. Oxford and New York: Oxford University Press.

—— and Camaioni, L. (1997). A comparison of the gestural communication of apes and human infants. *Human Development* 40: 7–24.

—— and Zuberbühler, K. (2002). Primate vocal and gestural communication. In M. Bekoff, C. Allen, and G. M. Burghardt (eds.), *The cognitive animal.* Cambridge, MA: MIT Press, 293–9.

Tomlin, R. (1986). *Basic word order: functional principles.* London: Croom Helm.

Turkel, W. (2002). The learning guided evolution of natural language. In Briscoe (ed.), 235–54.

Umilta, M. A., Kohler, E., Gallese, V., Fogassi, L., Fadiga, L., Keysers, C., and Rizzolatti, G. (2001). I know what you are doing. A neurophysiological study. *Neuron* 31: 155–65.

Uster, D. and Zuberbühler, K. (2001). The functional significance of Diana monkey 'clear' calls. *Behaviour* 138: 741–56.

Van der Helm, P. A. and Leeuwenberg, E. L. J. (1996). Goodness of visual regularities: a non-transformational approach. *Psychological Review* 103: 429–56.

Vargha-Khadem, F., Watkins, K., Alcock, K., Fletcher, P., and Passingham, R. (1995). Praxic and nonverbal cognitive deficits in a large family with a genetically transmitted speech and language disorder. *Proceedings of the National Academy of Sciences of the United States of America* 92: 930–3.

Vihman, M. M. (1996). *Phonological development.* Cambridge, MA: Blackwell.

Vogt, P. and Coumans, H. (2003). Investigating social interaction strategies for bootstrapping lexicon development. *Journal of Artificial Societies and Social Simulation* 6/1. <http://jasss.soc.surrey.ac.uk/6/1/4.html>.

Waddington, C. (1942). Canalization of development and the inheritance of acquired characters. *Nature* 150: 563–5.

—— (1975). *The evolution of an evolutionist.* Edinburgh: Edinburgh University Press.

Wallace, C. S. and Freeman, P. R. (1987). Estimation and inference by compact coding. *Journal of the Royal Statistical Society, Series B* 49: 240–65.

Warren, D. K., Patterson, D. K., and Pepperberg, I. M. (1996). Mechanisms of American English vowel production in a Grey parrot (*Psittacus erithacus*). *Auk* 113: 41–58.

Webelhuth, G. (1995). X-bar theory and case theory. In G. Webelhuth (ed.), *Government and binding theory and the Minimalist program.* Oxford and Cambridge, MA: Blackwell, 15–95.

Wechsler, S. and Arka W. (1998). Syntactic ergativity in Balinese: an argument structure based theory. *Natural Language and Linguistic Theory* 16: 387–441.

Wernicke, C. (1874). *Der aphasische Symptomenkomplex.* Breslau: Cohn and Weigert.

Westergaard, G. C. and Suomi, S. J. (1993). Use of a tool-set by capuchin monkeys (*Cebus apella*). *Primates* 34: 459–62.

—— —— (1994). Hierarchical complexity of combinatorial manipulation in capuchin monkeys (*Cebus apella*). *American Journal of Primatology* 32: 171–6.

Whiten, A. and Byrne, R. W. (eds.) (1997). *Machiavellian intelligence II: extensions and evaluations*. Cambridge: Cambridge University Press.

Wilkins, W. K. and Dumford, J. (1990). In defense of exaptation. *Behavioral and Brain Sciences* 13: 763–4.

—— and Wakefield, J. (1995). Brain evolution and neurolinguistic preconditions. *Behavioral and Brain Sciences* 18: 161–226.

Williams, G. C. (1966). *Adaptation and natural selection*. Princeton, NJ: Princeton University Press.

—— (1992). *Natural selection: domains, levels and challenges*. Oxford and New York: Oxford University Press.

Williams, S. L., Brakke, K. E. and Savage-Rumbaugh, E. S. (1997). Comprehension skills of language-competent and nonlanguage-competent apes. *Language and Communication* 17: 301–17.

Wilson, E. O. (1978). *On human nature*. Cambridge, MA: Harvard University Press.

Winograd, T. and Flores, F. (1986). *Understanding computers and cognition*. New York: Addison-Wesley.

Wisniewski, E. J. and Love, B. C. (1998). Properties versus relations in conceptual combinations. *Journal of Memory and Language* 38: 177–202.

Wolff, J. (1982). Language acquisition, data compression and generalization. *Language and Communication* 2: 57–89.

—— (1991). *Towards a theory of cognition and computing*. Chichester: Ellis Horwood.

Wolters, S. and Zuberbühler, K. (2003). Mixed-species associations of Diana and Campbell's monkeys: the costs and benefits of a forest phenomenon. *Behaviour* 140: 371–85.

Worden, R. (1998). The evolution of language from social intelligence. In Hurford et al. (eds.), 148–66.

Wray, A. (2000). Holistic utterances in protolanguage: the link from primates to humans. In Knight et al. (eds.), 285–302.

—— (2002). Dual processing in protolanguage: performance without competence. In Wray (ed.), 113–37.

Wray, A. (ed.) (2002). *The transition to language*. Oxford: Oxford University Press.

Wright, S. (1931). Evolution in mendelian populations. *Genetics* 16: 97–159.

Wunderlich, D. (ms.). Major steps in the evolution of language.

Yamauchi, H. (2000). Evolution of the LAD and the Baldwin effect. MA thesis, University of Edinburgh.

—— (2001). The difficulty of the Baldwinian account of linguistic innateness. In Kelemen and Sosík (eds.), 391–400.

Yates, J. and Tule, N. (1979). Perceiving surprising words in an unattended auditory channel. *Quarterly Journal of Experimental Psychology* 31: 281–6.

Yirmiya, N. and Shulman, C. (1996). Seriation, conservation, and theory of mind abilities in individuals with autism, individuals with mental retardation, and normally developing children. *Child Development* 67: 2045–59.

Zahavi, A. (1975). Mate selection – selection for a handicap. *Journal of Theoretical Biology* 53: 205–14.

Zipf, G. K. (1949). *Human behavior and the principle of least effort.* Reading, MA: Addison-Wesley.

Zuberbühler, K. (2000a). Referential labelling in Diana monkeys. *Animal Behaviour* 59: 917–27.

—— (2000b). Interspecific semantic communication in two forest monkeys. *Proceedings of the Royal Society of London B series* 267: 713–18.

—— (2000c). Causal knowledge of predators' behaviour in wild Diana monkeys. *Animal Behaviour* 59: 209–20.

—— (2000d). Causal cognition in a non-human primate: field playback experiments with Diana monkeys. *Cognition* 76: 195–207.

—— (2001). Predator-specific alarm calls in Campbell's guenons. *Behavioral Ecology and Sociobiology* 50: 414–22.

—— (2002a). Effects of natural and sexual selection on the evolution of guenon loud calls. In M. E. Glenn and M. Cords (eds.), *The guenons: diversity and adaptation in African monkeys.* New York: Plenum, 289–306.

—— (2002b). A syntactic rule in forest monkey communication. *Animal Behaviour* 63: 293–9.

—— Cheney, D. L., and Seyfarth, R. M. (1999). Conceptual semantics in a nonhuman primate. *Journal of Comparative Psychology* 113: 33–42.

—— and Jenny, D. (2002). Leopard predation and primate evolution. *Journal of Human Evolution* 43: 873–86.

—— —— and Bshary, R. (1999). The predator deterrence function of primate alarm calls. *Ethology* 105: 477–90.

—— —— Noë, R., and Seyfarth, R. M. (1997). Diana monkey long-distance calls: messages for conspecifics and predators. *Animal Behaviour* 53: 589–604.

Zuidema, W. (2003). How the poverty of the stimulus solves the poverty of the stimulus. In S. Becker, S. Thrun, and K. Obermayer (eds.), *Advances in neural information processing systems, 15.* Cambridge, MA: MIT Press, 51–8.

Zur, K. B., Mu, L., and Sanders, I. (2004). Distribution pattern of the human lingual nerve. *Clinical Anatomy* 17: 88–92.

Index